African pasts

MANCHEStER
1824
Manchester University Press

African pasts

Memory and history in African literatures

Tim Woods

Manchester University Press
Manchester and New York

distributed exclusively in the USA by Palgrave

Copyright © Tim Woods 2007

The right of Tim Woods to be identified as the author of this work has been asserted by him in accordance with the Copyright, Designs and Patents Act 1988.

Published by Manchester University Press
Oxford Road, Manchester M13 9NR, UK
and Room 400, 175 Fifth Avenue, New York, NY 10010, USA
www.manchesteruniversitypress.co.uk

Distributed exclusively in the USA by
Palgrave, 175 Fifth Avenue, New York,
NY 10010, USA

Distributed exclusively in Canada by
UBC Press, University of British Columbia, 2029 West Mall,
Vancouver, BC, Canada V6T 1Z2

British Library Cataloguing-in-Publication Data
A catalogue record for this book is available from the British Library

Library of Congress Cataloging-in-Publication Data applied for

ISBN   978 0 7190 6493 7 *hardback*

First published 2007

16 15 14 13 12 11 10 09 08 07   10 9 8 7 6 5 4 3 2 1

Typeset
by Action Publishing Technology Ltd, Gloucester
Printed in Great Britain
by CPI, Bath

for Helena,
Mary and Madeleine

let me seep into Africa
let this water
this sea
seep into me own me
and break my face into its moods
. . .
ah
africa
is this not your child come home

Mongane Wally Serote, from *No Baby Must Weep*

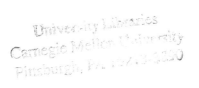

Contents

Figures

Acknowledgements

Although the gestation for this project has been the past thirty years since I was a teenager in apartheid South Africa, the immediate conception and research for this book occurred over the last five years, during which time I have had two children and taken on the headship of the Department of English at the University of Wales, Aberystwyth (UWA). Consequently, what was originally conceived of as a relatively tightly controlled project in terms of its research time stretched somewhat, and I have many to thank for their patience and indulgence with this project. The chief long-suffering supporter of this project is Manchester University Press, and Matthew Frost in particular, who always extended a supportive, accommodating and encouraging hand. I also owe the Leverhulme Foundation a large debt of gratitude for its endorsement of the project through a year-long fellowship in 2002, which allowed me the time to carry out most of the primary research. I am also very grateful to UWA, which offered me a sabbatical and the means and time to attend libraries around the UK, and especially the resources at SOAS. Librarians at SOAS, the British Library, the Hugh Owen Library at UWA, the National Library of Wales, and the University of Stellenbosch, South Africa, have all aided my research with professionalism and dedication.

I have had the opportunity at different times to discuss the project with numerous colleagues, students and friends, and I would select the following for their intellectual contribution, or indirect help: Peter Barry, Allen Cook, Tim Dunne, Andrew Hadfield, Christoph Lindner, Peter Middleton, Paule Ongoulem, David Schalkwyk, Tony Voss, Judi Woods and Kate Wright. I am grateful to Penny Siopsis for her permission to print *Patience on a Monument – 'A History Painting'* (1988), and the National Army Museum for permission to print Charles Fripp's *The Battle of Isandhlwana* (1885). Extensive efforts have been made to contact all other copyright holders, and the publisher and author would be pleased to hear from any party concerned. Earlier drafts of this book that have subsequently been rewritten or altered have been published as follows: 'Giving and Receiving: Nuruddin Farah's *Gifts*, or, the Postcolonial Logic of Third World Aid', *Journal of Commonwealth Literature*, 38:1 (Spring 2003), pp. 91–112; 'African Writing and Modernity' in Peter Brooker and Andrew Thacker, eds, *Geographies of Modernism: Literatures, Cultures, Spaces* (London, Routledge, 2005), pp. 126–35; 'Postcolonial Fictions', in Peter Nicholls and Laura Marcus, eds, *The Cambridge History of Twentieth-Century English Literature* (Cambridge, Cambridge University Press, 2004), pp. 736–50; and 'Reading Urban Spaces in African Texts', in Christoph Lindner, ed., *Urban Space and Cityscapes: Perspectives from Modern and Contemporary Culture* (London, Routledge, 2006), pp. 101–11.

Finally, this book has seen the light of day only as a result of the selflessness and unstinting support of Helena Grice, without whom I would be lost in the desert. I dedicate this book to Helena; and to our two girls, Mary and Madeleine, in the hope that in years to come they will discover the intricacies, excitements and differences of that vast continent that presses in upon us all – Africa.

Introduction

A people who do not preserve their memory are a people who have
forfeited their history. (Wole Soyinka, *The Burden of Memory, the Muse
of Forgiveness*)

In 1997, the Nobel Laureate Wole Soyinka delivered the Dubois
Institute Lectures at Harvard University, collectively called *The
Burden of Memory, the Muse of Forgiveness*. Soyinka's title provides
an overarching thematic concept for this book as a whole. For, under
the imperative of postcolonial theory, many recent critical studies of
African literatures have attended to the African representation of
history as a jettisoning of the politics of colonialism. However,
frequently this is stated without thinking through the associated
issues and allied debates, where history is associated with memory
and trauma in a cultural politics of national identity. Colonialism for
Africans is not an event encapsulated in the past but is a history
which is essentially *not over*, a history whose repercussions are not
only omnipresent in all cultural activities but whose traumatic
consequences are still actively evolving in today's political, historical,
cultural and artistic scenes. The aim of this book is to chart the ways
in which African literatures represent history through the twin
matrices of memory and trauma. My contention in this book is that
African literatures are continually preoccupied with exploring modes
of representation to 'work-through' its different traumatic colonial
pasts. African literatures (by writers like Achebe, Ngugi, Coetzee and
Soyinka) have always been preoccupied with the past, inextricably
tied up with the historical conditions of Africa's colonisation, charting the emergence of its independence, and scrutinising Africa's
contemporary neo-colonial and postcolonial states as a legacy of the
colonial past. Ranging widely across Africa's literary representations
of the past and exploring the various uses to which such invocations
of the past are put, this book will focus upon the growing interest in
African literatures and cultures. Writers will be drawn predomi-

nantly from three regions – East, West and Southern Africa – and from a number of different countries; and, although it will not ignore Francophone writers and the politics of indigenous-language writers, its principal focus will be upon African writers in English. African literature is not a homogeneous entity, and therefore, one needs to be constantly aware of the plurality of *literatures*, as well as the differing regional debates and historical contexts. The book will aim to provide a combination of critical argument about those central debates within African literary studies, alongside a focus on individual texts and writers that are central to the study of African literatures. I was predominantly brought up in white suburban Johannesburg, South Africa, and the pernicious effects, exclusionary tactics and oppressive policies of apartheid were a cautiously if regularly discussed subject in my family household (and this experience permeates Chapters 5–7 of this book, in which there is a detailed and contextualised case-study of recent South African writing). As a white South African now living and working within a western academic context in Britain, I am wary of myself perpetrating exactly the kinds of 'colonial' cultural appropriations of texts so roundly condemned by many African writers, and therefore my aim is to establish textual affinities without 'claiming' and 'owning' the literary texts. I will try to do this by integrating interpretations of African texts within a matrix of contemporary critical debates about memory and history within literary studies and postcolonial theory, with comments and observations on the future trajectories of African literatures by the writers themselves. My methodological approach to African literatures mirrors the same ways in which American literature is studied and debated. That is, people regard American literature as a coherent body of writing with running and developing themes that give the whole literary field intellectual coherence – themes like the frontier, the idea of the West and the Wilderness, contestations of notions of 'manifest destiny', the notion of the 'American Dream', the drive for cultural independence, etcetera. Hence, those studying American literature are not just studying separate authors who happen to be American. Rather, they are exploring a rich field of 'co-textuality' in which key ideas are taken up in different ways by authors across the generations and from different regions. My book aims to extend this approach to the field of African literatures, considering a set of characteristic themes that are recognised as constitutive of the field. In other words, the book will aim to lift African writing out of the area of 'postcolonialism' (in which all non-Anglo-American fields tend to become the same field) and help to perpetuate it as a distinct intellectual entity. The important focus will be on contextualising these African writers within specific debates about the problems of ethnography, history, memory, trauma and ethics. Yet, as with so many other cultures, history and memory are always vexed issues in African literatures. In many ways, the art of memory recalls one not to the life that has been lost but to the life that is yet to be lived. In this respect, history and memory are not merely literary tropes – they are the crucial sites where postcolonial national and cultural identities are being formed and contested.

History has been a site of contest from the moment the first European stepped upon the continent. The colonisers' actions of stereotyping the inhabitants, censoring their pasts, rewriting their histories and brutalising their traditions all find focus in a powerful and arresting image that might well form a thematic hub for this book, *Patience on a Monument – 'A History Painting'*, by South African artist Penny Siopsis (Figure I).

I Penny Siopsis, *Patience on a Monument – 'A History Painting'*

A black female figure sits nonchalantly peeling a lemon in the fore-ground, atop a pile of natural waste and debris cast off by civilisation, which includes fruit peelings, a skull, paintings, books, bowls of fruit, an outstretched hand, sundry art objects and a bust of a black man. Behind this figure stretches a vast vista sweeping backwards into receding time and space, depicting in minute detail a myriad school history textbook and other illustrations (photocopied, stuck down or affixed) of adventurers, missionaries, Boers, black warriors, slaves, colonial administrators, British redcoat soldiers, Voortrekkers, traders and others – all scenes recording South Africa's past from a dominant white patriarchal and prejudiced point of view. The black female serenely peeling her lemon and looking into the abstract distance appears as a conspicuously anti-heroic figure of 'Liberty leading the People', and distinctly echoes Walter Benjamin's angel which looks back at the debris of the past strewn behind it.[1] However, unlike Benjamin's 'Angelus Novus', Siopsis's figure is looking not backward but forward, apparently oblivious to the mayhem and violence behind it. Nevertheless, there are two visions of history here; and like Benjamin, Siopsis would appear to be suggesting that the teleological principle that rationally determines the course of history (the ideology of progress) is in opposition to a liberation that lies in grasping the memory of men whose forgotten voices in the past lay claim to justice. Dramatising the ways in which prejudice operates in those historical images and texts that appear objective, harmless and 'natural', Siopsis opens up a critique of the politics of representation and, in her own way, subverts and decon-structs the ways in which the 'other' has been (mis)represented in these widely disseminated 'educational' images. As a self-declared 'history painting', Siposis's picture symbolically represents the traumas and ruptures imposed upon the wider continent's peoples by colonialism, and aims to manipulate common 'western' ideological images to undermine the very historical narrative they tell.

The Hegelian denigration of Africa's benighted past has reap-peared like a structural hiccup (or perhaps, a conceptual stutter) in western views of Africa, views repeated with embarrassing regular-ity. Yet various historians have described African history as having been interrupted by colonialism, as the African nations' search for nationalism was diverted by imperial obstructions. Caroline Neale cites the following examples:

'The natural course of African history was savagely halted by European conquest and the centuries of the slave trade' (G. F. Pollock, *Civilizations of Africa: Historic Kingdoms, Empires, and Cultures* [Middletown, CT, American Education Publication Unit, 1970], p. 5). It is in this sense that Davidson (Basil Davidson, 'Questions About Nationalism', *African Affairs*, 76 [1977]: 39–46 [46]) refers to 'the restarting of the processes of African history after the long episode of colonial alienation,' as if African history were some independent force which had spent the colonial period behind bars, restrained, but biding its time. (Neale 1986: 116)

Frantz Fanon's critical oeuvre provided a significant reminder that white civilisation and European culture forced an existential deviation and rupture on the African, which amounts to an assertion that Africa did suffer a traumatic cutting, a severing from place and past, as a consequence of colonialism.[2] The choice for these African writers is not whether or not to have a past, but rather – what kind of past shall one have, and what shall be recollected and what forgotten? It is an issue of the control of memory: not only how to get a hold on the past, but also how to let it go.

In the years following the political decolonisation of Africa, the impetus for new historical writing was fuelled by a desire to achieve intellectual and cultural decolonisation through a revision of African history. In his exploration of the Western anthropological and historical discursive constructions of Africa, the historian V. Y. Mudimbe notes that colonialist histories 'speak neither about Africa nor Africans, but justify the process of inventing and conquering a continent and naming its "primitiveness" or "disorder", as well as the subsequent means of its exploitation and methods for its "regeneration"' (Mudimbe 1988: 20). Where colonial writing had sought to demonstrate that Africans remained outside the development of the modern nation-state, post-independence writing portrayed Africans as active within it. The result was a decade of writing that centred upon the triumph of African nationalism in a western mould, and on those aspects of the African past that were perceived as contributing to its evolution. African historians in the 1960s had to write the missing African history, erased by Europe and dismissed by its historians. To uncover these erased pasts (what Michel Foucault has termed 'subjugated histories') was as important as providing visions of a new future. Furthermore, as is well attested now by the events of recent decades, the ending of direct colonial domination did not necessarily spell the instant demise of imperialist ideologies. Postcolonial liberation has involved far more than a revision of economic and governmental infrastructures. Not only institutions and frontiers but a whole raft of imposed and ingrained assumptions, especially about white 'culture' and 'advancement', remained as a corrosive residue of the imperial iron worldview, long after independence itself. So one of the principal strategies of the novelists has been to aid in the reconceptualisation of culture, but also of history and memory, and to organise and articulate the trauma and disruption that colonialism brought about to African communities. Aided by such imaginative publishing ventures as Heinemann's landmark

African Writers Series (Low 2002), so many of these writers participated over the last half of the twentieth century in an (admittedly)
uneven and patchy, yet nevertheless continent-wide process of
cultural and imaginative realignment.

In attending to this cultural revisionism undertaken by African
nations, this book will examine the traumatic effects of African
cultures maimed by colonialism. Its chapters will be studded by the
literatures' prevailing metaphors of holes, gaps, lacunae, interrup-
tions, cracks and fissures. Writers from these different African
cultures register the shock of radical historical change. Since
cultural memory is necessarily overdetermined, past injury can be
ambiguous or even apocryphal and still be damaging. African literatures still dramatize the percussive shock of colonialism almost fifty
years after independence. It is an ambiguously intrusive past, part of
an ongoing symbolic transaction. Over the past decades, African
literatures could be regarded as a radar sweep of the continent's
social atmosphere, sensitive to patches of turbulence and movements
of undercurrents, where one can usefully locate unsettled imaginative conditions, and identify some of the paths of their development.
Yet the paths of this development follow complex trajectories.
Contrary to those models of African literatures as a linear and
sequential development from independence through nationalistic
fervour to post-independence disillusionment and beyond, African
literatures come back again and again to the problems of how to
represent the continent's past. In responding to the slings and
arrows of this traumatic colonial history, African literatures appear
to develop by a repetition of, a delayed iteration of and an obsessive
return to history and the past. For as we shall see in Chapter 1, a key
Freudian insight into trauma is that the impact of a traumatic event
lies in its belatedness, in its refusal to be simply located, in its insistent structure of spatial displacement and temporal deferral. Thus, it
should come as no surprise that in beginning to repair their identities and cultures, African authors inscribe belated and epiphenome-
nal post-traumatic cumulative stresses in their writing. As one
psychoanalytic theorist puts it, what is striking in the experience of
trauma is that its 'insistent re-enactments of the past do not simply
serve as testimony to an event, but may also, paradoxically enough,
bear witness to a past that was never fully experienced as it occurred.
Trauma, that is, does not simply serve as a record of the past but
precisely registers the force of an experience that is not fully owned'
(Caruth 1995: 151). Disturbances in the ground of collective experience are reflected in those after-shocks, shocks that leave the
stresses unassimilated and that induce changes in the central
nervous system of the culture. In clinical cases, therapy usually tries
to help the victim complete the blocked process of integration by re-

experiencing the crisis in a safe environment. African writing can be seen as part of this therapeutic gesture. The events of colonialism left indelible and distressing memories – memories to which the nation, continent and its subjects or citizens continually return. Trauma is psychoanalytical, because the injury or wound entails an interpretation of the mental injury. Nevertheless, trauma has its somatic consequences, and, as in Siopsis's picture, the injured body runs through the following chapters and fictions by African writers, showing how the African body is continually 'on show' in colonial and postcolonial discourse: objectified, manacled, incarcerated, whipped, tortured, branded, categorised, starved. Although the mind or body is afflicted, the injury demands to be interpreted, and if possible, integrated into the character's 'narrative memory'. In order to master the problem of reintegration, the victim may symbolically transform the traumatic event, compulsively re-experience it or even deny it. This book will explore the representation of these overwhelming experiences on the development of the psychopathology of the continent, as its writers register the dissonance of meeting long-denied realities that threaten their individual and collective self-esteem, negotiating the problem of how to tame and ultimately heal its wounds through symbolic transformations, where historical trauma is so often figured as personal amnesia.

Trauma thus does not hinge upon resemblance – it is indexical (i.e. of something else). Trauma opens an understanding of models of history that are no longer straightforwardly referential (based on simple models of experience and reference). For history to be a history of trauma means that it is referential precisely to the extent that it is not fully perceived as it occurs; or, to put it another way, that a history can be grasped only in the very inaccessibility of its occurrence. Consequently, African writing conceived of as an 'art of trauma' is inextricably bound up with the problems of language and representation. So, for example, the influential Kenyan novelist Ngugi's remedy to the catastrophe of colonialism is ultimately to write in Gikuyu since no other language will do; no other language will convey, for him, those interior states of mind of being that Kenyans want to discuss. He experiences the trauma of the fracturing of Kenyan culture and attempts the healing process in his own work and language. Trauma forces an intense address to the entire question of language and representation itself. For example, a writer like Achebe in *Things Fall Apart* and *Arrow of God* refashions English as a way of rendering traditional Ibo discourse and mindsets. Some criticism would make writers like Achebe and Soyinka into writers who speak of universal values, as modern metropolitan consciousnesses reconciling 'heritage' and 'progress'. Yet this modernity obscures the extent to which these writers participate in a sense

of the traumatic nature of African culture and history – albeit
without a nostalgia for the primitivist authenticity which hovers over
the polemic criticism of the 'Bolekaja' critics.[3] The writing in English
constantly traverses the split between familiarity and forgiveness. It
inscribes an alienation and a sense of loss into the African novel
itself, querying an understanding of mimesis, and making
Africanness a model for modernity (rather than Europeanness). This
book therefore explores the extent to which African writers answer
Adorno's call that the novel, if it 'wants to remain true to its realistic
heritage and tell how things really are, ... must abandon a realism
that only aids the façade in its work of camouflage by reproducing it'
(Adorno 1991: 32). In this respect, to what extent is the identity politics of the realist mode intimately allied to what Robert Young has
termed the logic of the 'white mythology' (Young 1990), the radical
separation of before/after, inside/outside, rooted in African literature? Can African literatures simply abandon realism? Or are their
self-identities partly predicated upon the model and example of their
oppressor, which is part of their tragedy? Yet even if history seems to
have staged the lack of self-presence of the colonised self as an ontological condition, consciousness and conscience begins with the recognition of the situation as it is, not with the projection upon others of
one's own handed-down identity, or the flight into nostalgic constructions of pure origins. Thus, the puncturing of realist representation
must also aim at puncturing the illusionary defence of African
nationalist purist self-identification. African writers demonstrate
that the traumatic nature of history means that events are historical
only to the extent that they implicate others, and that African
history, like trauma, is never simply one's own, that history is
precisely the way we are implicated in each other's traumas as ex-
colonial powers.

African literatures testify repeatedly to this traumatic rupturing –
a rupturing of national identity, of national history, of continental
integrity, of racial identity and of individual autonomy. African literatures demonstrate a recurring attempt to overcome this rupturing
process called colonialism, and its after-effects, or psychic after-
shocks. While postcolonial theory is clearly not new to psychoanalysis (one has only to think of Fanon's and path-breaking Bhabha's
work), nevertheless the intersection of trauma studies and postcolonialism is still in its infancy, albeit with 'a growing understanding of
postcolonial theory as a discourse haunted by the trauma of colonialism, a discourse permeated with traces of European guilt and indigenous victimization' (Libin 2003: 121). The provenance of trauma
theory is relatively recent, with Post-Traumatic Stress Disorder
(PTSD) being officially recognised as an ailment by the American
Psychiatric Association only in 1980. Although the physiology of

shock as a wounding of the mind first found widespread exploration in the work of figures like Freud, Breuer, Charcot and Janet, and then with the psychological effects of the two world wars, it has found its principal theoretical formulations in relation to cultural representations in studies of the Holocaust and, more recently, African American literature. Self-consciously situated in a matrix of ethics, aesthetics and politics, such studies have been principally concerned with the tensions between speaking and silence, between reclaiming lives by means of language and images in the face of stories of extermination, torture and oppression, and the problems of how an ethics of persuading and engaging a contemporary readership is affected by the aesthetics of representing the effects of mass extermination.[4] Such thematic analogies, despite their different historical and geographical specifics, are clearly the main issues at stake in African literature. Still, a traumatic event such as colonialism cannot simply be recuperated in one single text, representation, or 'working-through', and hence the proliferation of texts, attempts and forms of repetition throughout African literature. The event spills out sideways, always needing to be repeated or represented in an attempt to try and 'get it right' in an authentic manner. Trauma presents a gap between event and discourse. As one key conceptual theorist for this book, Dominick LaCapra, has written, 'Trauma indicates a shattering break or caesura in experience which has belated effects. Writing trauma would be one of those telling aftereffects ... It involves processes of acting out, working over and to some extent working through in analysing and "giving voice" to the past – processes of coming to terms with traumatic experiences, and their symptomatic effects that achieve articulation in different combinations and hybridized forms' (LaCapra 2001: 186). Much of African writing is involved in the goal of assisting in the effort to restore to the victims of colonialism (at least symbolically if posthumously) the dignity that the perpetrators of colonialism took from them – a restorative effort in which historical and literary discourse is itself engaged to some extent in processes of mourning and attempts at proper burial (important forms of working through the past). This is related in crucial ways to the problems of memory. What is of utmost importance, is what is constructed or allowed to enter into publically accessible memory which enables the past to be available (or is suppressed, distorted or blocked). This is not a book that laments the manner in which colonialism transgressed the African continent's cultural authenticity. There lies nostalgia and a cultural cul-de-sac. This is not an analysis of the ways in which African writers have sought to reconstitute the integrity of African culture corrupted by decades of hybridity within the new contexts of independence. As Kwame Anthony Appiah appropriately warns, the homogenisation of an African 'national heritage' is created by 'the careful filtering of the rough torrent of historical event into the fine stream of official narrative; the creation of [an] homogenous legacy of values and experiences' (Appiah 1992: 59). Rather these are often stories of broken languages, broken memories and broken identities. Accurate memory that confronts the traumatic dimensions of African history is ethically desirable in coming to terms with that past both for the individual and for the social collectivity. It is bound up with one's sense of self-understanding and with the nature of an African public sphere, including the way a collectivity comes to represent its past in its relation to its present and future. In this projection of an imagined future, the disillusionment, trauma and severance are balanced by a sense of exuberance and excitement. Yet a pugnacious sovereignty can be its own source of problems; and history (memory), especially personal histories (memories), teaches conflicting lessons about peoples' and nations' ethical trajectories.

A further related issue hovering in the background of these matters is the specific relationship of literature to trauma. Does literature go beyond the theory of trauma? Does literature possess an excess that can somehow get at trauma in a manner unavailable to theory? Do African literatures provide a 'traumatic realism' that differs from stereotypical conceptions of mimesis and enables instead an often disconcerting exploration of disorientation, its symptomatic dimensions and possible ways of responding to them within a specifically African context? Living in a post-traumatic experience – with the effects of colonial oppression, neo-colonial oppressions, racial barbarisms, racial genocides, autocratic corruption, and continued economic harshness and environmental crises (floods, droughts, diseases, animal extinctions, etcetera) – to the degree that Africa is a post-traumatic continent, what do the continent's literatures teach Europeans about trauma and the African past? Does trauma structure the literatures? Do the literatures bear witness or provide a testimony to this trauma? How is the *act of writing* interrelated with the *act of bearing witness*? In the light of these questions, my interest lies less in further defining trauma, so much as using the ideas and questions (which have often emanated from analyses of other traumatic experiences such as the Holocaust) to help in understanding the development of African literatures, their construction of history and memory, and how trauma unsettles and forces Europeans to rethink their notions of historical and literary mnemonic experience. In so doing, trauma will be examined as a cultural trope in various contexts and forms of writing. One aspect of the subsequent chapters will be an examination of how the tropes, lexicons and discourse of trauma theory in psychoanalysis allows one to focus more clearly on the problems of (re)telling the past without flattening or romanticising it, acknowledging its gaps yet seeking its import.

Focusing upon this moment of colonial rupture opens up a number of risks associated with the complicity or resistance of western theory when using it to relate to African literature. As I will repeatedly return to this issue in subsequent chapters, it is important to note now that postcolonial theory as a framework is too homogenising or simplistic when mechanistically or straightforwardly imposed to 'unlock' African literature; that the utilisation of theory is too 'centrist' a process that can have the effect of domesticating non-European texts. In fact, Stephen Slemon suggests that texts are far trickier, enacting or thematizing those very slippery processes that theory is constantly trying to pin down or formulate as a narratology, or as an economy of writing (Slemon 1990a). Although it has provided many of the conceptual and interpretative frameworks for discussions of African fictions, postcolonial theory is arguably a discourse that is distinct from African fiction. Postcolonial theory has often proved to be more about the West's view of the 'African other', or how European views have influenced African writers, than actually about the writings from these new nations themselves. In fact, theory has sometimes been guilty of homogenising the African world as an idealised movement of resistance to imperialism, demonising a European literary and cultural tradition against which the 'African empire' is implicitly or openly rebelling. There are clearly instances where African fiction is responding to ideas and debates originating in postcolonial theory, but usually that fiction is responding to more pressing political issues, a point made forcefully by Aijaz Ahmad (Ahmad 1995). Indeed, it is a moot point as to whether the theory has driven the fiction or whether the fiction has driven the theorisation. African writers often stand in an ambiguous relationship *vis-à-vis* the 'post' in 'postcolonialism': seeking to resist the homogenising tendencies of postcolonial and postmodern theory through a politicised self-consciousness, they are not blind to the potential for complicity with and contamination by the very influences that they seek to resist. Nevertheless, broadly speaking, African writing (along with writing from a host of 'ex-colonial' countries) has effected a new agenda in discussions of cultural value, and placed a new urgency on discussions of such issues as aboriginality, revisionist historiography, mappings, migrancy, landscape and language, oral and scribal traditions, responses to European texts (counter-discourses), gender mythologies, discovery and settlement, nationalisms, multiculturalism and cultural division.

In a now well-worn phrase, postcolonial literature has sought to 'write back against the empire' (Ashcroft et al. 1989). So, for example, the well-known Nigerian novelist Chinua Achebe's early fiction sought to rewrite the African perspective of Nigeria after hundreds of years of colonial rule, in which people's cultures, histories and religions were routinely denigrated and dismissed. Such novelists present the missing or excluded cultural histories of their peoples, such as Ngugi's novels about the Gikuyu during the transition from colony to independent Kenya in *The River Between* (1965), or novels by Elechi Amadi and Ayi Kwei Armah that seek to present indigenous life before colonialism in West Africa. Some of these writers also specifically engage with the aesthetic representations of European novelists, such as Achebe's engagement with Joseph Conrad and Joyce Cary, seeking to forge a national consciousness through the development of new cultural forms. The generic adaptation that has emerged in African writing has often been responsible for constructing new or hybrid genres from oral traditions, such as Amos Tutuola's *The Palm-wine Drinkard* (1952) or Ben Okri's *The Famished Road* (1991). Furthermore, there are instances where African writers have rewritten particular works from the English literary 'canon' with the intention of restructuring 'realities' from a peculiarly African perspective, such as J. M. Coetzee's *Foe* (1986). This approach to representing hidden or obscured cultural histories has been termed 'decolonising fictions' (Brydon and Tiffin 1993). However, the task of these writers has not been merely to find a non-repressive alternative to imperialist and colonialist discourse, but to resist repeating the repressive discursive structures in their new modes of writing. In writing back against the empire, these fictions from the 'periphery' have been profoundly instrumental in forcing the 'centre' to rethink and reconceptualise central aspects of western Enlightenment thought, such as concepts of history, issues of nationhood and the constructions of race, ethnicity and subjectivity. Constructions of a national culture go hand-in-hand with definitions of new citizenship, new subjectivities, and new social and political identities.

Focusing upon this moment of colonial rupture also runs the risk of privileging the postcolonial moment. Has postcolonialism given Africa its 'moment'? Is what is new and different in the present and future dependent on what has preceded it in the past? As I have noted, history and memory are always vexed issues, and no less so in African literatures. African writers return repeatedly to the problems of history, the difficulties in remembering the past(s) and the force of tradition. For example, the Ugandan poet Okot p'Bitek's *Song of Lawino and Song of Ocol* dramatises this conflict of modernity and tradition (p'Bitek 1984). The poems take as their central issue the defence of Acholi tradition against the encroachment of western cultural influences, as p'Bitek translates English words into traditional Acholi (or Luo as the Acholi language is sometimes called) verse patterns. The "Song of Lawino" tells the story of Lawino's complaint against her husband, Ocol, who neglects her because of her adherence to Acholi customs and traditions. Ocol, by contrast, endeavours to become as westernised as possible, rejecting his indigenous culture as backward and crude. Yet it is the strength of Lawino's voice that dominates the poem, reminding the reader of the human reality behind glib denials of the rudimentary, primitive 'bush people'.

Yet the past is never simply a matter of something over and done with. Memory is part of modernity and the modern nation. Memory and history form part of a literary politics of identity which plays dynamically upon a palimpsestual tension. It uses the future imaginary to negate, renegotiate or playfully compromise present authority. In turn, it can also reaffirm authority, or its possibility, by counteracting the traces of colonial and precolonial sociality within the postcolonial. This book will explore the unequal and vacillating relationship between memory and history within the context of African literatures. Since 'history' can be an aggressively exclusionary narrative, this book will argue that African writing constructs memory as a form of counter-history that subverts false generalisations by an exclusionary 'History'. A key conviction in this book is that a genuine potential for change is impossible without the development of a historical consciousness. The future is generated according to our understanding of the past. A nation that has no past knows not where it is going. This book is not simply criticising one way or another of representing the past. Rather, it recognises that there is going to be a use of different techniques at different moments and places – for example, that realism is not simply a tired form to be replaced by a vibrant innovative postmodern metafictional style, that African fiction cannot be understood if one is simply involved in the valorisation of an anti-realism from a partisan postmodern perspective. Nor is it the aim here to define or theorise memory in only one particular way. Rather, this is a contribution to an ongoing debate about the processes of memory, and about how memory (especially traumatic memory) is created and inscribed, particularly within an African postcolonial milieu. The book will investigate how certain versions of the past get to be remembered, which memories are privileged and what the loci are for memory within the context of African literatures. Chapter 1 will provide a theoretical framework for the arguments in this book, by establishing the main debates about African writing in relation to modernism and traditionalism, history and the present, trauma and the ethics of historical representation, and theories of memory as a challenge to the discourses of historiography and ethnography. In these respects, this book will, first, focus upon memory as a discourse in African writing, emerging as a product of discourse in the ways it operates in private and public life, and how memory is socially and historically constituted within differing African contexts; and, second, interrogate the invocation of memory within a number of other discourses (political, historical, ethical, autobiographical, gender, ethnic), enquiring how memory is called upon to legitimate identity, construct or reconstruct it, and asking how memory is narratively organised, and the ways in which narrative is related to other cultural forms of remembering.

The Economist of 11 May 2000 led with a story entitled 'Hopeless Africa', and tapped into the global media focus upon evolving African politics in the last two decades – South Africa and the end of apartheid, genocide in Rwanda and famine after famine in the Horn of Africa. More recently, this media focus has continued with its attention to the political thuggery in Zimbabwe, the G8 summit in 2005 and the 'Make Poverty History' campaign, all of which have raised the profile of Africa in all quarters. This political and economic interest has been matched by a growing number of books which deal with African writers and literatures in recent years; and the field of African literature and studies has been carefully constructed by a number of prominent scholars such as Jahnheinz Jahn, Jan Vansina, Ulli Beier, Eustace Palmer, Abiola Irele and Bernth Lindfors, and major organisations such as the African Literature Association. Yet despite this increasingly high profile, with writers of international distinction (Achebe, Ngugi), Nobel Laureates (Soyinka, Gordimer) and Booker Prize winners (Okri, Coetzee), it is clear that African writers do not seek to seduce their readership into forgetting the traumatic ruptures of their birth as 'nations'. Yet this is contradictory, since their writing is also a 'working out or through' of the trauma, an effort to try to come to terms with the effects of the rupture. So, they try both to raise consciousness of the traumatic past and to cure the consciousness of that trauma. There is an astigmatic focus in these writers – a double focus, a dysraphism. It is a strange expression that dominates – a blockage model – a feeling that repression is negative, but also a recognition that repression is never merely negative but also constructive and libertarian. There is a curious way in which many of these African nations are what they are because of the monstrously repressed traumatic rupture at their heart. Colonial trauma acts like a *pharmakos*, a poison and cure.

The following book attempts to trace this double focus on the consciousness and cure of the traumatic rupture in a variety of different literary contexts – myths of the past, social realist attempts to portray an accurate present (and by extension, past), postmodern rejoinders to the realist representations, the way in which gender is implicated in this traumatic consciousness, and the way in which this traumatic past is ironically replicated and intensified in the literature produced by those imprisoned by postcolonial African regimes. The book concludes with several chapters that focus upon the exceptional, barbarically self-conscious, social experiment in racial manipulation that was apartheid, and the manner in which this has preoccupied writers of all ethnic backgrounds from its very inception. In particular, it focuses upon the coalescence of anti-apartheid reaction in the poetry emerging from the 1970s and 1980s, and, more recently, upon the somewhat perplexed readjustments to a post-apartheid era in fiction. Roughly speaking, the book is organised into two parts: Chapters 1 to 4 focus on pan-African commonalities, while Chapters 5 to 7 offer more detailed, historicised and territorialised accounts of recent South African writing. Chapter 8 attends to a more overarching issue of the usefulness of metafictionality and postmodernity as terms to understand African literature, and also acts as something of a concluding assessment, especially since all the preceding chapters are arguably predicated upon perspectives of the representation of history that result from a 'postmodern' theoretical consciousness. Therefore, the trajectory of the book aims to be neither chronological nor inclusive, but typological and thematic in its investigation of the instances of traumatic irruption.[5]

Africa is hardly what might one call homogeneous. The culture and history are neither continuous nor uninterrupted. One needs to recognise the plurality of cultural experience when one is dealing with the differences of the specific instances of colonial eras in the East, West and South; the Islamic influences in the West, North and East; and the different colonial masters of parts of the continent and their linguistic and cultural legacies. Within this heterogeneity, one might well question the direction of Africa after the effects of colonialism. Is it meaningful, in the context of the plurality of African cultures in contemporary Africa, with the discordant and jarring hullabaloo of the marketplaces in Lagos, Accra, Nairobi and Bamako, or the wide deserts and savannahs of Mali, Somalia, Uganda and Kenya, or the highly surveilled high-tech malls and gated communities of South Africa, to speak of an African post-nation? Bearing in mind the immediate pressures of its burden of modern histories, how ought Africa tackle its looming future, yet without forgetting its recent, haunting past or stirring up wistful legends of validity as a way of keeping in check the ostensible futility and indecision of the present? Indeed, how does one account for the present, encircled as it is by constant states of emergency and the rival impediments of the past and future? I concur with Abiola Irele who argues that important books matter in the intellectual life of any country struggling out of the disjunctures and traumas of colonialism (Irele 1981).

Indeed, as the subsequent chapters will palpably show, despite their differing cultural, geographical and historical contexts, a large number of African writers repeatedly demonstrate an ethical acuity, a responsibility to forge a new consciousness, flying by those nets of language, nationality and race on the wings of recollection and memory.

Africa's literary archive registers the transformation of social memory by emergent fantasies, narratives and images of the past shaped by two converging forces: a growing acknowledgement of the aftershocks and responsibilities of historical traumas, and the adjustments made necessary by new landscapes of space and time in late postcoloniality. African literatures encapsulate several dominant features of contemporary cultural belief about the past: it is hidden; it can be recovered through memories graven by the force of trauma whose reversal requires an ethics of emotional sacrifice, as well as catharsis and the lifting of repression; and when recovered, the past will appear as a witnessable event in a specific space and time. As Africa begins to confront the potentially catastrophic trauma of massive devastation by HIV, the latest in the long line of the traumatic experiences of Africa, which threatens to become its newest nemesis, it is absolutely imperative that nations rise to meet the challenges of mass education and health policies if they are to avert a pan-continental calamity.

Everyone is talking about memory today, whilst what is less noticed is that this discourse of memory is a response to the degree to which the relation to the past has been disembodied, fractalised and repackaged by new practices of time and space emerging in scientific theory, new technology, new relations of production, and shifting discourses of political and social legitimation, which together have transformed and disoriented our understanding of experiences of both chronology and place, and therefore of history as knowledge of the past. As I have argued with Peter Middleton in our book *Literatures of Memory*, theories of repression and trauma are compelling because they offer solutions to the detemporalisation and anachronisms of modern experiences of spacetime, bypassing or inverting causality in the *Nachträglichkeit* of hindsight, but these solutions also easily collude with or wholly give in to dominant narratives of history (Middleton and Woods 1999). We argued in *Literatures of Memory* that there is a need for a more articulate ethics of history to develop out of this increasing preoccupation with memory, that would acknowledge the democratic and ideological contests over the making of pasts, as well as ceaseless constructions of identity and difference at work. Paul Ricoeur sees this happening only in the novel (sometimes too readily perhaps); he says that fiction 'permits historiography to live up to the task of memory' by revealing 'possibilities buried in the actual past' (Ricoeur 1985: 189 and 192).

Museums privilege history over memory because the story the museum aims to tell is one in which the inaccuracies and chronological idiosyncracies of memory have no role. History involves ordering and classification, the metonymic displacement of fragments for objects. However, theories of memory have always incorporated the notion of forgetting on several different levels. Something must be forgotten before it can be retrieved. Each act of remembering involves a selection, a leaving aside of that which is not chosen. Finally and most importantly, nothing can be completely forgotten until it is remembered. As we shall see time and again, memory is inextricably associated and implicated with the current allocation of ethical responsibility and the politics of blame. This dialectic between memory and forgetting creates the ethical trajectory that principally allows Africans, but also Europeans, to recall and then move on, to put aside the burden of memory and to open oneself to the muse of forgiveness.

Notes

[1]   'A Klee painting named Angelus Novus shows an angel looking as though he is about to move away from something he is fixedly contemplating. His eyes are staring, his mouth is open, his wings are spread. This is how one pictures the angel of history. His face is turned toward the past. Where we perceive a chain of events, he sees one single catastrophe which keeps piling wreckage upon wreckage and hurls it in front of his feet. The angel would like to stay, awaken the dead, and make whole what has been smashed. But a storm is blowing from paradise; it has got caught in his wings with such violence that the angel can no longer close them. This storm irresistibly propels him into the future to which his back is turned, while the pile of debris before him grows skyward. This storm is what we call progress' (From the Ninth Thesis, Benjamin 1992: 149).

[2]   Alternatively, one might agree with Ali Mazrui, who argues in *The Africans: A Triple History* (1986: 14) that the colonial experience is a relatively brief period in African history, which stretches for millennia. While this argument does have the effect of further downplaying Europe's role on the development of African history through relativising its historical impact, nevertheless it does seem to stubbornly ignore the representational impact that colonialism has had on African culture, nothwithsanding its brevity in terms of the continent's longer historical development.

[3]   For example, see Msiska 2000; and Kanneh 1998, in which she argues, in agreement with Anthony Kwame Appiah, that Chinweizu, Jemie and Madubuike's provocative thesis in *Toward the Decolonization of African Literature* (1983), is flawed by a 'cultural essentialism haunting the arguments ... where Africa becomes a totalised vision of otherness, summarised in the phrase, "Africa is simply not the West"' (Kanneh 1998: 39).

[4]   The provenance and genealogy of trauma theory are exceptionally well traced in Leys 2000, where she examines many of the key theorists, including the work of Sigmund Freud, Pierre Janet, Sándor Ferenczi, William Sargant and Cathy Caruth among others. Among what is now an extremely extensive bibliography, key recent theorists of trauma theory in relation to the representation of the Holocaust include Lawrence Langer (see later chapters), Dominick LaCapra (see Chapter 1), Horowitz 1997, Vice 1999, Schwartz 1999, Reiter 2000 and Eaglestone 2004. Other recent texts in the extending discussion of trauma theory and various sites of representation are Tal 1996, Herman 2001, Farrell 1998, Edkins 2003 and Eyerman 2001. Other texts

and theorists who are not mentioned above are more specifically discussed and cited later in this book's list of Works Cited.

⁵   This has meant that, despite the recognition that African literatures need to be continually historicised, nevertheless, a structural tension remains in the book, between an approach that implicitly predicates a pan-African sensibility in which 'memory' becomes the focus for an alternative model of history and an approach that suggests the distinctiveness of the experiences and 'concrete particularity' of specific cultures and groups. This may also mean that occasionally a certain elision occurs between the different positions of writers from groups that have suffered from discrimination and writers from privileged groups who address the inequities of political situations and regimes on their behalf. Whilst I recognise that sacrifices are bound to occur as a result, I hope that different strengths emerge from these two foci (of broad perspective against local particularity) as well.

1

Figuring African history, memory and trauma

Our struggle is also a struggle of memory against forgetting. (*South African Freedom Charter*)

'The writer in Africa and other countries in the Third World, because of his nearness (remember: he is a member of the privileged élite) to the central questions of decision-making and power, is engaged (unlike his counterpart in Western Europe and North America) in the unfolding of history in its rawness; engaged in the making of history' (Nuruddin Farah, quoted in Killam 1984: 192). So said Nuruddin Farah, the internationally honoured Somali novelist, juxtaposing state and individual power with the proximity of problems of mediating, representing and constructing history. Whether African writers are closer to history in the making (its 'rawness') than writers other from parts of the world is open to debate, but nevertheless discussions of African literature nearly always touch on history – the histories of peoples, cultures, nations and colonialism. Ethnicity is perceived to be a product of material history, constructed and re-articulated with regard to the particular historical location of groups in relation to a dominant culture. One critic has argued that history has been an enabling discourse for African writers, allowing them the opportunity and space to create a new 'African gnosis'. History and literature offer a discursive challenge to ethnographic discourses which sought to essentialise and objectify the African experience:

Thus, not all, but some writers – those preoccupied with history – wrote literature while aiming at creating the possibility of a new African gnosis. One of the shaping impulses behind their fiction was to counter the authority of European social 'scientists' who studied Africa and Europe's relation to Africa. The ambitions behind the cultural production of Africans in European languages are directed at the totalising discourses of the ethnographic description of African peoples and a European historiography into which Africa had been incorporated as a blank space, a void. (Coundouriotis 1999: 14)

History is thus construed as a counter-ethnographic discourse. Eleni Coundouriotis argues that ethnography is motivated by a synchronous impulse, a freezing of time and place, whereas 'Historical narration entailed the reinscription not only of narratives of development but of descriptions of place, a reclaiming of time and place' (Coundouriotis 1999: 44). Her principal argument is that ethnography is a conservative discourse, against which historical narration seeks to fight, providing a diachronic explanation for the initial colonial values. As a transgressive discourse, 'the practice of history by [some] novelists is a constant effort to cross the limits in which Africa has been circumscribed through its encounter with Europe' (Coundouriotis 1999: 118). As such, 'The literary conventions of the novel have always functioned for African writers as a site of contest where the limits of literariness are constantly challenged in order to initiate an alternative discourse of knowledge' (Coundouriotis 1999: 13). In this respect, writers such as Achebe, Ngugi, Soyinka, Okri, Gordimer, Coetzee among others are all faced with a problem, 'one of narrative method: how to write a history from the point of view of the dispossessed without re-enacting a further dispossession by taking over their point of view' (Coundouriotis 1999: 122). Memory is one site where this difficult task is repeatedly explored.

Memory may not be judged by using the same criteria of accuracy, coherence and analysis that conventional history assumes in its attempt at objectivity, for often in the course of remembering, historical facts are metamorphosed, lost or misinterpreted. It is the medium we employ to remind ourselves who we were, who we have become and who we will be. It vies with and undermines the linearity of conventional history, as Jacques Le Goff, one of the foremost theorists of the relation between history and memory, remarks when considering the increased significance of memory in recent decades: 'Today the application to history of the results of philosophy, science, and individual and collective experience tends to introduce, alongside these measurable categories of historical time, the notions of duration [*durée*], of lived time [*temps vécu*], of multiple and relative times, and of subjective or symbolic times. Historical time is rediscovering at a new, very sophisticated level the old time of memory, which is broader than history and supplies it with material' (Le Goff 1992: xx). Le Goff's idea of memory enlarging the scope of history demonstrates that, whilst memory inhabits territory that overlaps with history, it concerns itself with something other than historical accuracy. Often memory struggles to convey the reality of an unimaginable occurrence, and consequently employs figures and metaphors that transcend the boundaries of fact. Whilst colonialism did exist in historical fact, it may not be relegated simply to history; for memory, there can be no 'before' and 'after' the colonial age: the colonial is in the postcolonial. Testimonies by people who lived through the transition to independence in all those African countries reiterate this fact. Whilst they are able to write of a 'before' and 'after', colonialism does not seem to be 'over', managed or closed. African writers become cultural witnesses insisting on memory as agency in its power to intervene in imposed systems of meaning. The question of memory is therefore not only an epistemological one but also an ethical one; and the opposite term to forgetting, or to the forgotten, is not remembrance but justice.

Memory is regarded as having a demystifying effect. It can be used for a number of different challenging functions, as Foucault has reminded us.[1] It can be treated as a counter-hegemonic chronicle, in which an imagined 'other' history is narrated, thereby destabilising dominant histories. Ethnic literature in particular often reinscribes memory as history. There are ways in which personal memory shapes and is woven into group memory through what is selected, and linguistic and narrative strategies are sometimes designed to subvert the hegemonic narrative of historical events. African writers are frequently concerned with the problem of how to represent a release from the past without losing 'authenticity'; yet they are also deeply conscious that many literary and ethnographic constructions of African cultural 'authenticities' as against cultural hybridities can play into the hands of the essentialist racial hierarchies which featured so prominently in colonial representations of Africa. Yet despite the attendant problems, memory is often construed as a basis for an authentic self that can be liberated from the silence and suppression brought upon it by history. Then there are the disruptions to memory, psyche and identity, through displacement, slavery or colonisation. Reliving these disruptions of the past can be liberating. Language itself, as Bakhtin has demonstrated, has its own 'memory':

> As a result of the work done by all these stratifying forces in language, there are no 'neutral' words and forms – words and forms that can belong to 'no one'; language has been completely taken over, shot through with intentions and accents. For any individual consciousness living in it, language is not an abstract system of normative forms but rather a concrete heteroglot conception of the world. All words have a 'taste' of a profession, a genre, a tendency, a party, a particular work, a particular person, a generation, an age group, the day and hour. Each word tastes of the context and contexts in which it has lived its socially charged life; all words and forms are populated by intentions. Contextual overtones (generic, tendentious, individualistic) are inevitable in the word. (Bakhtin 1981: 293)

Many African writers are concerned with the effects of the vestigial traces of European colonialism not only in their current culture but also specifically within their various languages. Consequently, this book will examine the interrogations African writers make into language, representation and memory.

However, as David Palumbo-Liu has argued, there is a 'double dilemma' of history for ethnic groups. Although ethnic groups challenge the epistemological authority of history through memory, paradoxically, these memory narratives in turn have to lay claim to a more legitimate epistemology:

> The ethnic narrative presents an occasion for a subversive revision of the dominant version of history; it gives voice to a text muted by dominant historical referents; and it makes possible an imaginative invention of a self beyond the limits of the historical representations available to the ethnic subject. However, critics have paid less attention to the ways in which such acts of revision are highly problematic; to perform such acts, ethnic writers are often caught in a double dilemma. First, to make a space of articulation for themselves, to carve out an area for revision, they must first dis-place history, and yet such destabilization of the dominant history necessitates a preliminary critique of *any* history's epistemological claims. Any counterhistory, furthermore, must legitimate itself by laying claim to a firmer epistemology than that claimed by the dominant history. The question then becomes, how can one deconstruct the dominant history on the basis of its ideologically suspect nature, and *not* admit that one's revision is also overdetermined?
>
> Second, the formal properties of literary narrative engage ethnic writers in the ideologically problematic nature of closure. The narrative's ending may be predicated upon a stabilization of history in which the ongoing dialectical relationship between minor and dominant discourses is suppressed. What starts off as a contestive counterhistory may thus be objectified and stabilized as merely a smaller instance within the greater metanarrative of history. (Palumbo-Liu 1996: 211–12)

Thus, 'the insertion of counterhistory calls for an epistemological foundation that can challenge history's authority to narrate the past; that is, if one seeks to offer a counterhistory within literary narrative, then one must still subvert history via a discourse that is equally, if not more, stable' (Palumbo-Liu 1996: 212). In this dilemma, it is from memory, the repository of things omitted from history, that the ethnic subject often seeks to challenge history. Many of the texts studied in this book share methods of inverting the history-memory relation – they stabilise memory, imbuing it with the status of history, and destabilise history, critiquing its modes of assigning significance. In this double movement, African narratives frequently reinscribe memory as history; and, as Christopher Miller has argued in *Theories of Africans* (1990), the narratives stage a confrontation between ethnicity and the ethics of representation.

Many people have explored the topic of ethnic memory, but few have really explored the unequal and vacillating relationship between memory and history, especially within the context of African literature. How do history and memory creatively interact in African literature? Often spurred on by a conscious effort to limit forgetfulness, *lieux de mémoires* (to use Pierre Nora's resonant phrase) are products of the interaction between history and memory, of the interplay between the personal and the collective. Individual or group memory selects certain landmarks of the past – places, artworks, dates, persons, public or private, well-known or obscure, real or imagined – and invests them with a symbolic and political significance. Since 'history' can be an aggressively exclusionary narrative (consider Hegel's notorious exclusion of Africa from 'history', or Hugh Trevor-Roper's infamous notion that Africans are barbarians), in many cases, memory can become a form of counter-history that challenges false generalisations in an exclusionary 'History'. This proposition is advanced by Michel de Certeau, in which he argues that acts of memory introduce into the ordered space of the present other times and other forms of know-how (de Certeau 1984: chapters 3 and 9). The act of memory can become a 'tactic' which invokes excluded practices, actions and narratives. Memory resists the detemporalising moves of history writing which, by constructing narratives of the past as authoritative knowledge geared towards a predictable future, has to dominate the historical contingencies and specificities of the past. Memory 'spatialises' time by seeing the past as yet another aspect of the present. Memory, anecdote or folk-tale are fragments of the past as such, not determined completely by the ordering 'strategies' of the present.

Psychoanalysis, which is partly a hermeneutics of memory, tries to produce a way of dealing with the past rather than revolting against it. Events and actions in the past can be disruptive, and memory can be both the source of pain as well as of pleasure: as Freud explains, memory is the stuff of pathology and desire. Yet we need not be merely victims or survivors of our pasts: we are capable of making meaning and direction out of our past. Narrative memory assimilates the past and integrates it into our present. At the core of historical representation, narrative memory *transforms* the past as a condition of retaining the past. Whilst many African writers recognise that politically historical representation must communicate a distance, an otherness, they also frequently suggest that it must also convey something of how we connect to that past or otherness. In this respect, memory 'is by definition, a term which directs our attention not to the past but to *the past-present relation*. It is because "the past" has this living active existence in the present that it matters so much politically' (Johnson et al. 1982: 211). Freedom, therefore, can be brought about only through acknowledging the scars of one's history, not in escaping from them. Wole Soyinka has forcefully argued in his essays on the subject of trauma, memory and history that

> One does not shed the scales of centuries as simply as a snake sloughs off its winter – or harmattan – skin. Our proposition is simply one of recollection, or, to go back to our commencing code, memory. The need for the preservation of the material and spiritual properties by which memory is invested. Acceptance of both its burdens and triumphs or – better still – its actuality, the simple fact of its anterior existence and its validity for its time. (Soyinka 1999: 62–3)

As the African philosopher Tsenay Serequeberhan argues, African philosophy as the hermeneutics of the postcolonial situation is critically involved with memory and evocation: 'the critical remembrance, itself interior to the lived emancipatory *praxis* of the contemporary African, that cultivates, mediates, and revitalizes the origin or the source of this emancipatory *praxis*' (Serequeberhan 1998: 17). Contemporary African literature is involved in a hermeneutic effort to reconstruct and appropriate meaning within the parameters of a lived inheritance and tradition that has become estranged and crisis prone. The past acquires a particular significance for those subjects, peoples and communities for whom categories of the present have been made unusually unstable or unpredictable, as a consequence of the displacement enforced by postcolonial and migrant circumstances. Personal memory can be instrumental in installing a mobile sense of postcolonial identity. The present acquires its meaning only with reference to the disjointed and conflicted narrative of the past – in which references to official narratives about colonization and a historical memory are tangled up with personal memories and private recollections of past experience. As some historians state the case,

> Private memories cannot, in concrete studies, be readily unscrambled from the effects of dominant historical discourses. It is often these that supply the very terms by which a private history is thought through. Memories of the past are, like all common-sense forms, strangely composite constructions, resembling a kind of geology, the selective sedimentation of past traces. As Gramsci put it, writing about the necessity of historical consciousness for a Communist politics, the problem is '"knowing thyself" as a product of the historical process to date which has deposited in you an infinity of traces, without leaving an inventory'. (Johnson et al. 1982: 211)

It is making this inventory which preoccupies African writers, constituting the present-day African realities partly by the hybrid remnants of the colonial and precolonial past.

This activity has precipitated a crisis of memory in Africa today – a problematics of postcolonial memory (see Werbner 1998). Memory-work is examined at every turn, as representations of loss, insecurity, displacement and deterritorialisation occur in African literature. Much memory-work is future-oriented, as people struggle to keep traces of the past and the present alive for the sake of the future. In this way, memory can become a way of countering political nostalgia fostered by neo-colonial African governments (or what Ngugi has disparagingly termed in Kenya a 'comprador bourgeoisie'), and memory emerges as a modernist rupture with tradition. Focusing on the way memory is politicised in African writing, this book concerns itself with the way contemporary African subjectivities are made through nostalgia for a lost past, through buried, suppressed, textualised or scripturalised memory, through remembering the present and through the memory-work of rupture with the past. This first chapter frames the succeeding chapters of this book, in that it seeks to examine the relations between history, memory, trauma and African postcolonialism.

Memory and self

The crisis in memory is not simply a macro-historical 'crisis': memory is linked to identity-politics. The politics of representing the past, and the ways in which memory acts as the chain with missing links that connects the postcolonial subject to his or her disrupted history, form the principal focus of Nuruddin Farah's novel *Maps*. Farah gained an international reputation with his first 'Variations on the Theme of an African Dictatorship' trilogy, for his outspoken critiques of the Somali dictator General Mohammed Siyad Barre who ruled the country during the 1970s and 1980s. His second 'Blood in the Sun' trilogy deals with various unconnected characters living through the history of Somalia's struggle for the unification of the Somali-speaking territories from Ethiopia, and the legacy of Barre's rule – a Mogadiscio plagued by internecine warfare between clan factions in the 1990s. Farah's obsessive search for identity – personal, familiar, social, national – echoes throughout the trilogy. The first novel in the sequence, *Maps*, arguably the most challenging of the three novels, is about the development of a young boy, Askar, an orphan prodigy who has visions of his own birth (and his mother's death in childbirth) and whose mouth bleeds as if menstruating. Askar grows up under the nurturing – and titillating – embrace of his Ethiopian guardian, Misra, before he sets off to live and study in the capital Mogadiscio with his cosmopolitan aunt Salaado and Uncle Hilaal, where he becomes shaken by the war that took his father's life.

Elaboratively self-reflexive, the novel opens with the following address to Askar by the undisclosed authorial voice:

You sit, in contemplative posture, your features agonized and your expressions pained; you sit for hours and hours and hours, sleepless, looking into darkness, hearing a small snore coming from the room next to yours. And you conjure a past ...

Yes. You are a question to yourself. It is true. You've become a question to all those who meet you, those who know you, those who have any dealings with you. You doubt, at times, if you exist outside your own thoughts, outside your own head, or Misra's ...

As you sit contemplatively, your mind journeys to a region where there were solid and prominent shadows which lived on behalf of *others* who had years before ceased to exist as beings. As you sit, your eyes open into themselves, the way blind people's eyes tend to. Then you become numb of soul: in other words, you are not yourself – not quite yourself anyway. The journey takes you through numerous doorways and you are enabled to call back to memory events which occurred long before you were a being yourself. (*Maps*: 4)

This is the realm of the novel – history, the past, uncertainty, ghostly beings, otherness, quests and alterity. The repeated invocation of memory in the novel raises questions about the possibility of an easy distinction between memory and 'memory', between memory as unmediated natural fact or process, and the culturally mediated acts, schemata, and stories – the memory-work – that comprise our memories, and the way we think about them. During the narrative, it becomes clear that Askar's life is linked to the 'life' of Somalia. At the outset, his existence is an 'untalked-about secret' (*Maps*: 8), marginalised, suppressed and unrecorded in the face of his forced separation from his mother owing to her untimely death. Askar's existence becomes surreptitious, his name barely mentioned, in no better than a whisper, and he is merely a trace of his mother's former self: 'your mother's corpse was buried in haste and secretly too, your mother who left behind her no trace save yourself ... You did not exist as far as many were concerned; nor did you have any identity as the country's bureaucracy required. Askar! The letter "s" in your name was gently said so as to arouse no suspicions; whereas the "k" was held in the cosiness of a tongue couched in the unspoken secrets of a sound. As-kar!' (*Maps*: 8). In the absence of his own certain past, Askar becomes a mirror that reflects back to others their own identities and pasts: for example, Misra sees her past in Askar as a child: 'she saw a different terrain of land, and she heard a different language spoken and she watched, on the screen of her past, a number of pictures replayed as though they were real and as painful as yesterday' (*Maps*: 7).

As he grows up, so Askar seeks to work out his past, partly from his memories and partly from other signs. Askar rarely feels in control of his life and frequently feels the pawn of forces other than himself: 'Did I, as a result of this my stare, bring into existence a life of memories in which I am not the rememberer but the remembered?'

(*Maps*: 40). The novel is studded with frequent references to Askar's memory, as he tries to piece together the past and his role in the construction: 'I'll admit that many things are confused in my memory. My head, I feel sometimes, will explode with the intensity of the anecdotes I remember – events which in all likelihood didn't take place, not, at any rate, as I remember them' (*Maps*: 41). Faulty memory, untrustworthy memory (*Maps*: 73) and conflicting memories dog his life, as he worries about where dreams end and memories begin: 'I cannot vouch for the accuracy of my memory here. Possibly I have invented one or two things, perhaps I have intentionally deviated from the true course of events. Although I tend to think that I am remembering in precise detail how things happened and what was said' (*Maps*: 84). Askar is a subject who constantly doubts his origins and his identity, and realises that his future is uncertain as long as his past remains shrouded in mystery, 'like a man upon whom it has just dawned that a future is not possible without his disowned past' (*Maps*: 147). It emerges that the crisis of Askar's memory is also about identity, for when he takes personal identity for granted he is not self-conscious about the past; yet when identity is not in question, neither is memory.

Askar's growing self-consciousness is informed in part by the maps he uses to trace the shape of his people's land and his own allegiances. The metaphor of maps structures the narrative since it is the result of piecing together an outline of Askar's past and Misra's role in that past from clues, stories, dreams and memories. The link between the two characters is repeatedly discussed: as to where Askar ends and Misra begins, in terms of physical feeling, emotional psyche and personal identity: 'I seem to have remained a mere extension of Misra's body for years – you saw me when you set eyes on her. I was part of the shadow cast – in a sense, I was her extended self. I was, you might even say, the space surrounding the geography of her body' (*Maps*: 78). The topographical representation of space and its politics are a central issue associated with maps in the novel: personal territory, the connection with Misra's space (how Askar constantly tells us he is the centre of Misra's space), the gradual establishment of one's own space, the masculine space that comes with circumcision (*Maps*: 93–4), and the unification of national space. Gradually, Askar develops his own space, as he assumes his own agency: 'I took hold of a different "self", one that had no room and no space for Misra' (*Maps*: 96), although this space is rarely stable, since Askar is prone to experiencing states of existential uncertainty, as he does in one dream: 'And no one told me where I was, no one told me who I was' (*Maps*: 97). The metaphor of the map is used increasingly as Askar matures, to the point where it becomes a cognitive metaphor for all sorts of spaces: 'The sea is a map: it tells those who are literate in its language where they are, it reveals, to those who are able to uncover secrets, where the treasures are' (*Maps*: 167). Uncle Hilaal adds how it is easier to get rid of colonial powers from overseas than colonial powers that happen to be your neighbour, by which he means the territory of the Somali–Ethiopian dispute, the Ogaden. Permeating the entire narrative is the struggle for the unification of the Somali-speaking territories from Ethiopia and Haile Selassie, retrieving the Ogaden desert for the Somali nation (*Maps*: 87–8), and the various wars attendant upon foreign powers' involvement in Somalia's business. Ethiopian violence performed upon the Somali people, and the imposition of Amharic on them, 'an alien language with its alien concepts and thoughts imposed forcefully upon the mind of a child' (*Maps*: 88), remind the reader of the vestiges of colonial power in the region. Askar uses his body as a map to draw a new reunited Somalia on it thereby identifying himself with the 'mother-nation' but also reuniting himself with his father (*Maps*: 101–2).

Farah has always been conscious that neo-colonial subjectivity is precarious: 'A neo-colonial subject is born into uncertainty, lives in uncertainty, dies in uncertainty and operates on the frontiers of uncertainty. A neo-colonial subject is a person who is told, "You are not who you are"' (Meyer 1999). In a dream Askar meets a young girl to whom he confesses that although 'I who am a child of the age's spirit, I who am, in a sense, a maker of myself, I couldn't tell the girl anything' (*Maps*: 137). Accused of seeing only the surface of things, Askar is unable to trace his origins since he is undermined by his sense of an uncertain and multiple identity. This lack of certainty is reinforced by the epigraph to Part Two of the novel, which quotes Joseph Conrad: 'All is illusion – the words written, the mind at which they are aimed, the truth they are intended to express, the hands that will hold the paper, the eyes that will glance at the lines. Every image floats vaguely in a sea of doubt – and the doubt itself is lost in an unexplored universe of uncertitude' (*Maps*: 139). Pronouns used to address characters in the novel shift disconcertingly between 'I', 'You' and 'He', and the complex issue of identity arises once again as Askar gains a *carte d'identita* proclaiming him to be a Somali rather than a refugee from the Ogaden. The entire issue of what constitutes a Somali is a vexed one that is raked over by both Askar and Uncle Hilaal on several occasions. Askar has a strange sense of being *other*, of harbouring another inside him, a feminine half that he sometimes thinks is Misra, of being a schizophrenic self, split between two identities: 'I have the strange feeling that there is another in me, one older than I – a woman I have the conscious feeling of being spoken through, if you know what I mean ... And during the time I'm spoken through, as it were, I am she – not I' (*Maps*: 158). Even in the final lines of the novel, Askar oscillates in his sense of a unified identity: he asks 'Who *is* Askar?' (*Maps*: 258), then asserts his identity as answering to the name of Askar Cali-Xamari, only to eventually lapse into multiple identities in the final lines of the novel, 'allowing for his different personae to act as judge, as audience and as witness' (*Maps*: 259). One might compare this sense of internal otherness with the strange Shaman scene in the neighbour's house in the later stages of the novel, where the woman confesses to having another inside herself (*Maps*: 215).

Askar has always been obsessed with bodies from his infancy, and Farah calls the 'Blood in the Sun' trilogy 'body novels'. They are novels that explore how socioeconomic environments affect not only a person's concept of his or her own identity but also the physical body itself. In Somalia, people have been starved, tortured, beaten and killed. In these novels, Farah demonstrates that neo-colonial subjects are guests not only in their own countries and psyches, but also in their own skin. The reader is made to feel the blade of circumcision (both male and female), to taste menstrual blood (again, strangely, both male and female) and see the mutilation of Misra's body in the final pages. Blood in particular emerges as a key metaphor, especially the opposition between the body and the mind – also symbolised by blood and water. Blood signifies the importance of kinship relations in the society, but also makes one conscious of the violence that impregnates Somali life. Along with blood, other dominant preoccupations are death, life, the best means of communication with others possible, the relationship between mother and son, beginnings and endings, the conflict and opposition between the earth and the sky, and the opposition of male and female. The role of gender conflict within the novel is intimately connected to sexuality. While subverting traditional gender roles in much of his fiction, Farah also exposes the strong undercurrents of sexuality in Islamic society. Askar's Uncle Hilaal ends a lofty discourse on life, the cosmos and Freudian analysis with the bald insight 'Truth is body' (*Maps*: 236); and he adds in similar candid fashion, 'sooner or later, sex' (*Maps*: 245). And the sex Farah reveals is unashamedly polymorphic, as every sexual taboo – rape, incest, homosexuality, sex with animals and young boys – is entertained. The removal of body organs, through either amputation, violation or mutilation, circulates through the narrative. Askar's body or skin becomes 'mapped with routes which led him back to his past, a map which took him back to his own beginnings, a map showing earth roads, the rivers which rise in the region, a map whose scales followed a logic known only to himself' (*Maps*: 248). Eventually the body even becomes part of Askar's anxiety about narrative and memory:

Stories with fragmented bodies!
   Bodies which told fragmented stories!
   Tales about broken hearts and fractured souls!
   In the end, who is to say, but you, what you wish to relegate to an
unremembered past? (*Maps*: 161)

Most invocations of memory are part of a discourse about identity,
and thus the conceptualisations of the 'self' and 'subject' mutually
support one another. Memory and identity serve to reinforce one
another, as people's sense of who they are is closely linked to what
they think about memory, what they remember and what they can
claim to remember. This complex matrix of personal identity, representation and memory clarifies the manner in which the novel is
about separation and the traumatic effects of that separation.
Askar's life is mirrored in the life of Somalia and circumcision only
serves to reinforce this traumatic severance (*Maps*: 89). The initial
violent separation and its delayed repetition in Askar's life recurs
when the mother is identified with the nation: '"Somalia", a country
that was referred to as "Mother" in a tone suggesting a getting
together of her and the Ogaden/child separated from her' (*Maps*:
101). The question of national identity – the definition of what constitutes a nation, who are its people and what is its territory – recurs
throughout the novel: 'The image which has remained with me, is
that of a country made up of patchworks – like a poor man's mantle'
(*Maps*: 99). The splitting of the nation and the splitting of the
mother-child at birth are constantly implied: 'Imagine, Askar. A
nation with a split personality, Askar. How tragic!' (*Maps*: 126) – and
this splitting and separation mirrors the trauma of the Somali
people. Askar experiences a sort of Lacanian separation from the
fullness of the mother, but does not experience the concomitant entry
into the symbolic under the law of the father. Instead, he is left in a
sort of half-way house, neither joined nor separated, and his loss is
both lack and fulfilment as he continually oscillates between the
feminine and the masculine. The identification of Askar and the
nation is so complete that, when the Ogaden is recaptured by
Ethiopian hands after the Soviet-backed invasion, Askar falls ill on
that very day thereby uniting the illness of body with the illness in
national politics. In a time-honoured metaphor, Askar's body is
symbolic of the national body politic, and Askar's attempts at remembering his past are intricately connected with the traumatic rupturing of the national psyche: 'Our memories, our collective or if you
like, our individual pasts. We leave our bodies in order that we may
travel light – we are hope personified. After all, we are the dream of
a nation' (*Maps*: 129). Personal memory, internalised experiences of
selfhood and autobiographic narratives are always linked to social
narrative as is social memory to the personal. The politics of nation-

hood are clearly built upon memory, as every nation including Somalia needs to construct a past for itself. Disembodied as he is by his history, Askar attempts to organise his own complex autobiography and his narrative is an attempt to refigure himself. The circumstances of his own birth link him inalienably to the trials and tribulations of the emergent nation of Somalia. He perceives his narrative therefore as simultaneously the story of his own life and a mirror of the life of Somalia itself. Askar significantly eschews a linear, chronological mode of narration in favour of one that veers between past, present and future, or as the epigraph to the 'Interlude' section taken from Kierkegaard says, 'Life can only be lived forward and understood backward' (*Maps*: 123). The invocation of memory signals Askar's effort to forge association over dissociation, continuity over fragmentation.

Trauma

After every trauma comes a crisis in and of memory. *Maps* is not only about the primary importance of memory in the assertion of one's current identity in the face of unintegrated experiences from one's past, but it also displays the traumatic rupture caused by colonial violence that so many African countries have experienced. One is persistently reminded of the fact that Mogadiscio is an ancient hybrid city, criss-crossed with different colonial histories, that has been and to some extent still is the 'playfield' (*Maps*: 166) for foreign powers; and how typical this is of African politics more generally – for example, South Africa's incursions into Angola and the USSR's dalliances with Libya. Furthermore, Uncle Hilaal is acutely aware of the arbitrary way in which African countries have gained their names, betraying the vestigial signs of European colonialism, as does the diasporic history of the Somali people who have been scattered around East Africa (*Maps*: 155–6). Whether Askar's traumatic separation is Lacanian or not, the novel is structured by an experience of continually deferred integrations of overwhelming experiences from his past. Writing about the thoughts and feelings associated with traumas forces individuals to weld together the many facets of overwhelmingly complicated events. Once people can crystallise complex experiences into more recognisable shapes, they can begin to move beyond the trauma. As Cathy Caruth states, what is striking in the experience of trauma is that its 'insistent reenactments of the past do not simply serve as testimony to an event, but may also, paradoxically enough, bear witness to a past that was never fully experienced as it occurred. Trauma, that is, does not simply serve as a record of the past but precisely registers the force of an experience that is not fully owned' (Caruth 1995: 151). Askar's history is constituted by the

very incomprehensibility of its occurrence. It is a life story that
cannot be integrated into a completed story about his past. Caruth
argues that the registration of the traumatic events are closely
connected with the way they *escape* full consciousness as they occur.
Askar's narrative shows the importance of 'working-through' the
anxieties and fissures associated with trauma, as he tries to connect
the *slippages* of memory with the *accuracy* of remembrance. In this
respect, Askar is a reader and writer of his past, caught in a
hermeneutic spiral of interpretation as he continuously re-explores
the significance of earlier episodes in his life in the light of what
occurs later, especially under the guidance and tutelage of Uncle
Hilaal.

Indeed, memory and history have been among the principal
concerns of African writers since the advent of independences across
the continent after colonialism. Yet the relations between memory
and history are complex, and especially their import for aesthetic,
political and ethical issues. The subtle complexities of these issues
can be tackled in a number of questions: What facets of Africa's past
should be remembered and in what ways should they be remembered? Can one construe the period of colonialism in Africa's past as
a traumatic block to understanding that disrupts memory while
producing belated effects that overshadow or deflect attempts to
represent or otherwise address that past? Does the significance of
trauma in the African past present ethical and representational
issues even for groups only obliquely implicated in them? Do those
more unequivocally involved have special responsibilities to that
past and the way it is remembered in the present? Can – or should –
literary history define itself in a purely scholarly and professional
way that distances itself from public memory and its ethical implications? Or should it embed itself in memory as its matrix and muse?
To what extent is the complex and nuanced interaction between
history and memory evident in Africa's literary self-representations?
Can one legitimately expect art itself to take a special responsibility
with respect to traumatic events that remain invested with value and
emotion? I aim to explore some of these questions, for my focus in this
book is on the interactions among history, memory and ethico-politi-
cal concerns as they emerge in the aftermath of colonisation in
Africa.

The historian Michael Roth argues in *The Ironist's Cage* (1995)
that 'talk about memory has become the language through which we
address some of our most pressing concerns. This is because in
modernity memory is regarded as the key to personal and collective
identity ... Memory in modernity is seen less as a public, collective
function than as a private, psychological faculty; ... We are what we
remember, and this is one of the reasons why forgetting (and sudden

recall) arouses so much anxiety and excitement' (Roth 1995: 8–9). History and memory press in upon people when the foundations of communities begin to erode. Without the usual normative sources of authority, Roth argues that history emerges as important in assigning relative significance to particular elements in some narrative emplotment (Roth 1995: 9). Yet history writing also signifies a forgetting, since collective memory is in the process of disappearing. History is the traditional form for containing a disappearing past; yet conversely, once forms of community are gone, history forms a primary means of reconstructing or reimagining a community's traditions.

As Roth notes, one of the biggest obstacles to creating a usable past is the existence of trauma (Roth 1995: 10). The understanding of trauma in relation to the problems of representation has become a significant critical issue in recent decades. Trauma refers to those experiences which lie outside the scope of orthodox human experience. As Cathy Caruth argues, trauma is an *unresolved experience* not because of the event's *inherent content* but because recourse to an external frame of reference is unavailable. It is like the invasion of an 'unsifted beyond' into the psyche, the enduring presence of partially assimilated events. Seemingly bypassing memory, the traumatic event has been described by Caruth as a 'structural resistance to integration into memory' (Caruth 1995: 151–4). In her description, the traumatic event seems to bypass memory and be largely immune to revision in accordance with existing memories of other events. Trauma can be experienced in at least two ways: first, as an experience that cannot be integrated into one's own experience; and, second, as a catastrophic knowledge that cannot be communicated to others. Trauma therefore can have a twofold *structural disjunction* between an experience and its integration into narrative memory, understanding and communicability. Traumatic experiences are all located somewhere outside memory yet within the psyche.

Many regard trauma as confounding any temporal sense, in fact as lying outside history, or as Freud puts it, *zeitlos* ('timeless'). Yet, African narratives concerning the trauma of colonialism, are also explicitly concerned with history, with trying to reinsert the self into history. If indeed, these writers represent a trauma of being forcibly yanked out of history, there is an explicitly historicising thrust in many of these traumatic experiences. There is a conflict between an experience's resistance to absorption into any kind of larger interpretative context and its understanding as part of history. There is a tension between the 'timelessness' of the traumatic event and assigning the event to some form of historical context. The integration into consciousness of dissociated moments of a traumatic past also aims, in psychoanalysis, at the 'proper' forgetting of that past. The resolution of the traumatic event towards which psychoanalysis strives is a turning of the unassimilated past in the present into a future past, or pluperfect, a future in which the past is laid to rest as past. It is a conscious forgetting which is different from traumatic dissociation or repression. The clinical aim of psychotherapy is to defuse the traumatic memory into a life-story whose coherence had been upset by the unassimilated experience. Yet the attempt to turn the unassimilated event into meaning may be regarded as an effort to 'temper' the force of an event. Therapy aims at turning the force of the traumatic image into signification by loosening the frozen, dissociated memory and carefully allowing for its partial integration as a less threatening memory into the life-story. The difficulty of grasping the two temporal frames of trauma – past and the present – are a cause of the somatic symptoms, or in post-Freudian psychoanalysis, rupture is regarded as *constitutive* of the subject itself (for example, Lacanian).

As Freud has famously described in his theories of the 'talking cure', the traumatised individual's story must be heard on its own terms. The rigid traumatic memory and the language of the individual's mental patterns of making sense of the world must be 'unlocked' for a liveable version of the intolerably painful past to become again part of the outside world and then, as an event outside the psyche, to be reintegrated into the individual's sense of self. Freud's ideas on trauma pervade his work, but key discussions can be isolated in two principal essays, 'Remembering, Repeating and Working-Through' and 'Mourning and Melancholia'. In the former, Freud is concerned to differentiate between a patient 'acting-out' and 'working-through' the causes of his or her repressed memories. Importantly, 'acting-out' is a *repetition* though, not a remembrance: '[The patient] reproduces it not as a memory but as an action; he *repeats* it, without, of course, knowing that he repeats it' (Freud 2001a: 150). According to Freud, 'acting-out' is thus an obstacle to remembering, since remembering is supplanted by 'acting-out'. Remembering is the antithesis of 'acting-out': remembering is on the pathway to liberation, while repetition ('acting-out') is inimical to liberation and freedom, for no new consciousness or insight is gained into the past. The key for Freud is that the patient's resistance to therapy produces repetition: 'We have learnt that the patient repeats instead of remembering, and repeats under the conditions of resistance' (Freud 2001a: 151). Repetition is a pathological form of remembering, and, as Freud notes elsewhere, hysterics cannot get certain stories out of their system. Freud goes on to note that, therefore, one must treat a compulsion to repetition in an ill patient 'not as an event of the past, but as a present-day force' (Freud 2001a: 151). Significantly for my interests, we might construe many of the repeated African writers' returns to the traumatic event of colonialism as a compulsive repetition, which tells us less about that past and more about the energy of its contemporary persistence. By contrast, 'working-through' is a process whereby the patient opens himself or herself to the past in a performative manner. Returning to these issues in 'Mourning and Melancholia', Freud contrasts mourning as a devotion to a lost love-object that gradually ceases as 'respect for reality gains the day' (Freud 2001b: 244) with melancholia, which he regards as a 'pathological mourning' (Freud 2001b: 250). Melancholia 'is in some way related to an object-loss which is withdrawn from consciousness, in contradistinction to mourning, in which there is nothing about the loss that is unconscious' (Freud 2001b: 251). Freud notes that the closeness and shared characteristics of mourning and melancholia, are such that what distinguishes the latter from the former is a predisposition to 'obsessional neuroses' (Freud 2001b: 251). Pathologising African writing runs the risk of essentialising it; nevertheless, its characteristics of repetition would suggest a great deal of 'acting-out', which is markedly resonant with the stultification Freud finds in melancholia, where 'The complex of melancholia behaves like an open wound, drawing to itself cathectic energies ... from all directions' (Freud 2001b: 253). This 'open wound' is a fundamental disturbance embedded in all traumatic experience, which is its testimony both to the occurrence and to the hopelessness of its direct access. The persistent writers' interpretative problem thus becomes how to relieve the suffering of trauma, and to understand its nature without eradicating the compulsion and truth of its reality.

Trauma theory charts this path from the solitary muteness of trauma to the articulation of the recognition of a loss by inventing new forms for symbolic language and by acknowledging, as Kevin Newmark has shown, 'that the language we speak in order to understand ... trauma is also irretrievably marked by it' (Newmark 1995: 254). In this respect, these African narratives are often marked by a double effort to find an addressee to communicate the experience of the impossibility of an address, and of accounting for unresolved past experiences without allowing them to be relegated to the past. The question raised by these traumatic narratives is how to expose oneself to an experience that is defined by its absolute singularity and inaccessibility, without transgressing the narrative's demand to be recognised in its absolute singularity. Is it possible to acknowledge the true meaning of the traumatic events of colonialism without inevitably compromising and effacing them through the mental processes of recognition and its subsequent representation?

This book aims to elucidate African narratives within this context of history, memory and trauma, demonstrating how African writers make an active acknowledgement of the traumatic consequences of colonialism that continue to permeate African narratives, as they

seek to 'work-through' the trauma. It examines how these writers
conjoin trauma with the possibility of retrieving desirable aspects of
the past that might be of some use in counteracting trauma's extreme
effects and in rebuilding individual, national and social life. The
articulation of this critical goal owes an immense debt to Dominick
LaCapra's challenging and rigorous work on the associations
between history, memory and trauma in relation to the Holocaust.
His principal concern is with the ways and procedures people have
for confronting and dealing with their traumatic experiences.
LaCapra's studies of history, memory and trauma in relation to the
Holocaust are important for their insistence on the therapeutic
consequences of the processes of 'acting-out' and 'working-through',
as well as recognising the need for a discourse of ethical responsibility in negotiating the discourses of other people's histories and pasts.
Building upon Freud's pioneering work on trauma, LaCapra has
sought to reinvigorate and revitalise Freud's concepts of 'acting-out'
and 'working-through' as crucial to our understanding of negotiating
experiences that threaten to overwhelm us. LaCapra is careful to
elucidate crucial differences between 'acting-out' and 'working-
through'. According to LaCapra, post-traumatic 'acting-out' is a
process

> in which one is haunted or possessed by the past and performatively
> caught up in the compulsive repetition of traumatic scenes – scenes in
> which the past returns and the future is blocked or fatalistically caught
> up in a melancholic feedback loop. In acting out, tenses implode, and it
> is as if one were back there in the past reliving the traumatic scene. Any
> duality (or double inscription) of time (past and present or future) is
> experientially collapsed or productive only of aporias and double-binds.
> In this sense, the aporia and the double bind might be seen as marking
> a trauma that has not been worked through. Working through is an
> articulatory practice: to the extent one works through trauma ... one is
> able to distinguish between past and present and to recall in memory
> that something happened to one (or one's people) back then while real-
> izing that one is living here and now with openings to the future. This
> does not imply either that there is a pure opposition between past and
> present or that acting out ... can be fully transcended toward a state of
> closure or full ego identity. (LaCapra 2001: 21)

Rather than the stultifying experience of 'acting-out', 'working-
through' involves a sustained, problematic relation between witnessing and a critical comparative history that marks differences, including
those between the present and the past; it also involves the attempt to
acquire some perspective on experience without denying its claims or
indeed its compulsive force. LaCapra points out that Laplanche and
Pontalis's presentation of 'working-through' as countering compulsive
acting-out does not concede a simple ideology of liberation from the

constraints of the past. Working-through is a repetition, but involves a critical purchase on problems and responsible control in action which would permit desirable change. Laplanche and Pontalis define 'working-through' in the following manner: 'From the technical point-of-view, by the same token, working-through is expedited by interpretations from the analyst which consist chiefly in showing how the meanings in question may be recognised in different contexts' (Laplanche and Pontalis 1973: 488).

Elsewhere, LaCapra makes a further distinction between Freud's terms of 'working-through' and 'acting-out', which elaborates upon and defines Freud's terminology, his comparisons and analogies, in useful ways:

> I would also distinguish in nonbinary terms between two additional interactive processes: acting out and working through, which are inter-related modes of responding to loss or historical trauma ... I have argued elsewhere that mourning might be seen as a form of working out, and melancholia as a form of acting out. Freud, in comparing melancholia with mourning, saw melancholia as characteristic of an arrested process in which the depressed, self-berating, and traumatised self, locked in compulsive repetition, is possessed by the past, faces a future of impasses, and remains narcissistically identified with the lost object. Mourning brings the possibility of engaging trauma and achieving a reinvestment in, or recathexis of, life which allows one to begin again. In line with Freud's concepts, one might further suggest that mourning be seen not simply as individual or quasi-transcendental grieving but as a homeopathic socialization or ritualization of the repetition compulsion that attempts to turn it against the death drive and to counteract compulsiveness ... by re-petitioning in ways that allow for a measure of critical distance, change, resumption of social life, ethical responsibility, and renewal. Through memory work, especially the socially engaged memory work involved in working through, one is able to distinguish between past and present and to recognize something as having happened to one (or one's people) back then which is related to, but not identical with, here and now. (LaCapra 2001: 65–6)

'Acting-out' therefore is being stuck in a compulsive loop:

> In acting out, the past is performatively regenerated or relived as if it were fully present rather than represented in memory and inscription, and it hauntingly returns as the repressed. Mourning involves a different inflection of performativity: a relation to the past which involves recognizing its difference from the present – simultaneously remembering and taking leave or actively forgetting it, thereby allowing for critical judgment and a reinvestment in life, notably social and civic life with its demands, responsibilities, and norms requiring respectful recognition and consideration for others. By contrast, to the extent someone is possessed by the past and acting out a repetition compulsion, he or she may be incapable of ethically responsible behaviour. (LaCapra 2001: 70)

'Working-through' is therefore linked to a hermeneutic task, that of interpretation and critical analysis within an historical and social framework; and it seems to me that this is vital if the concept of trauma is likely to be useful for an analysis of the particularly vexed historical and political legacy of colonialism in Africa. Along with LaCapra, I would want to link the concept of 'working-through' to ethical and political considerations rather than keeping it in a narrowly therapeutic framework. 'Working-through' implies proce-dures which are not *ad hominem* but argumentative, self-interroga-tive and related to ways of action. Many African narratives fit into this perspective: they are a 'working-through' of the disruptive trau-matic events of colonialism, and are set on establishing new forms of agency and identity within a post-independence and postcolonial social existence.

Yet compelling and appealing as Freud's and LaCapra's arguments seem to me, they do nevertheless pose a rather stark oppositional structure that somewhat exaggerates the antithesis of therapeutic effects of 'working-through' and the stultifications of 'acting-out'. Surely things are more complex than such a simple binary would suggest and one needs to be cautious in theorising all African litera-ture in this simply conceived either-or configuration. Rather what one sees in African literatures are fictions that are more-or-less 'working-through', more-or-less 'acting-out' – in effect, more of a continuum than a polarisation. A more pertinent descriptive term might be 'uneven development'. There is a blurred spectrum between mourning and melancholia, between 'working-through' and 'acting-out', which suggests the room for confusion, elision, and blending of these states or modes.

If trauma is understood to be an indirect experience which is repeated after its forgetting, like a history whose traces cannot be effaced, one can begin to perceive African literature in interesting new ways. A characteristic feature of trauma is its metaleptic nature: trauma leads an encapsulated existence never manifesting itself as such until symptoms, sometimes decades after the event, point to an absent cause. Texts, in their process of searching and exploring themselves *produce* the traumatic object that *causes* it. They involve us in the exploration and eventually *produce* the desired representa-tion – a witnessing reading. The postcolonial subject appears to be mourning the gap that divides himself or herself from the possibility of interiority and self-presence that might have been had history been different. Much African writing charts an experience of the symbolic event of the entry into representation as a disruptive and violently fracturing moment, splitting body from discourse and initi-ating an endlessly repeated attempt at arriving at a signification of itself. It highlights the presence of a void or a gap opening up within representation and memory, and much of the writing works in this affective gap, writing in an English which, in its defamiliarisation and slips of the tongue, evokes the continuous spectral presence of what, for want of a better image, we may denote as the felt presence of the lapsing of the mother tongue. As Adorno argues about the 'affective demand to witness',

> We will not have come to terms with the past until the causes of what happened then are no longer active. Only because these causes live on does the spell of the past remain to this very day ... Just as violence keeps generating new acts of transgression, the wounds of the past will remain active and spoil the present, unless we heal them though mourning. We must become conscious, accept the past, and find words to voice and feel the desolation it occasions. (Adorno 1986: 29)

Although reading literature cannot replace the work of mourning imposed by history, reading the 'art of trauma' in African literature may engage the reader in a dialogue with that trauma that might open him or her up to acknowledge its hitherto repressed presence. Although Africa haunts modernity, it seems that its impact is still largely repressed. This book will argue that it will remain misread, enlisted in the service of transcendent truths or narcissistic play, unless we learn to receive and confront it in its sensuously embodied form as the 'art of trauma'. African literature performs a 'mimesis of loss' which is an ongoing process of self-conscious self-revision which keeps re-enacting the basic traumatic tension of colonialism at ever more sophisticated levels.

History maims individual ethical identity in ways that are not easily traceable to private choice or personal decisions. Therefore, this book, in many ways, is about *agency*. For agency is a central problem in postcolonial narratives, for agency is removed in trauma, thereby precluding the counter-ideological attempt to recount a history, reconstruct a sense of agency and rebuild an indigenous life. Does trauma paralyse and numb the victim and make immediate resistance impossible? Kai Erikson has explored the wider social dimension of trauma and observed that whole communities and peoples can be traumatised, where the tissues of the community or continental races can be damaged like individuals (Erikson 1995). Although he notes that trauma can *create* community, in which sharers of a traumatic experience can search each other out and provide support for one another in their shared distress, for the most part, trauma *damages* communal texture. Thus, when there are signs of resistance, especially in a post-traumatic situation, one needs to attend to their origin, since often these are signs of a 'working-through' of the problems. Jacques Le Goff has remarked upon the way in which history and memory seek to substitute the

dynamic idea of genesis for the passive idea of origins (Le Goff 1992:
xv). Since traumatised people often feel a vulnerability and fragility
as a result of losing a vital degree of control over the conditions of
their lives, African novelists are intent on regaining agency. In
'working-through' the traumatic effects of colonialism, African novelists are in effect turning what are in a sense, timeless, experiences,
into temporally located events and phenomena, giving them a story,
placed in time, with a beginning, middle and end, and thereby reconstructing and recovering a communal and national identity.
Nevertheless, one needs to be cautious against salvationist 'feel-good'
attempts in portrayals of the experiences of overcoming colonialism,
as an uplifting testimony to heroic strength and the indomitable
human will.

Although one must guard against becoming a surrogate victim,
this book aims at empathic witness to the muted trauma. With
LaCapra's help, I aim to write a book which recognises the crucial
aspect of 'empathy' to ethical historiography, or a poetics of ethics.
There are forms of historiography or critical practice which try to
write the history of others, which effectively denigrate, deny, or
suspend ethical judgement of, their experiences. The problem of
striving for an 'objective' account in representing trauma is that it
suspends judgement. It removes the problems of agency and responsibility in general. Empathic historiography and critical practices are
an attempt to overcome these blindnesses. What LaCapra terms
'empathic unsettlement' in historiography and critical practices is
necessary if one is to prevent harmonising or spiritually uplifting
accounts of extreme events from which we attempt to derive a reassurance or benefit (for example, an unearned self-satisfaction about
the way in which the human spirit can overcome adversity with
dignity and nobility). 'Trauma brings about a dissociation of affect
and representation: one disorientingly feels what one cannot represent; one numbingly represents what one cannot feel. Working
through trauma involves the effort to articulate or rearticulate affect
and representation in a manner that may never transcend, but may
to some viable extent counteract, a reenactment, or acting out, of that
disabling dissociation' (LaCapra 2001: 42). However, LaCapra
cautions against a situation where 'a virtual experience involved in
empathy gives way to vicarious victimhood, and empathy with the
victim seems to become an identity' (LaCapra 2001: 47). He also
cautions against those 'fetishized and totalising narratives that deny
the trauma that called them into existence by prematurely
(re)turning to the pleasure principle, harmonizing events, and often
recuperating the past in terms of uplifting messages or optimistic,
self-serving scenarios' (LaCapra 2001: 78).

African writers continually address the 'affect' of the trauma, creating a muted history which works its effects on everyday life in a manner disproportionate to the present occasion. They attempt to address the *feeling* attendant upon the historical suppression of cultural memory, and, unless it is confronted and mourned, it will continue to haunt the present. The writers pay attention to the 'feeling', the non-figurable, because people still feel that they have not told the story, or because empirical records have been obliterated or not kept. To understand the experience, historicism must break with the monopoly of history by cognitive phrases and venture forth to acknowledge what is not presentable under the 'rules' of knowledge. In this respect, African writers urge readers to read Africa in a new way. In dealing with colonisation and its vestigial effects, writers like Achebe, Ngugi and Soyinka describe what amounts to an 'event', a coming-into-historical-being, which permanently affected the representation of Africa, just as 'Auschwitz' permanently altered our understanding of the concept of history. Fascinated with colonialism as a deadlock of representation, they seek to 'tell' us something about the incomprehensibility of the violence of African colonial history which resists symbolization, even today. Slavoj Žižek defines the traumatic event as 'a point of failure of symbolization, but at the same time never given in its positivity – it can be constructed only backwards, from its structural effects' (Žižek 1989: 169). If we accept the peculiar temporal logic of trauma, which makes itself evident in displacement and deferral only as a result of the latency inherent in its structure, we may also come to read African writing as the latent record and location of such a return of the unexpressed of African history as symptom. Consequently, trauma brings a new notion of representation: a victim lives out and repeats the event that always escapes conscious articulation. Thus, in *Bones*, the Zimbabwean novelist Chenjerai Hove writes about the traumatic severances of children from their parents, about the disruption of family, and by extension, the crisis of the Shona people on the land, causing alienation and the interruption of natural links. The novel is structured in the form of fragmented recollections, of memories of people and the past, as a series of interconnected voices, jumping backwards and sideways in a variety of stylistic associative links, as the language carries the full weight of Shona idiom in giving Zimbabwean peasants a voice in conveying their struggle for liberation in a white man's world. Marita, a mother talking to her daughter about her past, states: 'my eyes have seen what you have not seen. Many wounds have healed on this chest of mine. Many wounds. Many scars. Most of us women are one big scar, a scar as big as the Chenhoro dam from which farmer Manyepo waters his crops, vast, never dying. I will say this to you, I am one big wound child' (Hove 1990: 8). Like so many other novelists in Africa, Hove's writing thus traverses a subjectivity that finds itself grappling with a void or gap that opens up in representation; and only through repetition and replay may the event which caused the trauma eventually crystallise into experience and narrative – if it ever does. In this respect, African writing is both performative and referential – the writing both enacts and describes the trauma. It is a psychoanalytical tenet that without attending to affect, there is no psychological change. The literary confrontation with the encrypted trauma helps the reader to 'change his or her mind', and to acquire a future-oriented perspective which opens new vistas.

Note

[1]   Foucault has a clear notion of 'counter-memory': 'The historical sense gives rise to three uses that oppose and correspond to the three Platonic modalities of history. The first is parodic, directed against reality, and opposes the theme of history as reminiscence or recognition; the second is dissociative, directed against identity, and opposes history given as continuity or representative of a tradition; the third is sacrificial, directed against truth, and opposes history as knowledge. They imply a use of history that severs its connection to memory, its metaphysical and anthropological model, and constructs a counter-memory – a transformation of history into a totally different form of time' (Foucault 1980: 160).

2

Purifying the language of the tribe: (pre)colonial memory

> I would be quite satisfied if my novels (especially the ones I set in the past) did no more than teach my readers that their past – with all its imperfections – was not one long night of savagery from which the first Europeans acting on God's behalf delivered them. (Chinua Achebe, 'The Novelist as Teacher', in *Morning Yet on Creation Day*)

Thirty years after Nigerian independence, novelists were still writing about the problems of organising the past, representing Nigerian history, deciding upon the best models or images in order to write that history, and understanding who makes history. One example of this prolonged anxiety is T. Obinkaram Echewa's *The Crippled Dancer* (1986). The novel is a coming-of-age story as the central protagonist Ajuzia details memories of his friends and recollects memories of significant moments in his personal development into a young man, as he gets embroiled in his grandfather's bitter, lifelong struggle with the village chief Orji. Even his childhood rivalry with the notorious rapscallion 'Bush Radio' turns sour, and Ajuzia gets sucked into a disturbing conspiracy – one that seeks to destroy his family's fortune by rewriting its past. Ajuzia's problem, like Saleem Sinai's problem in Salman Rushdie's *Midnight's Children*, is how to represent this past and where to place himself within this narrative. While Saleem tends to organise things somewhat egocentrically, placing himself and his actions at the centre of Indian independence, Ajuzia is less certain about his position in relation to the unfolding of Nigerian history:

> Ajuzia felt vague; his self-consciousness was dispersed through a sea of uncertainty; his thoughts of himself were merely passing glimpses, blurred like the shadows of hurried motion off the corners of one's eyes
> . . .
>   Ajuzia felt a need to substantiate himself. Just as a whale collected large quantities of plankton by filtering the ocean, so perhaps he could gather the diffuse elements of his personality by running the memories

of his nineteen years of life through his mind. Others also would be netted in the filter, but he himself was bound to be there somewhere. (*Crippled Dancer*: 1)

Organising the past by filtering memories is a key strategy for African novelists participating in the discursive construction of a national culture, and this activity is invariably also connected to establishing and consolidating a sense of personal and collective identity. Yet the problem, as with so many narratives, is where to start:

> But, like so many other experiences in his life, a return to the beginning was not possible. The parade marched past and did not return. More than that, he realised, even now, that his intellectualisations of the experience were more palpable than the experience had even been in reality. He had always stayed lost between thought and action, between the doer and the spectator. Would he ever experience anything in full and uncompromised measure? Would he ever be ready and fully prepared? Or would he always back or side-step into everything unawares? (*Crippled Dancer*: 5)

Reflecting here upon his first sexual experience, Ajuzia's concerns are to do with the fact that his life is always a mediated experience, that the past is always unrecoverable, that he is always unsure about the nature of his agency or passivity in relation to his experience, and that it is unclear as to whether his experiences are the consequences of conscious planning or happenstance. Echewa's novel extends these anxieties about representing the past and history, by instigating a debate amongst the characters concerning the nature of responsibility and obligations between fathers and sons, the sense among the elders in the society that the modern youth is rebellious and shows little respect for traditional authorities, and whether the sons ought to set right the problems experienced by the fathers. The general consensus though is of loss: 'So much was lost. So many people were lost. The issue really wasn't who was more lost than who else. Everyone seemed lost enough' (*Crippled Dancer*: 39). The older generations in the novel express a general sense of social fragmentation and leaderlessness as the old social order collapses. Yet the causes of this social chaos are complex, and are not simply attributed to the historical consequences of colonialism: some blame this want of direction, this 'world turned upside down' (*Crippled Dancer*: 31), on the initial arrival of the white colonists, while others consider that they are to blame themselves, owing to continual social back biting and internal division:

> So you see, even if our people are always saying that justice is like a brittle twig which cannot be bent, they are bending it, even while the words are still on their lips. The White Man may have brought evil of a

new kind, but there was a lot of evil native to us before his coming. Perhaps the new evil has impregnated the old kind, and their bastard offspring is now what terrorises us . . . . (*Crippled Dancer*: 40–1)

The novel is studded with metaphors and images of altered times and states, with the constant refrain that times have changed. The country collapsing into chaos is figured in the novel in a striking image of the removal of the Termite Queen, causing the other termites to run around in pointless and aimless directions. It is pointed out that the white colonists removed the Termite Queen (*Crippled Dancer*: 103–4). Nevertheless, the argument about purity continues, persistently circling around the question of who is responsible for the social crisis.

The novel is structured as a series of Ajuzia's memories of injustices and wrongdoings perpetrated by various people against him or his family. Ajuzia's attempt to work out his history is also therefore an attempt to work out the history of the community, and in a wider context, the nation:

Was he no more then he remembered? Merely the dim and transparent shadows of fleeting moments, marching by without footprints, swirling and dissolving, forming and reforming without substance? . . .

It had been a slow journey to where he was now. But then he was not quite sure where he was now, whether at a spiritual waystation or at a physical landmark. His consciousness was just barely beginning to come together, to jell like a thinly dispersed colloid precipitating slowly in a centrifuge. He was perhaps beginning to arrive after spurts of random motion. He had accumulated these memories, acquired something of a history. (*Crippled Dancer*: 100–1)

This begins a key passage in the novel in which the issues of history, memory, national identity and personal consciousness coalesce. Like Saleem in *Midnight's Children*, Ajuzia regards himself as identified with the birth of the nation, but is seeking to straighten out the nation's history – whether it is a cause for pessimism or life-affirmation, a cause for collapse or rejuvenation. All the metaphors of what the nation heralds are embedded in this passage, as well as the paradoxes and contradictions, of the role of the colonists (i.e. polluters or educators, stultifiers or enablers). The problem for Ajuzia, as for other characters, is one of metaphor. What image or metaphor adequately inscribes the past in a meaningful and enabling way?

And then look to the past? Find the past and reclaim it? Wash off the dirt and the grime and expose the nugget? Shake out the white termites from the wooden idols, take them out of their dank huts from under the shades of the ancient trees and leave them in the noon sun to dry and harden again? What really was this past that had been lost and needed to be found again? How long ago was it lost? Did anyone, including the oldest man alive, have any true memories of it? (*Crippled Dancer*: 106)

It is unclear what past has been lost and whether this past can actually be remembered. The image of the true past as a piece of gold buried under a sheen of ideological grime or dirt, is repeated (albeit in a gendered manner) a few paragraphs later:

> Was the future the girl who had been working all day in the dusty farm and was covered with dirt, soot and sweat, who at the end of the day would bathe off this repugnant grime and re-emerge once again as the beautiful bride? (*Crippled Dancer*: 107)

The figure of a new future emerging from a tainted past is seductively powerful, yet Ajuzia is never completely certain that this is a viable possibility. In fact, near the end of the novel, after the successful end to the witchcraft trial of his grandfather, Ajuzia envisages his village as an indistinct hybrid space, that leaves the questions that have absorbed him throughout the novel unanswered:

> He could not see the village now. It was swathed in shadows and in darkness, and he could only imagine it as he had seen it in these, the first twenty years of his life. It was only an image of in his mind, part memory and part imagination, half past and half future, mixed fractions of yesterday and tomorrow. The images would not resolve into a single form. They collided and clashed and splintered and splattered, showing neither symmetry nor a single principle of order. They were mangled centrifugal shapes.
>
> The images were of the village as well as of him, their combined history. He saw the crowd of that afternoon in the market square, a rag-tag mob of frightened men wilting under the stern gaze of the ASP. Among them were talismans and Saint Christopher medals (equally unavailing); *ofo* sticks and Bibles; animal-skin amulets and Speidel watchbands; trousers and loin cloths. Some of them woke up to cock-crows and others to Smith Alarm clocks – fractions of Europe and Africa, remnants and discarded parts, and scarecrows ...
>
> In all this, where was the truth, and what was its infallible source – Elders sometimes did not know and often lied. He chuckled as he recalled Orija's statement at the trial that ancestors were once living human beings, with all the virtues and vices of humans. Hence, to say that the truth was in the past with the spirit of the dead ancestors was no safer than to say that it was present with the consensus of the living. Where, indeed, was the truth? (*Crippled Dancer*: 225–7)

Faced with such overwhelming insecurity, the eponymous crippled dancer of the book's title emerges as the central image for Ajuzia to cope with the problems of dealing with the past (*Crippled Dancer*: 107). The crippled dancer is the key image of a man who kept dancing despite his physical incapacity, in the face of adversity. In this respect, the crippled dancer becomes a figure of someone who continues creating and living despite the weight and shock of past and previous impairments and shackles. Ajuzia regards the crippled dancer as the image of his future salvation, and, as the final lines of the novel make clear, 'Life was truly a court case, and he, Ajuzia, had best be like the crippled man of the popular proverb, and whether he had lost or won his case, he should go home swinging, swagging and dipping as if he were dancing' (*Crippled Dancer*: 227).

This novel is instructive in a number of ways, for Ajuzia's anxieties about subjectivity, memory and the past are echoed in a number of other African novels that reflect upon the nature of African history, how it is written and by whom. The combination of history, memory, national identity and personal consciousness form a matrix of ideas and concepts that are repeatedly played out during the course of the development of African fiction since various national independences. The novel's exploration of the problems of agency recurs throughout a number of other writers and novels, as they collectively ponder the structural position of Africans and Africa in the post-independence period. The remainder of this chapter will trace this problem of agency in several other authors' works, attempting to analyse its recurrence as a symptom of the traumatic nature of the historical interruption by colonialism of their respective cultural developments. In particular, this analysis will attend to the way in which many novelists have sought to retrieve or represent precolonial eras and societies, and consider the reasons for such representations.

As Echewa's novel exemplifies, frequently at the root of trauma is a sense of absence, loss, or lack. Yet when dealing with the consequences of traumatic rupture, Dominick LaCapra is quite clear that it is crucial to identify the differences between absence, loss and lack in that originary experience (LaCapra 2001: 56), since this enables managing the loss or lack without a concomitant erasure of the past, often perceived as a fall or exaggeratedly constructed as the abolition of meaning altogether. The ideology of a lost age or culture is specifically different from that of an absent age or culture, since the former implies the possibility of return while the other does not. As LaCapra argues, converting absence into loss gives anxiety an identifiable lost object, which allows one the hope that anxiety may be transcended: 'In converting absence into loss, one assumes that there was (or at least could be) some original unity, wholeness, security, or identity that others have ruined, polluted, or contaminated and thus made "us" lose' (LaCapra 2001: 57–8). One can deal with historical losses or lacks without necessarily adversely affecting the present and without 'promising secular salvation or a sociopolitical return to a putatively lost (or lacking) unity or community' (LaCapra 2001: 54). Crucial as these distinctions are though, LaCapra does caution one about the difficulties in making or attributing cross-cultural comparisons about absence, loss or lack: 'How to make this argument in non-ethnocentric terms, which do not simply privilege something presumably distinctive of, or unique to, one's own culture, poses a difficult problem in normative thinking' (LaCapra 2001: 54).

Various ways of conceiving history emerge after colonialism, as nations seek to restore their own sense of identity and integrity. This means that there are *types* and *models* of history vying with one another for explicable verifiability. Different narratives of the past had to contend with the censorship of the colonial power, which denied certain indigenous narratives the certitude of their pasts. However, once the colonial powers had left, new contentions began between respective narratives of the past, and on how these perspectives enabled (or disabled) certain events and actions in the *present*. Consequently, one can look at different narratives which treat of African pasts and analyse them for their ideological consequences, their *reasons* for viewing the past in that manner as opposed to another manner. This chapter will scrutinise those narratives which represent the past anterior to the arrival of the colonial powers, and in some cases, mark the arrival of the colonists. Understanding contemporary African modernity aright is an exercise in retrieval, but the results hinge largely on what is retrieved. Representations of sophisticated and cultured village communities emerge, along with more mythical treatments of the past. A recent article by Wole Ogundele contends that there is in fact a paucity of genuine historical fiction in African writing and he argues that myth replaces or displaces African history in the fiction of recent decades, and concludes that 'Postcolonial African literature responded (and still responds) with a more mythical than historical imagination to the historical experience that brought it into existence' and urges that the 'historical novel is better suited than mythical accounts [to give one the historical and cultural self-knowledge], and to explore issues of basic morality' (Ogundele 2002: 137). Whilst the political perspective in these assertions and the conviction that an informed investigation of the African past can only emerge through a greater degree of historical consciousness are certainly compelling, nevertheless, Ogundele omits the role of memory and traumatic memory in particular from his perspective. For it seems to me that the problem Ogundele identifies as a confusion of myth and history, as a paucity of the existence of historical fiction, as the substitution or displacement of history by myth, of a lack of clarity in the definition of what constitutes historical fiction and how this slips into a focus on mythology, is indicative of 'acting-out' the past rather than 'working-through' it. For as we have seen in Chapter 1, the compulsion to repeat this mythic focus or structure that Ogundele identifies, is itself part of a traumatic structure – trying to 'work-through' the past to 'own it', to reintegrate that past, no matter how much it evades the effort to do so.

Yet surely things are more complex than Ogundele's simple binary of mythical versus historical fictions would suggest. Rather what one sees are fictions that are more-or-less historical, more-or-less mythical in focus, more of a continuum than a polarisation. Just as I sought to adjust LaCapra's binary model between melancholia and mourning, between 'working-through' and 'acting-out', it seems that one is better conceiving of a more blurred spectrum between the mythical and the historical, which suggests exactly that room for confusion, elision and blending of these states or modes that Ogundele thinks so impairs African writing. It is the diverse blurrings on this spectrum with which this chapter will be concerned, investigating those representations that seek to retrieve the precolonial past and the history of colonisation, in the face of the dominant narratives of the colonial powers, for example, in Achebe's early novels, Okara's and Tutuola's fiction, Elechi Amadi's work or Ayi Kwei Armah's novels of the 1970s. This chapter will consider the various pasts that are evoked and recollected in different writers' works, their structural roles as histories, and the way in which memory forms part of the activity of writing history in an attempt to 'purify' the traumatic experience.

Precolonial history: Elechi Amadi

The erasure or eradication of a culture was one of the prime effects of colonial histories and had a profoundly traumatic impact upon African peoples. A great many postcolonial African writers have sought to revive or restore what was written out of existence by colonial historians, and to show that, despite the colonial perspectives, African societies have sophisticated and elaborate cultures. Chinua Achebe's *Things Fall Apart* is often regarded as the pre-eminent example of this process of recovery. As Achebe has famously and resoundingly made clear, he regarded his fiction as a corrective to the western colonial view of African culture:

> Here then is an adequate revolution for me to espouse – to help my society regain belief in itself and put away the complexes of the years of denigration and self-abasement ... I would be quite satisfied if my novels (especially the ones I set in the past) did no more than teach my readers that their past – with all its imperfections – was not one long night of savagery. (Achebe 1975a: 44–5)

> This theme – put quite simply – is that African peoples did not hear of culture for the first time from Europeans; that their societies were not mindless but frequently had a philosophy of great depth and value and beauty, that they had poetry and above all, they had dignity. (Achebe 1964a: 157)

Elechi Amadi, a Nigerian novelist who was a protégé of Chinua
Achebe, has also been actively concerned with the retrieval and
representation of a precolonial society, establishing the sophistica-
tion and cultured nature of the social activities and relations that are
eventually to be disrupted by the arrival of white European society.
His novel *The Great Ponds* (1969) is a narrative about the rivalry
between two villages, Chiolu and Aliakoro, over the fishing rights to
the Great Ponds, especially the Pond of Wagaba. The novel focuses
upon the characters of Olumba (the Chiolu hero) and Wago (the
Aliakoro hero), as well as the various witchdoctors and *ezes* (tribal
chiefs), and Ikechi, the young man who looks up to Olumba and
aspires to be like him upon maturity. The narrative is set roughly in
the early years of the twentieth century, just as British colonialism
in Nigeria was consolidating its foothold, and there are references to
the activities and encroachments of the white men. However, this
narrative is exclusively about the lives and beliefs of the precolonial
Nigerian peoples. It depicts their lives as culturally sophisticated,
socially stratified and hierarchical, albeit very male-oriented. In so
doing, the novel sets out to expose the myth that prior to colonial
arrival and rule, the indigenous societies were without order and
barbaric. Instead, the reader is presented with a society in which
there are extensive honour systems, deferential value systems and
strong family bonds. High emotions – love, honour, fear, anger,
triumph and despair – are the material of the book, and the cultural
fabric of the society is depicted in great detail.

There is a good deal of fatalism in the novel though, and if Amadi
depicts any sense of the model of history, then it is one that is prede-
termined, thoroughly guided by indigenous mythical and metaphysical belief systems. The book offers a precolonial past that is
sophisticated and complex, and yet that is also limited by its local
perceptions. For the novel causes a certain uneasy reassessment in
the reader with the final lines of the novel. The plot of the novel
concerns the inter-tribal warfare over the rights to the Great Ponds.
After a period where a third party is consulted to adjudicate, Olumba
is bound over to a ritualistic peace process. However, despite
forswearing further violence, people from both tribes continue to
keep dying, and these deaths are put down to the fact that the gods
are angry at the behaviour of various people in both communities.
Yet the final lines in the book step back from depicting the tribal
beliefs of witchcraft and medicine, by describing the ravaging effects
of the Great Influenza of 1918, which not only dates the book but also
gives a western explanation to the tribespeoples' belief system. What
is not clear is the extent to which Amadi is rationalising the metaphysics of the tribe's belief in magic and supernatural forces. The
implications of this are perplexing, since it would appear that Amadi

is suggesting that there is a macro-explanation and macro-rationalism embedded in European medicine that is unavailable to the tribal explanations through their indigenous beliefs. This leaves the novel precariously balanced as to the principal structure of belief – the tribe's or the European's – and by extension the model of history at work in the novel.

A similar problem concerning the fatalism of history, and the ensuing consequences for the passive or active nature of humans, pervades Amadi's other novels, *The Concubine* (1966) and *The Slave* (1978). *The Concubine* is a powerful story about the life and loves of Ihuoma and, in particular, her relationship with Ekwueme, and the terrible fate that the gods have ordained for her. After losing her first husband, Emenike, she is pestered by the village bully Madume, until he commits suicide after being blinded by a spitting cobra. Ekwueme then falls in love with Ihuoma, but his parents force him into marrying the immature Ahurole, although the marriage collapses. However, after gaining the village's consent to marry Ihuoma, advice from the village *dibia* or witchdoctor reveals that this marriage will also end in tragedy, since Ihuoma used to be a sea-god's wife, who has sought reincarnation to live among humans, and the sea-god has threatened vengeance against any man who dared to make advances to her. On the eve of his marriage to Ihuoma, Ekwueme is accidentally killed by an arrow shot by Ihuoma's little son, Nwonna. While the novel is particularly interested in the characters of Ihuoma and Ekwueme, especially the latter's psychological relationship with his mother and the implications for gender roles within the village society, the deaths of the respective men who involve themselves in Ihuoma's life do raise once again the extent to which the force of metaphysical fate guides the lives of the protagonists.

In the case of *The Slave*, the narrative focuses upon the protagonist Olumati and his return from the temple of the god Amadioha to claim his father's lands in the village of Aliji, with his sister Aleru's help. He gradually decides to marry Enaa, only to be pipped in his choice by his friend Wizo. The narrative depicts how he throws Aso, a rival, in a wrestling bout and how he is aided in his daily life by Adiba (Wizo's sister), when Aleru marries his friend Nyeche. Eventually, he leaves the village after having lost Enaa and his sister (who dies), returning to Isiali, where he returns to the temple of Amadioha. The title 'The Slave' refers to the eponymous Olumati, who it is feared is eternally linked to the temple of Amadioha, and from which he cannot ever be severed, therefore bringing trouble to anyone who forms a relationship with him. This is one of the reasons that ultimately prevents him from securing the hand of Enaa. The narrative is structured on the two-year period of Enaa's *mgbede* (a period of retreat before marriage), where 'at puberty a girl was given a long holiday before she took on the burdens of marriage. Mgbede could be as short as six months for girls of poor parentage or as long as two years' (Amadi 1978: 11). The story of Olumati's trials and predicaments occurs within this period of ritual time, before he leaves, rumoured as having returned to Amadioha's temple. Once again, this narrative hinges on the question of whether Olumati's life is prescribed by fate and the gods, or whether there are other rational explanations for his failure to reclaim his father's lands and life, and his return to Amadioha's temple. Is he a slave to the god (i.e. fated to be unable to break away)? Or is it because his life does not work out and he goes into religious retreat through rational choice? Once again, Amadi's novel leaves open the question of whether one is passive or active in fashioning one's life and history, since there are mutually exclusive answers to both sides of the issue. Yet the novel spends a great deal of time explaining the intricate rituals and rites attached to cultivation, palm-wine tapping, domestic life, *mgbede* and coming out, wrestling, family relations and commitments, the rights and wrongs of being a man and woman, the sophistications of good manners and poor manners, and so on. The book is clearly an evocation of early precolonial Nigerian life, and demonstrates the civilised and over-elaborate culture of the society. The tribespeople put great stock in tradition, the past, heritage, history, memory, the way things have been, and Amadi clearly implies that this past has been lost.

Accidents and coincidences do not necessarily mean the existence of supernatural forces, yet the novel does leave the explanation for the events in an ambiguous suspension. Amadi clearly wishes readers to consider the rational and the irrational aspects in our lives and to ponder the extent to which we attribute causes and relationships where the evidence for these is non-existent or barely visible. In addition to his narrative interest in the psychology of his characters, Amadi's fiction offers significant anthropological information, describing all sorts of sociological practices, such as marriages, cooking practices, courtship rituals, social hierarchies, gender roles, agricultural practices, and religious beliefs and customs. In so doing, he recorrects many of the missionary or colonial records that dismiss or deride African histories and their cultural practices as barbaric and immature, retrieving a loss rather than pointing to an absence. His writing is an example of postcolonial redress, reconstructing the past for the purpose of establishing self-esteem and integrity in the present, endowing the culture with a positive history that is untainted by racial prejudice. His aim is the restoration of cultural memory, albeit resisting the route to a simple cultural or historical nostalgia. In this respect, although occasionally appearing to succumb to the seductions of the mythical, following LaCapra's terminology, Amadi's fiction can be seen as an example of 'working-through' the trauma of colonialism, proffering a persistent investigation into the processes of representing a critical history that resists conceding a simple creed of deliverance from the chains of the past.

Oral narratives and the past: Tutuola and Okara

As many literary historians and cultural anthropologists have observed, oral narratives rely heavily upon the past through accumulated tradition (for example, see Vansina 1965 and Nwachukwu-Agbada 2000). Emmanuel Obiechina points out that oral tradition depends significantly on human memory for the perpetuation and communication of the cultural repertoire, and therefore it develops sophisticated mechanisms for aiding human memory (Obiechina 1975a: 33). Those writers who show a marked dependence upon the major influence of oral traditions in everyday African culture implicitly embed within their writing a retrieval of a past that is facing increasing pressure from modernity. Modernity is a rupture, and that rupture is largely consequent upon the arrival of European colonialism, and writers who seek to hold modernity at bay might be considered to be conservative. Several critics also point to the fact that some African novelists sought 'to rehabilitate the past by incorporating the oral tradition through a resort to local ethnic tenets and philosophy, beliefs, and attitudes to life and existence' (Nwachukwu-Agbada 2000: 68). In all this debate, there seems to be a debilitating conflation of several issues: a confusion of the oral with the folk-tale and mythical; a mistaken postulation of the oral with a cultural conservatism; and the fact that the oral tradition is only to do with the past. It would be a grave cultural error to equate a writer's admiration for the techniques of oral narrative as the mark of literary regression or as a sign of cultural conservativism. There is a complexity in oral narrative, with its swoops, spirals, digressions and reiterations; and such eminent scholars as Ruth Finnegan have impressed upon people that oral literature is not a thing of the past but a part of the current vibrancy of cultures throughout Africa (for example, see Finnegan 1970 and Adedji 1976). The oral tradition is not *lost*, since it pervades all aspects of African cultural life on a day-to-day basis. Furthermore, in some hands the folk-tale representation can act as an incisive contemporary fable, tearing the veil from colonial obfuscation and modern obeisance to received narrative versions.

Part of this interest in oral narratives is motivated by an interest in the *mythical or folk past*, an interest that emerges in numerous narratives and that has provoked considerable debate over the nature of the past that such narratives offer. A principal example of this folk style rests in the pasts evoked by Amos Tutuola's narratives, which are structured by oral folktale and allegory, and depend heavily upon the influence of the Yoruba folktale writer D. O. Fagunwa. Tutuola was lauded in Europe by the likes of T. S. Eliot and Dylan Thomas when he first published *The Palm-wine Drinkard* (1952), for what was perceived to be the linguistic exuberance and innovation that he brought to African literature (Thomas 1952). However, he was somewhat ridiculed or criticised for derivation (or at worst, outright plagiarism) in Nigeria, causing his reputation to undergo something of a re-evaluation in recent years. Abiola Irele has sought to disentangle the misperceptions about Fagunwa's influences over Tutuola, and has argued that Fagunwa's work in translating oral into written form has established him 'at the head of creative writing in the Yoruba language' (Irele 1981: 177). Irele suggests that Tutuola 'merely took over a form developed out of the folk tradition to a new level of expressiveness by Fagunwa' and there was a shift in attention from Fagunwa in Yoruba to Tutuola in English (Irele 1981: 182). Nevertheless, Tutuola individualised the Yoruba tradition that he bent to his purposes, and in densely packed narratives his 'imagery reflects an unusual capacity for perceiving and realizing in concretely sensuous terms a certain order of experience that lies beyond the range of the ordinarily "visible"' (Irele 1981: 186).

The Palm-wine Drinkard is a series of adventures that befall a man addicted to palm-wine, who goes in search of his dead palm-wine tapper. During the course of his search, he captures Death, overcomes the Skull, has a baby who plays all kinds of harmful pranks, is tortured by the inhabitants of the Heavenly Town, meets the 'Redpeople in the Red-town' and finally arrives at the Deads' Town where the dead palm-wine tapper is residing and who explains that he cannot leave, and the protagonist eventually arrives back in time to help save his own town from famine. Like Fagunwa, Tutuola fuses the supernatural and natural realms into a drama of human projections of the terrors and obsessions that haunt the imagination and consciousnesses of people on an everyday basis. Like Fagunwa, Tutuola 'has created the universe of his novels directly out of the African, and specifically Yoruba, conception which sees the supernatural not merely as a prolongation of the natural world, but as coexisting with it' (Irele 1981: 179). Indeed, O. Dathorne suggests that 'in the final resort Tutuola succeeds because his works remain enigmatic intrusions of the inexplicable past into an inquisitive present' (Dathorne 1971: 72). Tutuola's main intervention is to give the narrative an inflection in English, although in his imaginative use of Yoruba folklore many have criticised Tutuola for writing 'wrong' English, making him out to be 'quaint' or 'semi-literate' in the process, ignoring the fact that Tutuola's language is partly the palm-wine drinker's language and also reflective of the pidgin English spoken in West African speech (Dathorne 1971: 72). Emmanuel Obiechina has sought to clarify Tutuola's achievement, distinguishing Tutuola's ability to 'assimilate elements peculiar to the oral tradition to elements of the literary tradition: in other words, to impose a literary organization over essentially oral narrative material' (Obiechina 1975b: 144). Tutuola's writing effectively revisits a West African past that has been mythicised in Yoruba folk-tales and has been resurrected and thereby installed as part of the significant cultural history of Nigeria. In this respect, the oral tradition becomes the signifier of a past that has been censored by the rupturing cultural effects of colonial modernity and is now part of a process of postcolonial 'working-through'.

A further example of the resurrection and renewal of the folk and allegorical past occurs in Gabriel Okara's short novel *The Voice* (1964). Like most of Tutuola's narratives, this is also a quest narrative, in which the principal character Okolo (whose name means 'voice' in Ijaw) searches for '*It*'. '*It*' seems to be a moral value connected to the relationships one forges with one's community although '*it*' resists easy definition, and the reader acquires a knowledge of '*it*' only as the consequence of a cumulative synthesis of meanings during Okolo's search. This search causes Okolo to fall foul of his tribal chieftain Izongo, who ostracises and eventually expels him from his village because Okolo's quest for the meaning of life is perceived as a challenge to Izongo's leadership. Thereafter, Okolo ventures forth on a number of adventures, which take him to the neighbouring village of Sologa. During the course of these adventures, Okolo is given refuge by the socially marginalised woman Tuere, who is regarded as a witch. She proves to be steadfast in her support of Okolo, befriending him and ultimately dying in his company. Okara's novel is reminiscent of Tutuola's narrative style, partly in its dreamlike sequencing and partly in the somewhat fantastical scenes and characters that Okolo encounters, which are clearly part of what is owed to the oral narrative tradition and its vividness of event and immediate freshness of perspective.

The key aspect of *The Voice*, as many commentators have pointed out, is the language and style.[1] Okara has attempted to write English in a manner that echoes the idioms and rhythms of Ijaw, causing the English to have many repetitions and stylistic oddities in the adjectival phrases and metaphors. This has caused the novel to be picked out for its *poetic* style, as an experiment in language. For example, characters speak about their 'inside' meaning 'mind', or 'soul'. There are some excellent phrases, such as when Okolo goes anxiously and reluctantly to the Big One's house, he is described as walking 'with each step begging the ground' (*The Voice*: 80). The style also mimes the syntax of Ijaw, which often means placing the verb in an unusual position within the sentence. Certain passages of the novel clearly fall into the generic mode of parable, or allegory. For example, upon arrival at Sologa, Okolo meets a light and a wall, which, when followed, take him to a street in daylight, filled with all sorts of professions and daily activities (*The Voice*: 77–8). What occurs is an allegory that touches upon themes such as lawlessness, fear of power, the inadequacy of the law, authoritarian power and ignorance. It satirises the corruption and neglect evident in contemporary society, from the perspective of an oral and traditional narrative style.

Okara has written that he thinks that 'the immediate aim of African writing is to put into the whirlpool of literature the African point of view, to put across how the African thinks' (Okara undated: 4). In trying to combat a postcolonial situation in which English has been absorbed into African societies, and is at odds with the characteristics of the inner landscape that has been moulded by this entirely different culture and environment, Okara aims for an Africanisation of the English idiom, almost a transliteration. Instead of turning to the language of the once-ruling power, Okara turns his English to the African continent: 'a writer can use the idioms of his own language in a way that is understandable in English. If he uses their English equivalents, he would not be expressing African ideas and thoughts, but English ones' (Okara 1973: 137–9). The deliberate manner in which Okara works his different rhetorical devices and idioms is evident in the entire novel. Trying 'to keep as close as possible to the vernacular expressions' (Okara 1973: 137–9), the repetition of words, phrases, sentences, images and symbols, as well as short sentences and a high degree of the ritualisation of belief, actions and concepts, the symbolisation as a means of concretising experience, and the routinisation of everyday actions, all draw on the vernacular tendency of language to concretise experience. Abstract notions are rendered as physical realities. Obiechina describes Okara's practice as 'reification', endowing 'thingness' to abstract qualities (Obiechina 1975a: 174), although it is a process devoid of alienation. The metaphoric and hyberbolic elaborations, as well as the colloquial rhythms and the literalisation of action (i.e. 'Who are you people be?'), belong to the oral tradition. *The Voice* emerges as a quest not only for '*It*' but also for the frame of reference to the past culture embedded in indigenous cultural oral forms.

Okolo's journey and search echoes a familiar narrative structure. African narratives are repeatedly structured as quests. The structure of the quest, or the search for some lost thing, item, value or object, which may have previously existed and is now lost, but may also be something as yet unexperienced or metaphysically unknown, is a frequent theme. Prominent examples are Tutuola's *The Palm-wine Drinkard*, I. N. C. Aniebo's *The Journey Within*, Wole Soyinka's *The Road*, Gabriel Okara's *The Voice*, Ngugi wa Thiong'o's *Petals of Blood* and Ben Okri's *The Famished Road*. It has been observed that journeying on the road in African literature is a pronounced and observable metaphorical structure (Elder 2000). Sometimes this journey is figured as a physical journey during which characters move from place to place in search of the object. In other cases, this journey is more abstract, figuring an emotional or psychological quest, a search for some future maturity of vision, or knowledge of the state of things. Quest narratives in general need not inherently bespeak a traumatic origin or a traumatic past. However, the frequency and similarity of the structure of the quest occurring in the breadth of narratives written shortly after national independences within African countries might suggest similar structural paradigms in their cultural representations. In other words, I am suggesting that these quest narratives in African culture figure a paradigmatic traumatic structure that pervades postcolonial fictions, albeit of different nationalities and cultures across Africa. This traumatic structure is a pattern of loss, a pattern of searching for something that has been taken away, removed, interrupted, or a culture that has been forcibly wrenched or skewed. These quest narratives are therefore part of a fictional and cultural effort to recorrect a sense of cultural loss, but also of personal and social disruption and disorientation. Quests for answers to either subjective or social problems seem indicative of a desire for social *reorientation*, of the attempt to find a history, past or object that articulates more satisfactorily or more adequately the social fabric that is at a loss with itself. The narrative is an attempt to achieve social self-consciousness in the face of a period of enforced colonial *mésconnaissance*, alienation and anomie. In this reading, quest narratives are signs of a structural trauma and a cultural displacement that are in the process of being rectified and 'worked through', as delayed or deferred self-identifications are established in altered forms.

Tutuola and Okara resist presenting their mythical and folk pasts with any nostalgia. These are not pasts depicted for the purposes of envisaging a structural developmental progression into the future; nor are they pasts dependent upon some rose-tinted version of society before the ills attributed to the impact of an interruptive colonialism. These narratives do not refrain from presenting the petty grievances, the internal bickerings, the family vengeances, the political intrigues, the intertribal rivalries, the social corruptions or other features of social rifts. These are not pasts established primarily in contradistinction to the colonial pasts, or the neo-colonial presents, nor are they depictions of a past that is free from any social problems, economic hardships or forms of exploitation, in other words, a past that is harmonious, equal and democratic. They are indicative of a celebration of the characteristics of oral narratives, the free-and-easy nature of the protagonists, and the values of the societies that existed before colonialism. In this respect, they are narratives that utilise memory as much for the purpose of remembering the particular *modes of oral narrative* as much as for remembering that past itself. If there is a remembrance occurring in these narratives, it is a memory of a style of telling, of a form of narrating, which is itself indicative of a particular social structure that is coming under pressure from western or ex-colonial forms of narrative (i.e. the novel, or realism). Memory is therefore being used to preserve a form of the past in the *form* of the narrative. History is retrieved in form rather than content; the past is revisited principally in terms of a 'structure of feeling', rather than in terms of an ideological depiction of a certain way of life. The theatre of memory in these cases, is a production of language, and through this, memory acts to retrieve and preserve a syntax of the past, rooted in linguistic and narrative difference.

So far from succumbing to some quasi-nostalgic sentimentalism, Okara's and Tutuola's narratives testify to a culture concerned with a disappearing past, a past being erased by new modes of narrative, new forms of genre, and new structures of syntax. Their narratives are part of a general anxiety that history is being eroded by alien cultural forms which are unattuned to the nuances and significances of tribal mythological structures and to the labilities and flexibilities of indigenous forms of articulation. In this respect, these narratives form part of a technology of memory that aims for preservation and conservation. Yet this is in no sense a static form of preservation. Here it is form that is acting as the process of 'working-through'. For these narratives embed within themselves a finely nuanced hybridity, as they imbricate their indigenous knowledges and forms of speech with western influences and structures of consciousness. So while these narratives are concerned with the impact of foreign cultures upon indigenous African cultures, they do not turn a blind eye to the alternative expression of other cultures. In their use of the oral and mythical modes as a departure from the more orthodox modes of western narrative structure and technique, their writing enlivens the diversity of African culture and demonstrates how the past can be reinvigorated by preserving and activating the memory of once-forgotten narrative styles. This memory is conceptualised as a force in conflict with the counter-force of repression and censorship; and as such, recalling memory acts as a politico-cultural tactic in the effort to combat historical marginalisation.

Memory and healing: the archetypal case of Ayi Kwei Armah

For all their interest and fascination, if Echewa's, Tutuola's, Amadi's and Okara's fiction poses awkward imponderables over the matter of African self-fashioning, then the novels of Ayi Kwei Armah are far more emphatic in their depiction of the past and the problems standing in the way of establishing a clear sense of national identity. Armah's fiction is distinctly concerned with fashioning an African past by the intellectual retrieval of a usable past and alternative cultural histories. Commenting on the way in which the interplay between past and present in fiction raises consciousness about agency, Armah himself has said that:

> One of the virtues of Creative Writing is that apart from letting us see the way things happen to be now, it also opens our vision to the way things were in the past, and the way they might be in the future. In fact, at its best, Creative Writing engages the reader in a constant interactive process between the past, the present and the future, calculated to make educated persons not passive endurers of present conditions, but active protagonists aware of past causes, and willing to use their awareness to help shape future results. (Armah 1985: 994)

Derek Wright suggests that 'The gradual shift of emphasis in Armah's writing is away from the grim portrayal of a pre-colonial past of despotic privilege and greed, expressed directly in the essays and through the panoramic historical retrospections of the early novels ... towards a "literature of combat"' (Wright 1989: 50). Early novels like *The Beautyful Ones Are Not Yet Born* that emerge out of Ghanaian independence are critical of African leadership, bitter about the effects of corruption and disappointed at the loss of a communal vision. Nevertheless, his novels of the 1970s, for all the criticism they attract for their movement away from the specifics of history to a more mythical historical structure, are attempts to tackle the effects of traumatic history in a manner that deals forthrightly with the problems of 'acting-out' and 'working-through'. In his general introduction to *The Novels of Ayi Kwei Armah: A Study in Polemical Fiction*, Robert Fraser has argued that Armah's fiction is a record of postcolonial ennui, depicting how revolutionary fervour has guttered into political betrayal in post-independence Ghana. Yet it is not simply a fiction of political or ideological disenchantment, but one of passionate, meticulous and concentrated critical analysis. Taken together as a body of work, one can examine Armah's fiction as a trajectory of a writer analysing a problem, diagnosing the illness and, finally, prescribing a remedy. The fiction is a prime example of an African writer grappling with history as trauma, with Africa's present-day concerns as being the deferred and delayed consequences of actions in the past that were never adequately internalised, understood and integrated into national and racial consciousnesses.[2]

Despite its shifts in content, Fraser suggests that there is an aesthetic consistency across Armah's fiction, as it gradually moves to a broader historical perspective in the novels of the 1970s (Fraser 1980: 10). Indeed, a focussed project can be tracked across all the novels: 'There are certain symbols which transcend the divisions between the books, recurring in such a way as to amount to motifs pervading the whole of Armah's writing' (Fraser 1980: 12–13). Yet Derek Wright contends that Fraser's approach speciously flattens out differences in Armah's thought and writing: 'some of the weakest critical moments ... are to be found in the forging of spurious conti-nuities between individual novels' (Wright 1989: 12). Wright contin-ues by arguing that: 'It would be more correct to say that it is the intellectual shape of Armah's symbols which is recurrent, rather than the symbols themselves. For example, the idea of the cycle, either with its regenerative connotations or with its darker hints of vicious circles of entrapment ... But within the limits of this very loose pattern of consistency, each novel starts again with a new metaphoric pattern and is structured around its own independent symbolic centre' (Wright 1989: 14).

Often regarded as a key text reflecting on the dawn of African inde-pendences, *The Beautyful Ones Are Not Yet Born* (1968) depicts the life of a lonely and isolated yet honest railway worker (known in the novel as 'the Man'), who is married to a woman from whom he feels somewhat detached and separated, and the struggles he has in main-taining his honesty and sincerity within a sea of corruption. This corruption is personified in the person of Koomson, who involves the lonely husband's wife and her mother in some tax-evasion ploy when he buys a boat. Finally, as a result of a military coup, a new govern-ment seeks to root out the corruption of the old regime, and Koomson has to turn to 'the Man' in a desperate search for help and ultimately make an escape, which occurs by Koomson having to literally crawl through a mire of human excrement in the toilet to escape (this metaphor thereby literalising his previous existence). Indeed, the novel is riddled with images of fragmentation, illness, decay and disease, figured most graphically in the smell and the stench of the latrines. At one point in the novel, 'the Man' meets the 'shitman' returning from his job of cleaning the latrines, 'carrying other people's excrement ... The shitman is a man of the night and the very early morning, a man hidden completely from the sight of all but curious children and men with something heavy on their minds in the darkness of the night' (*Beautyful*: 121). This thematic treatment of excrement is ultimately associated with Koomson as an allegorical association with corruption. The book is principally a critique of the legacy of corruption left to the current neo-colonial generation by the white colonists and their administration; and it frequently speaks about the ways in which corruption permeates current neo-colonial petty officials, and the ways in which they use their power to ape the characteristics of the white colonists (imitating their dress, their food, their drinks, their cars, their acquisition of material goods, manners of speaking, etcetera): 'There is something so terrible in watching a black man trying at all points to be the dark ghost of a European, and that was what we were seeing in those days' (*Beautyful*: 95). 'We were ready here for big and beautiful things, but what we had was our own black men hugging new paunches scrambling to ask the white man to welcome them onto our backs' (*Beautyful*: 94). In the midst of this material glitter, 'the Man' wonders: 'It was not the things themselves, but the way to arrive at them which brought so much confusion to the soul. And everybody knew the chances of finding a way that was not rotten from the beginning were always ridiculously small ... What monstrous fruit was it that could find the end of its life in the struggle against sweetness and corruption' (*Beautyful*: 170–1).

The matter of political disillusionment with internal national politics is explored in chapter 6 with an old friend of 'the Man', called the Teacher. Chapter 6 is a central chapter and focuses upon the Teacher's perception of the crucial role of memory, and the ways in which people have been severed from their beginnings, or origins. 'There is nothing that should break the heart in the progressive movement away from the beauty of the first days. I see growth, that is all I see within my mind' (*Beautyful*: 73). The Teacher is also concerned with how memory can dissimulate the past: 'It is so surprising, is it not, how even the worst happenings of the past acquire a sweetness in the memory. Old harsh distresses are now merely pictures and tastes which hurt no more, like itching scars which can only give pleasure now. Strange, because when I can think soberly about it all, without pushing any later joys into the deeper past, I can remember that things were terrible then' (*Beautyful*: 74). As we shall see, Armah's fiction becomes progressively more preoccupied with the traumatic resurgence of the past in the present, and in particular, with the pathology of its treatment, or as the novel puts it: "The listening mind is disturbed by memories from the past" (*Beautyful*: 78). For the Teacher, the Ghanaian president Nkrumah serves to confirm the overwhelming rule of a weary recognition of a fat-cynical and power-grabbing elite. The current moral and political corruption is portrayed as the legacy of centuries of moral compromise, a history of duplicity that precedes independence, that precedes even colonialism itself. 'History is rotten through and through' (*Beautyful*: 28). The potent image of the wooden banister at the end of chapter 1 in *The Beautyful Ones*, constantly being polished to prevent deterioration but being undone and inevitably doomed to rot, is yet another of the novel's pessimistic observations about the irresistibility of pollution, corruption and rottenness:

> The wood underneath would win and win until the end of time. Of that there was no doubt possible, only the pain of hope perennially doomed to disappointment. It was so clear. Of course it was in the nature of wood to rot with age. The polish, it was supposed, would catch the rot. But of course in the end it was the rot which imprisoned everything in its effortless embrace ... [the wood] would convert all to victorious filth, awaiting yet more polish again and again and again. And the wood was not alone. (*Beautyful*: 14–15)

This does seem to place the novel in a state of general gloom and pessimism. The title of the novel indicates the fact that the nation is still awaiting the birth of hope and suggests that emancipation leads not to hope and freedom but straight to sterility, despondency and despair.

In many ways, the book is deeply pessimistic and finishes on a very depressed note; the corrupt regime is overthrown by a military regime, seen to be involved in corruption just as the old one was (see the bus-driver in last pages handing over a bribe to the soldier); in this respect, history seems circular, and there seems to be little sense that one might escape the system of bribes, corruption and backhanders: 'But for the nation itself there would only be a change of embezzlers and a change of the hunters and hunted ... Endless days, same days, stretching into the future with no end anywhere in sight' (*Beautyful*: 191). The final lines of the novel lend further to this sense of corruption: 'But then suddenly all his mind was consumed with thoughts of everything he was going back to – Oyo, the eyes of the children after six o'clock, the office and every day, and above all the never-ending knowledge that this aching emptiness would be all that the remainder of his own life could offer him. He walked very slowly, going home' (*Beautyful*: 215).

The novel seems to be arguing that, in the face of this corruption and its concomitant fragmentation of society, the people need to be made whole again: 'There was something so good about the destroyed people waking up and wanting to make themselves whole again' (*Beautyful*: 105–6). The problem, though, is that for Armah, Africans are still struggling for agency. 'The Man' in *The Beautyful Ones* is described as 'A victim of history' (*Beautyful*: 25) and many of Armah's characters are not free agents, determined as they are by social circumstances. Indeed, Armah is centrally concerned with subjects' relations to history, and the historical contexts of most of his novels are significant. The central context in *The Beautyful Ones* is disillusionment with Nkrumah's role in Ghanaian independence and the

larger history of centuries-old betrayals, a note that recurs in several
of the novels of the 1970s as they explore the backdrop of centuries of
oppression by indigenous exploiters, such as chiefs who sold their
people into slavery. Much of Armah's writing is an archaeology of the
reasons for delayed liberty in Ghana, seeking the factors that have
inhibited revolutionary success. In a significant passage in the
conversation between the Teacher and 'the Man', there is a discussion of freedom and slavery in which it is argued that people 'would
laugh with hate at the bringer of unwanted light if what they knew
they needed was the dark' (*Beautyful*: 93). The Teacher speaks cynically of the freedom of the people to choose – if they choose darkness
rather than light, who is to say they should not? Neil Lazarus argues
that the book suggests that 'the masses' are first afforded a vision of
freedom, and are exhorted to move toward it; then, once they have
wrestled themselves to within touching distance of it, it is snatched
from their grasp, and unfreedom is cynically reimposed in its stead.
Finally, to add insult to injury, this humiliation is compounded by
the official rhetoric, which in celebration proclaims Africa's independence. In independence, according to *The Beautyful Ones*, the
'masses' are still unfree (Lazarus 1992: 164). Contrary to S. A.
Gakwandi's view (Gakwandi 1977: 97; see also Gakwandi 1992:
106–7), Lazarus argues that it is wrong to perceive Armah's depiction
of the 'masses' as a hostile and critical attitude to all humanity, and
that one is equally wrong to assume 'Armah's hatred of crass materi-
alism, conspicuous consumption, and neo-colonial thinking as a
loathing of *mankind in general*' (Lazarus 1992: 164). Rather, Armah
focuses his bitter critique on the corruption of the neo-colonial ruling
classes, fat cats like Koomson made rich through exploitation of
sometimes gullible ordinary people.

The book is also about how power circulates and is meted out
within the society. Partly about the cynical rhetoric of socialism by
those in power, who have betrayed any real sense of democratic politics and economic equality, the novel depicts one oligarchy over-
throwing another oligarchy, with the power revolving around these
groups of people, leaving the ordinary people (like 'the Man') always
as the victims of the system, with a 'New people, new style, old dance'
(*Beautyful*: 185). The novel's unremitting pessimism is summed up in
the following passage, where history is represented as being caught
in depressing circularity:

> In the life of the nation itself, maybe nothing really new would happen.
> New men would take into their hands the power to steal the nation's
> riches and to use it for their own satisfaction. That, of course, was to be
> expected. New people would use the country's power to get rid of men
> and women who talked a language that did no flatter them. There would
> be nothing different in that. That would only be a continuation of the

Ghanaian way of life. But here was the real change. The individual man of power now shivering, his head filled with the fear of the vengeance of those he had wronged. For him everything was going to change. (*Beautyful*: 190–1)

Corruption is explored further in *Fragments*. Written from the perspective of several of the key protagonists, as Richard Priebe notes, this is yet another novel in which the liminality of Armah's 'anti-heroes' illuminates the diagnostic and analytical representation of a corrupt Ghana (Priebe 1976: 126): Baako, a 'been-to' (the phrase referring to his having 'been-to' Europe to study), who returns to work for Ghanavision and struggles to adapt to being back home in Ghana; Juana, a Puerto Rican doctor working at one of the key hospitals in Accra; and Naana, Baako's blind grandmother, who is prone to visions about the country and her family (Efua is his mother). Baako's notes on the 'been-to' likens the returnee to figures in the Melanesian cargo cults (*Fragments*: 223–5): the nature of the return, the hope of alleviating problems, the disillusionment are all related to the returnee as a ghost, interceding on behalf of those less fortunate. Yet Baako's breakdown is partly the 'fear of the return' (*Fragments*: 145–7) in which he does not live up to the 'been-to' image – no calm return from abroad with foreign materials, no limousine and no deep-freeze. Robert Fraser points out that one of the chapter titles, 'Osagyefo', is an Akan word denoting a glamorous redeemer. Consequently, 'Baako is the child who has been sent away to forge the weapons of deliverance. His function on his reappearance is hence a sacramental one' (Fraser 1980: 33), although, ironically, he fails to carry out the religious redemption, as he becomes increasingly disillusioned with the sickness in Ghana.

For Baako is finally beset by a grim realisation that the country is thoroughly corrupt (consider the description of the nauseous scene of Ghanaian society and politics in the chapter entitled 'Igya', in which 'the dance of memories ... drew him impotently back into unending waste, the stupid stream against which he was powerless even to set his own mind' (*Fragments*: 187)). Baako consequently resigns from his job that he feels is a dead-end, and, eventually, he either goes insane or is considered insane by his friends and family – this collapse seems to be brought on by the corrupt state of the country, which drives him to desperation. Much of the book's polemical critique concerns the administrative indifference and laziness of the state; Baako's sense of trying to make a difference or a contribution to the state after having been educated abroad is punctured by his experiences of corruption, uselessness and anxiety on behalf of the state's employees. There are some stunning passages of writing, where Armah is spellbinding in his focus – the murder of the dog in the traffic jam, in chapter 2, or the scene in which the lorry driver tries to ram his way on to the ferry, and gradually slides off, sinks and dies. Social violence is something that fascinates Armah, and these passages point to a senseless violence in society, where social and political frustrations and repressions are taken out on scape-goats.

Written as 'fragments', or bits and pieces of vision, almost as if there is a difficulty in providing a joined-up perspective of the society in Ghana, the novel is another critical diagnosis of the sick man of Ghana. In this respect, Robert Fraser argues that the fragments are to do not with the form but with the content. Yet the book does constantly interrupt one's experience of linearity and smoothness – and one may construe this as a style judged to reflect the crisis of the country in the postcolonial era. For example, one of Baako's film-scripts details a cinematic style that stresses the interruptive and fragmentary: 'THROUGH REPETITIVE USE OF IMAGE AND SOUND IMPRINT IDEA OF VIOLENCE, UNPLEASANT, STRONG, IRRESISTIBLE, ATTACKING THE VIEWER, INVAD-ING HIS EYES, ASSAULTING HIS EARS … FREQUENT DISSO-NANT LEAPING SOUNDS BREAKING IT UP' (*Fragments*: 207). These filmscripts are rejected by Baako's employers at Ghanavision, because they find them unacceptable to the apolitical interests that they are attempting to feature. His scripts for something on the slave-trade, and on racial histories associated with Ghana, are also refused as dissociated with Ghana's past. Baako is also too outspo-kenly critical of the obsequious, fawning and corrupt society in which he finds himself. Whilst meditating on the analogies of the 'been-to' and the cargo cults, 'A fractured thought crossed his mind. The urge to trap it before it disappeared made him forget the general pain of his body' (*Fragments*: 223). Baako's urge is exemplary of the novel: it is a series of fractured thoughts attempting to dissect the general pain of the nation. It is worth noting the way in which the text is studded by capital headlines throughout the novel, as posters, texts, slogans and other verbal tags cut into the consciousness of the char-acters, demonstrating another 'fragmentary' consciousness at work. Naana, a blind seer, has an authority by dint of her age that allows her to perceive ethical realities and truths denied to the rest of society – age gives memories of things before the present materialis-tic rush. Her final musings before she dies offer another interpreta-tion of the 'fragments': 'The larger meaning which lent sense to every small thing and every momentary happening years and years ago has shattered into a thousand and thirty useless pieces. Things have passed which I have never seen whole, only broken and twisted against themselves. What remains of my days will be filled with more broken things … But then every cracked bit of a moment some other mystery traveling past caught my eye, my ear, and the trouble of the time before was made deeper, not replaced, by a worse confusion' (*Fragments*: 280–1). This is not unlike a Lyotardian realisation that metanarratives have collapsed and all that is left are micro-narratives which do not add up to a greater whole, leaving one to manage with the tattered halves of a once-realised social entirety.

These realist evocations of a troubled and traumatic neo-colonial state, where the crisis in the past resurfaces in the form of a society riven by a number of different social tensions, gets a different twist in Armah's fiction of the 1970s. *Two Thousand Seasons* (1973) is constructed as part of a literary struggle of memory against forgetting. In this novel, the principal theme is racial memory and an inherited trust of communal integrity, of some spiritual ancestry running through the centuries. Armah's novel demonstrates that one needs to remember as part of a self-critical process in reconsidering choices and locations. As Robert Fraser notes, 'In any post-colonial state, the way that the future of the nation is envisaged is inextricably bound up with the particular construction put on the past' (Fraser 1980: 67). The past depicted in this novel is not a nostalgic or sentimental one – there are just as many negative issues in the past precolonial times as there are after the colonists arrive. It is set in precolonial and early colonial times, during which white slave-traders arrive, in order to enslave the Ghanaian population for trade with the Americas. The narrative follows the lives of a band of tribes-people who form a resistance group, confronting the slavers with guerrilla warfare and it shows how the tribal elders capitulate to the white colonists' seductions (arms and alcohol), becoming complicit in the oppression of their own people motivated by greed. The narrative is cast in a certain mythic mode and it makes a great deal of the prehistory of Ghana (when it was organised along tribal lands and boundaries).

As Derek Wright contends, although it is dormant but not dead in the early works, history becomes more explicit in Armah's works in the 1970s: 'The past itself, which assumes many different guises in the first two books, is endowed with a new singleness and simplicity by the dogma of "the Way"' (Wright 1987: 12). 'The Way' is the pivot upon which the ethical centre of Armah's novel swivels in his postulation of reciprocity as the epitome of African identity, or 'our way, the way' as he continually characterises it: 'Reciprocity. Not merely taking, not merely offering. Giving, but only to those from whom we receive in equal measure. Receiving, but only from those to whom we give in reciprocal measure. How easy, how just, the way' (*Two Thousand Seasons*: 17). This is an ethic that seeks to counter any hierarchical relationship established in the act of giving, through a generosity that can work only if the *otherness* of the other is accepted, and through which there is no attempt to identify and thereby integrate that other. In seeking undistorted relationships through a transfiguration of giving and receiving, the non-identity of the other person and culture must be respected and preserved. It entails an ability to receive the other's specificity, and this receptivity is entwined with an ability to extend ourselves generously toward others and otherness. Giving ought to establish personal qualitative relationships between the subjects doing the transacting. In the midst of the self-apotheosis of contemporary liberalism, this counter-vision of receptive generosity is rooted not in sovereign self-interest but in a non-assimilating openness to others. *Two Thousand Seasons* narrates the fragmentation of the social wholeness by the arrival of invaders, white settlers, and the ways in which various elders betray the people into enslavement for their own profit. The slavers over-throw this unity of spirit, the lost 'reciprocity', 'connectedness', or 'our way, the way'. The vestigial remnants of this ethos of 'the way' lies in the band of young resistors and the tribal elder Isanusi, who lives in self-exile in remote areas of the forest. In teaching the young followers how to understand the fragmentation and degeneration of their society, Isanusi says: 'See the disease, and understand it well' (*Two Thousand Seasons*: 200). Generally more optimistic than in his former novels, Armah here forges a central image of the water being released to irrigate the desert areas, as an indication of fertility and liberation. A sense of democracy and hope pervade the novel, and culminates, in the final paragraph, which contests the bleaker versions of African history, with history figured as a flowing river, unblocked and running: 'What a hearing of the confluence of all the waters of life flowing to overwhelm the ashen desert's blight! What an utterance of the coming together of all people of the way' (*Two Thousand Seasons*: 206).

In many ways, Armah's novel is curative vision, presenting a philo-sophical discourse of diagnosis and prescription for a redemption that masquerades as a narrative and commentary on that narrative, that self-reflexively poses as a memory of itself. Armah is a nameless participant in the 'we' of the novel, rejecting any distance between the author and the narrative.[3] The text emerges as an articulation of a collective memory in contradistinction to the violators of African identity. Carefully structured on the issue of remembrance and forgetting, the novel turns again and again to memory as a corrective to the existential deviation and dissociation foisted upon Africans by white colonialism and its effects: 'We will not betray this remem-brance: that all unconnected things are victims, tools of death' (*Two Thousand Seasons*: 8). One critic observes that in the novel 'the recol-lection of the past is a "remembrance" rather than "history." "Remembrance" suggests that memory fails, that only what is rele-vant is remembered for the present and for posterity, while "history" implies inclusiveness, accuracy, and objectivity' (Izevbaye 1992: 32). The novel does not purport to portray an accurate or totalised past, for its history is cast in the epic and mythic mould, with types of people in the action – 'the destroyers', the 'ostentatious cripples', for example. The book reconstructs the past for the purposes of social direction in the future, attempting to relocate Africans at the centre of their own sphere of signification, reinventing and reinscribing the matrix of this meaningfulness in reciprocity. It produces a narrative that treats the enslavement of West Africa as a traumatic episode in its history, a trauma through which its people are still attempting to work. This narrative is a 'working-through' of that trauma.

If *Two Thousand Seasons* begins to construct a history of regeneration through rupture, *The Healers* (1978) makes this history of African trauma and its palliative explicit. Robert Fraser's argument is that, in rewriting the Second Asante War as a 'restatement of a neglected and misunderstood phase of the colonial past' (Fraser 1980: 85), *The Healers* is therapeutic – that the discourse is pathological, diagnostic and psychoanalytical:

> There is a marked therapeutic value to much of Armah's work. We can now see that he is concerned fundamentally with the ethical quality of a nation's life, a potential for exuberant health he sees as having been strangled by an infection of foreign origin. In the first two books we were treated to some rather gruesome medical illustrations. Increasingly, however, his vigilance has directed itself less to the pallor invading the surface than to the causes lurking beyond immediate notice, the sad aetiology of their growth. (Fraser 1980: 2)

Fraser argues that *The Healers* 'is a therapeutic work which aims to close the wounds left over and festering from centuries of implied cultural abuse' (Fraser 1980: 82); and that, whereas *Two Thousand Seasons* depicts history as an endlessly flowing stream, or a repetitively eternal cycle, where the historical method is 'deductive', *The Healers* is 'inductive', setting out to demonstrate the reasons for the failure of a culture (Fraser 1980: 84). *The Healers* poses as an alternative to the official militarist ideals of the Asante nation, showing it to have its roots in the spiritual activity of the healers. The novel concerns Densu, a young man who seeks out the aid of his friend Damfo, a member of a group of healers who live in contemplative seclusion in the dense forest, when Densu is accused of intrigue and the murder of a friend, competitor and prince. In the description of the tribal games at the outset of the novel, one sees that the original Akan wholeness has been fragmented by social competitiveness and a notion of purely individual advancement. The concomitants of this individualism – slavery, the rise of an oligarchic ruling class, social fragmentation into jostling ethnic sub-groups – blight the entire community's life. The healers seek to wean people away from these false idols. As someone who has been treated by the healers, the murdered prince's mother, Araba Jesiwa, speaks to Densu of numerous things:

> She talked to him of renewal – of the purging of falsehoods out of the abused self, of the flushing out of poisons from body and soul. She talked of the regaining of contact with a truer self abandoned in the past because false selves had offered the illusion of greater convenience. She talked of the incredible joy of the rediscovery of the authentic self, when the self too long exposed to lies was set free at last to roam along the paths to truth. She talked of remarriage, the finding of a soul closer to her own, and the quickening discovery of the body that held that soul. (*The Healers*: 68)

Araba Jesiwa's 'remembrance of her long nightmare' (*The Healers*: 69) is clearly a moment of traumatic recollection, a 'nightmare' which was a period of self-alienation, now overcome through the therapy performed by Damfo. Damfo performs what we might perceive to be psychoanalytic therapy, causing her to talk about forgotten memories (*The Healers*: 70), echoing Freud's 'talking cure'.

Araba Jesiwa's narrative about being healed by Damfo in the forest, about being told how to regain her true self and put aside the false self to which she had succumbed, could be read as a parable about the history of Nigeria itself, and Africa more generally. An important passage occurs when Jesiwa explains to Densu the different selves in her life, and how these have been corrupted by different forces: 'Of his conversations with Araba Jesiwa, Densu kept sweet memories. They were memories of the search for the true self, the natural self; the attempt to let the true self reveal its nature and follow its own path in life; the avoidance of force, deception, and manipulation in relationships with close ones; the constant reliance on inspiration to do the work of the spirit' (*The Healers*: 78). When Densu eventually records his own first conversation with the healer Damfo, he says that Damfo talked about the healers' work as one of making a wholeness in the people, of correcting a division that has crept into the people after years of social life. His explanation boils down to explaining that healers are especially astute *readers of signs*, of the written world:

> 'Does a healer know languages others don't know?'
> 'You may want to understand it that way. You know how full of sounds the world is. Some of these sounds we are taught to understand. Most we don't understand, ever. In the universe there are so many signs. A few we understand, the way farmers know what clouds mean, and fishermen understand stars. But most signs mean nothing to us because we aren't prepared to understand them. The healer trains his eye – so he can read signs. His training is of the ears – so he can listen

to sounds and understand them. His preparation is also of the nostrils
– life and death have their smells. It is of the tongue, and the body's
ability to feel.' (*The Healers*: 80)

Arguing that the people have been seduced by visions other than the
ones that the people and the nations know themselves, Damfo
discusses his healing work within the context of a nation's alienation
(*The Healers*: 82): indeed, even the concept of the 'nation' is a sign of
alienation among the people. Damfo continues to describe the
healing work as a process of restoring a people's memory, a way to
overcome a wilful forgetting of the natural disasters that caused the
divisions in the first place:

> The events that have shattered our people were not simply painful
> events. They were disasters. They were strange, unnatural catastro-
> phes. Those who survived them could only survive in part because they
> found ways to forget the catastrophes. When you're still close to past
> dangers that threatened to wipe you out, even remembrance pains you.
> Our people forgot a lot of things in order to survive. We even went
> beyond forgetfulness. To forget thoroughly the shattering and the
> dispersal of a people that was once whole, we have gone so far as to
> pretend we have always been these silly little fragments each calling
> itself a nation. (*The Healers*: 82)

Damfo then continues to say that the highest work of healers is 'the
bringing together again of the black people' (*The Healers*: 82).
Healing is reunification, through the evocation of the memory of
unity, buried like the unconscious of the people. The healer's act is to
allow the people to speak their unconscious unity, and thereby overcome the alienation of the nation. As Fraser puts it, 'The hurt runs
deep, the running sores only suggesting at the gross infection of the
whole social organism. It is here that the writer can help, applying
his healing art and bracing the spirit by reference to a vision of social
confidence sufficient to dispel the gloom of accumulated self-loathing'
(Fraser 1980: 103). This method of excavating and 'working-through'
hidden and dim memories, is a key procedure to reunifying the
people by offering diagnostic and therapeutic narratives
(Nwahuunanya 1995).

There has been some considerable debate about the effectiveness of
Armah's political project. Derek Wright suggests that 'It is true that
Armah's novels do tend to reduce "the complex process of history" to
the suspiciously perfect symmetry of cyclical patterns. Neo-colonialism reincarnates colonial and post-colonial evils that were never
really expelled' (Wright 1989: 6). Kofi Anyidoho has pointed out that
a great deal of recent scholarship on Armah has scrutinised his peculiar dialectics of historical reconstruction and mythopoesis.[4]
Nevertheless, Anyidoho concludes that 'Armah's chosen objective is a

revolutionary and visionary ideal; the visionary ideal is not simply a retrieval of a past ideal but a reshaping of a future world free from the destructive factors of past and present conditions. A historian with his eyes on the future is under no obligation to merely reconstruct past events (Anyidoho 1981)' (Anyidoho 1992: 41). Anyidoho makes a strong argument about the manner in which Armah constructs a *collective heroism* in *The Healers*, in which all major victories for the people of 'the way' are won through collective heroism, while the traditional epic hero's path to fame and to glory is contrary to the spirit of 'the way', reciprocity and communal struggle (Anyidoho 1992: 43). Despite the whys and wherefores of Armah's representation of history, he is clearly concerned to develop an overwhelming counteraction to the colonialist distortion of history. Wole Soyinka describes this literary opposition as 'the visionary reconstruction of the past for the purposes of social direction' (Soyinka 1976: 106). In fact, this historical reconstruction is particularly prominent in Armah's most recent fiction, *Osiris Rising* (1995) and *KMT: In the House of Life* (2000). Arguably his most far-reaching investigations of African pasts, these two novels are part of Armah's consistent and unrelenting preoccupation with reclaiming Africa's place in world history. As one critic has noted, 'With the appearance of Armah's sixth and seventh novels, *Osiris Rising* and *KMT: In the House of Life: An Epistemic Novel*, the representation of African history in fiction could be said to have reached the stage of maturity. [The two novels are concerned with] finding a cure for Africa's past and present ills, so as to trigger the transformation required for the long-awaited future regeneration' (Ayivor 2003: 38). Taken together as an oeuvre, Armah's fiction of healing and memory acts as a critical inscription of the legible form of trauma, but also as an attempt to foster creative imaginations of un-actualised potentialities for the future.

Loss or lack?

This chapter has sought to explore the extent to which the colonial and the postcolonial epochs can be construed as traumatic resulting from a pre-oedipal imaginary unity (or community) with the mother (for example, a precolonial society) that has been lost through the intervention of (the name of) the father and the institution of the symbolic under the sway of the phallus (the colonial power). Is that imaginary unity a misrecognition (of absence as loss) (for example, in Armah, or Amadi)? Does not this structural model itself problematically set up the African as mother and the European as father, since it engenders an unhelpful confusion in the nature of the African trauma by implying that colonialism is a movement from nature to culture, in which colonialism acts as Africa's entry into language or a validated symbolic structure? Is subjectivity predicated upon the constitutive nature of originary melancholic loss? Absence projected as loss implies a regenerative process or ultimate salvation or redemption. Yet is the arrival of the European equatable to an *original trauma*, over which African culture persistently pores in an 'acting-out' and 'working-through'? If so, how does African writing manifest itself, and when is that trauma 'worked-through'? Or does this predicate a misrecognition (i.e. absence or loss)? In other words, there never existed that unity, and consequently a different narrative of African history emerges, for example one where division did exist before the colonists arrived, and the colonists imposed a certain sort of unity-through-culture, which never really unified. Therefore, that history emerges as a series of different conflicts, where the resolution of one might not imply resolution of another, where there are uneven and differential historical trajectories as a result. In this case, one is dealing with *lack* rather than absence or loss. A lack need not necessarily involve a loss. The conversion of absence into loss or lack, notably through the notion of a fall from a putative state of grace, at-homeness, unity or community, is a difficulty. The fiction of the writers concerned in this chapter demonstrate repeated efforts to combat versions of history as loss or lack. Nevertheless, in the proposed alternative models of the past, these African writers testify to the traumatic nature of that past, where rather than restoring and healing wounds, history is at best a pathologist rather than the physician of memory.

Notes

[1]   For example, see Arthur Ravenscroft's introduction to *The Voice*: 15.

[2]   For considerations of history as the critical site of Armah's therapeutic analysis, see Lindfors 1980; Wright 1987; and Wright 1990.

[3]   The narrative of the 'plural voice' that emerges at the end of the novel has been described as one of the most significant formal aspects of Armah's work. See Webb 1980.

[4]   'Some have accused him of over-simplification, falsification of historical events resulting in "fantasy" (Achebe, 1982, *TLS*, 26 Feb.), or "a cartoon, comic-strip history" (Lindfors 1980). Others have applauded his work as a much-needed and effective projection of the creative imagination from the past, through the present, into the future. The mythic value of his work receives special attention (Amuta 1981; Fraser 1980; Ngara 1982; Okpewho 1980 and 1983; Soyinka 1976)' (Anyidoho 1992: 41).

3

Critical and traumatic realist pasts

Freedom could be found only in acknowledging the scars of one's history, not in escaping from it. (Michael S. Roth, *The Ironist's Cage*)

Festus Iyayi's influential call in the 1970s for a realism to supplant what he perceived to be African writers' obsessive preoccupation with the past was part of a desire to focus African fiction on the current troubles blighting the continent. His fiction calls upon Nigerians to look to the crises of the present, rather than dwelling on the past. Albeit a rather blunt and un-nuanced clarion call for realism (the problems of which I will return to later in this chapter), in ostensibly eschewing history, Iyayi practised a social or critical realism that would force into the public eye the issues of state corruption, class exploitation and the manipulation by wealthy social elements of the poorer classes. An exponent of critical realism in novels like *Violence* (1979) and *Heroes* (1986), Iyayi explores the complex political problems in contemporary Nigeria, ranging across issues like the reasons for and consequences of the Nigerian Civil War and the development of hotels for tourist purposes. He rubs the noses of his readers in polemical argument about the dirtiness and grubbiness of contemporary Nigerian life, rather than focusing upon precolonial village life, the transposition of folk-tale myths or mythical fantasies about African pasts. The novel *Violence* (1979) focuses upon the lives of two sets of people in contemporary Nigeria, starkly mapping a comparison between the poverty and apparent impotence of Adisa's and Idemudia's lives against the wealthy lifestyles of Queen and Obofun. Whereas Adisa and Idemudia struggle to make ends meet, are met with unemployment problems and suffer domestic strife as a consequence, Queen and Obofun are middle-class business people on the take: their nefarious deals in order to promote and secure their wealth and their racial position are the subject of the book's political daggers. Obufun attempts to seduce Adisa and, although he eventually gets his way, it is a pyrrhic victory since she does not let this disrupt her marriage to Idemudia. When Idemudia finally finds out about Adisa's adultery, he eventually realises what sacrifices have been made to keep his family together with its basic domestic necessities of food and shelter. The novel demonstrates in graphic and hard-hitting ways how their marriage came close to collapsing, how it has ironically strengthened through being the economic pawns and playthings of the wealthy, but, more generally, how people are always in a process of self-abandonment.

Violence is insistently materialist and polemical in its critique of the decadence in Nigerian society. In good Marxist fashion, materialist analysis drives off and refutes the metaphysical on several occasions. In a discussion about throwing away excess food, the rejoinder makes it clear that human agency cannot be exonerated by attributing actions to God: "'Everything is God's work". "*Kai* is not God's work, it's man-made'" (*Violence*: 20). Elsewhere, there is an exhortation against religion and God, since they do not provide food and material benefits to the starving masses (*Violence*: 220). While a patient at hospital, Idemudia attends the patients' theatrical production for a visiting government bureaucrat. The play is entitled 'Violence', and it concerns corruption and nepotism within the legal system. The Judge in the play acknowledges that he is protecting the propertied classes (*Violence*: 184), while the Counsel for the Defence has a polemical speech about the exploitation of the masses (*Violence*: 185–6). The play is a not-so-subtle device to implicate the State and the legal system in the hegemonic control that oppresses the poor population, although the government bureaucrat ignorantly misses the irony in the play and applauds the production. The novel takes its title from this play, and concerns the violence perpetrated by the system of capitalism on the mass of the people through economic exploitation, corruption, nepotism and moral decadence. As so often with social realist fiction, the narrative reads as a recipe for social evils and the novel offers numerous examples of the ways in which people's lives are degraded through poverty and how society is tainted by exploitative actions; and it presents a systematic critique of the legal, governmental and medical systems. For instance, the novel depicts a high mortality rate at an early age of between 35 and 40, with people rarely surviving to 50, owing to the lack of adequate health services, which reinforces the message that malnutrition and disease are rife amongst women (*Violence*: 71–2); in order to make ends meet, many people are forced to sell their own blood for pin money, with the attendant health risks (*Violence*: 155–6); and there are instances of the arbitrary implementations of justice, such as Papa Jimoh's jail experience of wrongful arrest without compensation (*Violence*: 82–4).

The point at which Idemudia is admitted to hospital offers the novel further opportunity of commenting upon the medical services: 'The doctor put on his glasses again but his mind went back to the dark tunnel of the numberless sick, their abject poverty and from that to the helplessness of their position. He couldn't understand why in the midst of so much disease, the government concentrated on building hotels instead of hospitals. He simply couldn't understand' (*Violence*: 55). The doctor's criticism of despair and hopelessness among people (*Violence*: 56) is reinforced when Idemudia's health improves and he begins work on Queen's building site, since the exploitative procedures become starkly evident. The building site operates without regard to safety rules, and is open to stark economic exploitation through 'scab' labour, spontaneous sacking and the inequality of treatment of employees (*Violence*: 240). Idemudia's consciousness is raised as he experiences the violence outlined in the hospital play, with the debasement of his humanity and working circumstances likened to slavery and prison labour (*Violence*: 243). One long passage explicitly lays out the exploitation of the masses by the hegemonic overclass and, in a clear socialist realist style, paints a Marxist analysis of the economic and labour situation (*Violence*: 247–8). Accompanied by a vicious satire on the making of money – any way is a good way, especially in the name of the government (*Violence*: 281) – the novel concludes as a searing indictment of social circumstances and bureaucratic corruption within contemporary Nigeria.

Set in the Nigerian Civil War, Iyayi's second novel *Heroes* (1986) merely serves to reinforce his deeply critical and derogatory depiction of Nigerian society. The narrative charts the gradual awakening of political consciousness in Osime Iyere, a Nigerian journalist writing for the Federal forces, who slowly realises that the war is being fought for and on behalf of the political and economic gain of the officer and government elite on both the Federal side and the breakaway Biafran side. After several incidents where Iyere witnesses grotesque travesties of Federal justice, gross military incompetence and negligence by Federal generals, and overt acts of military corruption, the novel concludes that the ordinary soldiers of both sides are brutalised and brainwashed by the elite into committing inhuman actions from which they would normally recoil. Osime Iyere's stark conclusion is that

> The soldiers have the defeat while the generals have the victory. ... ten years from now ... the generals on both sides will have come together and told themselves that the war was a temporary distraction, that it arose as a result of miscommunication problems and that there was nothing to remember or forgive in it. They will have congratulated themselves on effectively reducing the number and strength of their real

adversary, the working class, and mapped out for themselves other
strategies for maintaining their hold on the country. (*Heroes*: 214)

In what amounts to a somewhat desperate conclusion to the novel, it
is suggested that Iyere's newfound political consciousness and the
likemindedness he has found among some soldiers are the awaken-
ings of a sleeping giant among the ordinary soldiers and citizens of
the nation.

Although Iyayi is concerned with the neo-colonial state, he represents these neo-colonial regimes as perpetuators of colonial structures of power. Military and government officers effect their control
in a systematic way to oppress the 'working classes', echoing the
white colonial exploitation and enfeeblement of the 'black masses'.
Substituting a class oppression for what was a racial oppression, the
grammar and syntax of these neo-colonial regimes are violence and
pure force, and this exists alongside a declaration of ostensibly
'protecting' the people from their own 'infantilised' selves. The
regimes bring violence into the home and the mind, just as the colonial structures were an implementation of cultural violence reinforced by the possibility of physical violence. Yet just as violence was
often the precursor to decolonisation, so violence is the precursor to
Iyayi's sense of social dehierarchisation or social egalitarianism.

So for all Iyayi's efforts to concentrate critical and political attention
on the troubled present of African life, he cannot escape the past. It
surfaces throughout his fiction like a bad dream, a Freudian rupture of
the bad present. Iyayi's aesthetic ideology of social or critical realism
becomes one more moment in the deferral and displacement of Africa's
structural problems induced by colonialism. Although the form of
Iyayi's fiction occurs in the realist style as a mode of the present and
presence, it is evident that he cannot escape the past, and even the ideological assumptions made in realist fiction about perspective, referentiality and psychological character implicitly involve Iyayi's
representations in Africa's colonial past. Yet why do African writers
appear attracted to realism so frequently in their fiction? Is this
realism the same realism that European writers have used for so long,
and that in recent decades has become so blighted by the taint of
aesthetic conservativism? There are instances where realism in postcolonial literature does simply appear to be a naive unmediated access
to the Real through direct reference. In another treatment of the
Nigerian Civil War, Eddie Iroh's novel *Toads of War* concerns the late
stages of the war as Nigeria overruns Biafra. The two protagonists are
Kechi Ugboma, a onetime air-hostess, who has effectively turned into a
high-class prostitute to government officials; and Kalu Udim, an ampu-
tated officer from the front line, who has a score to settle with his erstwhile boss (now one of Kechi's lovers), Chima Duke. The title of the book
refers to the succubi of the war – those who prey upon the war through

profiteering and racketeering – for example, the Chima Dukes of this world. The phrase 'toads of war' is used several times by the ex-soldiers and lowly public to refer knowingly to the scandalous degree of corruption amongst the official in society. Iroh's book is something of a popular novel, which aims to satirise the collapse of the Biafran cause: politically it would seem that he feels the massacre of the Igbos needed to be prevented; but in terms of the way the war was conducted, the book appears to depict savagely a state of ignorance, self-satisfaction, and egotism amongst the powerful classes (and the parasites who cling to them). History and memory work only as instances of a time when the traditional values of Igbo culture had once been part of daily life: this emerges in the play that Kechi and Kalu go to see entitled *Veneration to Udo*, which is described as a 'call to cleansing', and in the final stages of the book, when Kalu remembers a friend's poem, which refers to 'the treachery of history', and concludes with 'Then shall memory cease to be my woe / And I too shall learn to court my foe' (*Toads of War*: 136). The populist style of this book suggests a realism that appeals to a wide readership that regards realism as a mode reinforcing historical and social truth.

However, realism should not simply be seen as an epistemological response, but should be construed as a social force that has consequences for material practice as well as the understanding of events. In his collection of essays entitled *In My Father's House*, Kwame Anthony Appiah outlines a staged development to the evolution of a decolonised African writing, the first of which is the unavoidable stage of 'realism'. Although he regards this as only a useful phase en route to the second stage of African writing – the post-realist, postcolonial stage – Appiah claims that this first generation of African literature (spanning roughly 1955–65 and including such works as Achebe's *Things Fall Apart*), is anti-colonial and nationalist. The texts of this first era are also triumphant, since they are 'imaginative recreations of a common cultural past crafted into a shared tradition by the writer' (Appiah 1992: 149). The most successful mode for this task is realism, which, for Appiah, presents what he perceives to be a naive depiction of an illusory past. Yet is realism inherently conservative? Depicting African social life need not necessarily involve a treatment of the mythical or folk culture. Indeed, like Iyayi's fiction of the 1970s and 1980s, many African literary representations are resolutely realist, eschewing an engagement with the fantastical by facing head-on the trials and tribulations of contemporary postcolonial nation. However, realism is often assumed to be the perpetuation of imperialism or colonialism. Realism is regarded as a conventional, conservative, nationalist form, which serves only to legitimate and normalise everyday states of affairs, without challenging or questioning the structures or ideologies that underpin them. In other words, realism is incapable of resistance. In Timothy Brennan's view, realism inscribes nationalism on the nation (Brennan 1990). Realism is regarded as a discourse of authenticity, and post-structuralist postcolonial critics are inevitably suspicious of such a discourse. Nevertheless, critics like Lewis Nkosi and Laura Moss have mounted a cogent case for needing to be more discriminating about the usefulness of realism within a postcolonial literary context: 'There is a need, however, for these critics to distinguish more clearly between the realism used in the service of imperialist beliefs written by authors who look in from the outside in a fallaciously objective manner and the realism produced by authors who are indigenous to the postcolonial locations of their narratives' (Moss 2000: paragraph 4; see also Nkosi 1998). While it may be the case that some realist fiction does indeed buttress the structural edifices of colonialism, other texts may contain resistance to the 'real' material oppressions of postcolonial societies. Therefore, in lessons taught by Bakhtin's work on the novel, one needs to maintain the possibility that realism is not monolithic and that it does have the *potential* for cultural, social or political critique. Yet one must be cautious in arguing that a literature that aspires to have a role in liberation ought to address itself to the necessity of people reclaiming their history and identity from the cultural terrorism and depredation of the colonial period. Such a generalisation might seem to suggest that the colonised peoples are a homogenous mass with a shared 'history' and 'culture', and this assertion carries undertones of essentialism with the call to a precolonial past as some sort of redemptive process.

Yet in a very compelling study entitled *Traumatic Realism* (2000), Michael Rothberg has addressed himself to the question of what constitutes a redemptive realism in fiction, and how this mode is related to the past, memory and trauma. Rothberg argues that, because postcolonial writers are interested in the possibility of critique, their focus is not just oriented toward the past. Rather, their writing creates a constellation between the past and a series of postcolonial developments in Africa − including the persistence of the very modes of thought, structure and language that made colonialism possible. Postcolonial writers, through a constant reference to the sites and activities of colonialism, force a revaluation of the time of postcolonialism − now no longer perceived as a progressive passage from before to after but as threatened from within by potentially deadly repetition, or if one wishes, a state of 'acting-out'. The historical imperative of thought and critique in African writers' fiction thus corresponds to an ethical and political imperative to prevent the recurrence of colonialism, an imperative that entails a critical programme of cultural (re)construction and public education, or a 'working-through'. It is noticeable in narratives about apartheid and imperialism or colonialism among postcolonial writers that the desire for realism and referentiality is a strong characteristic feature. This is possibly because it is so difficult to construct a narrative out of extremity, or because so much of the narrative must turn on absence, and that as a consequence, a commitment to documentation and realistic discourse has come to figure prominently in confrontations with colonialism and apartheid. Yet realism's aim to make absent objects not only present but credible also raises suspicion in many who live in the aftermath of colonialism. Rothberg suggests that 'Traumatic realism develops out of and in response to the demand for documentation that an extreme historical event poses to those who would seek to understand it' (Rothberg 2000: 100). Furthermore, 'The "possibility of *knowledge*" – the epistemological claim – that inhabits realist texts and desires makes it difficult merely to dismiss realism as ideology, even when the constructionist, aesthetic side of the realist project is foregrounded'. Rather ideology ought to be reconfigured as a form of 'cognitive mapping' (Jameson) rather than *error*, which it would be perverse in dismissing (Rothberg 2000: 102).

Ngugi, history and memory

> I talk about the past mainly because I am interested in the present.
> (Ngugi wa Thiong'o, cited in Michael Green, *Novel Histories*)

That critical or social realism should inalienably be concerned with the present is, of course, quite illogical. Ngugi wa Thiong'o, in a Marxist analysis of the function of the writer, has identified three ways in which the writer is affected by the prevailing political environment: first, the writer is inevitably a product of history, time and place; second, the writer's subject matter is history; third, the product of a writer's imagination becomes a reflection of society (Thiong'o 1981b: 72). These three factors lead to the production of the 'realist' novel, with the realist novel being understood in this context as a product of novelists 'look(ing), historically, at the crises of their own immediate time' (Williams, R. 1984: 14). As Ngugi has maintained, 'Literature has often given us more and sharper insights into the moving spirit of an era than all the historical and political documents treating the same moments in a society's development. The novel in particular, especially in its critical realist tradition, is important in that respect: it pulls apart and it puts together; it is both analytic and synthetic' (Thiong'o 1981b: 72). Ngugi wa Thiong'o in particular has made history and the exploration of history a principal feature of his critical realist fiction: 'The novelist is haunted by a sense of the past. His work is often an attempt to come to terms with "the thing that has been", a struggle, as it were, to sensitively register his encounter with history, his people's history' (Thiong'o 1972: 40). In narratives that bear witness to the contested historical experience of Kenya since the 1920s, Ngugi has constantly probed the ethical problem of how the novelist can represent history without compromising it or becoming imprisoned within the past. Though he is attracted to Marxism as an instrument for a historical understanding of colonialism and a political explanation of postcolonial or neo-colonial culture, it has not been able to account for, or indeed give meaning to, all historical events that Ngugi himself has witnessed, experiences that, as he notes in several places, come back to his mind every time he tried to write about the past. Ngugi seems to be constantly separated from that past: he writes from the position of one who remembers the recent African past vividly, but does not seem to be connected to this past except through its remembrance and – ultimately – its representation in narrative. For as it is repeatedly outlined in *Petals of Blood*, history seems to be blocked by the very narratives designed to represent it. For Ngugi, fiction is something that rejects the split between private and public, and embodies the collective experience and reality, and demonstrates the community's way of looking at the world. In his explorations of the questions of language, power and knowledge, his fiction is as much about literary form as it is about ideological preferences. In searching for a non-alienated mode of representation, fiction by writers like Ngugi stages their agonising reflections on the ideology of literature and the complex relationship between history, memory and aesthetic form.

James Ogude's significant study *Ngugi's Novels and African History* explores the change in Ngugi's theory and representation of history, tied to the changes in Kenyan political circumstances. This change is a movement from a more complex picture of the moral dilemma that faced the loyalists and fighters during the violent period of the 1950s, to a fairly linear history of the movement in which one has neat camps of the abhorred collaborators on the one hand and the patriotic fighters on the other in his later postcolonial novels. In other words, the complexity of the war in the earlier novels gives way to a Mau Mau simply seen as the ultimate expression of Kenya's anti-colonial struggle. Furthermore, one of the principal causes to which Ogude attributes Ngugi's shift in his thesis of history is Kenya's disposition in the 1970s to underdevelopment and dependency on colonial structures of economy (Ogude 1999: 11–12). In this respect, Ngugi dramatises the continuation of the class war against the colonising oppressor in his later fiction. The possibilities of a syncretic culture in the early novels gives way to a hostility towards anything western: 'If reconciliation, both to oneself and to community, is central to the structural organisation of the texts in the earlier novels, class conflict is central to the organisation of the later texts' (Ogude 1999: 13).

History and memory are unquestionably the structuring devices of the early novels. In *The River Between* (1965), Ngugi's focus is on members of the Gikuyu tribe in Kenya, during and slightly after the arrival of the white settlers at Siriana Mission. *The River Between* takes its title from the river Honia that flows between the two ridges, Makuyu and Kameno, where the Gikuyu tribe has its home, with one side (Makuyu) organising itself upon traditional customs and values, and the other (Kameno) upon Christian and white values. The novel concerns the lives of several of the key protagonists in these clusters of people. First, there is the story of Chege and his son Waiyaki, and their developing and maturing relationship, with their different aspirations for the future: it depicts Chege's traditional life with his tribal beliefs and customs, and Waiyaki's mixed and somewhat confused existence, vacillating as he does between traditional and western education. In parallel, there is Joshua's relationship with his family. Joshua, a converted Christian and evangelical proselytiser, loses his daughter Muthoni, who wishes to be circumcised in the usual tribal manner, but who still regards herself as a Christian. Nyambura, her sister, watches in fear of the consequences of this split in the family. Finally, there is Livingstone, the white missionary running Siriana School and Hospital, who seeks to educate Waiyaki into the ways of the white culture. *The River Between* is pervaded by the conflict between traditional and Christian or western cultures, and Ogude argues that 'Christian religion is used to inflict what Ngugi calls a "psychological wound ... on the whole generation". Ngugi's position is that religion is a tool for oppressing workers' (Ogude 1999: 29). Furthermore, Ogude adds that 'In addition, cultural and educational institutions are seen too by Ngugi as tools for mental captivity in the postcolonial state' (Ogude 1999: 29). Yet the conflict in *The River Between* is also a generational struggle that crosses all boundaries, seen, for example, in the way Muthoni from a Christian background gets circumcised in traditional ritual; or the way in which Waiyaki, brought up in traditional values, has a western missionary education, but goes through the traditional circumcision rituals, all the while conscious of the ambiguity of his position from the perspective of Livingstone.

In the novel, memory largely plays the role of taking one back to traditional values and precolonial cultures. In Waiyaki's case, there are hints that memory plays a vestigial role, making him dimly aware of something he cannot quite understand or see. It is similar to a Kristevan *chora*, a symbolic existence only fleetingly and improperly understood or conceived. The vestiges of the traditional past are the tribal unconscious, desperately being shored up by people like Chege against the white settlers' values and education. Chege takes Waiyaki to the sacred grove as an initiation into that remote place, that past from which people are growing away. It is exactly like the psychoanalytical model of Lacan and Kristeva, in which people dimly recognise their castration or separation from an organic wholeness. The tribal past equates to the lost symbolic realm, while the present equates to the semiotic realm, under the rule of the Father (God and the White colonist). Chege and others seek to show the way back, to reconnect people to that symbolic past. This involves showing Waiyaki the ritual medical ways, telling stories of the past myths, keeping initiation rites going (it is said when Waiyaki is circumcised and the blood drips on to the ground, 'Henceforth a religious bond linked Waiyaki to the earth, as if his blood was an offering' (*River*: 52–3)).

Waiyaki also experiences an alienation and separation from his culture as a result of his education: 'He felt a stranger, a stranger to his land' (*River*: 69). His alienation is the consequence of the troubles and splits between the tribe over the issue of beliefs and values. In response, Waiyaki 'still felt hungry and yearned for something that would fill him whole, a thing that would take possession of the whole of himself. That something seemed beyond him, enmeshed, as he was, in the ways of the land. ... It was his eyes that spoke of that yearning, that longing for something that would fill him all in all' (*River*: 81). Waiyaki experiences a yearning for that memory of a past that was whole, a loss precipitated by the advent of colonialism, and entrenched by the teachings of Christianity and the missionaries. For Ngugi, land ownership and tilling are the basis of precolonial communal and social cohesion. When the colonists appropriate the land, crisis ensues in the Kenyan social fabric. As Ogude notes, 'Thus, one might deduce that, for Ngugi, the history of conflict in Africa is the history of colonialism and how it affected the African populace' (Ogude 1999: 28). The association of the land with a precolonial cohesion does raise questions about nostalgia permeating this memory of the past, although the land issue is so intimately connected in Ngugi's view with the traumatic rupture caused by colonialism. Even in his later novels (like *Petals of Blood*), which veer away from representing colonialism, Kenya's neo-colonial troubles are still perceived to be a vestige of land acquisition and exploitation:

[Nyakinyua] was not alone: a whole lot of peasants and herdsmen of Old Ilmorog who had been lured into loans and into fencing off their land and buying imported fertilisers and were unable to pay back were similarly affected. Without much labour, without machinery, without breaking with old habits and outlook, and without much advice they had not been able to make the land yield enough to meet their food needs and pay back the loans. Some had used the money to pay school fees. Now the inexorable law of the metal power was driving them from the land. (*Petals*: 275)

The extent to which education itself is inherently a contamination of the culture, or whether education could be culturally manipulated, or whether education contaminates the purity of the tribe, is another argument within *The River Between*. The metaphor of disease and ill-health riddles the book, and the Makuyu's effort to preserve its purity and 'healthiness' makes them keep Joshua and Christianity at bay, as well as the negative effects of the missionary education: 'Waiyaki was superstitious. He believed the things that the people of the ridge believed. Siriana Mission had done nothing effective to change this. His father had warned him against being contaminated by the ways of the white man. Yet he sometimes wondered. Was the education he was trying to spread in the ridges not a contamination? ... Was he trying to create order and bring light in the dark?' (*River*: 83). Wrestling with his own conscience and struggling to balance the opposing influences of his father Chege and Miss Livingstone, Waiyaki is constantly in search of a means to reconcile the various factions on the ridges. He even begins to doubt that his stress on education is the correct path: 'I had not seen that the new awareness wanted expression at a political level. Education for an oppressed people is not all' (*River*: 160). Finally, Waiyaki reaches a more moder-ate conclusion, that white culture is not entirely *essentially* corrupt-ing, but that indigenous beliefs and customs rooted in the past need to be preserved for the sake of their own identity, or else people would be culturally asphyxiated, like Joshua: 'A people's traditions could not be swept away overnight. That way lay disintegration. Such a tribe would have no roots, for a people's roots were in their traditions going back to the past, the very beginning, Gikuyu and Mumbi ... [Joshua] renounced his past and cut himself away from those life-giving traditions of the tribe' (*River*: 162–3).

In the hour of Waiyaki's last speech, he is motivated and impelled by vestigial memory of his father, of ancestors and of the land: 'And he remembered his father, Mugo wa Kibio, Wachiori, Kamiri, Gikuyu and Mumbi. And he remembered Kerinyaga as he had seen it that great day with his father' (*River*: 168). Memory supplies the strength to proceed and build for the future. Waiyaki reminds the tribes-people of their history in order to make a political argument about the present: 'He turned to the people and in simple words reminded them of their history. "It was before Agu and Agu, at the beginnings of things, that Murungu, the Creator, gave rise to Gikuyu and Mumbi, father and mother of the tribe. ... You remember ...". He spoke of the great heroes of the tribe and mentioned Demi, Mathathi, Wachiori, Mugo wa Kibiro and Kamiri' (*River*: 170–1). Memory of the past gives the people a means of 'working-through' the traumatic interruption of colonialism, of providing a firm rock in the midst of the torrent of foreign cultural beliefs and practices. Yet the conclusion of the novel seems to be a triumph for the forces of ignorance and blindness, impelled by the power of the crowd. The struggle mutates from Christian versus traditional customs, to individual versus collective; and Waiyaki is sacrificed to the collective will to power. Biblical rhetoric and metaphors of sacrifice and judgement pervade the last pages of the novel, while the path of enlightenment through education is closed by 'darkness'. The novel's conclusion seems to suggest that some ideologies of purity and racial cleanness can have a greater power than collective development. The 'oath' wins out over 'unity' and 'education'.

The River Between is a book about the cultural consequences of colonial education and religion; there are hints at the other important issues, such as the question of land rights, but these appear to be a secondary concern. A far more complex and sophisticated novel, *A Grain of Wheat* (1967) continues exploring the ways in which history affects the contemporary political consciousness, although it is oddly structured by a sense that the passing of time does not bring changes. Memory also works like Proustian memory – the novel opens with the reminiscence that 'He liked porridge in the morning. But whenever he took it, he remembered the half-cooked porridge he ate in detention. How time drags, everything repeats itself, Mugo thought; the day ahead would be just like yesterday and the day before' (*Grain*: 4). Ngugi's version of history is somewhat cyclical, since he perceives the colonial as an allegorical version of the post-colonial or neo-colonial state. History has turned full circle, and oppression has merely arrived in the form of a different bourgeoisie. As one character in *A Grain of Wheat* states, 'Whatever happened yesterday could happen today. The same thing, over and over again, through history' (*Grain*: 122). This cyclical model of history is enforced by the novel's narrative structure of flashes backwards and forwards, piecing together the past and the present as if they are both part of a broken whole, a whole broken by bitter experiences of disruptive actions. The narrative structure – jumping backwards and forwards – is intended to force the reader into recognising that the present and the past are intricately interrelated, if not exact repetitions of one another.

A Grain of Wheat also dramatizes conflicting accounts of the past and models of Kenyan history. Chapter 2 of the novel delves into the history of 'The Party' and the development of Kenyan resistance politics with the advent of the earliest colonial settlers in Kenya. A roll call of Kenya's leaders is presented, among them Waiyaki: 'Then nobody noticed it; but looking back we can see that Waiyaki's blood contained within it a seed, a grain, which gave birth to a political party whose main strength thereafter sprang from a bond with the soil' (*Grain*: 15). This clearly echoes the epigraph to the novel drawn from I Corinthians 15: 36–7: 'And that which thou sowest, thou sowest not that body that shall be, but bare grain, it may chance of wheat, or of some other *grain*.' This Biblical passage is to do with spiritual rebirth after life, and the novel clearly envisages such rebirth within the context of Kenyan politics as predicated upon a close bond with the soil. This 'bond with the soil' is yet another example of the Kristevan vestigial cultural memory at work, a dimly perceived link, albeit now severed, with a lost past. Opposed to this collective, vestigial memory is the colonist's different conception of history. The white colonial administrator John Thompson has an interest in the history of the British Empire as a mission, and he has a sudden realisation that he could play a role in that mission. This is a vision of history as manifest destiny, as the propagator of a new world order, of the 'principle of Reason, of Order and of Measure' (*Grain*: 62). His conception, entitled 'Prospero in Africa', is basically a project of racial prejudice wrapped up in the rhetoric of equality and civilisation. As his diary entries gradually show, Thompson is prone to exactly the same racial prejudices as the entire history of 'enlightened' liberal European thought.

Yet Ngugi's portrayal of the Europeans (the Thompsons and Dr Lynd) oscillates between the empathetic (not the sympathetic) and the stereotypical. He can see that colonial existence unwinds a different sort of life for European women from the grandly patriarchal role for the men, and that it opens up a streak of viciousness and brutality in the colonial administrators. By the same token, Ngugi is not without criticism of the neo-colonial state. The book is scornful of the actions of African MPs and their somewhat undemocratic existences, and deeply critical of the backhanders that go on with the corruption of the police. As Paul Connerton has persuasively demonstrated in *How Societies Remember*, rituals are actions of memories: "'It is like our elders who always poured a little beer on the ground before they themselves drank," Wambui now said. "Why did they do that? It's because they always remembered the spirits of those below. We too cannot forget our sons"' (*Grain*: 24). Memory is constantly evoked as a means of impelling people forward. This is part of the constant appeals to the earth, the soil, land, as part of the people's inheritance and national identity. It is memory that acts as a prompt to subversive political action against the ethical colonial power:

'Do you ever forget?'
    'I try to. The government says we should bury the past.'
    'I can't forget ... I will never forget,' Gikonyo cried. (*Grain*: 79)

The narratives relayed by Gikonyo and Mumbi to Mugo on separate occasions are in the form of memories. These memories are clearly important, having the effect of a partial expiation of their past sins, and also allow people to rehearse the past in an attempt to set the record straight. So there is a 'talking cure' at work, and a type of struggle for history going on – why did they act as they did? were the past circumstances responsible for their actions? who betrayed Kahika? was it Karanja or someone else? what was Mugo's past, which appears to have dark actions implicated in it? Narratives carry within themselves unrealised projections of alternative lives: 'How was it that Mumbi's story had cracked open his dulled inside and released imprisoned thoughts and feelings? The weight of her words and the face of General R. dissolved into acts of the past' (*Grain*: 195). Ngugi's novel acts in a way similar to that of Mumbi's story – it opens up dulled insides and releases imprisoned thoughts and feelings. In this respect, Ngugi is engaged in retelling history as a form of expiation and ethical recovery, acting as a 'working-through'. 'Things of yesterday should remain with yesterday' (*Grain*: 198) warns Warui to Mugo, about the rumours of the return of the deaf and dumb boy to this mother after being shot in the Emergency. As a general warning, these allude precisely to the struggle in the novel between letting these memories surface in state of Uhuru, or letting bygones be bygones. The novels of Ngugi are clearly an effort to counter that insistence by the government, since the novels are precisely about getting that past narrative written and piecing the past together in the face of efforts to smother it, either by the colonial historians or by the neo-colonial rulers. Angela Smith notes the strength of the imagery of the eye in the early chapters of the novel, thematising the issue of perspective, and how the history you have determines the present you see. This is important in the context of the novel that is structured upon fragmented perspectives that are only really brought together in the final pages. Like Smith, I would agree that *A Grain of Wheat* mimics the fragmented nature of the society, although, unlike Gakwandi, I do not consider the novel to be structurally flawed because of this structure (Smith 1989: 52–5).

While the early novels are quite clearly concerned with the conflicts arising from Kenyan communities in tension with white colonial settlers, later novels are concerned with the legacy of the colonial interruption. *Petals of Blood* (1977) represents Kenyan history as dominated by the struggle between black consciousness and economic oppression, which has led to a debate between a racist analysis and an economic analysis of the problems facing the country. The importance of history for Ngugi is stated everywhere. He envisages the role of the writer as a spokesman for the people, and part of that role is to mediate between native and foreigner, between past and present. Identity is all-important, and the past holds the key to it. Ngugi writes at one point in 'The Writer and His Past' in *Homecoming* (1972): 'Here I want to argue that what has been – the evolution of human culture through the ages, society in motion through time and space – is of grave import to the poet and the novelist. For what has been, especially for the vast majority of submerged, exploited masses in Africa, Asia and Black America, is intimately bound up with what will be: our vision of the future, of diverse possibilities of life and human potential, has roots in our experience of the past' (Thiong'o 1972: 40). Again, in *Homecoming*, he writes: 'The novelist is haunted by a sense of the past. His work is often an attempt to come to terms with "the thing that has been", a struggle, as it were, to sensitively register his encounter with history, his people's history. And the novelist at his best must feel himself heir to a continuous tradition ... swimming, struggling, defining himself, in the mainstream of his people's historical drama. At the same time, he must be able to stand aside and merely contemplate the currents' (Thiong'o 1972: 40).

Ngugi has repeatedly stated that a writer must be somehow detached and yet engaged: the aesthetic problem of balancing these two aspects is one of his preoccupations. Ngugi's themes are explicitly political: he brings out the betrayal felt by Kenya's freedom fighters when the rewards of independence went not to them nor to the common people for whom they had fought but to the men who had remained loyal or aloof in the Emergency and acceded to wealth and position in the new nation. *Petals of Blood* is dogged by this postcolonial disillusionment. The novel depicts a racial oppression being replaced by a class oppression: Lenin's *Imperialism: The Last Development of Capitalism* (a book to which Ngugi frequently refers) makes it quite clear that both are part and parcel of the same development of capital.

How, Ngugi asks, does such an outcome fit with ideas of past and future glory, or of the simple conflict between white oppressors and black liberators? As with much of Ngugi's writing, questions about the relevance of history recur insistently throughout *Petals of Blood*. Yet history is seen not to be something divorced from the daily lives of people. The protagonist Karega is constantly concerned with the relationship between the present and the past, and finds this connection crystallised for him in a conversation with Wanja:

'Tell me, Karega, do you always think about the past?' ...

'To understand the present ... you must understand the past. To know where you are, you must know where you came from, don't you think?'

'How? I look at it this way. Drought and thirst and hunger are hanging over Ilmorog! What use is Ndemi's story? I am drowning: what use would be my looking back to the shore from which I feel?'

'The fact that they did things, that they refused to drown: shouldn't
that give us hope and pride?'

'No, I would feel much better if a rope was thrown at me. Something
I can catch on to ...' she was silent for a few seconds. Then she said in
a changed tone of voice. 'Sometimes there is no greatness in the past.
Sometimes one would like to hide the past even from oneself.'

Karega suddenly realised that she was not talking about an abstract
past. (*Petals*: 127–8)

Karega's obsession with the past is here challenged by Wanja, and he
is forced to confront the past as more than an academic exercise in
thinking one's way out of the long reach of the colonial past. Ngugi
deals with history through the confused and shifting efforts of the
characters in trying to understand their personal histories, in which
the conflicts, while occurring in the context of the Emergency, are felt
as personal ones. In this way, Ngugi makes the connection, so often
elusive, between political situation and human action, creating at the
same time a psychological narrative, a masterful whodunit and a
treatise on the possibilities and limitations of political action, all
conveyed not by simplifying but by exploring the complexities of his
characters and their situation.

In the context of this exploration, various models of history emerge
in the book: 'How and where did Karega fit into the picture? This was
a case of history repeating itself, and indeed for him at that moment
the cliché seemed to acquire new significance. Yet did anything ever
repeat itself?' (*Petals*: 59). The significant issues are whether history
progresses in a linear fashion, whether it is cyclical, whether history
is revolutionary, or whether it moves in some other mode. Walter
Benjamin has taught us that history is one of the main things that
any victor or oppressor seeks to write. The whole novel is conceived
of as a narration of the various histories that make lives, cultures
and beings: the history of the colonial regime; the history of the individual characters; the history of capitalist development after Uhuru,
or Kenyan independence. Contrary to this pressure, chapter 4 opens
with an attempt to write a different history: the history of Kenya as
it is known to a Kenyan, rather than as it is told by the white colonialist oppressors:

For there are many questions about our history which remain unanswered. Our present day historians, following on similar theories
yarned out by defenders of imperialism, insist we only arrived here
yesterday. Where went all the Kenyan people who used to trade with
China, India, Arabia long long before Vasco da Gama came to the scene
and on the strength of gunpowder ushered in an era of blood and terror
and instability – an era that climaxed in the reign of imperialism over
Kenya? But even then these adventures of Portuguese mercantilism
were forced to build Fort Jesus, showing that Kenyan people had always

been ready to resist foreign control and exploitation. The story of this
heroic resistance: who will sing it? Their struggles to defend their land,
their wealth, their lives; who'll tell of it? What of their earlier achievements in production that had annually attracted visitors from ancient
China and India? (*Petals*: 67)

Here is the history of Dedan Kimathi, those 'legends passed from
generation to generation by the poets and players of Gichandi,
Litungu and Nyatiti' (*Petals*: 68–9); and of 'Old Masai and his brave
band of warriors' (*Petals*: 70). This is the history that is positively
endorsed in the novel, the lives of the peasant characters and their
memories of a Kenya that predates the arrival of the colonisers. It is
a censored history, left to the legends passed from generation to
generation for its survival. Memory sustains this past despite the
structural and systemic pressures exerted by subsequent colonists to
repress the very existence of the people before the colonists' arrival.

In fact, the novel eventually poses at least two significant models
of history. One model in the novel identifies with the imperialist
heritage, colonial and neo-colonial, and it sees imperialism as the
motive force of Kenya's development. The more rapidly Kenya loses
its identity in the West and leaves its fate in imperialist interests,
the faster will be its development and its movement to the modernity
of the twentieth century. This is the particularly clear affiliation in
the novel of a corpus of intellectuals who write manuals in praise of
colonialism: *Petals of Blood* represents this Trojan Horse rhetoric in
the 'theories yarned out by the defenders of imperialism' (*Petals*: 67).
Another instance of this disguised partisan colonial ideology occurs
in the books that the lawyer lends to Karega, which turn out to be
endorsements of the political and financial status quo of the state
authority that is already practising a neo-colonialism:

> He one day sat down and wrote to him. Send me books, he appealed, for
> somewhere in the high seats of learning in the city somebody was bound
> to know ... he vaguely hoped for a vision of the future rooted in a criti-
> cal awareness of the past. So he first tried the history books. ...
>   But instead of answering these, instead of giving him the key he so
> badly needed, the professors took him to pre-colonial times and made
> him wander purposelessly from Egypt ... To the learned minds of the
> historians, the history of Kenya before colonialism was one of wander-
> lust and pointless warfare between peoples. (*Petals*: 198–9)

Instead, Karega turns to international politics: 'He tried political
science. But he plunged into an even greater maze ... occasionally
there were abstract phrases about inequality of opportunities or the
ethnic balancing act of modern governments' (*Petals*: 199). The issue
of race versus class, and race versus economic system becomes
blurred: Karega looks for 'truth', whereas he perhaps ought to be
looking for a group to which he wants to be affiliated. As the Lawyer

reminds him, there are no unbiased, disinterested histories: all history is a fiction employed by various groupings to legitimate, or give more credence, to a specific power structure (*Petals*: 200).

The second, other model of history identifies with the line of resistance in all nationalities. It looks at the activities and actions of ordinary Kenyan men and women, as the basis of Kenya's history and progress. The starting point for these people is democracy – to get the peasants and workers of all varieties in Kenya to unite. This is not a call for isolationism, but a recognition that national liberation is the basis of an internationalism. At the close of the novel, Ngugi reinforces the possibility of revolutionary action towards the transformation of society: 'The true lesson of history was this: that the so-called victims, the poor, the downtrodden, the masses, had always struggled with their spears and arrows, with their hands and songs of courage and hope, to end their oppression and exploitation' (*Petals*: 303). Yet this exploitation is sometimes altered: sometimes through direct action, like the workers' march on Nairobi in *Petals of Blood*; but at other times through the work of trade unions. The trajectory of the novel is from perceiving racial struggle as the root cause of the state's problems to eventually seeing the problems as class-based; and this largely results from Ngugi's increasingly Marxist perception of the problems facing Kenya and its colonial past.

Where *Petals of Blood* showed an increasing perplexity with the convolutions of history, *Matigari* (1987) is a biting satire on Kenyan neo-colonial society, which makes little or no concession to the complexities that preoccupied Ngugi's earlier fiction. The novel is based upon the Gikuyu mythical character who returns to his home looking for his family, and finds that the ideals for which he was fighting have become corrupted and betrayed: the people are oppressed, the lands are exploited, the laws have become overtly partisan in favour of the ruling hegemony, morality has been overturned, and Matigari's specific history has been desecrated. The narrative works at the level of allegory, an allegory that is specifically about a neo-colonial bourgeois elite exploiting and mimicking the oppressive capitalist mechanisms of the ex-colonial structures. Matigari emerges time and again as a sort of Messianic character, 'like a father to his children' (*Matigari*: 57), who appears to possess mystical characteristics: the children's stones do not hit him; he is not searched before going into jail; he challenges authorities without personal injury; and he is familiarly known as 'The Seeker of Truth and Justice' (*Matigari*: 62). The novel is overtly polemical in its political critique, such as the debate concerning conflicting values of individuality and communality (*Matigari*: 48–9). Any notion of individuality is accused of being a white concept, while communality is construed as a black concept. This overturns the values of the social and the ethic of supporting one another, and suggests that communalism pulls the individual back, preventing him from forging ahead.

Yet despite this narrative of simpler perspectives, the memory of lost former times permeates the strength of Matigari's rhetoric. When addressing his fellow prisoners in jail and sharing his food with them, the vestiges of the forgotten past and communality are what strikes the political chord: 'Something in Matigari's voice made them listen to him attentively. There was a sad note about it, but it also carried hope and courage. The others now fell silent. His words seemed to remind them of things long forgotten, carrying them back to dreams they had had long before' (*Matigari*: 56). The scene in the jail is a somewhat flimsy caricature of types – the worker, the drunk, the teacher – as can be seen in the worker's speech (*Matigari*: 59). Nevertheless, the root problem with the neo-colonial power elite is the repression of history: 'The ruling party of messengers was trying to imprison the real history of the working people behind bars and in detention camps' (*Matigari*: 161). This echoes *Petals of Blood*'s endorsement of the people's history, of the Marxist view that the oppressed are the source of future change.

Despite the historical aporiae noted by Ogude in Ngugi's fiction – such as the representation of a solid and united Mau Mau movement fighting collectively for a common interest; or a linear tradition of continuity in the anti-imperialist struggle, with little sense of a tension between the loyalists and the colonial state; or the uneven relationship between the loyalists and Mau Mau and the colonial state, which was never a linear one – nevertheless, it is clear that Ngugi regards his intervention in history-making and understanding the past as the key to overcoming the ruptures instigated by colonialism and to implementing meaningful social change within Africa and Kenya in particular. As Ogude states, 'Ngugi's return to the past is a common feature in his narrative. The past is often evoked by Ngugi as a challenge and at times a parallel to the present state of chaos. Where colonialism denied histories and traditions, Ngugi seeks to found a sense of self in a recovery of history, a recuperation of tradition' (Ogude 1999: 46). Ogude's implication that there is something redemptive in Ngugi's attention to historiography is not just pointing to an act of reclamation or a recovery of something lost (i.e. a culture removed or censored by colonialism), but also to an act of freeing and deliverance in an ethical and psychological dimension. Simon Gikandi speaks about Ngugi's relation to the past as something that 'haunts' him, something that recurs as he tries to work out what the past means to him, and how that past affects his present (Gikandi 2000: 7–8). Gikandi also speaks about the 'blockages' to Ngugi's understanding and making of meaning. All of these concepts are closely linked to the psychoanalytical notion of trauma – how memory returns and interferes with the present, how the return of the past is linked to structures of trauma which need to be 'unblocked' or 'worked-through'. Ngugi's writing is redemptive in precisely this sense of exorcising this 'ghost' and using writing as a process of social transformation and 'working-through' the trauma. Ngugi's return to the past reminds one that, like Pierre Nora's and J. Young's work on 'sites of memory', memory is not inherent to a discursive or factual place but has to be manufactured through the repeated reinvention by human agents. Only through this narrative reinvention can the full effects of physical and psychological trauma be 'worked-through', on both a personal and a national scale.

Other realisms

Jacques Lacan argues in *Four Fundamental Concepts of Psychoanalysis* that trauma is the result of the structure of the subject's 'missed encounter' with the real allowing the past to remain in the present, rather than acting as a pure discontinuity. Trauma is not simply an instance of the modernist rhetoric of discontinuity and fragmentation. Rather trauma is *Nachträglichkeit* (deferred action or after-effect) – both a return of the repressed and a reordering of the past. Michael Rothberg identifies two ways to deal with this: first, an epistemological approach, i.e. a question of reference and knowledge of the past event; and second, an ethical approach, i.e. what is the proper ethical stance to take in relation to the past? It is in these two approaches that Ngugi's fiction can be seen to demonstrate Rothberg's argument that 'Realism is a production, not just a reflection' (Rothberg 2000: 103). Ngugi's realism is an example of what Rothberg names "traumatic realism", which is counter-ideological precisely to the extent that it does not construct an imaginary outcome but rather attunes readers to recognise the absence of the Lacanian 'real', or that 'missed encounter'. 'Traumatic realism' therefore produces knowledge but refuses consolation (Rothberg 2000: 156). Ngugi is a novelist who writes in a largely realist mode but who does not subscribe to the association of realism with nativist politics. Ngugi's realism both suspects and questions the normal, the habitual, and subverts and poses a challenge to the assumptions of colonialism or the interpellative ideology of imperialism. Realism can repeat and distribute familiar scenes but without the intention of sanctioning or endorsing them. Indeed, through its representation of the everyday, realist literature within a postcolonial context often seeks to change the dominant political system. In Stephen Slemon's view, realism can proffer a *contextualised* state of affairs that denaturalises and defamiliarises an accepted everyday state (Slemon

1990b). Slemon also argues that there is an order of ethnographic epistemological dominance in realism that establishes the author as an object gaining access to the 'truth' of the subject. This ethnographic gaze implicit in the structures of realism can be redirected to subvert and upset existing power relations. Slemon sees a necessity for the decolonisation of modes of literary representation, such as the critical assumptions associated with realism. As Laura Moss has argued, many critics have all too prescriptively assumed that a form can be endowed with a single ideology (Moss 2000: paragraphs 24–5). Within the context of postcolonial literature, there is a need to reinvestigate the counter-discursive possibilities of realism, and this might take the form of noting the dialogism, the multiple perspectives inscribed in realism.

Indeed, despite Kwame Appiah's correlation between realism and nativism, there are several other novels that could be regarded as post-nativist but that are not post-realist. Wole Soyinka's *The Interpreters* is one case in point. As with other realist novels, this novel repudiates the idea of a single national past. The novel is about a group of five Nigerian friends, who are professionals (some failed, some successful) in various roles, and focuses upon their various social situations and perspectives on contemporary Nigerian life: Bandele and Kola (university lecturers); Sagoe (journalist); Sekoni (engineer and sculptor); Lasunwon (lawyer); and Egbo (foreign office). Full of ideals, they gradually find they are pushing up against hidebound tradition, vested interests and widespread corruption. Much of the book demonstrates the various inequities and moral degenerations in Nigeria – political corruption, moral corruption, sexual degeneracy – and this extends into political life as well as professional life (for example, the descriptions of the newspaper offices, and the corruption in the civil works programmes). Egbo, one of the principal characters, makes a choice as to whether to become a teacher or to take on his father's role as tribal chief. He opts for the teaching role, but is never quite able to shake off the past. Much of his role in the book is questioning the role of the past in the present, as he does in a conversation amongst three of the friends, which opens up this debate at one point:

> And he only plunged again into the ancient, psychic lie of still sediments, muttering, how long will the jealous dead remain among us!
> 'Why do you continue to brood?' Always Bandele knew exactly when he flogged his mind over the decision of Osa. 'You brought yourself to the point of choice, that had to happen, you know.'
> 'Even that choice is a measure of tyranny. A man's gift of life should be separate, an unrelated thing. All choice must come from within him, not from the promptings of his past.'
> 'You continue to talk of the past as if it has no place with us.'

'It should be dead. And I don't just mean bodily extinction. No, what I refer to is the existing fossil within society, the dead branches on a living tree, the dead runs on the bole. When people die, in one sense or in the other, it should not matter what they were to us. They owe the living a duty to be forgotten quickly, usefully. Believe me, the dead should have no faces.'

'You and Sagoe should get together,' Kola said.

'He is a politician.'

'Meaning? You tell me what new African doesn't spew politics.'

'You see? You don't even know what I am talking about. Can't you get it in your head that your global or national politics don't really count for much unless you become ruthless with the fabric of the past.'

'So what are you complaining about?' Kola said.

'Nothing. Nothing as far as my head goes.'

'But otherwise ...?'

Impatient now, Egbo cried 'Is it so impossible to seal off the past and let it alone? Let it stay in its harmless anachronistic unit so we can dip into it at will and leave it without commitment, without impositions! A man needs that especially when the present, equally futile, distinguishes itself only by a particularly abject lack of courage.' (*The Interpreters*: 120–1)

The characters argue about the usefulness of the past in the context of living the present and planning the future. Whether one can cut off the past, or whether one is continually negotiating with it in the present, is the source of the contention. This ideological argument is mirrored in the structure of the novel. The temporal line of the novel jumps backwards and forwards, into the past and into the future and gradually, the novel builds up a picture of the histories of the five friends. Although the novel peters out a bit, it nevertheless presents savage satires on the nouveau riche in Nigeria, as well as the social pretensions of academics, professionals and government employees – especially those aping European characteristics.

Soyinka's realism concerns itself with getting the past straight, and he approves of fiction that insists on 'a strict selectivity from the past in the designing of the future' (*The Interpreters*: 116). It has little truck with the populist or the mythical. The Ghanaian poet Kofi Awoonor, on the other hand, in his novel entitled *This Earth, My Brother* ... (1971), clearly dovetails a hard-hitting realism with mythical modes. The aspects of poetic prose are clearly evident in some of the chapters (the parallel '*a*' chapters), where the print is slightly smaller and tends to be more imagistic and metaphorical as opposed to the social realist prose of the other chapters. The novel also presents a quite savage satire on the new bourgeoisie which has sprung up after the departure of the colonial power. The principal character is the barrister Amamu, a 'been-to', who has returned from London to practise law in Accra, Ghana. His life seems to be listless and aimless, lacking direction and goals beyond the acquisition of social status. The society appears to be decadent, corrupt, morally bankrupt and at odds with itself in terms of social division. This can be seen in the description of the squalor and putrid foulness of 'the dunghill of Nima' (*This Earth, My Brother* ...: 28), the shanty-town on the outskirts of Accra where the servant Yaro lives:

> No river runs through Nima. Only a large open gutter that stinks to heaven. [Accra] itself grew with vengeance. Nima grew alongside it like an ever growing and eternal dunghill. ... The conspicuous landmark is the Harlem Café. Another set is the two septic latrines, a fitting memorial to Nima, the city within a city, Nkrumah once said he would make it. These latrines are ever full. Those in a hurry take a shit right on the floor. Near the septic latrines are huge dunghills which in the language of the Accra City Council are called refuse dumps. No one ever removes refuse in Nima. (*This Earth, My Brother* ...: 151–2)

An additional schism in the novel is between those who have been brought up as Christians and those who have remained attached to their indigenous religions. Various Christian hymnal lyrics recur throughout the novel, which almost act as an ironic commentary on people's actions. The narrative alternates between mythical and historical narratives: the past appears to be lost in a mire of greed and cultural and moral blinkeredness. There is a significant overlay of myth and metaphysics in the narrative. When it occurs, Amamu's death appears to be a return to the mythical past, in so far as he returns to the almond tree of the mythical memory at the beginning of the book, and feels that he returns to his lost mythical lover. Richard Priebe notes this liminal ambivalence in Awoonor's novel, suggesting that Amamu 'is a man between two worlds, two traditions, and he is striving to effectively put the European side of his self in the service of his African side' (Priebe 1988: 66), and the novel presents two perspectives, a realist and a mythic consciousness. As Priebe shows, this negotiation between the realist and mythic is something of a preoccupation in West African fiction, and one can think of instances of this in the novels of Achebe, Okri, Soyinka, Tutuola and others. As Professor Sackey, a character in Kojo Laing's novel *Search Sweet Country* (1986), states: 'the Ghanaian is indestructible because he has got formed in his head, deep ravines of opposites; if he feels too hot with one being or with one presence, he just hops onto another, thousands of miles away if necessary. And there's something I find very odd: there is not territory between the supernatural, and the purely factual ... you get the factual explanations that do not fit superfactual situations, and you get supernatural answers that fly off at a tangent to the merely factual' (*Search Sweet Country*: 240). Realism itself (like any literary form) is clearly not a 'pure' form, and realisms clearly do stray into the territory of 'super-realism', myth, or 'magic realism'. Yet as Adewale Maja-Pearce cautions, 'The point is not that people should be denied their myths, but that they shouldn't mistake them for the real thing' (Maja-Pearce 1992: 32). This area of stylistic 'cross-over' and hybridity will be picked up and explored more fully in Chapter 8 below.

Traumatic realism and 'postmemory'

Delving into and retrieving the past has often been influenced by Marxist models of history and their particular influence upon the representation of national and racial identity. This chapter has focused principally upon the problems thrown into relief by realist fiction and its attempts to interrogate the colonial past. It has sought to examine how the fiction of principally Ngugi wa Thiong'o, but also the novels of people like Soyinka, Iyayi and Iroh, have constantly probed the ethical problem of how the novelist can represent history without compromising it or becoming imprisoned within the past. It has argued that, although Marxism provided some writers with an instrument for understanding postcolonial culture, it could not account for, or indeed give meaning to, recurrent traumatic historical events every time one tried to write about the past; and it investigated how these writers sought to resolve their agonising reflections on the ideology of literature and the complex relationship between history, memory and aesthetic form. For as Ngugi repeatedly outlines in his novel *Petals of Blood*, history often seems to be blocked by the very narratives designed to represent it. Once one begins to discuss the relations of history and memory, one is inevitably caught up in the ramifications of what constitute models of history. What so many African writers demonstrate in their writing in the postcolonial epoch is that postcolonial history has a traumatic structure – it is repetitive, discontinuous and characterised by obsessive returns to the past and the troubling of simple chronology. In this respect, the various articulations of the colonial era and the postcolonial epoch are not simply belated but uneven. The postcolonial itself marks a crisis in representation, a self-reflexivity entering the realist novel, inflected by a modernism that talks about itself and its representational practices. Trauma lies in the rupturing of a progressive temporality and the modernising dynamic of developmental innovation. Within the context of postcoloniality, 'traumatic realism' does not produce seamless, untroubled accounts of the everyday. Where realist discourse relies upon stability, stabilising structures and perspectives, which is precisely the discourse of colonialism that sought to portray Africans in stereotypical ways, fixing them as lazy, conniving, good-for-nothings that had to be guided out of their error-prone and ignorant ways, 'traumatic realism' resists this ideological pressure. One problem of continuing to use the mode of orthodox realism is that one runs the risks of continuing to portray a social fixity, albeit this time about contemporary societies. Thus, although the object of representation has changed, the mode of representation is still tainted with the erstwhile oppressor's (colonist's) stigma. The mode of realism harks back willy-nilly to representations of history as stable, monolithic and monologic, precisely at a moment in postcolonial political history when writers are seeking to challenge monological portrayals and to produce more dialogical pictures of social interaction. Although memory itself can be regarded as an act of repetition since we must 'repeat' the scene in our minds in order to remember it, the remembrance is not, however, simply a repetition – it is a representation. For Nietzsche, repetition carries with it a negative connotation because it is allied with the past of 'tradition, custom, history, habit, style, and convention that colonize the mind and restrict the creative potentiality of human beings' (Nietzsche 1909: 35). Representation is partly about agency and change through self-conscious manipulation of images and signs. As people like Michael Rothberg and Stephen Slemon have demonstrated, 'traumatic realism' resists an ideological permanence and solidity in favour of a troubled, interrogative and inquisitive historiography. The memory of survival and victimisation denies and resists any resemblance or congruence with other human experiences, affirming difference and the need of the non-survivor who reads or listens to *not* understand, *not* to admit consonance. This is due to the emotional and intellectual sense that understanding perhaps trivialises and facilitates the barbarism. Consequently, there is some call for a 'traumatic realism' that somehow attempts to come to terms, affectively and cognitively, with limit experiences involving trauma and its after-effects. Consequently, 'traumatic realism' resists any easy subsumption into crude associations of realism with colonialism or the ideology of imperialism. In this respect, 'traumatic realist' texts are the preservers of what Marianne Hirsch has so compelling termed 'postmemory', in her exploration of the ways in which family photographs seek to perpetuate ancestral histories:

> Postmemory is a powerful and very particular form of memory precisely because its connection to its object or source is mediated not through recollection but through an imaginative investment and creation. That is not to say that memory is itself unmediated, but that it is more directly connected to the past. Postmemory characterizes the experience of those who grow up dominated by narratives that preceded their birth, whose own belated stories are evacuated by the stories of the previous generation shaped by the traumatic events that can be neither understood nor recreated. (Hirsch 1997: 22)

Although Hirsch is specifically interested in developing this notion in relation to photographs (or what she calls 'imagetexts') of Holocaust victims, Hirsch acknowledges that this concept may usefully explain other second- (or indeed, third-) generation memories of cultural or collective traumatic events. African 'traumatic realist' texts therefore act as the custodians of postmemory, in what is for the most part an unredeemed topography, a landscape that persistently upsets and disturbs the easy arrangement of the past, and where 'postmemory' refers to those texts that are haunted by memories that they have inherited from their families, or from the culture at large.

4

Gender, memory, history

In any case, the question is not just the past or the present, but which factors out of both the past and the present represent for us the most dynamic forces for the future. (Ama Ata Aidoo, *Our Sister Killjoy*)

Within African literature, room must be made for women ... room we will fight for with all our might. (Mariama Bâ)

Abdul JanMohamed has argued that a dialogue with colonial discourse constitutes 'a fundamental component of contemporary African literature' (JanMohamed 1983: 279). Frantz Fanon has also argued that African politics and culture are structured upon a racial allegory – black/white, good/evil, superior/inferior. However, these positions obscure the fact that African literature is also structured upon a sexual allegory – male/female, good/evil, superior/inferior, subject/object, self/other – and suppress the fact that women's writing is as much an interaction with gender as with race or coloniality. Histories specific to women in an African context can frequently be obscured by the dominant preoccupation with a racial identity or ethnicity. When Chinua Achebe was asked the question, 'Do you write fiction about women the way a woman writer does?', he gave the simplest and obvious answer: 'How could I?' Yet one feminist study of African women's writing has a chapter entitled 'How could things fall apart for whom they were not together?' (Stratton 1994: 22). This implicit critique of the silences and exclusions in Achebe's canonical novel *Things Fall Apart* points to the way that, for all the consciousness of sexual difference, this has not translated into African men's representations of African women's experience.[1] The ways in which novelists such as Bessie Head, Flora Nwapa, Ama Ata Aidoo, Grace Ogot, Miriam Tlali, Mariama Bâ and Buchi Emecheta deal with the past and the counter-discourse of memory to raise consciousness about the particular problems of gender, colonialism and history will be the focus of this chapter. While African women's writing does not exclude the need to liberate African peoples from neo-colonialism and other forms of race and class oppression, there is the recognition that a feminist consciousness is necessary in examining the position of women in African societies.

Yet not all African women novelists unite under a common feminist banner (for example, see Newell 1997: 1–3; and Nasta 1991: xiii–xxx).

Indeed, they do not all necessarily desire the same changes. Deriving from various cultural, religious, ethnic and geographical formations, some defend traditional securities while others seek to overturn the nightmare of tradition. Often they show their female protagonists as torn, confused, in a mileu of cross-cultural conflict. The tragic alienation caused by the desire for Europeanisation, the persistent debilitating effects of constructing images of the African mother as Mother Africa, as well the ways in which the images of African women as concubine, prostitute, supermother, wife, earth as muse support or distort the creation of a female *mythos* and how they conform to the realities of women's lives, are some of the principal features of this chapter. Despite such representations of women as positive possibilities of transcendence in Ngugi wa Thiong'o's depiction of Waaringa in *The River Between* (1965), or Sembene Ousmane's portrayal of N'Deye Touti in *God's Bits of Wood* (1962), women for the most part are consistently marginalised and 'othered' in past and current debates about African writing. Women's utilisation of memory and oral history to resist and challenge the identification of women with the 'petrified' cultural traditions of the past and the allocation to male characters or narrators of the role of regaining control over the historical development of their societies is one of the main strategies of much African women's writing. This traditional alignment of women with space and men with time effectively removes women's agency, eliminating their ability to prompt historical change to their political conditions. African women's writing demonstrates the need to think history and the past from the perspective of gender as well as from the perspective of race. Frequently these narratives are first-person narratives of women determined to make sense of their past and to inscribe themselves within and against the cultures that subtend that experience; and this process of discovery becomes the source of rebirth and reconciliation, the mode of healing of the narrating self. In particular, I hope to make clear how the realisation of different pasts and the processes of articulating those pasts are highly political – they trace the path to social consciousness. Without seeking to write a complete history of the development of this political consciousness in African women's writing, I shall examine various case-study examples to articulate how that writing is part of a collective effort to redefine the roles of womanhood. Women writers especially have been interested in reap-propriating the past so as to transform people's understanding of themselves, valuing memory as a viable alternative to oppressive history. Their voices echo the submerged or repressed values of African cultures as they rewrite the 'feminine' by showing the arbitrary nature of the images and values which western culture constructs, distorts and encodes as inferior by feminising them.

Memory-work and the 'double yoke'

The fact that over the years African women's writing has been over-looked by many male critics of African literature has been widely noted in recent decades. A great deal of critical work in the past fifteen years has gone into rectifying the absences, exclusions, igno-rances and the omissions in the work of important African literary scholars. One of the pathbreaking works in this area was Lloyd W. Brown's book entitled *Women Writers in Black Africa* (1981), which sought to rectify the omission of women writers from the histories and development of an African canon of writing. However, it was perhaps *Ngambika: Studies of Women in African Literature*, edited by Carole Boyce Davies and Anne Adams Graves (1986), that plotted a specifically feminist course for African women's writing. The intro-ductory essay by Boyce Davies identifies a tension found in the works of many African literary critics, whom she argues write out of the increasing awareness of the necessity of balancing both 'the need to liberate African peoples from neo-colonialism and other forms of race and class oppression, coupled with a respect for certain features of traditional African cultures', and 'the recognition that a feminist consciousness is necessary in examining the position of women in African societies' (Boyce Davies and Adams Graves 1986: 1). Boyce Davies then delineates the issues relating to African women's writing, and the representation of African women in fiction written by men, as well as addressing the need for an African feminist criti-cism. She lists four major areas that need addressing at the crux of modern African feminist theory: first, the development of the canon of African women writers; second, the examination of stereotyped images of women in African literature; third, the study of African women writers and the oral tradition; and, fourth, the study of African women writers and the development of an African female aesthetic. In many ways, this agenda of critical revaluation and recu-peration is still involved in providing critical essays and accounts of the work by women writers who have been omitted from the surveys of African writing, and on promoting the work of younger, more recent African women writers like Tsitsi Dangarembga, Yvonne Vera, Lindsey Collen, Calixthe Beyala and others. This positive discrimination has also been undertaken quite effectively by the establishment of small African presses dedicated to publishing the work of African women, such as Flora Nwapa's Tanga Press in Nigeria, and the politically conscious Femrite based in Kampala, Uganda. Unsurprisingly, critical work concerning individual authors has both enlarged and extended over the years, especially as an individual author's oeuvre has grown or been excavated from anonymity. Only very recently has serious critical attention been given to the ways and strategies adopted by African women writers as a group rather than as individuals in combating patriarchal values and developing an account of an African female aesthetic. This is partly due to the fact that, pervasive though they may be, patriarchal values operate and insert themselves into social structures in different ways in different regions of the continent (see for example the different treatment of women between the Yoruba and Ibo tribes noted in Buchi Emecheta's *The Joys of Motherhood* (1979); or the differences in male expectations of women in Islamic societies such as those described in Mariama Bâ's *So Long a Letter* (1980); or the various customs and traditions attendant on marriage in the Luo tribe in Kenya in Grace Ogot's *The Promised Land* (1966); or the various practices in southern Africa, like those described in Bessie Head's novels, in particular *A Question of Power* (1974), where the protagonist Elizabeth suffers a psychological breakdown with a 'storm in the head': 'It had taken such drastic clamour to silence the hissing record in her head, but it had left a terrible wound' (*Question of Power*: 52)). Consequently, women critics have had to attend to the regional, cultural and historical specificities of the critique of patriarchy in specific novels since the 1960s. However, more recently, especially with the advent of the powerful interventions of postcolonial theory, criticism of African women's writing has shifted to the shared concerns, the common strategies and the collective visions of these writers.

   Yet postcolonial theory has not always proved to be a satisfactory 'fit' with African women's writing. Many African women writers explicitly distance themselves from the term 'postcolonial', such as Ama Ata Aidoo, who has said that 'colonialism has not been POST-ed anywhere' (quoted in Boyce Davies 1994: 152), and Buchi Emecheta. In her book entitled *Black Women, Writing and Identity*, Carole Boyce Davies has been fierce in her critique of the appropriateness of the term 'postcolonialism' to African women's writing: 'post-coloniality represents a misnaming of current realities ... It is too premature a formulation, it is too totalising, it erroneously contains decolonizing discourse, it re-males and recenters resistant discourses by women and attempts to submerge a host of uprising textualities' (Boyce Davies 1994: 81). Boyce Davies considers postcolonial theory to be a western category of thought that excludes people living the practical realities of life in modern-day Africa, and that colonialism and neo-colonialism are complicit in reinforcing traditional gender inequities in African society. Likewise, other African women writers have sought to distance themselves from the concepts of feminist theory. This scepticism and reluctance of African women writers to be labelled as feminists, owing to the associations of westernisation carried in these terms, is not to imply that African women's writing is not politically committed.[2] On the contrary, in the words of Ogundipe-Leslie, African women writers frequently display a triple commitment 'as a writer, as a woman and as a third world person' (Ogundipe-Leslie 1987) as they work out and clarify for themselves the politics and activism of women's rights in Africa.

If colonialism posed a traumatic disruption to African male novelists, then African women novelists have suffered a 'double yoke' of traumatic disruption in their cultural histories. Not only have they had to contend with the alienation and dispossessing effects of colonialism but they have had to navigate and negotiate the frequently strenuous and rigorous exclusions and marginalisations posed by a deeply entrenched structure of patriarchal power. Florence Stratton has pointed to the way in which male critical attitudes in a range of introductory texts to African literature have basically ignored or excluded African women's fiction. As Stratton shows, this invisibility of African women is also evident in attempts to theorise colonialism. She picks on one example from Abdul JanMohamed's *Manichean Aesthetics*, where she quotes him discussing the subtle manoeuvres of colonial cultural structures:

> [Colonialism] puts the native in a double bind: if he chooses conservatively and remains loyal to his indigenous culture, then he opts to stay in a calcified society where developmental momentum has been checked by colonization. If, however, the colonized person chooses assimilation, then he is trapped in a form of historical catalepsy because colonial education severs him from his own past and replaces it with the study of the colonizer's past. (JanMohamed 1983: 5, cited in Stratton 1994: 7)

However, as Stratton points out, females are relatively barred from education. Numerous novels testify to exactly this exclusion, both by male novelists (John Munonye's *Oil Man of Obange*) and by women novelists (Flora Nwapa's *Efuru*, Tsitsi Dangarembga's *Nervous Conditions* and Goretti Kyomuhendo's *The First Daughter*). So it is really a *male* double bind. Colonialism, Stratton argues, posed quite another set of problems for women:

> For, as feminist scholars in various fields have argued, colonialism is not neutral as to gender. Rather it is a patriarchal order, sexist as well as racist in its ideology and practices. What these studies indicate is that women's position relative to men deteriorated under colonialism.

They also show that, while pre-colonial women had more freedom than their colonized descendants, male domination was nonetheless an integral part of the societies they lived in. Under colonialism, then, African women were subject to interlocking forms of oppression: to the racism of colonialism and to indigenous and foreign structures of male domination. (Stratton 1994: 7)

As many African women's novels demonstrate, this 'double yoke' of oppression has taken some considerable effort to articulate, not least because, in their eagerness to throw off colonialism and champion native culture, many influential male writers have unwittingly or not reinforced well-worn images and stereotypes of African womanhood. The consequence of this is that African women writers have had to contend not only with resisting the white colonists' negative portrayals of *Africanness* (perpetuated later by some acquiescent white feminism (Bush 1996: 5)) but also with unpicking the complex mixture of African males' representations of *femaleness*. This has oscillated between negative denigrations of women, and a celebration and idolisation of African *femaleness*, which disguises a deeper-seated traditionalism and, in some cases, conservative fear of femininity. Omolara Ogundipe-Leslie has pointed out that the various stereotypes of African women in literature have been the 'mother' and the 'houri', or the rural woman and the sophisticated city woman (Ogundipe-Leslie 1987: 6). Perhaps the most famous character is Cyprian Ekwensi's portrayal of Jagua Nana in *Jagua Nana* (1961), a charming, colourful and impressive prostitute who moves through a whole panoply of vibrant, amoral characters who have rejected their rural origins and adopted the opportunistic, pleasure-seeking urban lifestyle of Lagos. Similar portrayals of women as prostitutes include the figure of Kechi Ugboma in Eddie Iroh's *Toads of War* (1979) and other examples abound in African literature, especially the more sensationalist fiction. This eroticisation of the African woman, Ogundipe-Leslie maintains, demonstrates 'that many male writers conceive of women only as phallic receptacles' and that the myth of the naive, rural woman is necessary 'to buoy-up [the African male's] conservatism and his yearning for that pre-colonial and patriarchal past where he was definitely king as father, husband and ruler' (Ogundipe-Leslie 1987: 6, 8).

In handling these problems, African women writers have inevitably resorted to 'memory-work' as a means of unravelling the patriarchal patchwork quilt of history. Shuttling between rewriting the history that men have written about women and writing a new history that has been omitted from narratives by men, these women's writing make clear that the past is a crucial element in forging an African future, not just for women but for all people on the continent. As Barbara Bush's discussion of the ways in which black women develop and redefine their own identities, there are 'vital links between recorded history, "long memory" and present, lived experience, for the collective memory of the black "holocaust" and ensuing long-term trauma remains alive and burning in the black diasporic consciousness' (Bush 1996: 3). Yvonne Vera's novel *Nehanda* (1993) is a good example of this structure: written in a semi-mystical mode, the eponymous central protagonist Nehanda who has been chosen by the ancestral spirits to galvanise an uprising against the invaders of the land, experiences 'that gaping wound everywhere. The wound has been shifting all over her body and she can no longer find it' (*Nehanda*: 2). Nehanda's role is to connect the current generation with memories of the past and the ancestral spirits, and thereby present a vision of an alternative future: 'Hope for the nation is born out of the intensity of newly created memory. The suffusing light dispels all uncertainty, and the young move out of the darkness of their trepidation, into the glory of dawn ... The newly born come into the world bearing gifts. They walk and speak. They have eyes that hold memories of the future, but no one is surprised: they have received their sight back' (*Nehanda*: 111–13). *Nehanda*'s endorsement of the validity of memory and testimony of oral transmission in recalling the history of the oppressed is becoming increasingly recognised as a legitimate political stance; and African women's writing has increasingly sought to place these aspects at the centre of its strategies of resistance. Certain images, memories, of *precolonial* gender roles have aided in supporting a modern-day feminism. One of the key issues in 'working-through' the trauma of African women is the alleviation of passivity, or the reclamation of agency; and, as we shall see repeatedly, one of the ways of understanding the development of African women's writing is locating a movement from the woman being the *object* of patriarchal ideology to asserting herself as the *subject* of her own narrative and life. This trajectory is a characteristic feature in African women's writing and, as I will show in further examples, it coincides with their 'working-through' of the displaced, unintegrated experiences forced upon them by colonialism and patriarchy. My focus on memory of the past and the traumas it has produced in African women's writing is partly to shift the attention away from anthropological interests in 'structure' to a more political and psychological interest in 'agency'. For memory is often regarded as subversive of 'official' history, and oral narrative in particular is often regarded by historians with suspicion, as an unreliable source for factual accounts of the past, prone as it is to condensation, ellipsis, dramatic exaggeration and rhetorical embellishment. Nevertheless, these methods of 'memory-work' constitute a vital force in the recuperation of lost experiences, suppressed activities and marginalized writers. Indeed, many women's novels take the form of memoirs or retrospective analysis of a life. For instance, there is Ramatoulaye's moving letter detailing to her friend Aïssatou the distressing material and psychological results for her life consequent upon her husband's death, in Mariama Bâ's *So Long a Letter* (1980); or the memoir written by the mother Elizabeth Sera to her alienated daughter Mercy spelling out the difficulties in her life that have led to that estrangement, in the Ugandan Ayeta Anne Wangusa's novel *Memoirs of a Mother* (1998); or the thinly disguised allegory of the corruption and despotism in Uganda under Idi Amin in Mary Karooro Okurut's *The Invisible Weevil* (1998), in which the central image of the weevil eating the nation is both political and literal disease; or the way in which *lack of memory* structures Mabel Dove Danquah's marvellously ironic short story 'Anticipation' (1947), about a polygamous king whose uncontrollable desire causes him to marry his forty-first beautiful young bride, only for her to gently remind him after the payment of the dowry that he had married her two years previously (see Opoku-Agyemang 1997).

'Memory-work' is thus a crucial aspect of rewriting the social and political position of women in Africa. The different ways in which some African women's narratives can recognise, order and reorder representations of pastness forms a major focus of this chapter. The frequent identification of memory with oracy and history with literacy is a misleading, gender-laden prescription about African women's writing that preserves a social hierarchy based upon a masculine ideology of his principal agency in constructing history. Elizabeth Tonkin's interesting study of oral narrative and its relation to history entitled *Narrating Our Pasts* (1992) challenges these misconceptions and demonstrates that oral history is an important historical resource in her examinations of how oral histories are constructed and how they should be analysed. She argues that oral accounts of past events are signposts to the future, as well as being social activities in which narrators claim authority to speak to particular audiences. For these reasons, 'memory-work' cannot be dismissed as being a 'weak' form of history, especially within the context of oral-based social structures. As Tonkin states, 'To tell history is to act, albeit to act in a verbal mode' (Tonkin 1992: 11). For Tonkin, memories are a form of social reproduction and are less individual than one is prone to think in an age of individualism. Hence, recourse to memory in narrative can be an activation of social structures that have been ignored, the excavation of social and political roles that have been neglected and the resuscitation of alternative modes of social behaviour. The appropriation of oral performance and oral narratives is instrumental in African women's writing affecting existing power relations. 'Memory-work' tied to oral narrative is critical to the ability to transform and not simply to represent existing gender power relations.

This 'memory-work' also needs to consider alternative *forms* of 'memory'. Paul Connerton's *How Societies Remember* (1989) distinguishes different forms of memory. He argues that most studies of memory as a cultural faculty focus on written (or inscribed) practices and how these are transmitted. Connerton, on the other hand, concentrates on the bodily (or incorporated) practices and provides an account of how these are transmitted in, and as, traditions. Connerton argues that images and recollected knowledge of the past are conveyed and sustained by ritual performances, and that *performative memory* has been badly neglected. In the analysis of African women's writing, performative memory frequently emerges as a memory inscribed on bodily practices, especially in terms of the expectations of women as mothers and bearers of (preferably) male children, as the possessions of their husbands, as the public expressions of male domestic power, as marks for physical violation and in initiation ceremonies that make women's bodies spectacles for the male gaze.

Unfixing stereotypes of African womanhood

The invocation of the past, history or tradition can be a negative as a well as a positive action. In the case of the former, it can be a means of tying one down to conservatism, of holding one back, of impelling one into roles, customs or positions already carved out and set aside for people. In the case of the latter, it can be a means of connecting with something that is lost, severed, removed or hidden, of finding or discovering a past that enables one to construct a present identity. It can also be a means to working out a position in the present, seeing all the disguises and deviations that have severed that past.

One such conservative invocation of the past occurs in the frequent nostalgic representations of African women as mothers. The observation of this feature in African writing has not gone unnoticed, and a substantial body of critical and analytical work tracing the idealisation of the African mother now exists. Many women critics refer to the long historical tradition of the iconic African mother under male patriarchy, and how this precolonial image has been consolidated and perpetuated by more contemporary representations since the end of colonialism, such as those celebrations of African womanhood by Négritude writers. For example, one might point to the representations of woman as a metaphysical symbol of a continuous cycle of birth and rebirth in Léopold Senghor's poetry, in which mawkishly idealised pictures of African womanhood are created in such poems by Senghor as 'Femme Noire', 'Nuit de Sine', 'I Will Pronounce Your Name' and 'Spring Song', and poems by David Diop as 'To My Mother' and 'To a Black Dancer'. As Florence Stratton points out, this trope of 'Mother Africa' as a fertile, sensuous, faithful and nurturing

woman reproduces 'in symbolic form the gender relations of patriarchal societies' (Stratton 1994: 51). Stratton continues:

> The trope elaborates a gendered theory of nationhood and writing, one
> that excludes women from the creative production of the national polity
> or identity and of literary texts ... A feminized Africa thus becomes the
> object of the male gaze ... The relationship is one of possession. He is
> the active subject-citizen. She is the passive object-nation. (Stratton
> 1994: 51)

This objectification of women, Stratton argues, is complicit with one
of the nightmares of Africa, namely the European male imperialist's
penetration and domination of the 'dark', 'mysterious' continent.
Consequently, many women writers are concerned with deconstruct-
ing these phallocentric images of masculine power, images that have
clearly structured the male psyche for many centuries, and proved to
be deeply traumatising for women in their effect. Mariama Bâ can
only have been thinking of these debilitating representations when
she wrote:

> The woman writer in Africa has a special task. She has to present the
> position of women in Africa in all its aspects. There is still so much
> injustice ... In the family, in the institutions, in society, in the street, in
> political organizations, discrimination reigns supreme ... As women, we
> must work for our own future, we must overthrow the status quo which
> harms us and we must no longer submit to it. Like men, we must use
> literature as a non-violent but effective weapon. We no longer accept the
> nostalgic praise to the African Mother who, in his anxiety, man can
> confuse with Mother Africa. Within African literature, room must be
> made for women. (Mariama Bâ, quoted in Schipper 1987: 46–7)

Literature as an effective weapon in the war against patriarchal
oppression, is precisely what motivates many African women's
narratives. As Bâ points out, the targets are those long-established
practices that subordinate women in particular ways, such as
marriage, motherhood, the bar to education, the acceptance of second
or third wives, the social rules governing patrimony and patrilin-
eage, and the imperative in providing a male heir.

A discussion of the responses to patriarchy and misogyny by
African women's writing would seem deficient without reference to
Mariama Bâ's now famous novel *So Long a Letter* (1980). Although
initially written and published in French, it was translated into
English almost straight away, and proved to be a controversial novel
right from the outset owing to its outspoken views on women's rights
in an African Islamic culture. *So Long a Letter* is a sequence of reminiscences, some wistful, some resentful, recounted by Senegalese
school teacher Ramatoulaye, who has recently been widowed. In a
letter to her friend, Aïssatou, Ramatoulaye writes of her emotional

struggle to regain her life after her husband Modou's abrupt decision to take a second wife without her knowledge. Many have regarded the act of polygamy and its aftermath as the main focus of the novel, but I concur with Obioma Nnaemeka's closely argued and persuasive argument that that the novel actually shows that Ramatoulaye finds her oppression less from the polygamy and more from her husband's betrayal of trust and the ways in which patriarchal society turns a blind eye to men's philandering and ensures women's compliance (Nnaemeka 1997a). Although a second wife is sanctioned by the laws of Islam, Nnaemeka shows how Modou's action is a calculated betrayal of Ramatoulaye's trust and an abrupt rejection of their thirty years of marriage. The novel opens with an explicit invocation of the past:

> If over the years, and passing through the realities of life, dreams die, I still keep intact my memories, the salt of remembrance. I conjure you up. The past is reborn, along with its procession of emotions ... We walked the same paths from adolescence to maternity, where the past begets the present. (*So Long a Letter*: 1)

Constantly preoccupied with the past, her previous relationship with her husband and her previous friendship with Aïssatou, Ramatoulaye writes the letter on the moment of her husband's death, a moment dreaded by Senegalese women as 'the moment when she sacrifices her possessions as gifts to her family-in-law' (*So Long a Letter*: 4). Ramatoulaye's precarious financial position produces rancour and bitterness, as she finds herself indebted to the second wife and the mother-in-law. The material effects upon Ramatoulaye's life are considerable, since, after her husband Modou marries his second wife, 'his new found happiness gradually swallowed up his memory of us. He forgot about us' (*So Long a Letter*: 46), as he redirects his wealth to his new wife and her mother in the most arbitrary ways. In fact, when Ramatoulaye learns about the other wife, she talks about her shock at the news and this leads into a general concern with the fate of women whom she likens to 'a ball; once a ball is thrown, no one can predict where it will bounce' (*So Long a Letter*: 40). Indeed, this image of the lack of control over one's life is compounded a little further on in Ramatoulaye's letter when she unsurprisingly likens a woman to a piece of discarded male clothing: 'the cases of many women, despised, relegated or exchanged, who were abandoned like a worn-out or out-dated *boubou*' (*So Long a Letter*: 41). In a key speech concerning her feelings, Ramatoulaye rejects this position firmly when Modou's brother proposes marriage to her: 'I am not an object to be passed from hand to hand' (*So Long a Letter*: 58). Ramatoulaye's primary need is to become an active participant in society, to *produce* culture instead of remaining a passive term within a given system of exchange.

Despite the persistent reminders of women's second-class status, Ramatoulaye is also clear about the initiatives that can improve women's lives. One principal way is through the value of education: 'To lift us out of the bog of tradition, superstition and custom, to make us appreciate a multitude of civilizations without removing our own, to raise our vision of the world, cultivate our personalities, strengthen our qualities, to make up for our inadequacies, to develop universal moral values in us' (*So Long a Letter*: 15). Resistance to the conservative effects of tradition is part of Ramatoulaye's new political consciousness: 'We all agreed that much dismantling was needed to introduce modernity within our traditions. Torn between the past and the present, we deplored the "hard sweat" that would be inevitable ... We were full of nostalgia but were resolutely progressive' (*So Long a Letter*: 18–19). At another point in the letter, she remarks upon the power of books and their social and educative value in transforming the consciousness of society (*So Long a Letter*: 32), and in the final analysis it is clear that writing is a means of surviving her abandonment and sustaining her life in the face of her loneliness. A further way in which the novel clarifies the way forward for women's equality is through economic independence. Ramatoulaye makes several observations about the difficulties in bringing up her twelve children, and the dual lives of the working woman and her domestic situation (for example, see *So Long a Letter*: 20). As Ramatoulaye later points out, society forgets that a man's economic success depends upon the hidden economic benefit he gains from his wife: 'In a word, a man's success depends on feminine support' (*So Long a Letter*: 56). The letter to Aïssatou does become a women's political manifesto of sorts, since Ramatoulaye gives vent to her feminist concerns to do with gender inequalities (*So Long a Letter*: 60), and the final pages of the novel are given over to the difficulties of bringing up children as a single mother. Indeed, the book seeks to (re)define motherhood (*So Long a Letter*: 82–3) within the context of redefining the role of a women within Senegalese society.

Ramatoulaye writes to Aïssatou partly because she has also gone through a similar experience with her husband Mawdo Bâ, who sought to justify his polygamous marriage and its devastating effects upon Aïssatou by pointing to the 'supremacy of the (male) instinct' (*So Long a Letter*: 34). The self-appointed superiority of male power and its effects upon all walks of women's lives features persistently throughout the novel. As a series of reminiscences, the novel is structured upon these memories of male power and influence as a constant sore, or *wound*, in women's lives. In writing to Aïssatou, Ramatoulaye acknowledges their shared experiences as a psychological scarring: 'I know that I am shaking you, that I am twisting a knife in a wound hardly healed; but what can I do? I cannot help remembering my forced solitude and seclusion' (*So Long a Letter*: 26). The theme of the wound runs throughout her letter to Aïssatou like the experience of a trauma: 'I've said the essential, for pain, even when it's past, leaves the same marks on the individual when recalled … Forgive me once again if I have re-opened your wound. Mine continues to bleed' (*So Long a Letter*: 55). In a novel that explores the traumatic wound as it converges with redemptive memory, Shaun Irlam notes that 'Aïssatou's "rupture" repeats and externalizes a psychological rupture first introduced by the male practice of polygamy and the emotional oppression of women. She replies to a ruptured society created by the male subject with a defiant counter-rupture' (Irlam 1998: 84). Irlam's sensitive and detailed deconstructive analysis of the provocation of memory and the space of writing demonstrates how writing acts as a *modus scriptus* that articulates the ambivalent therapeutic and traumatic spaces inhabited by women in the novel.

Novels dealing with these matters of a woman's role in African society continue to be too numerous to mention. Suffice it to say that the first African woman's novel to be published, *Efuru* (1966) by Flora Nwapa, dealt with many of these issues and they are still in debate nearly thirty years later in novels like the Zambian Tsitsi V. Himunyanga-Phiri's short novel *The Legacy* (1992), the Ugandan Ayeta Anne Wangusa's novel *Memoirs of a Mother* (1998), the much-acclaimed *Purple Hibiscus* (2004) by Chimamanda Ngozi Adichie, in which the protagonist Kambili's prosperous and generous Catholic businessman father, respected and revered in the wider community for his support of charities, proves behind closed doors to be a despotic, controlling and ultimately extremely violent man; or finally, the more recent coming-of-age novel entitled *Everything Good Will Come* (2005) by Seffi Atta. Yet this history of literature as a weapon can take different trajectories. There is the approach in which literature is a subtle and ironic exploration of women's positions within a society as in the novel *Efuru*, or in the novels by the Kenyan novelist Grace Ogot; and then there is the approach that bludgeons readers with blunt depictions of masculine selfishness and violence that act as polemical calls-to-arms. *The Legacy* is an example of this latter literature of protest, a sharp, critical portrayal of the degrading beliefs and practices of male-dominated Zambian society. The sketchy plot is a court hearing to rule on the property claims of Moya Mudenda's husband's relatives upon his death, which threaten to leave her without any of the financial and material accumulation for which she and her husband have fought so vigorously during their marriage. The rules of inheritance, through which men subjugate their wives to the precedence of the claims of the male's relatives, lead, by way of a remembrance of Moya's past life with her husband and their children, to an interrogation of the general state of women in contemporary society. The novel turns polemical towards the end, with a series of rhetorical questions and statements about the ironies and paradoxes of women's lives:

> I, too, saw myself as one whose potential was limited by the fact that I was a woman.
>
> I never really saw my strengths, only the weaknesses that society was quick to point out to me.
>
> What is more amazing is that there are a number of women who are doing the same thing daily and who are not getting the recognition they deserve.
>
> Does the fault lie with our culture? our society? our men? or with us women?
>
> Why have we allowed our lives to be led in this manner? In the manner that our mothers and grandmothers led their lives. Times have changed and so should our lives.
>
> It is funny that the men have been allowed to adjust their lifestyles to suit the changing times but women have not ...
>
> What is happening to our society? How can we go forward when one half of the population is being left behind in the name of culture?
>
> I have gone through life never stopping to question what was happening to me, simply existing.
>
> I should have questioned my life long before this. (Himunyanga-Phiri 1992: 56–7)

This is the fiction of protest, didactic and outspokenly critical, the plot merely a thin veil over the determination to advocate an interrogation of contemporary social politics concerning gender rights. The result is less a novel and more an occasion for a manifesto urging upon women the necessity of fighting back against the inheritance system by legal and other means, rather than passively accepting the status quo and thereby acquiescing in their own subjugation.

'A great big void': Tsitsi Dangarembga and women's memory

African women's fiction of the past two decades has thus shown a marked transition to a more confrontational stance. This is no more emphatically displayed than in Tsitsi Dangarembga's controversial novel *Nervous Conditions* (1988), which dissects African women's position as victims of a vestigial patriarchal colonialism. In fact, as many commentators have argued, the novel shows women negotiating the difficulties of feminism and nationalism in a postcolonial age (for example, see Okonkwo 2003; McWilliams 1991; and Thomas 1992). Depicting the teenage years of the young Shona woman Tambudzai in the 1960s and 1970s as she develops through her education and as she negotiates the various prejudices within her family, the novel concentrates on the ways in which women are marginalised and excluded from certain spheres of social activity like education and economics. Structured as Tambudzai's first-person account as she moves from her father Jeremiah's impoverished farm to the mission school run by her uncle Babamukuru and finally on to the exclusive Sacred Heart convent school which is mostly white, the novel explores the issues of postcolonial identity and strategies of resistance to co-optation into the colonial elite of white Rhodesia. From the outset of her young life, she is made aware that her gender relegates her to a low priority within the general family structure:

> The needs and sensibilities of the women in my family were not consid-
> ered a priority, or even legitimate. That was why I was in Standard
> Three in the year that Nhamo died, instead of Standard Five, as I
> should have been by that age. In those days I felt the injustice of my
> situation every time I thought about it, which I could not help but do
> often since children are always talking about their age. Thinking about
> it, feeling the injustice of it, this is how I came to dislike my brother, and
> not only my brother, my father, my mother – in fact everybody. (*Nervous
> Conditions*: 12)

This opening of the novel has caused quite a stir, since it describes a young girl's flagrant disapproval of the patriarchal and wider familial structures within African society. Establishing her rebellious streak at a young age, Tambudzai quickly articulates the complex oppressive structure of women in her society: 'Easy! As if it is ever easy. And these days it is worse, with the poverty of blackness on one side and the weight of womanhood on the other. Aiwa! What will help you, my child, is to learn to carry your burdens with strength' (*Nervous Conditions*: 16). Tambudzai develops an interrogative stance towards her circumstances, finally learning from her brother and implicitly from her father that she cannot go to school because she is a girl, at which point 'My concern for my brother died an unobtrusive death' (*Nervous Conditions*: 21). Tambudzai becomes irritated by her father's sense of what is 'natural' (*Nervous Conditions*: 34) in terms of gender roles within the family: 'He thought I was emulating my brother, that the things I read would fill my mind with impractical ideas, making me quite useless for the real tasks of feminine living' (*Nervous Conditions*: 34). She is constantly denigrated by her father for reaching above her gender role, striving for an education that is not hers, aspiring to a future which is not his vision for her.

Yet although Tambudzai feels excluded by the processes of male power, she also feels the warmth of inclusion in the female domestic roles, even if they are socially engineered by men: 'Exclusion whispered that my existence was not necessary, making me no more than an unfortunate by-product of some inexorable natural process' (*Nervous Conditions*: 40). 'It was comfortable for to recognise myself as solid, utilitarian me' (*Nervous Conditions*: 40). She learns from her grandmother, especially history, which is important to her sense of identity: 'She gave me history lessons as well. History that could not be found in the textbooks' (*Nervous Conditions*: 18). This oral history through stories about the family, about the past and the way it affected the development of the family, is crucial to an understanding of how the present came into being. For example, the grandmother speaks about the dispossession of the family's lands by the avaricious white settlers: 'It was truly a romantic story to my ears, a fairy-tale of reward and punishment, of cause and effect. It had a moral too, a tantalising moral that increased your aspirations, but not beyond a manageable level' (*Nervous Conditions*: 19). However, ultimately, through years of tolerating the status quo, her grandmother's history also reinforces female passivity: 'the message was clear: endure and obey, for there is no other way' (*Nervous Conditions*: 20).

Unconvinced by this argument, this 'other way' is what Tambudzai seeks, and her ambitions to see beyond the horizons outlined for her by her father and family are fuelled by the return of her cousins from a period of residence in England. When Tambudzai is given the opportunity of living with her schoolmaster uncle Babamukuru and his wife Maiguru and to attend his mission school, she studies hard and begins to see the potential that education brings. Yet this education is not without its problems. Tambudzai notices the way in which her cousins return from England unable to speak their native Shona, and how her brother Nhamo also begins to lose Shona and speak in English when he attends school. The consequence of this is the gradual erosion of one's connection to one's community, just as Nhamo is alienated from his cultural roots, language and family, as 'This restricted our communication to mundane insignificant matters' (*Nervous Conditions*: 53). Nevertheless, despite these conflicts, Tambudzai regards education as the opportunity to shake off her shackles, and craves the development of a new self, as her language shows: 'encouraged to consider questions that had to do with survival of the spirit, the creation of consciousness, rather than mere sustenance of the body. This new me ... Of course, this emancipation from these aspects of my existence' (*Nervous Conditions*: 58–9). She regards her transfer to the mission school as her 'reincarnation' (*Nervous Conditions*: 94), and becomes aware of different selves: 'The self I expected to find on the mission would take some time to appear. Besides, it was not to be such a radical transformation that people would have to behave differently towards me. It was to be an extension and improvement of what I really was' (*Nervous*

Conditions: 86). Tambudzai's principal education in the novel is that gender is not an essentialism, and that it consists of roles that one plays, more often than not roles that are forged by men. Education as the route to new possibilities and new identities, albeit fraught with a number of hazards along the way, is a motif repeated in a series of African women's novels.

Tambudzai's journey of self-discovery is mirrored in advance in her cousin Nyasha's journey. Yet the general pattern of Nyasha's revolt against bourgeois values – her mini-revolution – proves at first to be misunderstood by her family and Tambudzai, who see it as an ingratitude and an ignorance of the ways in which people in Zimbabwe generally live. Nevertheless, despite the apparently liberal values of her uncle's family, Tambudzai gradually learns that Nyasha's revolt against her father is not merely waywardness and ingratitude, but a revolt against stifling patriarchal values. Various scales fall from Tambudzai's eyes, as she begins to see the effects of her uncle's patriarchal power. She learns how her aunt Maiguru sacrificed things in England to help her husband despite gaining her own MA degree (*Nervous Conditions*: 103), and begins to realise that all is not what it seems with regard to women's affairs in the world. Nyasha's fight with her father precipitates a new perspective in Tambudzai, namely the realisation that patriarchal violence happens everywhere: 'The victimisation, I saw, was universal. It didn't depend on poverty, on lack of education or on tradition. It didn't depend on any of the things I thought it depended on. Men took it everywhere with them ... What I didn't like was the way all the conflicts came back to this question of femaleness. Femaleness as opposed and inferior to maleness' (*Nervous Conditions*: 118). When her mother leaves home for a period of time in protest against her husband's actions, Nyasha gives vent to her sense of claustrophobia, arguing that there is nowhere to which she can break out and escape, that patriarchy and the stifling atmosphere that she experiences pervades every aspect of her life. Nyasha's eventual bulimia is a manifestation of her struggle against her father (*Nervous Conditions*: 203), but more widely a struggle against patriarchy in general and, it has been argued, a 'quasi-voluntary bodily resistance to colonialism' (Sugnet 1997: 35–6). Nyasha articulates her unconscious recognition that oppression is the source of repression in this act of performative memory, where her body effectively inscribes a protest against the accumulated years of male strictures against women. Nyasha's breakdown, when it comes, is the consequence of her consciousness of the oppression under which she lives, and she understands a chain of oppression stemming from colonial interference through her father and mother, down to the two girls. Consequently, one could argue that Nyasha's breakdown is a direct effect of colonial trauma working through the social system and emerging as a traumatic result in Nyasha's life.

Gradually, all the women in the novel show differing signs of a variety of struggles and assertions against patriarchy.[3] The final page of the novel explains that the narrative records Tambudzai's expansion of consciousness about her society, its oppressive forces and where it positions her as a black woman. While Tambudzai manages to surmount the obstacles placed in her way, Nyasha is the representative of the tragic consequences of the twin pressures placed upon African women by male gender expectations and by (neo-)colonial exclusions. Indeed, the novel is deeply concerned with the schizophrenic psychological effects of these two pressures, and how women struggle with the problems of an inadequate history to which they can attach themselves in a meaningful and integrated fashion.[4] Dangarembga herself speaks of the lack of a 'tangible history that [Zimbabwean people of my generation] can relate to', and she suggests that this 'great big void' is the source of Nyasha's collapse (Dangarembga 1992: 191). Furthermore, as Dangarembga continues to argue, the novel is centrally concerned with a kind of critical rewriting emerging from a subversive memory:

> I think this problem of forgetting – remembering and forgetting – is really important. What is interesting is that Nyasha as an individual does not have anything to forget: she simply doesn't know ... She obviously feels some great big gap inside her and that she ought to remember it because this is her heritage. And she really doesn't come to the consciousness that even the reasons for this gap are so far out of her own control that she doesn't have to tear herself to pieces to have to rectify the situation. Tambudzai on the other hand I think is quite valid in saying that she can't forget because she has that kind of experience Nyasha is so worried about forgetting because it's not there for her to remember. Tambudzai is so sure that this is the framework of her very being that there is no way that she would be able to forget it. It is, as she says, a question of remembering and from what you remember picking out what is going to be useful in the future as you progress. (Dangarembga 1992: 191–2)

The narrative is Tambudzai's therapeutic way of staving off a similar collapse, a way of 'working-through' the trauma. She remembers in order that others may not have to remember. Tambudzai prevents any 'sickness' of her own through her progressive awareness of the past. In unearthing her childhood memories and emotions, she understands more and more about the patriarchal system that is the source of the repressive mechanism of her unconscious. In other words, she understands repression to be a consequence of oppression; oppression of children by parents, of the body by culture, of the colony by the imperial capital. In doing so, Tambudzai moves from being the *object* of her family's patriarchal ideology to asserting herself as the *subject* of her own narrative and life. This trajectory is very common in African women's writing, and it coincides with their 'working-through' of the displaced, unintegrated experiences forced upon them by colonialism and patriarchy.

Oppressive memories

The controversial francophone Cameroonian novelist Calixthe Beyala made a notorious impact upon the African literary scene with her two strikingly outspoken novels written in the mid- to late 1980s. *The Sun Hath Looked Upon Me* (1987) and *Your Name Shall Be Tanga* (1988) concern the hidden lives of women, usually the result of male violence perpetrated upon the women. Openly tackling taboo subjects, Beyala's two novels squarely confront the Négritude poets' figurations of women as Super Mothers, and as an incipient decon-structionist Beyala's fiction undoes the phallogocentric structures of masculine power. Although she acknowledges the erotic desires of women, she does not merely reproduce these as heterosexual desires; rather, she redirects these desires towards women, and substitutes alternative emotional structures for misogynistic social power. The novels chart the lives of women struggling with the need to articulate their dim recognition that masculine power has ruptured and riven their connection to humane feelings and emotional or psychological health. As one critic has put it:

> All of Beyala's novels locate and speak for that sense of a limit to communication – and in most of her work this is intensified into an acute sense of alienation and of the compulsion to silence imposed on this. In every case the alienated subject is female and her alienation is from the society of men – that is, from the expectations men generally have of her and the way these expectations are formalized and legit-imised within the community, not just by men but also by conservative women acting as their accomplices. (Dunton 1997: 211–12)

The Sun Hath Looked Upon Me is set in the grim world of urban pros-titution, giving voice to the multitude of women who are trapped in African ghettos. Ateba, a young African slum dweller, has her world rocked by the arrival of Jean Zepp, the lodger, who forces a sexual relationship upon her; an old neighbourhood prostitute dies; and Ateba's best friend is killed by a bungled abortion. Trapped between traditional values, male demands and the need to survive, Ateba seeks to end the tyranny of men, whom she holds responsible for this suffering. The novel opens with a preface by an invisible narrator outlining her hidden, silent knowledge, of acts attributable to the arrival of men in the world. The narrator envisages the novel as a correction to history: 'I wanted them to learn how the confusion of values, ideas, feelings, memories had ended up by killing history all the way back to its beginnings' (*The Sun*: 2). Framed by this preface, the novel then becomes the narrator's powerful portrayal of Ateba, her dawning thoughts about selfhood and realisations of identity as she emerges into adulthood. A quiet and unassuming teenager, taking care of her demanding and tyrannical Aunt Ada's needs, Ateba creates imaginary women to whom she talks as a substitute for her mother Betty who abandoned her when she was small. Living in the slum area of a city known as the 'Quartier Général' or the 'QG' (where inhabitants are known as 'qugees'), their life is desolate and poverty-stricken, and an income is derived from Aunt Ada renting out rooms in her house. The reader is introduced to the lodger Jean Zepp at the very beginning of the narrative, as he takes a room in the house. Zepp is absorbed in his own misogyny and his own enjoyment of violence to females: 'he loves fear; he loves suffering, he loves the abyss' (*The Sun*: 9). Ateba's first speech in the novel asserts a resigned acceptance of self: 'I am who I am' (*The Sun*: 7). Despite this, Ateba's imagination reflects upon male violence and she is aware all too often that she is 'other', defined by man. Ateba is later described as 'the nothing that makes the whole' (*The Sun*: 22), and she frequently ponders the general nothingness of women, their absence (*The Sun*: 22). This is structurally reinforced by the 'men whose idea of women is merely that which they are not' (*The Sun*: 101).

Although initially intrigued by Zepp, she is quiet, silent, and pent up in front of his violent speech to her, as he forcibly imposes himself upon her. Her tears are her realisation that she is not in full possession of her own identity, that she is in fact a victim of masculine power, that she has been severed from a once purified existence now tainted by the advent of man:

> She weeps, she asks her tears to come, to keep coming, to transform her life into one gigantic lake and to purify it, to sanctify her life. Since man has darkened her with slander, as he has sullied her with his hands. Oh! If only the stars knew this! Before, Ateba was woman. She was thousands of women. Was she beautiful? One couldn't say that she was beautiful because ugliness didn't exist, seeing that beauty was an accident in the life of man, and since he was running around the streets shouting out his disgust with the rest, with all that was not himself. (*The Sun*: 9)

Zepp, as a man, manages his liberation through the oppression of women: 'He will look at her body, he will welcome it into his memory in spite of himself, himself notwithstanding. In order to set himself free, he will call on suffering, on punishment' (*The Sun*: 10). Zepp's oppressive actions are a traumatic interruption of Ateba's life: 'But like a bruise, her body preserves the imprint of him who only a few moments earlier leaned into her. To keep on trying is useless since the memory is opened up' (*The Sun*: 11). Zepp causes a wound to surface, or he is that wound itself. Ateba figures herself as the

embodiment of the persecuted woman: 'She feels that they're touching her, that she's engulfed in hatred. She is these thousands of
women from whom the children have been torn away. Hatred has to
be ... She is an exile. Hatred is justified ... They've driven her from
her land. If she doesn't hate she'll skid around' (*The Sun*: 12). Women
are represented as palimpsests of the history of masculine sexual
violence: 'They are books, enormous quantities of books, in which are
inscribed the monstrous crimes of man's inhumanity to mankind'
(*The Sun*: 15–16). In this mixed state of physical disgust and nostalgic yearning, Ateba desires a new world, a woman's world, free of the
corrupting masculine hand. Although censored by social pressures,
Ateba's later love for Irène (*The Sun*: 107) is one manifestation of this
desire. Yet Ateba lives and suffers a traumatic anxiety, an unspoken
crisis in her past, which manifests itself in frequent fainting fits:

> A sudden anxiety paralyses her when she enters the house. She's under
> the impression that she has suddenly been plunged into a maze with
> unknown offshoots running from it. The spirits of ancestors spring up.
> Their groans illuminate the house and transform it into an enormous
> inferno. Ateba shrieks, her voice leaves her, the screams flow back into
> her body, one on top of the other. She can no longer command them, she
> no longer wants to be in command ...
>
> Unsteadily, Ateba straightens up again. She holds on to the wall to
> steady herself and wipes her forehead. Since Betty left her, she's been
> having these fainting spells. They are not merely the whims of an aban-
> doned child. It's something else, an anguish that wounds her, eats away
> at her, bores into her before setting her whole being on fire ... She is no
> longer the same, she's not quite herself any more. Sure, she is still
> obedient and, as always, she washes, she cooks, she gives rub-downs.
> But deep inside herself other words are being born which she fiercely
> holds in out of fear of Ada, of others, and above all of herself – since she
> no longer knows, she no longer sees, since she's standing on the edge of
> the abyss, since madness is calling her ... She constructs dams to
> contain it. Dams with known landmarks, so that rationality won't
> escape her again, so that she won't catch the madness again. (*The
> Sun*: 19)

Although one might be tempted to ascribe Ateba's fears, mixed
emotions and stressed anxieties to adolescent psychology, this would
ignore the way in which the novel explores the definition of African
womanhood as the consequence of construction and determination by
patriarchal sexual violence and misogyny. Ateba's existence becomes
symptomatic of the condition of womanhood. The novel repeatedly
extends Ateba's experiences and realisations as those of 'many
women'. During the circumcision ritual of a neighbour's son, the
invisible narrator pointedly states: 'I sing and evoke the memory of
women torn apart by this sex organ so carefully prepared for
manhood' (*The Sun*: 21). Indeed, men are constantly associated with

violence, power, physical and sexual dominance. Zepp's 'attitude of supreme judge' and 'Temperamental god!' (*The Sun*: 23), leads Ateba to understand 'more clearly why these male bodies have managed to bring humanity to its knees. They are of the ilk that destroys, pillages, mutilates, but manages to wash its hands of it all in the wink of an eye. In his eyes she reads his desire to subdue her one day, just for the pleasure of humiliating her' (*The Sun*: 23). Even when Zepp makes what appears to be a reconciliatory overture to Ateba, relations between men and women still prove to be a source of acute anxiety for Ateba:

> 'I want us to become friends,' he says without any preliminaries.
> 'Oh!'
> 'Is that all you have to say?'
> A veneer of ice engulfs and buries her. How can you describe it? What do you call it? How do you allow it to settle. Anxiety? Happiness? Man wants to become woman's friend ... It will be necessary to join his thinking with hers; man will leave his place, he will approach her, he will kneel down at her feet, he will no longer be his own master. She will let him direct her fantasies, he will speak to her with love, with gentleness, he will proclaim to the heavens all that unites them from now on. But why do the stars that pierce the sky not unite with the sun? Why doesn't dawn join with dusk? When will morning come, but which morning? Is it a question of this morning, or yesterday morning? Woman will no longer know since man will bump up against the obstacle of happiness, since he will forget love in favour of the flame of desire ... He will no longer admit he never wanted to join in with woman's dream, but rather with her flesh. (*The Sun*: 39)

From the outset a rapprochment between the sexes appears inarticulable and fills her with dread and trepidation. Just imagining man surrendering his domination, his desire, to the woman's 'dream', appears to be a fantasy in itself, as far as the novel's perspective on gender is concerned. Such a unity of mind and action is as likely as day and night merging as one – an unthinkable concept. As far as Beyala is concerned, there is an unbridgeable gulf between the sexes, and one that poses an interminable future of strife.

Ateba is consequently exiled, alienated and isolated. Her messages in bottles are sent into a void, communications with imagined recipients but they are all one-way messages with no response (*The Sun*: 26–7), or addressed to an abstract concept of 'Woman': 'Woman. You fulfil my need for love. To you alone can I say certain things; I don't have to be me any more, I can melt away in you, for I say them better to you than to myself ... Without you, I would be but the shadow of a life that apologises for living' (*The Sun*: 41). Ateba's messages are not dialogues but monologues, severed communications. We are repeatedly told that Ateba can no longer remember, that her memory is impaired by a lack of adequate support. In fact, she is severed from memory as well as meaningful dialogue (*The Sun*: 26). Furthermore, the novel associated man with history. At one crucial moment as Jean Zepp forces her into a brutal sexual act, Ateba seeks to escape back to the sea in her imagination, but finds that it is severed from her by man:

> Crouched. On her knees ... The moon, the sun, the stars want it so ... Unless ... unless she can go back into the sea. But the sea is no longer. Man has imprisoned it in memory; there is no more sea, the sea has become a myth ... And if she were to stop the flow of history by tearing his sex organ off with her teeth? ... But Ateba Léocadie does nothing, says nothing. All she has left are her tears which she tries to hold back, and that as usual, form a screen behind which she contemplates her helplessness.
>
> One truth has just forced itself upon her, still fuzzy, certainly, but a truth nevertheless: historically, as things stand today, whatever she might do, whatever she might say, she will always be wrong. This is man. (*The Sun*: 24–5)

In this respect, history places women in the wrong since it is written and constructed by men. Ateba is seeking to rediscover a womanhood not defined by men. It is no accident that her realisation occurs when Ateba's agency is apparently curtailed by male sexual violence and domination. Masculinity dominates history and memory, and thereby obstructs Ateba's agency, her determination, and her reconnection with a past wholeness, which is metaphorically constructed in the image of the sea. The past, in the form of tradition, acts as an obstacle to Ateba: 'Everywhere [she] runs into the stumbling blocks of tradition. Everywhere they accumulate, obstructing the view, clogging her throat, scratching the hand so shyly stretched out towards the light. Alone' (*The Sun*: 56). Yet in other ways, the past in the form of her lost mother Betty, who abandoned her in her childhood, represents for Ateba all that is desirable. Ateba constantly seeks her mother, to recover that past when Betty was with her, before abandonment. *Before*. This word reverberates throughout the novel: *before* man arrived, *before* Ateba was abandoned, *before* Zepp arrived, *before* Ateba lived with her Aunt Ada, *before* ... Constantly assailed by images from the past, painful remembrances, parts of her memory, Ateba's present life is ruptured by a traumatic absence which she struggles to articulate. In many respects, Betty, the absent mother, is the key traumatic absence in Ateba's life. She keeps going back to memories of Betty – Betty invades her present, despite being absent, *because she is absent*: 'To crack the wall of the past. To shred the memory. To find her present once again, confused and fragmented by endless talk. To find Betty again ... Betty ... To find the signs again. To retrace the chapters of a life. To find Betty again. Her smells. Her tastes. Her wishes. To catalogue the woman so as to find herself. To not be a qugee. To not quite be a qugee. To find her own elsewhere hidden in Betty's secrets' (*The Sun*: 56).

Severed from herself, Ateba seeks her own wholeness: 'To find herself again. To bring back to life that part of herself that had gone away. To move about in order to thaw out. To walk a different way' (*The Sun*: 52). Ateba basically desires to be purified. Standing in the rain, she imagines herself to be symbolically cleansed:

> She is under the impression that each drop of water is making her immaculately clean and taking her out of the QG and the black filth of its sewers. She is under the impression that she is rediscovering purity, that purity which custom claims to hold on to by sheer force, perfuming it with theories and sullying it with inconsistencies. (*The Sun*: 91)

Never in complete control of her identity, Ateba gradually becomes aware of the schizophrenic existence that she is forced to play, although this realisation itself brings a degree of self-control: 'woman, mistress, man's woman. She has found her role, she almost feels better; suddenly she becomes two Atebas. The woman and the actress. The ordinary and the extraordinary' (*The Sun*: 99). The final action of the novel appears to be a sublimation of her love for Irène, and the murder of her male client seems to be part of the some retributive vengeance for all the hatred of man piled up inside Ateba, and for the death of her abused female friend Irène.

If *The Sun Hath Looked Upon Me* appears to be somewhat partial in its view of masculinity, Beyala's novel *Your Name Shall Be Tanga* (1988) shows little adjustment to this perspective. Two young women are thrown together by injustice and violence in the same prison cell. The first one, Tanga, has experienced nothing but debauchery and poverty since the day that her father raped her, and she has been subjected to all sorts of abominations and vices meted out by a corrupt society. She is now about to die and the police want to force her to talk. The second woman, the white woman Anna-Claude, is a police stooge and labelled mad, although she is not as mad as her tormentors claim. One is African, the other of French-Jewish origin. One is young, the other old. Yet they are both hoping for love, and as prison life deteriorates, they grow closer.

The two female protagonists constantly seek to block out their memories: 'I stop time, I suspend the ladder of imagination, I clamber up, I change my clock, put a veil over my past' (*Tanga*: 13). Structured as a remembrance of her past despite herself, Tanga narrates her grim story of incest, prostitution, bereavement and crime, making it evident that men are explicitly answerable for much of this, inextricably associated as they are with sexual violence and power (for example, Hassan on pp. 15–16). Men accuse women of devouring speech, pasts, histories and words, yet Tanga's realisation of womanhood comes with her experience of sexual intercourse with a man: 'Woman's existence comes to me now. I hadn't known it, yet I recognise it. A memory engraved in the darkness of time' (*Tanga*: 19). Womanliness emerges when male sexual violence is perpetrated against women, and it is a sort of vestigial role and type buried in Tanga's memory and past, a sort of knowledge that has lain dormant in Tanga's unconsciousness. The male prison warders, for example, conform to type: they are vicious misogynists, cruel beyond belief, barbaric and inhuman (see *Tanga*: 32). Ultimately, Tanga is perplexed about the feasibility of life in such circumstances, especially when many women are caught in what she sees as a self-destructive sexual loop: 'How do you live in a country that goes along upside down? Turn towards the sky? ... Prisoners caught within the barbed wire of tradition, the women roam around muck-filled streets, forever and always following the sex organs that tear them to pieces' (*Tanga*: 90). Tanga has been the object of constant abuse from both her father and mother, as well as masculine society more generally, and her present is wracked by 'wounds of unhappiness' (*Tanga*: 45), the consequences of traumatic memories of a past that refuses to be internalised, 'the poisoned remnants of pain, every trace left by its calloused steps' (*Tanga*: 45). Indeed, Tanga's story to Anna-Claude constantly reminds the reader of Tanga's violations, trauma, pain and hurt as the result of a series of male sexual assaults: 'I find myself vanquished again, forgotten as always ... But in Iningué, all that the earth produces is pain like a growth in the flesh' (*Tanga*: 68). Tanga's life appears to be haunted by her unassimilable past, in which 'Everything becomes a sterile list. All that's left is fear and disgust with the departing dream' (*Tanga*: 70).

Rather than utilising the past or memories to rewrite the present, Tanga's life is constantly victimised by past memories, occasionally triggered by words or phrases that take her back to forgotten scenes in her childhood:

'Life is so very hard!'
How many times have I heard those words? Once – a thousand times perhaps! ... And always they had the power to take me back to the past. (*Tanga*: 84)

Acting like a verbal madeleine cake, the phrase triggers memories which cause the trauma to emerge. Tanga's life is dogged by past experiences that resist integration into narrative memory, into understanding and communicability: 'The past attacks me, always the past' (*Tanga*: 89). This molestation by events which refuse to be tamed eventually leads Tanga to proclaim 'I want to shut off my memory. It's persecuting me' (*Tanga*: 93). Tanga desires to wipe out the past, to erase memories, and to organise her present into an acceptable order. In the face of her collapsing world, the chaos and disorder that structure her every memory and living moment, Tanga is obsessed with getting order into her life or story (see *Tanga*: 20 and 21, 'I'll put order into my own story . . .'): 'I want to undo my life. Too many misfortunes have tied it into knots. I want to iron it out, to put it in order at the end of the path that love has traced' (*Tanga*: 80). It is in the act of narration that Tanga finds a means to this end: 'The story must be – to challenge the disruptive elements that are unsuited to the enlightenment of the state of grace; to plunge into reverie to cross the threshold of the impossible universe. To invent' (*Tanga*: 89). In fact, Tanga's narrative opens up unviolated spaces: 'Then silence filtered into the word, into a space where consciousness did not become obliterated as the earth is obliterated along the road upon which men tread' (*Tanga*: 129). Furthermore, Tanga's narrative gradually establishes a liberating relationship for Anna-Claude: 'With her deepening knowledge of Tanga, she brings back uninhabited periods of time, forgotten practices, formed under the reign of hatred. She tells herself that she stands at the frontier of eternity and that it is her role to bequeath to men the fermentations of History' (*Tanga*: 61). While the final page of the novel seems to gesture towards an identification of Anna-Claude and Tanga as a result of their gradual solidarity of consciousness in a rebuttal of exploitative and abusive forces, there are points in the narrative at which both women resist, or show pain, as they attempt to connect their identities. Indeed, Anna-Claude cannot simply soak up Tanga's narrative because it is a such a painful experience. Furthermore, Anna-Claude has arrived with an agenda of her own – the search for a man – although her description of life in Paris suggests a confused, empty existence. Connecting with Tanga offers Anna-Claude an opportunity for self-affirmation as a woman struggling to define herself. Yet while Tanga and Anna-Claude may have similar needs for self-discovery, it does not automatically follow that their needs fuse together to become one assured female identity. It is fair to say that, when faced with the brutality of the prison system, the women find comfort and support from one another. Nevertheless, as Tanga points out, Anna-Claude is in the final analysis barred from assuming her identity as a result of her different race and nationality. Anna-Claude's apparent descent into madness also suggests that the further she focuses upon Tanga's identity, the more she is damaged by the brutality of men (see Nfah-Abbenyi 1997).

These are unquestionably pessimistic and uncompromising novels. Beyala's first two novels, set in a deteriorating and collapsing Africa, are pervaded by imagery of death, decay and detritus, and depict a collapsing home in which children are sexually abused, and mothers and fathers act as pimps for their own children. As Ayo Abiétou Coly notes, 'In that continent which is gradually falling apart, the African is neither an "under developed person" of the precolonial era, nor the so-called "developing individual" that the "suns of independences" were supposed to bring. He/she is an individual who is disappearing and disintegrating' (Coly 2002). Despite Coly's generalist description, Beyala specifically represents this disintegration as that of women who are the victims of masculine violence. Ateba and Tanga are classic cases of trauma. This trauma is unequivocally the conse-quence of patriarchal brutality. Their narratives show women strug-gling to come to terms with unresolved experiences, battling with a past that refuses to be theirs, wrestling with a history that resists absorption into a narrative to which they can lay claim as rightful authors. These narratives are an attempt to unlock an intolerable past, and to gradually reinsert themselves into a history as agents through a process of 'working-through', relegating these surfacing memories firmly to the past as they forge a better present and future. Beyala's two novels expose the debilitating myths that obscure the unpleasant facts of life in many neo-colonial environments with their rigidly defined social roles. While *Your Name Shall Be Tanga* may well be a multi-purpose manifesto directed against the oppression of children and the market exploitation of women (see Darlington 2003), the novel is also part of a concerted fictional demystification of western ideologies of Africa. Beyala attempts a demystification of those myths while seeking to construct a different world: where woman is no longer a *male* construct, a sexual object of male fantasy and imagination, but rather a polysemic female subject that articu-lates and discloses the conflicts, contradictions and traumas of her historical situation.

'A nothingness so strong that it was a presence': the violation of colonialism in Lindsey Collen's *The Rape of Sita*

The debilitating connection of colonial violence and trauma and the sexual oppression of African women is nowhere made clearer than in the novelist Lindsey Collen's powerful book *The Rape of Sita* (first British edition 1995), winner of the 1994 Commonwealth Writers Prize for the African Region. Right from the Preface, this is a 'fallen' novel, a 'knowing' novel, which plays with the conventions of realism and flirts with the paradigms of postmodernist fiction (*Rape*: 1–5). The narrator, Iqbal the Umpire, worries away at the linearity of narrative, concerned with the status of truthfulness, authenticity and credibility. Genuflecting to oral narrative and its properties in the opening section, the story begins by telling of Mohun Jab, Sita's father and revolutionary union activist, how he sires Sita and how she then meets her lover Dharma. The novel dwells on accidents and moments of coincidence, and how these interrupt or influence people's actions. In this respect, Iqbal arbitrates over a narrative that embraces stories of broken languages, broken memories, broken identities, all of which gradually piece together the broken life of Sita. Indeed, Sita and Dharma are heroine and hero of mythical proportions – Sita is a strong, wise, powerful woman leader, and Dharma has charisma and strength. Collen's choice of the name of Sita stirred up a furore with Hindu fundamentalists, causing a backlash not dissimilar to the Rushdie Affair, in which Hindus objected to the transposition of sacred names into profane contexts (Collen 1994). These characterisations clearly echo the novel's intertexts of Shakespeare's *The Rape of Lucrece*, T. S. Eliot's 'The Waste Land', William Blake's 'The Tiger', Adrienne Rich's 'Diving into the Wreck' and the Rāmāyana, the ramifications of which have been illuminatingly explored by Sue Thomas (Thomas 1997).

The novel also makes clear from the outset that the 'truthfulness' of this narrative is tied up with memory and the processes of recollection (*Rape*: 23). The problem with which Sita has to grapple is that she has a 'hole' in her memory, a blank memory where 'At least twelve hours were missing from her memory' (*Rape*: 32), and where 'No memory was left' (*Rape*: 33). Sita's narrative is the recovery of this lost period of her life, dredging the various 'clues' to the lost memory from her 'diving': 'So that night, she went to work on it. With a will of iron. And she dived again and again all night. Diving into her memory. Relentless, she was. Diving into the unconscious. With cold determination. Diving into that opaque, dark, murky underworld' (*Rape*: 33). This image of diving down into the waters of the unconscious, searching, is a significant image for hunting the repressed, forgotten memory, an association that the narrative explicitly links with a traumatic event in her past: 'In 1987, five years later, that is five years later than the lost night, Dharma and Sita had gone to Reunion, and she had an episode of illness of some kind ... The memory of it was there ... Crystal clear. And never having been so much as looked at, let alone interpreted, worked out, analysed, it was as alive in her memory as if it had been yesterday. She looked at this memory. This clue. She had a bout of transitory madness. Insanity. Psychosis. No less' (*Rape*: 34). Sita is here clearly trying to come to terms with a traumatic episode in her past as she searches her memory for the signs of the disruption: 'Must it be, she thought in horror, for a memory of some form of duplicity? Of lies? Was there shame in it? Was there guilt?' (*Rape*: 35). Then eventually Sita finds something, 'The presence of an absence. The hole' (*Rape*: 35). This is analysed and interpreted in the following passage: '*What she had found: Rage. The rage of the history of wounded womankind.*

*And with it: Slavery. The slavery of humans historically doomed to be
unable to move'* (*Rape*: 37, original italics). As we shall examine, the
key nexus for the novel is the interconnection between womankind,
slavery and trauma. This section of the novel depicts Sita searching
her memory for the traumatic event that has produced a blockage in
her memory. It is a series of staged revelations as she explores her
memory, unpacking the different signs and vestiges of the forgotten
event. The consequences are a variety of emotions – anger, hate,
rage, frustration, feelings of imprisonment, objectified in the oscillat-
ing series of images of a hole, ball, knot, well and hall. The word that
is frequently used to describe Sita is 'sequestrated', as she constantly
feels hemmed in by the rape and its traumatic memory. This traumatic event is also linked to the deferred articulation in language:
'*What happens to a sentence deferred?*' (*Rape*: 37). Sita's answer is
that 'The words had been an introduction, prepared and never
spoken' (*Rape*: 38). Echoing the women silenced by rape in Ovid's
Metamorphosis and in T. S. Eliot's 'The Waste Land', this whole
process of self-reflection by Sita corresponds closely to a description
of a psychic trauma, and it gradually becomes clear that the narrative is predicated on precisely the model of a 'working-through' of the
past in order to 'cure' the present.

Moving through this passage of self-exploration is Sita's impression that 'buried' is a key word, a word that quite literally 'haunts'
her (*Rape*: 38). This seems like a nightmare, as the word 'buries'
resonates through her memory and triggers the sequence of events
that leads to her murderous action. This word recurs throughout the
narrative, since at a later point Sita confronts the word again,
'haunting her and taunting her' (*Rape*: 82): 'Two sets of meanings
jostled for her attention. The metaphorical. Burial to cover something up, to hide something, to forget something, to put something
out of sight, and out of mind ... And then the literal sense. Burial
after a death' (*Rape*: 80–1). Associated in her mind with T. S. Eliot's
'The Waste Land', Sita explores the possibilities of murder, death
and resurrection. In all cases, Sita finds it links to an unusual
memory: 'It's a kind of memory but it's not like an ordinary memory.
It's horrifying and recent and undigested. It's monstrous. She finds
her own anger. Staring at her. Raw. Can one behold such a thing?'
(*Rape*: 82). This is the full effect of the trauma, figured as an interruption in Sita's life. This persistent interruption also occurs in the
shape of a crowd of listeners (Iqbal is always giving metanarrative
advice), and in a repetitive stylistic feature of the narrative in which
sentences of quite well-known phrases are left unfinished, such as
'Into the heart of' (*Rape*: 104) and other unfinished sentences. Such
indecisive utterances are indicative of Sita's inability to articulate
her full awareness, her full consciousness. The following strain of

Sita's consciousness literalises the manner in which her ability to communicate has been interrupted, arrested, truncated and traumatised by the past event: 'The scene of the. Of something she has gone through, but had lost, and which she had no idea was in her memory. Of something she had done, but couldn't remember it. Was it something terrible? She didn't know at all' (*Rape*: 106). Sita's consciousness is then linked to the collective memory: 'And yet this fact united her with all the other people in the bus. As though they too had terrible memories that they didn't know they had. Of submission, of humiliation, of defeat. And they, like her, remembered an anger so vast as to be impossible to keep in mind, in brain, in head. Murders' (*Rape*: 106). The depiction of Sita as a strong woman striving to resist her own oppression is linked to her role as a champion of the oppressed, an inspiration to the weak, as her painful and angry search to come to terms with her past extends beyond her physical violation to encompass other forms of powerlessness and oppression.

Gender is the principal context in which this trauma occurs. At times, there is a blurring of gender in the novel: Iqbal is a man who thought he was a woman (*Rape*: 42), while Ton Tipyer the stonemason is described as 'a man like a woman' (*Rape*: 41). It has been suggested that this 'androgynous subjectivity' and 'destablisation of gender' identity is part of a concerted attempt to undermine 'the vestiges of colonial mentality' (Thomas 1997: 125). However, it is generally the female that is the important gender in the novel; as Iqbal says when describing the monkey-god Hanuman, 'he could do with his own hands what women can do with their bodies: produce, reproduce, create, make, invent. He was magic' (*Rape*: 41). The development of Sita's political consciousness does derive from Ton Tipyer, yet more importantly, from her mother Doorga's line. The matrilineal family of Sita is persistently outlined and the narrative makes clear that Sita comes from a powerful line of women, beginning with the power that is her mother Doorga:

> Doorga was a legend in her own life. And what's a legend, if not someone who tries to get into the flow of history, out of the mud of the past, into a realm of rationality that humankind deserves?
>
> Sita was brought up with a sense of history, and a sense of progress, and a very sound sense of the role of the individual in society. Neither an omnipotent fancy of herself, not an important image of herself. (*Rape*: 95)

Doorga infiltrates history and pulls myth into reason. Sita's and Doorga's lives are about shaping and determining their own lives and those of others themselves, and they stem from a long line of famous and influential women called Anjalay and Olga Olande. These are women who have claimed agency and control, and believe in the power of education to endow people with agency: 'Wisdom. Knowledge of things past and expectation of things to come' (*Rape*: 94), as Doorga instructs her daughter Sita. These are women bound by the common devotion to social reform through the enlistment of the working class against all forms of oppression. Indeed, the political context of such women's actions occur within a repeated history of Mauritius and Réunion as British and French colonies, and the institution of slavery that occurred thereon. In this context of patriarchal colonialism, 'From slave days some women have kept the laughter as a weapon against oppression' (*Rape*: 84).

Mauritius has been a Dutch, French and British colony, and the colonial history of Réunion and its vestigial effects are insistently on Sita's consciousness: 'In everyone she saw the same feeling. The same outline. As if drawn by a good artist with one stroke of the brush: *submission*. In a word ... Even in the early morning, you wake up to it, she thought. Another day of being colonized. The word went round and round in her mind: colonized' (*Rape*: 105). Colonisation is explicitly linked with all forms of oppression, but especially that of women, as male colonial administrators and businessmen perpetuate a modern-day enslavement based upon gender: 'French colonial servants, professionals, businessmen and sailors, and other nondescript officials of the *metropole*, were there. They were there to meet tarted up *Reyone* girls ... The men treated them like toys ... looked at them like you look at an animal in the zoo ... Like young slave-prospectors buying new womanslaves. Sheslaves' (*Rape*: 108). Patriarchy's voyeurism, its objectification and specularisation of women, its power through the male gaze, is explicitly correlated with colonisation. When Sita considers her aggressor, Rowan Tarquin, she is overcome by nausea: 'Is it the effect, she thought, of two hundred years of colonization, dominating me in one fell swoop? "I have taken into my body what everyone here has felt for two hundred years? The ghosts of the past are so alive that they have started to haunt me?"' (*Rape*: 109). Later, when the event of the rape is described, Sita construes her situation as an explicit 'working-through' of the oppression of women and the oppression of colonisation: 'Perhaps the revolt she had felt on the part of the girls was not against a rapist, but against colonization, she had thought. It was both. They are the same thing' (*Rape*: 149). Tarquin is described as a crude patriarchal thug: 'He was still in this woman-hating state. A state. The state. The colonial state. The capitalist state. The state of power. The state of repression. The patriarchal state. The state. *Something rotten in the state*' (*Rape*: 149). In Sita's case, 'She felt the rape of centuries against women descend on to her shoulders. Like the weight of chains. Like the head-locks fastened on women slaves. The patriarchy was what made her the victim. Only in patriarchy is rape a weapon. She knew it. She'd often learnt it before. Now she was being made to go through it' (*Rape*: 150). Entrapment, slavery, colonialism, patriarchy and the oppression of women are unequivocally connected. In this culmination, this is the closest that *The Rape of Sita* comes to explicitly establishing the correspondence of Sita's physical violation as a woman as a precise extension of the logic of patriarchal colonial rule, and the trauma caused by that rape is equated to the trauma caused by colonisation. The blockage in being able to articulate her violation is the gap that trauma presents between discourse and event:

> She missed her cue.
>
> Like a conundrum, the fact of her very thinking about the dilemma was, at least in part, the cause of her missing the moment of a good decision in the dilemma. And she missed her cue.
>
> And life went on as if she did not have those words to say, as if there wasn't anything waiting inside her head to be said. Life went on. (*Rape*: 178)

Ultimately, the novel is about the ability to speak, to narrate one's life, to find the words to put one's life into acts and arrange its events into a meaningful and understandable pattern, despite the fact that life continues regardless of this act of articulation. Yet one might question exactly who is speaking for whom in this novel. Collen's subject-position is complex. Born in South Africa, Collen is now a Mauritian resident writing about Indo-Mauritian society; and this itself raises complicated questions about the viewpoint of representation, even if the author does not finally feel that the position from which she writes is a crucial determinant in her act of narration. The rape is associated in the novel with the ability of having agency and being able to speak and mean 'no' and 'yes' (*Rape*: 180). Women like Sita seek to make history and to exercise their agency, while rape is an action that seeks to pull women back into passivity, a 'victim of the male's will to act' (*Rape*: 180). Iqbal's final words are about the reasons he has written Sita's story, as a record of the events, partly as a release for Sita's daughter as a hope for the future and partly as a vision of future freedom and unison of genders:

> And with our minds that work together. And in unison. We will all be man and we will all be woman. And we will love ourselves as we are.
>
> And we will have wanted to be free. Freedom. And then we will be free. And we will have wanted to be equal. Equality. And then we will become equal.
>
> Such are the hopes of Iqbal for another story. Another history. In the future. (*Rape*: 197)

As Sue Thomas argues, 'Iqbal implies that the ideal nation-family needs to give "women" the space and time to absorb rape and "announce" it publicly' (Thomas 1997: 133). The 'working-through' of Sita's trauma is to open up a new era in the lives of women as well as the lives of Mauritians, as they forge their future political independences.

Conclusion

The impact of African women's writing upon the African literary scene has been significant in the past quarter of a century. Male writers increasingly acknowledge the power of women's writing, as well as the crucial role that women play within the continent's political future. Writers like Ngugi, Ousmane, Farah and Achebe are more genuinely involved in taking into account women's perspectives on matters, in ways that are more than simply paying lip-service to them. As I suggested in my opening paragraphs to this chapter, many of these African women's narratives are first-person narratives of women aiming to define their past and to engrave themselves within and against the cultures that buttress that experience; and this process of discovery becomes the source of a mode of healing of the narrating self. Indeed, one might construe what happens in African women's literatures as a form of 'scriptotherapy', in that 'the subject of enunciation theoretically restores a sense of agency to the hitherto fragmented self, now recast as a protagonist of his or her life drama. Through the artistic replication of a coherent subject-position, the life-writing project generates a healing narrative that temporarily restores the fragmented self to an empowered position of psychological agency' (Henke 1999: xvi). The 'sick' woman is 'cured' thanks to her progressive awareness of the past. She succeeds in unearthing her childhood experiences and emotions, focusing more and more on the patriarchal system that is at the source of the repressive mechanism of her unconscious. In other words, she understands repression to be a consequence of oppression; oppression of children by parents, of the body by culture, of the colony by the *métropole*. Trauma violently shatters the (perhaps fantasised) image of the integrated subject and the effort to heal psychic wounds invariably involves a need to substantiate or reconfirm the self, which often entails convictions of transcendence. Yet such transcendence needs to be treated cautiously, since it is only through narratives that insistently undermine and overturn the discursive dependence on colonial tropologies and their explicit inscription of physical and psychical violence on the female body, that any 'working-through' can begin to be achieved. As Ama Ata Aidoo states, 'In any case, the question is not just the past or the present, but which factors out of both the past and the present represent for us the most dynamic forces for the future' (Aidoo 1977: 116). In analysing and reading African women's writing from the past thirty years, a clear trajectory emerges: of an increasingly more strident and outspoken stance against all forms of oppression in general and the oppression of women in particular. In marked contrast to the much more conciliatory tendency of their predecessors, many writers of the last ten years seem determined to take control of their own lives, wresting a space for their own actions, and steering a new course to women's histories. As the francophone Ivory Coast writer Véronique Tadjo states in *A Vol d'Oiseau*, 'It is time to keep [men] at arm's length and to teach them a new alphabet' (*A Vol d'Oiseau*: 54, my translation). Writing that new alphabet means constructing new letters and new forms, and forging anew the future through a 'working-through' of the gendered past.

Notes

[1]   See Innes and Rooney, who argue that African women's literature explores the *aporiae* in African men's writing: 'In Achebe's early novels of rural Igbo life, the roles and experiences of women may be said to be marginalised. Writers such as Flora Nwapa, Ama Ata Aidoo, and Buchi Emecheta recapitulate Achebe's point of departure, addressing colonial blindspots, while they address the blindspots in this very point of departure, with regard to both gender and writing' (Innes and Rooney 1997: 194).

[2]   Anthonia Akpabio Ekpa describes the history of the development of African feminism, and distinguishes its preoccupations from those of western feminism, especially what she perceives to be the exclusionist aspect of western feminism. See Ekpa 2000.

[3]   Anthony Chennells observes that *Nervous Conditions* identifies oppression not merely in Rhodesian settler racism, but also in the conservativeness of male-dominated Shona society, and that the effects of colonialism on the colonised differ between men and women. See Chennells 1996.

[4]   Neil ten Kortenaar argues that *Nervous Conditions* displays a compulsive doubling and splitting of characters, as the author splits herself structurally between the two protagonists. See Kortenaar 1997.

5

Imprisonment narratives: history through the eyes of hostages

a prison, even though entirely surrounded by walls, is a splendidly illuminated theatre of history. (Milan Kundera, *The Book of Laughter and Forgetting*)

Narratives of imprisonment have become a defining genre of African writing in the second half of the twentieth century. Many influential writers and politicians of colonial, neo-colonial and postcolonial Africa have been imprisoned for various reasons, and their accounts of detainment have provided Africa with some of its most stimulating and provocative writing. Diverse people such as Elechi Amadi, J. M. Kariuk, Maina wa Kinyatti, Jack Mapanje, Ken Saro-Wiwa, Wole Soyinka, Ngugi wa Thiong'o and Koigi wa Wamwere have been imprisoned by various African regimes; and the writing is as equally diverse in its manifestation, ranging across autobiography, letters, poetry, diaries, memoirs and political essays. These imprisoned authors have more often than not been imprisoned for their political or ideological beliefs that have been (or still are) at odds with the militaristic, dictatorial or ethnically different leaderships of their indigenous nations. Situated almost as a sub-genre within this body of African imprisonment narratives is the vast range of writing that has emerged as a painful testimony to the barbarities of that singular institutionalised racist ideology of apartheid, and the accounts by political detainees incarcerated on Robben Island and other South African high-security prisons: this includes works by people such as Breyten Breytenbach, Dennis Brutus, Jeremy Cronin, Michael Dingake, Moses Dlamini, Ruth First, Bram Fischer, Denis Goldberg, Helen Joseph, Ahmed Kathrada, Mosiuoa Patrick Lekota, Hugh Lewin, Mac Maharaj, Caesarina Kona Makhoere, Nelson Mandela, Govan Mbeki, Indres Naidoo, Lillian Ngoyi, Molefe Pheto and Albie Sachs. The sheer quantity of publication representing this particular country's history of political detainment testifies not only to the sheer tenacity of the system's opponents, but also to the world's appalled fascination with the politics of apartheid.[1] Many of these apartheid imprisonment narratives will find ready comparison-points with those of people like Soyinka and Ngugi, although the acuteness of the 'peculiar institution' of apartheid clearly does not pertain to their experiences.

Nevertheless, most of these imprisonment narratives derive from instances where the political regime has detained and tortured writers either for their political beliefs or as a result of racist ideologies. My principal contention is that these imprisonment narratives are themselves part of the consequences of a continental trauma of colonialism. Imprisonment narratives intersect with trauma in two ways. First, in the cases of the individuals, the incarceration acts as a traumatic rupture to their daily lives, relationships and careers. Second, as a genre, imprisonment narratives form part of a national and continental literature of trauma, or in those instances where there are accounts of torture, a 'literature of atrocity'. In both these cases, the interesting issue is the way that many of these narratives turn to querying the construction of the past, the representation of history, and the workings and function of memory, in the array of defence mechanisms and attempts to rationalise the barbarities of the state's actions. Furthermore, in attempting to understand the past, and figure out the reasons for one's imprisonment and torture, most of these narratives are forced to grapple with the problems of representation itself. For it is one of the ugly paradoxes of this sort of writing, where one is testifying to human brutality, that the literary representation of such acts achieves at best a 'terrible beauty'. The experiences of these detainees in prisons, in a similar way to those of the Holocaust, lie outside reason. In this respect, we might tentatively consider these testimonies as belonging to what Lawrence H. Langer has termed 'the literature of atrocity' (Langer 1975: xii). Consequently, these imprisonment narratives find that the traumatic disruption causes a crisis in the representation not just of the traumatic event itself but of the self.

Representing what Maurice Blanchot has termed an 'impossible reality' – the oxymoron duplicating the frustrated efforts of language to enclose irreducibly intractable material – tests all the writers (Blanchot 1986: 8, 29 & 38). The difficulty lies in our perception of brutality *as* reality, when brutality becomes the problem of the everyday and horror *is* normality. These witness narratives insistently return to themes that illustrate the aesthetic problem of reconciling normality with horror: the displacement of consciousness of life by the imminence and pervasiveness of death and torture; the violation of the coherence of the self; the assault on physical reality; the disintegration of the rational intelligence; and the disruption of chronological time. Although they dispel many traditional views of human nature and motive, moral theory, Enlightenment values and the heroic temper, these witnesses are not immune to the disparity between the events they record and their audience's expectations, or even their own. Most of the stories nurture not ethical insight but confusion, doubt and moral uncertainty. The gradual erosion of familiar reality, its displacement by a different, scarcely recognisable, threatening, amorphous externality providing no reassurance or support for the tottering spirit of the victim, is the overriding preoccupation of these witness narratives.

These accounts keep returning to the ways in which a system tries to break the individual from the community, to sever the individual from history; only to have that individual resist the system and reinforce individual identity against the domination, 'which, through an enforced isolation from the rest of humanity, forges in suffering new and stronger forms of solidarity with that community' (Clayton 1991: 137). In other words, these imprisonment narratives frequently manifest what might be called a dialectic of identity. The more insistently the state seeks to bury or erase the detainee's identity and his or her community, the more emphatically these narratives assert personal identity and call for stronger bonds of community. Foucault's description of imprisonment and the 'economy of suspended rights' (Foucault 1979: 11) focuses upon modern conceptions of penality and disciplinary power that are directed against the detainee's body, in particular the production of docile bodies. Yet the dialectic asserts resistance and active bodies, often inserting the activity into the very interstices of the penal system, or (as we shall see) the literal walls of the prison itself. Developing 'new bases of affiliation' with fellow inmates and detainees, these writings are 'potentially constructive' of a new discursive category that describes a collective experience emerging from a set of social relations that gives rise to a 'secular ideology' that is not based on bonds of race, ethnicity or, crucially, gender. For political detainees, attempts 'to silence their voices', to remove them from public political discourse, result in this proliferation of 'imprisonment narratives', which are themselves a rich source of documentation of 'memory writing'. As many theorists of autobiography have argued, repetition and memory are clearly crucial issues associated with the genre. Yet in the face of this assertion of selfhood and personal identity, how is one to read and treat these imprisonment narratives in the age of poststructuralism, when deconstruction and Lacanian psychoanalysis have exploded both the concepts of representation and of the self? Or when Michael Sprinker can contend that contemporary autobiography is marked by 'a pervasive and unsettling feature in modern culture', namely 'the gradual metamorphosis of an individual with a distinct, personal identity into a sign, a cipher'? (Sprinker 1980).

Does imprisonment impose a strangeness on the subject, alienating the self, in so far as the self becomes an unsettled, divided and dispersed being, in which self-reference is undermined, and the reality of subjectivity as dispersed and divided is mirrored in an equally fragmentary and discontinuous text? In this respect, can it be said that the pressures of imprisonment are similar to those of the decline of the subject in the paradigm shift of western culture? For if imprisonment is conceived of as a way of cutting one off from history, segregating and removing one from the community, then these memoirs, diaries, autobiographies and prison narratives are the result of a paradoxical struggle of power: the nation seeks to 'deface' the detainee, only for the detainee to give voice and face both to the self and to historical abstractions like a nation or a people in the memoir, testimony, or autobiography. Ngugi writes:

> The fact is that detention without trial is not only a punitive act of phys-
> ical and mental torture of a few patriotic individuals, but it is also a
> calculated act of psychological terror against the struggling millions. It
> is a terrorist programme for the psychological siege of the whole nation.
> That is why the practice of detention from the time of arrest to the time
> of release is deliberately inverted with mystifying ritualism. (Thiong'o
> 1981a: 13–14)

Therefore, prison narratives can be seen as attempts at 'national personification', or 'national re-facement' or re-embodiment. African imprisonment narratives – autobiographies, memoirs, diaries – like the similarly hybridised novels studied by Bakhtin, 'are pregnant with potential for new world views, with new "internal forms" for perceiving the world in words' (Bakhtin 1981: 360). Through analysing and differentiating the modalities of silence in imprisonment narratives, one can see that the writers question the authority of language (especially language that passes for history) and speak to the resources as well as the hazards of silence. They articulate – question, report, expose – the silences imposed on themselves and their peoples, whether in the form of cultural decorum, political necessity, external or self-censorship, or historical or political invisibility; and at the same time, through their manners of telling and through their 'fictions', they demonstrate that silences – textual ellipses, non-verbal gestures, authorial hesitations – can also be articulate. In their exploration of these and other problems to do with identity, memory and aesthetic form, imprisonment narratives need to be recognised as an ideological act in their own right, to be read as a politically charged rewriting of the traditional genre of autobiography, but also as crucial documents in the testimony to national and continental trauma. These narratives enact what bell hooks calls 'a politicisation of memory that distinguishes nostalgia, that longing for something to be as it once was, a kind of useless act, from that remembering that serves to illuminate and transform the present' (hooks 1990: 147). As hooks goes on to say, 'In much new, exciting cultural practice, cultural texts ... there is an effort to remember that is expressive of the need to create spaces where one is able to redeem and reclaim the past, legacies of pain, suffering, and triumph in ways that transform present reality. Fragments of memory are not simply represented as flat documentary but constructed to give a "new take" on the old, constructed to move us into a different mode of articulation' (hooks 1990: 147). Often future-oriented, these imprisonment narratives call for the possibility of a pluralistic conception of self and society, recognising our differences as well as our similarities.

'Interstices of freedom': language and representation

In the face of all the moral power and ethical force of Lawrence Langer's analysis, one needs to speak hesitantly about an aesthetic of atrocity. For writing has its limitations; this is one of the first truths one learns when it comes to people's pain. The journey from documentation to art, from the gross barbarities perpetrated in Kamiti Prison, Pretoria Central or Robben Island to their record in memoir or novel, is one that goes through difficult and grimly challenging terrain. When the body is in pain, what does torture do to language and representation? Can torture be represented 'aesthetically'? How can trauma performed on the body be represented in writing? Can one speak about the 'aesthetics of incarceration'? One of the characteristics governing much of this prison literature is that reality often exceeded the power of the imagination to conjure up images commensurate with the experience that the artist wished to record, with the result that the writer was confronted with the dilemma of converting into literature a history too terrible to imagine.

Theodor Adorno has pondered many of these issues in relation to representations of the Holocaust, and in his essay 'Engagement' he quotes Jean-Paul Sartre's *Mort sans sépulture*: 'Does it still make sense to go on living, while there are people who beat others till the bones in their bodies are broken?' (Adorno 1992: 87). Indeed, how can one represent the inexpressibly inhuman suffering of torture, without doing an injustice to that pain? There is something disagreeable, almost voyeuristic, in converting the sufferings of victims into works of art. A transfiguration occurs through the principle of aesthetic stylisation when the horror of the event disappears – as the senseless fate and brutalisation of lives proves to have meaningfulness after all. The prospect of art denying what it seeks to affirm (the

hideous sadism and brutality of dehumanisation in torture) raises
the spectre of a paradox for author, reader and critic that is not easily
circumvented. The transfiguration of moral chaos into aesthetic form
depends to a large extent on how a writer exploits his or her material. Two things are at work in 'the literature of atrocity': historical
fact and imaginative truth. The texts are not simply patients
etherised on the table of history: literature seeks ways of exploring
the implications and making the barbarisms and torture imagina-
tively available. Literature steps up to fill in the gaps of history's
deficiencies ... and runs the risk of erasing them.

Elaine Scarry very cogently argues that torture shatters language.
Her book *The Body in Pain* is a remarkable study of the mechanics
and dynamics of torture, in which Scarry explores the ways in which
the dynamic between the torturer and the victim leads to several
consequences. One of the principal issues is the extent to which
torture wrecks the usual descriptive and communicative aspects of
language. Torture, she argues, is language-destroying because pain
has no referential content, since pain 'more than any other phenomenon, resists objectification in language' (Scarry 1985: 5).
Constructing a typology of pain, Scarry explores the availability of
sites for registering varieties of pain, and quantifying it. Yet writing
is an attempt to overcome what Scarry describes in her semiotics of
pain as its 'resistance to objectification' (Scarry 1985: 56). Words
become a substitute for prisoners' wounds, and their memoirs and
diaries reinscribe the marks that violence has etched on their flesh,
a vanishing 'calligraphy of cruelty' (Ellmann 1993: 86). Writing seeks
to make visible the hidden and untranslatable pain suffered by the
victim of torture. Writing acts to subvert the strategy of isolation: it
enables authors to defy the loneliness of bodily experience, because
their words themselves become a form of pain, their letters a form of
penetration. Writing is also a discipline of memory. Detainees write
their lives to create their own memorial but also to disgorge their
minds of history, the frozen past. Yet rather than merely writing to
rid themselves of the past, disremembering, emptying minds of the
burden of the past, it is actually to reinscribe a different past, to
write a different history.

If torture shatters language, then the question is how one under-
going this torture of detention can articulate one's experiences. One
route is to model one's account on other imprisonment narratives,
and one is constantly aware of a generic intertextuality among these
narratives. Language, self-representation, the ability to write,
finding the means to write, securing one's writing against warders'
cell raids, are the repeated themes of all these imprisonment narratives. As Ioan Davies describes in his much overlooked study *Writers
in Prison*, this battle for representation is partly a process of over-

coming the limitations of one's physical space: 'To understand prison writing it is important to understand space and the reading of that space ... The language of prison space is therefore one in which eyes, voices, limbs interact in a moving out from the cell with its definite physical contours and back into the cell from the more obvious dimensions of the power/ideology that attempts to control' (Davies 1990: 59–60). Writers seek to form a counter-inscription against the cell's prior inscription upon the body; and prisons are a constant struggle of 'inscription/erasure, where the writer, compelled by his own hand to rewrite the prison by writing himself on to it, in turn finds his writing eliminated' (Davies 1990: 63).

In fashioning a consecutive chronicle of imprisonment, survivors who record their accounts unavoidably introduce some kind of teleology, investing the incidents they experience with a meaning, be it nothing more than regaining one's freedom. Telling modifies what is being told, an axiom of modern narratological literary theory. Memoir testimonial is shaped by certain literary conventions: chronology, description, characterisation, dialogue, and the invention of a narrative voice. This voice seeks to impose on apparently chaotic episodes and random acts of sadistic violence, a perceived sequence, *whether or not that sequence was perceived in an identical way* during the period that is being rescued from oblivion by memory and language. Writing invites commentary, reflection, interpretation. For it is the case that

> Written accounts of victim experience prod the imagination in ways that speech cannot, striving for analogies to initiate the reader into the particularities of their given world. This literature faces a special challenge, since it must give readers access to a totally unfamiliar subject ... Written memoirs, by the very strategies available to their authors – style, chronology, analogy, imagery, dialogue, a sense of character, a coherent moral and political vision – ease us into their unfamiliar world through familiar (and hence comforting?) literary devices, striving to narrow the vast imaginative gap that separates what he or she has endured from our capacity to absorb it. The impulse to *portray* (and thus refine) reality when we write about it seems irresistible: the literary often feels that it transforms the real in a way that obscures even as it seeks to enlighten. (Langer 1991: 18–19)

In other words, literary allusion, metaphor and analogy modify the uniqueness of these experiences. Whilst these witness writers are seeking some untransfigured actuality of what they recall, they are nevertheless keenly alive to the difficulty of this aim, and hounded by what language means for the reader and what it means for the victim – 'pain', 'cold', 'tiredness': they are always aware of this predicament of ambiguity, of the dual thrust of language.

One clear example of this consciousness of the aesthetic predica-

ment occurs in the collection of poems entitled *Inside* by the South
African Jeremy Cronin, who was imprisoned for terrorism in Pretoria
Maximum Security Prison between 1976 and 1983. The South
African government prison regulations prohibited 'creative writing',
almost in clear recognition that literature can afford the detainee
some form of 'escape', or 'transcendence' of limited conditions. The
poems are about Cronin's period of detainment, and they construct
what he terms a 'geography of the mouth' (Cronin 1987: 51), displaying a mastery of language and allowing his desire to 'let flesh be
made words' (Cronin 1987: 52). Written and published during the
time of the State of Emergency in the 1980s in South Africa, the
whole volume embodies the spirit of resistance and what it means to
be an exile in one's own country. Cronin seeks to prise open the many
layers of 'occupation, defiance and conquest' in South African
English, and 'to disturb history, the tongue bumping against
repressed parts' (Cronin 1987: 51). Aiming to produce a poetry that
embraces the rich variety of linguistic articulation in South Africa,
he writes about the need 'To learn how to speak / With the voices of
this land' (Cronin 1987: 64). In a poetry structured by the metaphor
of imprisonment both 'inside' prison and 'outside' in apartheid South
Africa, Cronin charts the processes of how sounds forged in solitary
confinement 'may // someday, grow into words' (Cronin 1987: 55), and
work towards the definition of a democratic society. The poems are
clearly partly memories of the events and descriptions, but they are
also retrospective evocations of the time and space of the detention.[2]
They wrestle with Blanchot's 'impossible reality', with the paradox of
whether and how to make aesthetic what is not aesthetic, how to turn
unpleasantness into an aesthetic object.

As many writers make clear, language and representation acts as
yet another site of struggle and conflict between jailer and detainee.
Cronin writes about the surreptitious ways in which his poetry had
to be secreted in crevices in the prison walls and in his memory in
order to avoid confiscation. Indeed, prison narratives repeatedly
mention the efforts to combat the various ways in which these
writers in detainment are censored, barred from possessing writing
implements and materials, and their experiences of how language is
repeatedly distorted.[3] The South African Afrikaans poet Breyten
Breytenbach, detained for political subversion in the 1970s and early
1980s, writes extensively about what it means to be a writer in
prison, severed from one's usual writing environment and smuggling
one's writing out of prison in order to save it. For Breytenbach, as for
many of these writers, writing is a means of survival: 'Writing
becomes for me a means, a way of survival. I have to cut up my environment in digestible chunks. Writing is an extension of my senses.
It is itself a sense which permits me to grasp, understand, and to

some extent to integrate that which is happening to me. I need it the same way the blind man behind his black glasses needs to see' (Breytenbach 1984a: 155). Yet Breytenbach is aware of the paradoxical double bind of language within prison: 'But at the same time I soon realize that it becomes the exteriorization of my imprisonment. My writing bounces off the walls. The maze of words which become alleys, like sentences, the loops which are closed circuits and present no exit, these themselves constitute the walls of my confinement. I write my own castle and it becomes a frightening discovery' (Breytenbach 1984a: 155). Both Soyinka and Ngugi also confront the debasement of language, and the imposition of silence; both struggle to find a new language of resistance in their books (see Lovesey 1995 and 1996). Soyinka insistently seeks to 'rescue words from a debasement to which they were constantly subjected by my gaolers' (Soyinka 1972: 14). This is an experience also explored in exacting and sensitive detail by Albie Sachs, a barrister who was arrested in Cape Town in 1963, and held without trial for 168 days in solitary confinement at three different prisons as the South African security forces tried to wear him down and extract information about the political activities of his former clients. Sachs describes the significance attached to reading (the Bible is the only book he, like all South African prisoners, is given), writing and representation while in prison, and the extraordinary lengths to which he goes in order to write with fishbones and cheese sauce. This occurs before he is eventually given paper and pencil by the prison officials, an experience he ecstatically likens to the first glyphs chalked by prehistoric man ('I am early man learning to write, a child making its first marks' (Sachs 1990: 161)). Sachs repeatedly mentions the way in which writing provides desperate intellectual stimulation to stave off loneliness; and yet he is aware of being dogged by the psychological terrors of opening himself to the authorities in his writing, as well as finding that without physical freedom, his writing always remains stunted:

> My special thoughts, the insights I have gained, the new emotional depths I have sounded within myself, all these must remain secret until I come out. The police must never be allowed to see into my mind. They must never be allowed to get hold of and to crush my thoughts, for the police are book-burners, destroyers of things delicate ... My mind lives in my body, and my body is caged here in a tiny world which is like a zoo without visitors ... What I need is direct stimulation, so that my senses have immediate contact with the world of movement and emotion. In order to write I must live. It is not merely enough to stay alive. (Sachs 1990: 245)

Hugh Lewin, another apartheid detainee, also describes in his book *Bandiet* the agony of having paper and pens withheld by the prison

authorities, as well as the value attached to reading books in detention, especially when the prison guards played arbitrary and tyrannical games with book allowances (Lewin 1989: 82). Time and again,
these apartheid narratives also mention the restrictions on the
number of letters that one was officially allowed to send and receive
– one every six months of exactly 500 words, interpreted and
censored with stunning accuracy and obstinacy. It is clear that
narratives of prison are also, at least at their point of conception,
imprisoned narratives – writers are barred from access to paper and
pens.

In *The Hunger Artists: Starving, Writing and Imprisonment*, Maud
Ellmann explores the tangled meanings of writing and hunger,
showing how starvation produces a strange excess of words in
contrast to the savage reduction of the flesh. *The Hunger Artists*
reveals uncanny affinities between the labour of starvation and the
birth of letters, diaries, memoirs, books, exposing a terrifying logic of
disembodiment. Ellmann's study reinforces how in instances where
these narratives depict hunger strikes, the threat of withdrawing
from food becomes part of the prisoners' armoury against the prison
authorities. Wole Soyinka's hunger strike in *The Man Died* is a good
example – 'he rejected *food* in order to protest against the dearth of
words that he suffered in his solitary confinement' (Ellmann 1993:
106). Hunger signifies the appetite of his intellect: 'To feed my body
but deny my mind is deliberate dehumanisation' (Soyinka 1972: 223).
Emaciation of the body, for Soyinka, intensifies or distils his writing,
since his fasting coincides with an avalanche of missives to the prison
officials.

In all these instances, writing and representation are a significant
part of the politics of reterritoriality and deterritoriality in prison.
This politics of negotiating spatial arenas is a complex one: prisoners
tend to constantly have to rewrite their selves, but also to rewrite
their space, their territory, and thereby seek to claim it, arrogate it,
insert themselves into it, to strip it of its transcendental significance,
and to deconstruct its abstract mechanisms. In some cases, the
writer embodies the prison, materialises it, senses and negotiates it;
in other cases, it is made metaphorical. In the former case, the prison
is deterritorialised, so that it ceases to have effective power; in the
later, the prison is reterritorialised, becoming the adjunct of an
abstract mechanism, the function of a higher power. In this counter-
hegemonic inscription of the self, 'Every prison writer writes against
the grain of the dominant language that provided the rules of enclosure' (Davies 1990: 162). In other words, all prison writing is deconstructive of hegemonic power. The key issue for the detainee is his or
her need to write one's own text in counter-position to the one
imposed by the authorities: 'Prison is essentially about playing out a

script written by others: the prisoner can play it out by acting out the part assigned to him (as criminal hero, stool-pigeon, simpleton) or he can rethink the entire imposition of text on himself in order to establish his own authenticity. The task is to be the author of his own stories, and that can only be achieved through dialogue between the inner and outer selves' (Davies 1990: 116).

The lexicon available to prison writers is problematic, and may well lead to erroneous conceptions of the reasons for writing and portraying one's imprisonment. For example, it has been frequently noted that imprisonment and artistic creation have a long history of connection. Artistic creativity is often conceived of as a release from constraints, and writers like Ioan Davies and W. B. Carnochan have noted this link: 'Whether fictional or autobiographical, the literature of prison concerns the interplay of constraint and freedom and therefore, analogously, also concerns its own creation' (Carnochan 1995: 427). Ideas of struggle have persistently underpinned the plot of prison literature, since one frequently reads of the prisoner as being on the road to some transcendence of limitations.[4] In some cases, the prison narrative has become a metaphor of confinement, in which modern life finds the 'human condition', that of being trapped in a tiny cell in some remote corner of the universe. It is there in the modernists Beckett and Kafka, but one can see a similar conceit emerge in Wordsworth's poetry, as in the sonnet 'Nuns fret not at their convent's narrow room'. It is thought that the prisoner's situation confers a special understanding – from suffering comes insight: confinement constitutes an injunction to reflection. Among the ideas we are forced to question as we read these memoirs and prison narratives is the comforting notion that suffering has meaning – that it strengthens, ennobles or redeems the human soul. Joseph Brodsky has written that incarceration is 'an integral metaphor of Christian metaphysics as well as practically the midwife of literature' (Brodsky 1996: xi). A Christian vocabulary of redemption and salvation frequently hovers over these testimonial narratives. In fact Ioan Davies has suggested that, in some respects, one could argue that the long history of prison writing in relation to Christianity becomes the jailer of the African writers, since the metaphors against which prisoners have to battle in conceiving their space and the reasons for their incarceration are frequently determined by the historical and ideological structures of the former. Language is often perceived to be a fulcrum tipping us from one lexicon of hope to another of despair. Indeed, detainees frequently note that the only text that their jailers allow them is the Bible. Yet their anguish can never be soothed by a thesaurus of consolation. Although clichés abound in prison writing,[5] the most compelling testimonies are those that resist the temptation to squeeze their experiences into familiar literary premises.

Detainment literature plays a vital role in raising questions about the integrity of language and identity and the dominion of history itself. Its unsettling contours force us to confront the estrangement of the world in which we live from the one we long to inhabit – or nostalgically yearn to regain. The need to wrest meaning from such estrangement (and the atrocities that lie at its root) continues to goad us. We should not mistake survival for renewal, and celebrate the triumph of humane continuity over the forces of autocratic state power. Whatever 'beauty' prison literature achieves, it is tainted by the misery of its theme. In these landscapes of agony, as they shift between hope and despair, seizing on the tiniest rumour or snippet to verify their yearning for release, we are given glimpses of the dual world of promise and doom that nurtures detainees and continues to haunt many of the survivors today. Any aestheticisation of imprisonment runs the danger of romanticising the experience and thus depoliticising the reasons and effects of physical incarceration. Indeed, to what extent are these prison narratives dogged by the grammar of heroism and martyrdom? One needs to be careful about the nature of the resistance in these narratives. 'Resistance' carries a rhetorical force that is loaded with romantic associations that often override the brutal details that deromanticise it as it unfolds. Indeed, there must be a resistance to romanticising survival as heroism; staying alive is not to be confused with an intrepid will to survival.

The self in prison

Resistance is a struggle with the self. Breyten Breytenbach makes this struggle clear when he links an 'ethics of resistance' with the myth of Icarus' and Daedalus' escape from the Minotaur's labyrinth, through the constant struggle to construct an 'I' with which to escape the restrictive maze (Breytenbach 1984a: 240): 'Beyond flying or dreaming or walking. You must move against the death-producing System which is a structure, knowing that your flight and your search is a *process* (the way all living structures are), becoming that which you are: a metamorphosis' (Breytenbach 1984a: 240). For such testimonies as these, imprisonment narratives reveal the consequences of a gradual attrition of the qualities of inwardness, freedom and individuality, an estrangement from nature until one is alienated from the very sense of modern identity. These narratives chart a frontal assault on human liberty and freedom. An inviolable assumption of choice is the keystone of moral speculation – and these narratives testify to the deliberate and systematic brutalisation of that assumption. They are a testimony to the rigorous battering of modern ethics and polity to do with the self. As we examined in relation to gender in Chapter 4, being placed outside or beyond the limits of human agency is tantamount to being placed beyond what we recognise as integral, that is, undamaged, human personhood. External circumstances compel one to enter a disintegrative milieu, as personhood is inevitably traumatised. Partly in order to reflect this damage but also to protect oneself against it, both D. M. Zwelonke and Breyten Breytenbach create fictional selves in their narratives as a means of combating the incessant brutalisation of the self.[6] *In* 'Why I Write', the opening chapter of *Robben Island*, Zwelonke explains his choice of narrative persona: 'For various reasons I have written it as a work of fiction. Fiction, but projecting a hard and bitter truth; fiction mirroring non-fiction, true incidents and episodes. The characters are all fictional, including, in a sense, myself' (Zwelonke 1973: 3). Breytenbach's narrative, constantly switching backwards and forwards with its introspective dialogue with the imaginary 'Mr. Investigator', is fully conscious of the ontological instability in one's life – with the different masks, personae and characters that we adopt in our lives in different circumstances: 'Isn't the whole process of our being, this looking for a name?' (Breytenbach 1984a: 13). Breytenbach reinforces this instability at the beginning of chapter 3, 'From Room to Room', through the disorientated stream-of-consciousness that mimics the destabilisation of time and space as a result of the interrogation procedures:

> From room to passage, to bathroom, to corridor, through the grills, through the gate, by car careening down narrow lanes of darkness past the blind man. From room. To room. To room. To room …
>
> It was the second day or perhaps it was the third, no, it was the first day. Then it was the fourth day, I mean it was the second day, it must have been the morning of the second day. On that morning, the morning of the third day, they took me back to the Compol Building and the questioning continued. (Breytenbach 1984a: 34)[7]

Yet as we examine definitions and redefinitions of self emerging from these detainment narratives, we must keep in mind that each of them represents a combat, more often than not unconscious, between fragment and form, disaster and intactness. The whole of chapter 4 in *The Jail Diary of Albie Sachs* is preoccupied with exploring the detachment and self-alienation brought about by detention in isolation: 'This image, I feel is me, the Albie who would respond if someone called my name. My body could be anybody's body, but the face is mine' (Sachs 1990: 41). Sachs is hyper-conscious of the collapse, separation and necessary re-erection of the self whilst in prison: 'It is I staring at myself. What is more, I am aware of the whole process as though there is yet another self which watches the I staring at myself. I am a mirror bent in on itself, a unity and yet an infinite multiplicity of internal reflections' (Sachs 1990: 252). This detachment and self-alienation is indicative of the effects of enclosure, and Sachs is continually forced to reconcile this for himself: 'How does one cope with a sentence of many years imprisonment? The answer is, I suppose, that the world of jail becomes one's new world ... The prison walls are one's horizon. One adapts to life in this special world and finds new sources of stimulation and satisfaction to replace the old' (Sachs 1990: 270). Keeping the self together, ensuring the security of the 'I' in the face of compelling disintegrative forces, is an overriding concern expressed in virtually every African imprisonment narrative.

These imprisonment narratives emerge in a variety of forms – letters, memoirs, diaries, notes, retrospective narratives, political essays, poetry, fictionalised autobiography and autobiography. Yet despite the identity of their generic form, they all tell a personalised narrative, which 'is best approached within the general category of autobiography, and more especially as confessional narrative. It shares with autobiography that combination of a process of self-discovery with the art of self-invention' (Jacobs 1991: 125). So one might ask what are the uses of autobiography within a specifically political context? Cheryl-Ann Michael has argued that such texts trace the linearity of political development or consciousness that masks an erasure of differences between past selves and the present 'I' or subject, thereby furthering the writers' iconic stature and political convictions (Michael 1995: 74). These autobiographical narratives are frequently a *staging* of memory, marked as they often are by self-fashioning, subjectivity, collective memory, confession and the social construction of their past childhood. Linda Anderson envisages autobiography working in two complementary ways: 'Autobiography becomes both a way of testifying to oppression and empowering the subject through either their cultural inscription and recognition' (Michael 1995: 74). As the narratives of apartheid detainees like Moses Dlamini and Caesarina Makhoere make clear, autobiography can have an emancipatory project among postcolonial writers and subjects, 'that teleological narrative of "becoming a self"' (Anderson 2001: 106), as the hegemonic neo-colonial regimes seek to sever them from their freedom and human rights. African prison diaries 'create and affirm an identity for a particular group', relying on 'encoding a particular readership and on employing a discourse linking community and selfhood which is also, ultimately, a historical discourse' of trauma (Anderson 2001: 106–7). Therefore, memories become not so much individualised instances of some general truth but 'interpretive devices', ways of interrogating the relation between individual experience and theoretical problems. A memory becomes an image that allows for an understanding of a social or political landscape, which means that discursive positions and material locations are imbricated in each other.[8]

Imprisonment narratives are counter-hegemonic to the extent that they expose the repressive mechanisms and show scant regard for the rule of law within specific regimes. They focus on points of incoherence or contradiction within the political and ideological discourses of the dominant power within the nation.

> If we then also regard autobiography more broadly as part of a historically and formally changing discourse of self-representation, it is possible to interpret it as a political site on which human agency is negotiated within and against institutions on the grounds of truth. If this is so, then autobiography may also be a site of resistance, especially as it engages the politics of looking back and challenges the politics of how the past and present may be known in relation to a particular version of history. (Gilmore 1994: 80)

If these imprisonment narratives are to be regarded as autobiographical in some sense, then they are marked as much by a resistance to the autobiographical as by an embracing of it.[9] John Paul Eakin has argued that there are two dominant paradigms in critical approaches to autobiography, which pose an irreconcilable controversy about the ontological status of the self in autobiography. Some theorists have argued that autobiography is a mode of self-restoration. For James Olney, on the one hand, autobiography is a 'theatre of possibility', a site for gaining knowledge of the self. As Eakin states, 'For Olney ... language is not a mode of privation, but an instrument of possibility and power to be placed at the service of self-definition' (Eakin 1985: 189). By contrast, for Paul de Man, autobiography is a genre of self-effacement, of de-facement of the self, a privation of discourse. Autobiography is a 'figure of deprivation', rather than a theatre for self-expression, self-knowledge and self-discovery. As a post-structuralist, de Man argues that the writer is *written* by the language he or she deploys, and the self is displaced from the text. Consequently, nowadays there is a focus on autobiography as detour, mediated, displaced, defaced stories – mediation, obliqueness, as shock and surprise, the sudden eruption of subjectivity, often figured as a face. Sachs's narrative displays a unique self-consciousness of the ways in which the isolated detainee is seduced by selfishness: 'More and more I cease to regard the world as something existing independently of myself. I am the centre of the universe. It is my fate that gives significance to destiny ... I am aware of my selfishness and disappointed at its grossness. I know on the one hand that it is largely a by-product of my isolation, and a reflection of the struggle my personality is subjected to in order to survive the assaults being made on it' (Sachs 1990: 89). Yet Sachs is equally aware that he needs to resist this selfishness in order to retain his sense of personal integrity, and he produces an ironic critique of this existentialist position:

So this is what existentialists feel – each individual is separate, alone, encapsuled in himself. They go through life aware of this all the time, even when they are at the dinner table, walking past people in the street or making love. Such a man lying wrapped in the limbs of his lover is lonelier than I in this cell; his intimacy is less than mine is with the unknown whistler. These thinkers are wrong to generalise as they do. Man is not naturally isolated and alone; the crowd is not his enemy. If that were in fact so, solitary confinement would not affect one so viciously. It would be a release, a happiness. No, man is interdependent in his very depths. He disintegrates in isolation, but flourishes through association. The urge for love and communication is the strongest of all drives. (Sachs 1990: 97)

Prison narratives work much like a combination of these two modes – self-restoration and detour – as a result of the environment in which the writing takes place (i.e. secretive), and the repression of the self (i.e. written as a self-assertion). Most of these narratives are also riven by uneasy mirror imagery – distorted mirrors, anamorphic visions – uneasy mirrors of 'race' and identity, and their distorting reflections, masks and mimicry, especially in apartheid narratives. Echoing Sachs's reflective self-examination, Breyten Breytenbach also constantly plays with a pun on 'mirror' and the French word 'mourir' ('to die') – the book he writes whilst in prison is entitled *Mouroir* – since he regards autobiography as a form of dying and seeing oneself. In this sense, these memoirs, diaries and autobiographies might be regarded as the performance of identity, or 'facework' if you will.

Two basic premises seem to be at work in these prison narratives: first to articulate the experience of oppression first hand as a precondition for political and social change; and, second, that collective testimony is one of the best means of achieving this end, so that neither the reader nor the author sees the autobiographical narrative as a matter of individualism. For as Laura Marcus notes, there appears to be a shift in the representation of the self in autobiography: 'This shift, if that is what it is, from the self-consciousness of autobiography (which may conceal a cultural demand for confession) to the ethical responsibility to testify, has important implications for conceptions of the status and value of self-writings and for concepts of experience and our relationship to it. It would seem to entail a move away from self-reflection towards a sense that we are all witnesses of history's tragedies and may be summoned to testify to our knowledge of them' (Marcus 1994: 213). Marcus importantly notes the ethical implications that have emerged with the autobiographical impulse, especially within recent decades. It is striking that much postcolonial writing in Africa has seen the emergence of themes of crime and reparation, and that memory and autobiography, and conceptions of history, are now dominated by these themes. A great deal of these narratives concerns the politics attached to 'speaking out' or 'remaining silent'; and in partial recognition of this state of affairs we may (after Shoshona Felman) characterise this age of African writing as the 'age of testimony' and 'witness' (Felman and Laub 1992).

The body under torture

The term 'political prisoner' has a varied use and lacks a universally agreed definition, and hence Amnesty International uses the term 'prisoner of conscience': 'Someone who is incarcerated for his or her beliefs or for peaceful expression or association.'[10] This definition includes the *advocacy* of violence but excludes the *use* of violence. However the United Nations has defined torture in a Declaration on Torture, in which *Article 1* states:

1. For the purpose of this Declaration, torture means any act by which severe pain or suffering, whether physical or mental, is intentionally inflicted by or at the instigation of a public official on a person for such purposes as obtaining from him or a third person information or confession, punishing him for an act he has committed or is suspected of having committed, or intimidating him or other persons. It does not include pain or suffering arising only from, inherent in or incidental to, lawful sanctions to the extent consistent with the Standard Minimum Rules for the Treatment of Prisoners.
2. Torture constitutes an aggravated and deliberate form of cruel, inhuman or degrading treatment or punishment.[11]

This makes quite clear that torture includes psychological as well as physical maltreatment, and detention without trial in solitary confinement would constitute a clear breach of the UN's Declaration. In this respect, most, if not all, of these narratives deal with torture, either through clear acts of physical brutality or through psychological contravention of the UN Declaration, by prolonged periods of solitary confinement, or detention without trial.

Moses Dlamini states at one point in his imprisonment narrative that 'Prison in the conditions of oppression in a country like South Africa – as indeed in most Third World countries – is a place where you are stripped of every vestige of human dignity – debased, demoralised, dehumanised, so that your spirit is broken to accept the perverted logic of the oppressor' (Dlamini 1984: 9). Commenting on how detainment in a South African prison is a microcosmic experience of social life within the whole of South Africa, another apartheid detainee, Michael Dingake, also notes how 'Prisons denature, dehumanise, depersonalise, decivilise and de-everything their victims' (Dingake 1987: 121). *My Fight Against Apartheid*, Dingake's chronological autobiography of his political involvements that resulted in a prison sentence on Robben Island, is strewn with intellectual ratio- nalisations and investigations of Marxism, white Christianity, apartheid, politics and economics. This book describes all aspects of life on Robben Island, recounting how the prison was used as a labo- ratory experiment in political detention, and it frequently turns into a propaganda manifesto for the ANC's political project, finishing as it does with an encomium to Nelson Mandela and an exhortation to continue the struggle against apartheid. Another book that deals with detention, imprisonment and torture on Robben Island in a graphic manner is Indres Naidoo's *Island in Chains* (1982). Naidoo, among the first South African Indians to be incarcerated on the Island, presents sharp, generous and often witty insights into both his fellow captives and his captors and puts ample flesh on the bones of what might, in less capable hands, have been a tedious polemic. The degradations and calculated sadism inflicted on prisoners – common and political alike – in the 1960s and 1970s is almost beyond belief (what energy it must have taken the warders to keep thinking up new torments!). Yet Naidoo's achievement is greater than merely recording the heinous details of apartheid's brutality. For this is also a story about humanity and inventiveness. Stripped of all privacy and modesty, crowded into cells with eclectic abandon (ANC prison- ers, members of the PAC, gangsters and recidivists), detainees learned to live with themselves and each other with good humour, compassion and even grace. Frequently narrated in the form of snap- shot incidents, the book goes into very great detail about the daily humiliations, the barbaric treatment of the 'politicals' by the warders, while the lack of medical attention is described as one of the most brutal inhumanities, with sufferers of significant illnesses either being told that they were lazy or simply dismissed out of hand (Naidoo 1982). Torture can manifest itself in cool denial just as much as in overt acknowledgement of a prisoner.

The inexpressibility of pain results largely from our inability to know another's pain, and to know how intense it is. Scarry seeks to isolate the metaphors that structure pain, and one can isolate which metaphors structure these prison experiences (of bodily damage, mental damage), and then study how these are related to issues of national identity. Scarry argues that our only means of conceptualis- ing pain 'entails an immediate mental somersault out of the body into the external social circumstances that can be pictured as having caused the hurt' (Scarry 1985: 16). Ultimately, torture is an act of display: 'having as its purpose the production of a fantastic illusion of power, torture is a grotesque piece of compensatory drama' (Scarry 1985: 28). For Scarry, torture is finally a process of performative translation, 'the conversion of absolute pain into the fiction of absolute power' (Scarry 1985: 27). As apartheid detainee Emma Mashinini states at one point: 'These people have fine ways of torturing you. They let you torture yourself' (Mashinini 1989: 65).

Elaine Scarry argues that the founding trope of torture is to reduce the world 'to a single room or set of rooms' (Scarry 1985: 40). This ontological reduction is one to which these prison narratives repeatedly return: Ruth First's opening remarks concern the restricted space of her cell (First 1982: 10); and Albie Sachs details how 'Everything is divided into significant fractions, for these are the dimensions of my world. The day is split up by mealtimes; morning, afternoon, and evening further split up by activities' (Sachs 1990: 58). When Sachs is moved from one prison to another, he needs to re-establish his order and pattern: 'Day by day I will explore and map this strange universe, penetrating the chaos with my ears and eyes, building up an ordered existence out of bits of information the guards may let slip from time to time' (Sachs 1990: 114). The debilitating effects of solitary confinement are repeatedly stressed by numerous testimonies as one of the worst aspects of detainment: 'There is no world outside. There is no outside I am aware of. *I cannot see out of my cell*' (Sachs 1990: 14); while another apartheid prisoner notes that 'Solitary is very disorienting, a torture in itself ... Certainties give hope; indeterminacy breeds despair' (Jenkin 1987: 42–3); and Ruth First mentions the isolation and the debilitating effects of uncertainty (First 1982: 74). This tactic of isolation is clearly part of the torture. Scarry points out that not only is the room or cell the space that happens to house the instruments of torture or the setting in which beatings occur but that the very room 'is itself literally converted into another weapon, into an agent of pain. All the aspects of the basic structure – walls, ceiling, windows, doors – undergo this conversion' (Scarry 1985: 40). Virtually to a person, these detainees observe the moment when they notice that prison hides or closes out the sun or natural light from their daily existence (see, for example, Pheto 1983: 76 and 154). Scarry also comments upon how the words for torture are often borrowed from the lexicon of domesticity suggesting an ominous affinity between the two domains, but that also calls attention to their similarity only as a prelude to announcing their annihilation. Breyten Breytenbach notes precisely this threatening lexicon of domesticity when he observes that warders or interrogators speak about forms of torture as having to 'use "the telephone" on you, or "the parrot", or "the submarine"; they may have you leave through "the Bantu exit"!' (Breytenbach 1984a: 29). Elsewhere, narratives describe how Pretoria Prison is familiarly called 'Beverly Hills'. Indeed, the boundaries between the domestic and the public, between the inside and outside, fundamental to a concept of the self, dissolve, because prisoners are put in disorienta-

tion programs for interrogation, severed from the outside and generally prevented from having contact with the 'outside' world. As
Breytenbach puts it, under the conditions of solitary confinement,
the jailers and Security Police eventually come to believe their own
fictions, and these are then perpetrated upon the prisoners: 'You'll
understand why, under such conditions, the line between reality and
illusion is effaced. For, to the extent that they believe something to
be real and act accordingly, that thing does become real'
(Breytenbach 1984a: 49).

In torture, Scarry argues, 'the pain is traditionally accompanied by
"the Question"' (Scarry 1985: 28). The scene of inquisition is usually
described in these prison memoirs and diaries: the torture or interrogation room is the *mis-en-scène* where power materialises in the spectacle of pain. Breyten Breytenbach's entire imprisonment narrative
is structured upon a parodic address to 'Mr. Investigator' and this
presents a curious insight into the symbiotic relationship between
victim and interrogator, how the jailer is tied to the captive in a sort
of master–slave dialectic of bondage: 'That it has been like this from
the beginning of time – you and I entwined and related, parasite and
prey? Image and mirror-image? You are my frame and my field and
my discipline ... In you I live' (Breytenbach 1984a: 56). In the addendum to his memoir, Breytenbach continues this analysis in 'A Note
on the Relationship between Detainee and Interrogator', where he
points out the 'macabre dance' or 'fatal game' between the two
parties, in which 'violator and victim (collaborator! violin!), are
linked forever perhaps, by the obscenity of what has been revealed to
you' (Breytenbach 1984a: 341; 343). In their description of the
mechanics of interrogation, most prisoners depict the occasion where
they are initially given paper and pen and told to write down their
life story, or their knowledge of all events relevant to their 'case', and
to let the interrogator decide when the correct version of events has
been written. So 'the Question' is frequently not even known before
an answer is extracted, which is part of the terror of uncertainty that
overwhelms so many victims of interrogation.

Many of these imprisonment narratives are obsessed with the
body, the consequence of a system that constantly turns the body into
a spectacle upon which power is performed. Albie Sachs notes that
this somatic introspection is a direct result of torture through solitary confinement:

> The immediate animal shock of being shut in has subsided a little and I
> start to reflect on my position. A process of self-observation and analy-
> sis has begun and with the passage of the days has reached the stage
> when self-exploration has become a settled part of my daily programme.
> So complete is my isolation, and so bare my circumstances, that the only
> object which acts as a source of stimulation is myself. I have become

intensely self-aware, physically, emotionally, intellectually, and the eye with which I look at myself is merciless. Every blemish is exposed, and what virtues I find I dissect and separate, so that my personality is taken apart after the fashion of a plastic skeleton dislocated for the purposes of demonstration. Looking at the various disassembled parts, I often wonder how they can ever be integrated into one nature. (Sachs 1990: 40)

The emergence of this disfigured self is a direct result of bodies becoming a battleground with the state authorities; and the body can be maimed in many ways, not only through mutilation. Indeed, there is a persistent invasion of the body in apartheid jails, from a so-called 'carry on' on Robben Island, when warders were instructed to 'carry on' with their batons, beating and thrashing prisoners with anything to hand, including pick-handles and lengths of rubber pipe (see Naidoo 1982: 113–15, and Zwelonke 1973: 45); to general bodily friskings ('While their hands searched our bodies in the most humiliating way possible, they told us that here the white man was boss, and they hurled as many insults at us as they could, crude insults, repeated over and over again, as though they could not be in our presence or touch our bodies without saying something vile, reminding them and us of their power to do with us exactly what they liked' (Naidoo 1982: 54–5)); to the humiliating *tausa* that was performed before guards who examined prisoners' anuses for concealed contraband. Many apartheid imprisonment narratives detail this degrading ritual, among which Indres Naidoo's description might be taken as a searing example:

> All one thousand of us had to strip stark naked and stand in about ten lines in front of the warders. They waited until every one of us was ready, totally naked, with clothes over our arms, and then an officer ordered us to go, one by one, and hand the clothes over to a warder who would search them thoroughly, every fold and stitch ...
>
> Next, it was the turn of our bodies and we were commanded to do the *tausa*, and we saw the other prisoners going through the routine of leaping in the air, twisting round, clapping their hands over their heads, shooting their legs wide open and coming down bent over with their rectums exposed to the warders. Most of the prisoners in for ANC activities refused to follow suit. (Naidoo 1982: 64–5)

Resistance by PAC and ANC prisoners to this barbaric dance is an attempt to protect the integrity of the self, and resist the relation of power that is enacted in the spectacle of nudity: 'The guards would smack our naked bodies all the time with their batons and hoses, or just come up to us and kick us, even while we were trying to sort out our clothes. They were not especially angry, this was just their normal way of reminding us of their presence' (Naidoo 1982: 65). These imprisonment narratives also describe outright acts of physical sadism by warders (such as the infamous Kleynhans brothers on Robben Island, or the warders at Pretoria Central), who perpetrated quite appalling practices in premeditated and brazen ways.

Kate Millett warns against the fact that torture is a panoptic process which is aimed at invading all one's spaces, turning them outside in (Millett 1994). Furthermore, she warns against the medicalisation of torture – its compliance with torture and eventually treating its consequences – as a removal of the issue from politics and a removal of justice from torture. Under the penal medical gaze, Millet continues, '[The prisoner] faces medicine, not law, an important distinction since law would exonerate him and medicine has yet to decide the case. And so the victim of state brutality in a client state applies not for redress or restitution but for healing in the place from whence the harm emanated. There is an imperial circularity here. Short-circuitry as well: the political has been psychiatrized, privatized, personalized into marginality; the social reality of dictatorship, the politics of cruelty have been banalized into a "case". Telescoped, trivialized, shrunken' (Millett 1994: 313). The complicity of the medical profession with prison torture is widely documented in these narratives: for example, the derisory medical treatment meted out to inmates on Robben Island; the withholding of dental treatment as punishment and intimidation in Soyinka's narrative; and the pathetic medical attention described in Albie Sachs's diary.

The mechanics of torture are usually also a process of emasculation. If imprisonment narratives represent penal systems riddled with ideologies of incarceration linked to race, skin colour, food, creativity and politics, then they are also deeply embedded in ideologies of gender.[12] Women prisoners tell a specific gendered story about how the prison becomes a stage where warders make the prison a scene of the body's subjection, where they appear to relish the *spectacle* of male power even more than the exercise of it in torture. Women's imprisonment narratives repeatedly return to the mechanics of panoptic power, and how these organise everyday life. Emma Mashinini, a South African trade union official imprisoned in Pretoria Central Prison, remarks of the cell's Judas-window: 'It was a frightful thing, that window ... All I could see was their eyes. It was very, very frightful. I couldn't get used to it. I thought, it's like an animal, to see those two eyes, and I'm in a cage. It was frightening' (Mashinini 1989: 64). The gaze through the Judas-window literally forms her image, capturing her even in her naked intimacy with the stain of perpetual visibility. The particular perspectives of women detainees and their deprivations within a system that was wholly patriarchal and militaristic in its organisation and ethos is recounted on many occasions.[13] So many imprisonment narratives embed a masculinist ideology depicting man-the-active and woman-the-passive, where men tend to position themselves as the actors in history, making and shaping it. However, the process of imprisonment is not merely physical torture but a process of mental debilitation, where the target of drawn-out isolation is repeatedly described as the destruction of the faculty of reason. Sachs points out that 'Prolonged solitude and inactivity produce emotional effects whereby rational thinking is displaced' (Sachs 1990: 166); Tim Jenkin notes that 'It is the solitary that messes you up. Left with your own disturbed thoughts you are unable to think things through rationally' (Jenkin 1987: 42); while in Zwelonke's *Robben Island*, Bekimpi's dreams deal with the need to resist irrationality and to adhere to reason (Zwelonke 1973: 146–51). Rightly or wrongly, this subversion of reason is perceived by many writers as an attack on masculinity, and a broader subversion of the male actor in history. Torture of the body works on breaking the strength of individuals; torture of the mind aims to break the strength of collectives.

The roles of history and memory

Under such physical duress and bodily torture (be it to male or female, white or black, prisoners), memory functions as a major buttress against the mental and physical assaults launched against the psychologies of detainees. In the face of all sorts of adversity, detainees constantly have recourse to memory as a means of combating the deliberate attenuation of one's past and personal identity. In his moving and inspirational memoir *The Jail Diary of Albie Sachs*, Sachs discusses solitary detention and the ways in which it affects memory, shifting the focus from the long-term past to the minutiae of daily prison life, causing him to forget things that do not belong to quotidien routine: 'It's amazing how clear my memory is. That is, for things that have happened since I was detained. I keep forgetting things that I have to do, and my recollections of the world outside are extremely faint, yet the events of my detention stand out sharply' (Sachs 1990: 185–6). The decline of memory is something that needs to be actively resisted. Commenting upon the techniques of subtle suggestion during interrogation, Sachs states: 'Until I saw this addendum I was beginning to doubt my own memory. The months of isolation had tended to wipe my mind clean of past recollection ... By isolating me from the world in which the relevant events had taken place, they had succeeded in destroying my independent recollection of what had happened ... My mind is simply bare of memory, unable to recall the past but still resistant to suggestion' (Sachs 1990: 219). Sachs realises that fantasies become a means to lift him out of his physical incarceration and mental limitation: 'With a minimum of outside stimulation available to sustain a reasonable level of emotional and psychological activity, it is extremely difficult to think and to feel in a coherent and satisfactory way. Memory and fantasy become increasingly important as aids to mental and emotional activity, but as time goes by memory of the outside world is replaced by recollections of my days inside, as though my life has begun in prison' (Sachs 1990: 42). Although writing specifically about the Holocaust, Lawrence Langer has drawn up an economy of memory, and he has argued that 'Testimony is a form of remembering. The faculty of memory functions in the present to recall a personal history vexed by traumas that thwart smooth-flowing chronicles. Simultaneously, straining against what we might call disruptive memory is an effort to reconstruct a semblance of continuity in a life that began as, and now resumes what we would consider, a normal existence' (Langer 1991: 2). Langer argues that these two voices compete with one another – and all witness narratives are riven by this duality: of the present ruptured by the past.

The famous Russian prisoner Alexander Solzhenitsyn remarked upon how in prison even one's thoughts were not free: 'The thoughts of the prisoner – they're not free either. They constantly return to the same things' (Solzhenitsyn 1963: 22). Trapped in this perpetual 'groundhog day' existence, it is noticeable that these prison memoirs return insistently to history, and the ways in which history is represented and conceived, and the role of memory in constructing a useable and sustainable past. For memory is constantly part of preventing the disappearance of one's own history. In recalling their individual memories, detainees are frequently led into recounting their communities', national, or ethnic groups' histories. Indeed, many of these imprisonment testimonies are heavily polemical about national politics, dictatorial government, apartheid and the abuse of human rights. These narratives are concerned with how memory acts within this resuscitation of the past, and whether memory is pitted against a structured history imposed from without. For detention without trial is more often than not an attempt by the political authorities to remove someone from daily life, and thereby to remove someone from history. This is curious because it implicates the 'great man' theory of history, an admission that the active agency of individuals can alter the fabric of society and the course of history. This flies in the face of all those structural notions of history, such as Marxist, Freudian, Foucauldian, or post-structuralist positions that argue that individuals do not have the power to shape the course of political ideology, since there are greater structural forces at work over which the individual has no control. So there is a sense in which the imprisoning regime is blind to its own failure, since its activities of detention and torture are ultimately unable to stave off the social and political changes from which it is trying to protect itself. Arguably, in a paradoxical twist, the imprisoning regime is actually reinforcing and adding to those structural changes, in that the greater the imprisoned and detained population, the greater the international pressure and scrutiny is brought to bear upon the practices and policies of that particular regime. Mass imprisonment without trial is an implicit acknowledgement of the failure of the regime's ability to maintain its own political power, the collapse and erosion of its own hegemony, as Stuart Hall's important study of the establishment, maintenance and ever-threatening fragility of hegemony in *Policing the Crisis* makes clear:

A crisis of hegemony marks a moment of profound rupture in the political and economic life of a society, an accumulation of contradictions. If in moments of 'hegemony' everything works spontaneously so as to sustain and enforce a particular form of class domination while rendering the basis of that social authority invisible through the mechanisms of the production of consent, then moments when the equilibrium of consent is disturbed, or where the contending forces are so nearly balanced that neither can achieve that sway from which a resolution to the crisis can be promulgated, are moments *when the whole basis of political leadership and cultural authority becomes exposed and contested*. When the temporary balance of the relations of class forces is upset and new forces emerge, old forces run through their *repertoires* of domination. Such moments signal, not necessarily a revolutionary conjuncture nor the collapse of the state, but rather the coming of 'iron times'. It does not follow either that the 'normal' mechanisms of state are abrogated. But class domination will be exercised, in such moments, through a modification in the *modes of hegemony*; and one of the principal ways in which this is registered is in terms of a tilt in the operation of the state away from consent towards the pole of coercion. It is important to note that this does not entail a suspension of the 'normal' exercise of state power – it is not a move to what is sometimes called a fully exceptional form of the state. It is better understood as a – to put it paradoxically – an 'exceptional moment' in the 'normal' form of the late capitalist state. What makes it 'exceptional' is the increased reliance on coercive mechanisms and apparatuses already available within the normal *repertoire* of state power, and the powerful orchestration, in support of this tilt of the balance towards the coercive pole, of an *authoritarian* consensus. In such moments the 'relative autonomy' of the state is no longer enough to secure the measures necessary for social cohesion or for the larger economic tasks which a failing and weakened capital requires. The forms of state intervention thus become more overt and more direct. Consequently such moments are also marked by a process of 'unmasking'. The masks of liberal consent and popular consensus slip to reveal the reserves of coercion and force on which the cohesion of the state and its legal authority finally depends; but there is also a stripping away of the masks of neutrality and independence which normally are suspended over the various branches and apparatuses of the State – the

Law, for example. This tends further to polarise the 'crisis of hegemony',
since the state is progressively drawn, now in its own name, down into
the arena of struggle and *direction*, and exhibits more plainly than it
does in its routine manifestations what it is and what it must do to
provide the 'cement' which holds a ruptured social formation together.
(Hall et al. 1978: 217)

It is useful to quote this passage extensively, since Hall et al. make
quite clear how the machinery of the state is linked to policing the
effective control of the population when social disagreement occurs.
Analysing in minute detail the *'repertoires* of domination' increasingly applied by the South African government to its citizens in order
to enforce compliance with the ideology of apartheid, Don Foster
explicitly linked Hall's analysis with the increasing crisis in the
white hegemony in South Africa that occurred with the advent of the
Nationalist Party in 1948 (Foster et al. 1987). Foster et al. demonstrate how this 'crisis of hegemony' manifested itself in the sequence
of repressive measures implemented by different apartheid
Nationalist governments, in which detention without trial was
merely one in a raft of coercive measures that sought to bolster the
sagging white hegemony. As I shall examine in Chapter 6, many of
the acts and legal measures were designed to deny black South
Africans any sense of human entitlement or rights, thereby removing
a sense of integrated selfhood.

The treatment of history and memory in these prison narratives is
not simply a case of constituting the lost part of the self though.
Oliver Lovesey has argued that these texts are not to be thought of
as autobiographical in the recognised sense, since the essence of the
African prison memoir often focuses upon an individual's confrontation with the search for national identity. Allegorising the structuring of national histories, these imprisonment narratives' treatment
of the writing of history offer 'a counter-discourse, not a confession or
a justification, which exposes the colonial legacy in the discourses of
neocolonialism, and its traces in the discourse of nationalism'
(Lovesey 1996: 210). Indeed, Lovesey explicitly argues that 'the isolation of the individual from the community (and the resultant existentialist despair) is linked to the nation's traumatized self-alienation'
(Lovesey 1996: 211). Kate Millett has written that 'Detention without
trial is not only an assault on one politically committed person but
also "a calculated act of psychological terror", which is aimed at
everyone, a program of the "psychological siege of the whole nation"'
(Millett 1994: 203). Ngugi, for his part, agrees, and also argues that
for him 'detention is not a personal affair' (Thiong'o 1981a: 28; xi).
Consequently, the comments of the narrating self in Ngugi's
Detained develop into critical analyses of Kenyan history and culture
in general, as acts of resistance inside jail become part of a resistance

outside jail. In fact, *Detained* makes itself part of a Kenyan 'resist-ance-culture', borrowing from two traditions in its various quotations and allusions to radical poets – Marxism and nationalist liberalism – which gives *Detained* a specifically historical perspective (Afejuku 1990). Tim Jenkin, in his thrilling account of his detention and famous escape from the maximum security prison in Pretoria that held the white political detainees under apartheid, entitled *Escape from Pretoria*, also regarded detention as an act of state political violence that had to be resisted. As Jenkin states, 'For us an escape was a political act, not an individual flight for freedom. It was this implicit trust in each other as comrades that made escape possible' (Jenkin 1987: 95). In other words, the act of escape, as much as the act of writing his imprisonment narrative, is an act of political defi-ance and resistance to an unacceptable ideological system. Indeed, dissatisfaction with the ethical and political premises of their cultures or societies pervades these testimonies. Writers such as Ngugi, Soyinka, Dingake and others repeatedly link their political detention to the dilemmas of their African nations. Their writing attempts to resist the depoliticised, dehistoricised nation space that is the desired consequence of their enforced isolation within time and space in solitary confinement in national prisons. These imprison-ment narratives are an attempt to break the plot of monotonous daily drudgery that severs one from social and political life, by connecting their individual histories to the nation's story. What we might term 'anguished memory' can be defined as discontent in search of form – it is memory that is aware of the fact that the self is always excluded from the original event, and thus imprisons the consciousness that it should be liberating.

Remembered histories as political counter-discourses act as a self-preservation mechanism and sustain the detainees in many of these narratives. Just such a process is evident in *Robben Island Hell-Hole: Reminiscences of a Political Prisoner*, the memoir of Moses Dlamini, sentenced to a six-year term and imprisoned on Robben Island for two and a half years as a Pan African Congress (PAC) activist. His record of imprisonment is studded with calls-to-arms, invocations of militant resistance and nationalist and patriotic chants. His narra-tive is structured as a series of flashbacks interwoven into the account of his time on the Island, seeking to demonstrate by retro-spect what caused Dlamini's political consciousness to be raised, how and when he got involved in political activism, and how he eventually came to be associated with the PAC in 1961. Later in the memoir, at the point that he is interrogated about his political activities by one of the prison officials on the Island, Dlamini rails against the policy of the Bantustans in South Africa (effectively the balkanisation of South Africa into racially separated homelands), as well as the general polices of racial segregation instituted by apartheid (Dlamini 1984: 134). Time and again, the narrative connects his personal incarceration with memories of the past and the history of the nation. A further example of this explicit link where imprisonment causes a meditation on the past and history occurs in the Nigerian novelist and political activist Ken Saro-Wiwa's prison diary, *A Month and a Day*. This becomes the occasion for an historical account of his role in the long-running political struggle against the Nigerian government's exploitative treatment of the Ogoni people, who suffered the oppression of the rest of Nigeria and multinational oil companies as they sought to extract the oil lying under the Ogoni tribal lands. In an explicit link, Saro-Wiwa caustically observes: 'You can tell the state of a nation by the way it keeps its prisons, prisoners mostly being out of sight' (Saro-Wiwa 1995: 224). Similarly linking the personal and the historical, at one point in his prison memoir, *The Man Died*, Wole Soyinka describes how he was chained while writing his notes for the prison officer. His manacles prompt a vestigial racial memory of slavery, and he senses that they define his humanity in some way, and this racial memory in turn causes a meditation on oppression:

> It was nothing new; vicariously, by ideology or form of racial memory, this contradiction may be felt, is felt, with vivid sufficiency to make passionate revolutionaries of the most cosseted life. Abstract, intellectual fetters are rejected just as passionately. But in the experience of the physical thing the individual does not stand alone, most especially the black man. I had felt, it seemed to me, hundreds of years before, as I believe I did experience the triggering of a surely re-incarnated moment when at school I first encountered engravings of slave marches in history books. Even when I met my first lunatics under the care of traditional healers, chained at the ankles to curb their violence, the degree of non-acceptance of such therapy bordered, I often think, on racial memory. Surely it cannot be a strictly personal experience. (Soyinka 1972: 39)

Here is an example of the way in which the past returns to haunt the present, a personal memory becoming a racial memory, triggered in Proustian fashion by a tool of neo-colonial oppression. Werner Sedlak has argued that Soyinka presents himself as a politically committed artist, since his narrative is underpinned by African communalism and mutual aid (Sedlak 1996). Rejecting Karl Jaspers's existentialism (Soyinka 1972: 88–90), *The Man Died* effectively becomes a meditation upon the strengths and weaknesses of communalism and individualism, offering a vision of a political future based upon memories and histories hitherto repressed by the state.

Memories of the past can also be historical memories which themselves possess political portent. *Robben Island*, D. M. Zwelonke's semi-fictional account of the detention of his PAC protagonist called Bekimpi on Robben Island, narrates how the Island has constantly been associated with political racism and segregation. Known also as Makana Island (in memory of the Xhosa leader Makana the Left-handed, 'the first victim of colonialism', who was exiled to the Island by the British in the nineteenth century), the 'devil island' became known as the University of Makana, where influential political detainees like Nelson Mandela and Tabo Mbeki continued amongst themselves to consider, diagnose and plan for the demise of the apartheid regime. Zwelonke's narrative depicts how Bekimpi constantly resorts to memory as a necessary political strategy in combating the effects of isolation. On one occasion, a song sung by fellow prisoners invokes the past names of figures in the history of apartheid repression, such as Makana, Simon Khuboni, Pahle and Mountain Langbon, and concludes with the words 'Your names shall not dry from our lips. / Immortality has become a platitude, / A conso-lation of no value to you; / Yet we shall remember' (Zwelonke 1973: 49). Later in the book, Bekimpi has a dream about the missing past and how the lack of a past prevents self-knowledge in the present: 'Our past is empty and it has no beginning; / Our future is blurred and it has no destination'; 'We do not know the beauty of our land, because of misinterpreted histories'; 'Fare thee well, brother, and rediscover yourself; / Discover your past; discover your base ... / For there lies our survival' (Zwelonke 1973: 84–5). Unsurprisingly, we learn that Bekimpi's period in solitary confinement concusses him. During the course of his dreams, fantasies and recollections of the past, he finally realises that he has been revisiting the past and that this is partly what has been sustaining him, although he is finally shocked by the memory of the death of Nompi (his earlier girlfriend) in the electric chair, as she refuses to betray his whereabouts. Memory is figured to him as a cat to his rat:

> The whole weight of this memory, like a big boulder, rolled on him; he squeezed into a corner, but it reached him there. He was like a cornered rat in an empty cupboard, and the memory was a monstrous cat advanc-ing, ready to claw. He did not want to think about Nompi, but this whole review of the past was bringing him to it. The memory came in the guise of hallucination, of daydream. It was the only way it could come, through his struggles to suppress it. He pretended he was Zweli ... It revived the name with its bitter memories, the name which Bekimpi had decided to forsake after the tragedy of his girl. (Zwelonke 1973: 126–7)

Memory hunts him down, ready to assault him, in a manner that actually reminds him of a bitter past before the bitterness of the Island life.

As any observer of a court trial would know, it is to be acknowledged that witnesses do not always have the most accurate recall of events. Yet calling into question the reliability of these prison testimonies – for example, questioning whether memory can accurately retrieve the missing past after so much time has elapsed – appears to be a misuse of terms and contexts. For torture and prison memory is insomniac – it never went to sleep to be later reawakened. Memory is both an escape from the past but also a shroud that covers one's life, ever-present in one's daily life. The paradox of how one survived this traumatic 'death' event is one of the urgent but unspoken topics of these testimonies.

Chronotopes of incarceration

Prisons contrive in every way to make one feel powerless. In this respect, prisons seem to share with melancholia the deprivation of agency. Yet prison writing is better construed as a 'working-through' to regain agency and self-control in the face of the traumatic, enforced removal of one's individuality; and there are few, if any, instances of 'acting-out' in these imprisonment narratives, since the genre essentially eschews the passivity and stultification associated with melancholia. Generally speaking, these narratives are often regarded as a genre of self-confession, of articulating a philosophy of bare survival and of enacting strategies of resistance. They are all these. Yet they are also narratives of traumatic experiences, of trauma in terms of the state terror performed upon victims' consciousnesses and bodies. In seeking some defence against these traumas, one occasionally finds that the prison narrative is converted into an occasion for sublimity, a transvaluation into a test of the self or group and an entry into the extraordinary. For example, there are parts of Breyten Breytenbach's prison narrative that do just this. Instead of becoming the vents which pose the problematic question of individual or national identity, the excess of trauma can become an uncanny source of elation or ecstasy, as in the sublime. Dominick LaCapra cautions against this, since he considers this as indicative of a romanticisation of traumatic experience. As we saw in Chapter 1, LaCapra argues that writers ought to practise what he calls 'empathic unsettlement' in historiography and critical practices, if they are to guard against gaining sweet succour from the synthetic construction of spiritually elevating versions of acute events.

Nevertheless, these prison memoirs form a genre that is raw and bleeding. Crossing racial boundaries, consecutive narrative form is disrupted which in turn duplicates the traumatic disjunctions of prison life itself. They bear witness to an agonising contradiction: frequently, the survivor's need to share and have validated a traumatic memory through the act of testimony stands in conflict with a second, and equally important, need to mitigate the memory's affective charge. A survivor may feel both psychologically and morally compelled to commemorate or testify to an event, even though his or her mental well-being depends on reducing the event's affective impact. Time and again in these narratives, we see survivors playing out these contradictory impulses at a formal level: between desire for realism, and recognition that realism is wretchedly inadequate to the specificity and uniqueness of the traumatic experiences. For these are narratives in which trauma motivates their language, their consciousness and their actions: trauma at the personal level, and trauma at the national level. Imprisonment narratives bespeak an act of national crisis in terms of the threat to the dominant hegemony, and, as a consequence, a state of trauma induced in the detainees. These narratives testify to a state of national trauma, as well as regional or continental trauma in their stages as postcolonial nations and regions. Consequently, these narratives also confront us with the challenge of enlarging our notion of what African history may be, what these detentions have made it, and how it urges us to reconsider the relation of the past to the present and a tentative future. There might be those who are very wary of accepting these testimonial imprisonment narratives as a form of history. Yet as we have seen, prison writing does project theories of history and representation. The chronotope (as articulated by Bakhtin) captures the simultanaeity of spatial and temporal articulations in cultural practices: in the production of chronotopes, 'time, as it were, thickens, takes on flesh, becomes artistically visible; likewise, space becomes charged and responsive to the movements of time, plot and history' (Bakhtin 1981: 84). Prison writing is chronotopic – fixated upon time and space, it both thickens and magnifies the two. One could go so far as to say that these African imprisonment narratives are inherently chronotopic, demonstrating a heightened awareness of time (history) and space (nation). This chapter has sought to provide an analysis of the testimonies of that chronotopic African trauma on the space and time of representation whilst suffering the barbarities of torture during political imprisonment. As legacies of the colonial imagination, they threaten to be a permanent hole in the ozone layer of history, through which infiltrate memories of a potentially crippling past. These testimonies remind us how overwhelming and perhaps ultimately insurmountable are the tasks of reversing its legacy. Providing a unique insight into the representations of the vestigial trauma in modern Africa, these narratives search for value while contending with worthlessness, allowing us to observe the evolution of ethical consciousness in the most barbaric and primeval of circumstances, seeking to shape history and some semblance of moral continuity in the face of the illogic of atrocity.

Notes

[1] For example, see Driver 1975 and Jacobs 1992, both of whom suggest a mordant sub-genre of apartheid prison narratives, the 'Robben Island genre'.

[2] See Horn 1994: 137–42, who tracks the significance of memory to the self-preservation of the incarcerated writer.

[3] See Schalkwyk 1994: 23–45, for an extremely subtle and intelligent comparison of these two writers.

[4] See Wole Soyinka's preoccupations with transcending the body in prison (Soyinka 1972: 39, 43, 140ff, 212, 225–6, 249, 251 and 255). Tim Jenkin also writes about the fantasy of transcending one's physical incarceration by trying to fly over the prison walls. See Jenkin 1987: 175–6.

[5] Sheila Roberts notes that 'there are predictable elements in any prison-experience and these do run the risk of becoming hackneyed through repetition in writing. It seems to me that prison literature might be more vulnerable to cliché than other kinds because of the very circumscription of the prison environment. There are, for instance, countless images of birds as symbols of freedom; expected references to the smallness of space and the expansibility of time; the frequent transformation of women – mothers, wives, girlfriends – into otherwordly [sic] or saintly figures; and the inevitable glorification of life on the outside' (Roberts 1985: 65–6).

[6] Jacobs 1986 argues that this projection of a metafictional self in these prison narratives is a form of self-protection, a 'shield for the "I"'. See also Roberts 1986.

[7] J. M. Coetzee finally regards Breytenbach's prison poetry as a form of diversion and a process of self-deflection: 'But the very gesture of blaming, so widespread in his writing, mirroring the blaming of him by censor and judge, belongs to an ultimately futile strategy of demonization and explusion.' See Coetzee 1996: 232. Compare this with Jolly 1996: 99, where she considers the poetry 'a vital act of self-defence'.

[8] See the very astute analytical study of the core components of autobiographical acts in Smith and Watson 2001.

[9] See Harlow 1987: 120, who distinguishes prison memoirs from autobiography because they are not written as 'a book of one's own', but as collective documents, testimonies written by individuals to their common struggle.

[10] Definition from Statute of Amnesty International, as amended by the 26th International Council, 16–23 August, 2003 <http://web.amnesty.org/pages/aboutai-statute-eng>.

[11] United Nations, *Declaration on the Protection of All Persons from Being Subjected to Torture and Other Cruel, Inhuman or Degrading Treatment or Punishment*, adopted by General Assembly resolution 3452 (XXX) of 9 December 1975.

[12] See Schalkwyk 2001: 1–36, in which he argues that white and black women detainees forge their different strategies for survival.

[13] For two anthologies of narratives, poetry, interviews and accounts of women imprisoned by the apartheid regime, see Russell 1990, and Schreiner 1992.

6

Embedding memory, seizing history: South African resistance poetry in the 1970s and 1980s

> Over three centuries have passed in our land,
> leaving feeble strings of our history
> to hold the decaying effigies of our past.
> (Oswald Mtshali, 'Effigies Are Falling', *Fireflames*)

In August 2000, in the remote veld of what is now Kwa-Zulu Natal, a north-eastern province of South Africa, a team of archaeologists began digging up the past as the first stage of a projected five-year survey of the Anglo-Zulu battlefield of Isandhlwana. Named after the impressive mountain that towers over the site of the battle (the word 'Isandhlwana' comes from the mountain's resemblance to the second stomach of an ox), Isandhlwana is the site of one of the most ignominious and humiliating defeats that the British Army ever suffered, albeit commemorated heroically in Charles Fripp's famous painting *The Last Battle of Isandhlwana* (1885) (Figure II). Approximately twenty thousand of Cetshwayo's Zulu warriors wiped out an entire British column of fifteen hundred soldiers and their African allies, sent into the Zulu kingdom to crush the uprising nation in 1879.[1] This was by any stretch of the imagination a remarkable Zulu victory, where breathtakingly courageous warriors armed with assegais (short, close-quarter, stabbing spears) and cowhide shields, overcame highly trained European soldiers armed with Martini-Henry rifles that could hit their target at about two hundred yards. It was a defeat that sent shock-waves rippling through the Empire, an event that has understandably been erased from the easy memory of the British and subsequent Afrikaner rulers of South Africa.

Almost a century later, the memory of that Zulu victory rose again

II Charles Fripp, *The Battle of Isandhlwana* (1885)

in the midst of further bitter armed conflict, this time in the 'South-western Township', or Soweto as it is more infamously known, in Johannesburg in June 1976. In a poem entitled 'Isandhlwana', Duncan Matlho digs up that past, evoking and manipulating the images of that victory over white colonialism as a stirring battle cry to the young students resisting the armed apartheid riot police in the now infamous shanty town. I quote the entire poem for the reader's benefit – the notes are in the original text.

Isandhlwana

> Isandhlwana
> mayihlome![1] the war-cry
> the impala horn
> the tom-tom drums on the lips
> of the hearts of plumed warriors
> time ticked the forces of defence
> waiting waiting waiting
> poised for the night to clear the morn
> the shrubs shrugged the minutes
> where justice lurked heaving sighs
> of determination on the forest's brow –
> Isandhlwana
> hearts steeled
> then a skip, a majestic leap over a brier
> over a boulder – aha – over injustice
> crush!

to a singing clash of spears
done –
it was done – it had to be
guilty groans arose
with a wave of triumph
scorning that sea-belched-vermin
the hilly sages and the sombre valleys
answered – Isandhlwana
the name that never lost its sting
its step astride on ancestral braves
rose striding the thorny blast of freedom
cutting Goch Street[2] on its golden pants
stood granite firm in Dobsonville[3]
spear-spit fire in Rustenburg[4]
and laughed as it broke loose
in Louis Trichardt[5]
Isandhlwana – the victory
i am Isandhlwana
hold your tongue and listen
you whose tongues and insolence
have decreed this waste this night
    the owl has hooted
    on the bones once more
this time Cetshwayo[6] has consulted with Makanda,[7]
Makanda with Moshoeshoe,[8] Moshoeshoe
with Sekhukhuni,[9] Sekhukhuni with Ramabulana,[10]
Ramabulana with Nghunghunyana[11]
    all in the nerve of the spear
in the heart and lips of the clenched fist
and Luthuli[12] has decreed
let the Spear sing ...

[1] Mayihlome! = Ready for battle
[2, 3, 4, 5] Places where African National Congress (ANC) guerrilla units were involved in armed action
[6, 7, 8, 9, 10, 11] All were leaders of resistance to colonisation
[12] Chief Albert J. Luthuli, president-general of the ANC from 1952–60, and winner of the Nobel Peace Prize in 1959

(Matlho 1980: 136–7)

Contrary to the picture of British soldiers in a heroic pose staving off the onslaught of native warriors in that far corner of the empire made famous in Fripp's painting, Matlho's poem reverses the image, presenting the heroic war-cries of the victors echoing down the century, urging on the youth of Soweto to their freedom. The poet turns the student 'charges' and pitched battles with the riot police into the glorious victory of Cetshwayo's troops at Isandhlwana. The poem is studded with references to traditional symbols like 'the impala horn' and 'the tom-tom drums', the 'plumed warriors', as well as a roll-call of major historical leaders of resistance to colonialism. This poem is reminiscent of Duncan Matlho's other poem 'The Skin Shield our Pride' (Feinberg 1980: 120–2), Rebecca Matlou's poem 'A Soldier at War (To the Year of the Spear)' (Feinberg 1980: 126–8) and Dikobe wa Mogale's 'Baptism of fire', in which Isandhlwana and the victory with spears is invoked once again (Mogale 1984: 9–10). History is used to justify, exonerate and support current political action, as well as inspire the actions of the current generation. Invocations of the ancestors and the poem's pervasive image of the ritualistic 'washing of the spears' – a symbol of Zulu triumph and manhood – all effectively summon the past as a mechanism for inspiring political victory in the present.

Duncan Matlho's poem is characteristic of the manner in which history is recuperated by the Soweto and other resistance poets for political purposes in the 1970s and 1980s. Many of the poets involved in the so-called 'Soweto poetry renaissance' in South Africa, the most prominent being Oswald Mtshali, Mafika Gwala, Mongane Serote, Daniel P. Kunene, Sipho Sepamla, Ingoapele Mandigoane, Keorapetse Kgositsile, James Matthews, Njabulo Ndebele, Chris van Wyk and Don Mattera, as well as a number of other black South African poets in the 1980s and 1990s such as Mandlenkosi Langa, Essop Patel, Lesego Rampolokeng, Seitlhamo Motsapi, Mzwakhe Mbuli, Alfred Qabula, Ilva Mackay, Farouk Asvat, Christine Douts and Shabbir Banoobhai, have sought to wrest back their expropri-ated histories and pasts. Their poetry figures as a repository for popular memory and consciousness and for mobilising a collective response to alienation and domination. The poetry also maintains a powerful sense of national and liberationist identity. Barbara Harlow has argued that the resistance poems, challenging the stan-dard patterns of western modernism as they do, 'actively engage in the historical process of struggle against the cultural oppression of imperialism, and assert thereby their own polemical historicity' (Harlow 1987: 37). The polemical quality of many resistance poems, the bareness and minimalism of their language, is part of the offen-sive, representing part of the critical attack on forms of cultural imperialism. Political riots are not fought in iambic pentameter. This poetry is not the rarefied, transcendent discourse of inner contempla-tion of the Romantics; instead it is a much rawer, starker albeit inte-gral, part of the ideological foundations of a new social order.

This chapter will address several areas and interrelated questions. How do these poets utilise history or invoke memory for their politi-cal purposes? What sorts of memory do they invoke? What models of history are the sources for their historical tropes and figures? Can these memories and histories be formal as well as content? i.e. are the figures of history encoded in the forms of verse they write, or the literary forebears or traditions to which they appeal? Do poetic appeals to memory or history differ generically from fiction or drama? The discussion of these issues will demonstrate the extent to which the Soweto poets were responsible not merely for rejuvenating black South African literature in the years following the vigorous state censorship in the wake of the Sharpeville Massacre in 1960 (which drove so many black writers into exile and silence), but they were also instrumental in utilising the past as a way of helping construct a realisable political and cultural alternative in the future, a 'post-apartheid vision'. With the raw and bloody memory of Sharpeville and the traumatic and brutal treatment of the Soweto schoolchildren in the June '76 Uprising sharp in their minds, these poets explicitly recognise and articulate the history of experience of apartheid as trauma, as a past that continues to upset and desta-bilise black society, as well as South African society more generally. This poetry is characterised by a repeated return to the past, to a recovery of erased histories, to censored indigenous memories, and this is symptomatic of a culture in the grip of a political racial trauma. Not simply propagandist art, nor merely art promoting a simplistic 'race revenge', these poets collectively testify to the way in which art can provide an effective mechanism for past-traumatic stress relief through the rereading and recuperation of history, the past and alternative memories. The recuperation and 'working-through' of these 'histories-under-erasure' are a crucial element of the nation-building of the new South Africa.

Black consciousness and aesthetics

It is necessary at the outset to identify two groups of poets in the late 1960s: the Sharpeville and the Soweto poets. Generally speaking, the Sharpeville writers are Dennis Brutus, Arthur Nortje, Cosmo Pieterse, Keorapetse Kgositsile and Masizi Kunene; while the Soweto poets are James Matthews, Mafika Gwala, Mongone Serote and Sipho Sepamla, with Oswald Mtshali straddling these two groups. Dennis Brutus distinguishes two sorts of poetry evident during these years: first, a poetry of protest, which is a poetry of personal response to oppression, based on justice, rights and human dignity; and, second, a poetry of resistance, which is a poetry of confrontation, provocation and defiance – a call to action (Knipp 1993: 131).[2] Many of the Soweto poets' work combines self-assertion and the ideology of the Black Consciousness Movement (BCM), with elements of Négritude and aspects of African American black aesthetics. Piniel Shava notes how the ideas of militant Soweto poets were partly borrowed from Négritude, and that blackness was celebrated as a militant concept: that Black Consciousness's 'concern with the past of black people is closely connected with the BCM's emphasis on the pride and dignity blacks ought to feel from being black' (Shava 1989: 103).[3] It is important to understand the extent to which Black Consciousness provided a significant impetus to the aesthetic renaissance of black culture, and was not merely a means of establishing an alternative political rhetoric to that of the predominantly socialist and economic ideological orientation of the rival political organisation, the African National Congress.

Black Consciousness emerged as a political ideology in South Africa in the late 1960s. The years following the Sharpeville Massacre in 1960 were a time of intense repression. Among other things, the African National Congress (ANC) and the Pan Africanist Congress (PAC) were banned under the Unlawful Organizations Act of 1960, house arrest and detention without trial in order to silence political opposition were introduced, censorship powers were extended by means of the Publications and Entertainment Act in 1966, and the security police system was consolidated and extended with the establishment of the Bureau of State Security (BOSS) in 1968. In spite of these repressive measures, frustration with the state policy of 'separate development' led to the emergence of a new black political movement, Black Consciousness, which took root particularly among the black youth. In an action that was to have far-reaching political ramifications, the student leader Steve Biko and his black student supporters split off from the multiracial National Union of South African Students (NUSAS) in 1969 to forge the black South African Students' Organisation (SASO), which was to become one of the most prominent black consciousness bodies. Paradoxically, the state initially encouraged Black Consciousness in the mistaken belief that it was furthering the kind of tribal division that apartheid was expediently seeking to enforce.

As Steve Biko argued in 1973, Black Consciousness was founded upon 'the realisation of blacks that the most powerful weapon at the hands of the oppressor is the mind of the oppressed' (Biko 1979: 92). Black Consciousness emphasised the psychological and political liberation of black people and reasserted the communal values of a black humanism. In his influential essay 'Black Consciousness and the Quest for a True Humanity', Biko defined the ideology as follows:

Black Consciousness is an attitude of mind and a way of life, the most positive call to emanate from the black world for a long time. Its essence is the realisation by the black man of the need to rally together with his brothers around the cause of their oppression – the blackness of their skin – and to operate as a group in order to rid themselves of the shackles that bind them to perpetual servitude. It is based on a self-examination which has ultimately led them to believe that by seeking to run away from themselves and to emulate the white man, they are insulting the intelligence of whoever created them black. The philosophy of Black Consciousness therefore expresses group pride and the determination of the black to rise and attain the envisaged self. (Biko 1979: 91–2)

From its inception, the Black Consciousness Movement broadened in scope and influence, culminating in the Soweto uprising of 1976, when black school pupils took to the streets in protest against the enforcement of Afrikaans as the medium of instruction in schools. Townships all around South Africa took up the issue, and it spread from the youth to all other sectors of the community. Nevertheless, the overall impact of black consciousness on workers was limited. Leading Black Consciousness organisations, including SASO, the Soweto Students' Representative Council, the Black Communities Programmes, the Black Parents' Association and the Black People's Convention, were declared unlawful by the state in 1977.

Black Consciousness involved an active process of historical and cultural recuperation, as Allan Boesak, a leading black anti-apartheid campaigner, asserted that Black Consciousness may be described as:

the awareness of black people that their humanity is constituted by their blackness. It means that black people are no longer ashamed that they are black, that they have a black history and a black culture distinct from the history and culture of white people. It means that blacks are determined to be judged no longer by, and to adhere no longer to white values. It is an attitude, a way of life. (Boesak 1978: 1)

Steve Biko urged that 'part of the approach envisaged in bringing about "black consciousness" has to be directed to the past, to seek to rewrite the history of the black man and to produce in it the heroes who form the core of the African background' (Biko 1979: 29). This echoes Frantz Fanon's description of the process of deculturation in the colonial context, by which the colonised subject is forced to accept the superiority of colonial culture, and which produces a deep-seated alienation in the colonised subject. Indeed, Biko frequently invokes Fanon's ideas in his writings (Biko 1979: 61–72, and see also Shava 1989: 103), especially the Fanonist process of self-empowerment founded upon a rediscovery and promotion of indigenous cultural values and traditions after a phase of deculturation. As Fanon puts it, 'The culture, abandoned, sloughed off, rejected, despised, becomes for the inferiorized an object of passionate attachment' (Fanon 1970: 51). Despite the revaluation of the past as the 'true culture', Fanon cautions against an over-hasty endorsement of a past that has often become ossified: 'The culture put into capsules, which has vegetated since the foreign domination, is revalorised. It is not reconceived, grasped anew, dynamized from within. It is shouted. And this head-long, unstructured, verbal revalorization, conceals paradoxical attitudes' (Fanon 1970: 52). This prompt embrace of indigenous values and traditions mirrors the preoccupations of Black Consciousness and many of the Soweto poets, in asserting the value of black identity and cultural institutions. Nevertheless, these poets for the most part sidestepped the potential pitfalls and paradoxes described by Fanon. This was largely due, in the context of South African apartheid, to the ways in which black culture had continued to develop outside official discursive spaces and was thus not historically static. Conferences and cultural festivals in the 1970s promoted the ideas of Fanon, American black power rhetoric and the Négritude of north and west Africa; and literature, particularly poetry, was regarded as pivotal in asserting black culture, with poems like Mafika Gwala's 'In Memorium' (Gwala 1982: 8) embedding this Black Consciousness ideology in all aspects of the aesthetic.

What has come to be called Soweto poetry first began to appear in the mid-1960s, particularly in the magazine *The Classic*, which took its name from the laundry that fronted the shebeen in which the magazine was started in 1963. Soweto poetry received an enormous impetus from the huge success of Oswald Mtshali's *Sounds of a Cowhide Drum*, published by Renoster Books in 1971. Ursula Barnett's significant study of black South African literature argues that Mtshali's volume started a whole new era of black South African poetry, 'by looking upon poetry as a form of communication, rather than as the intellectual pursuit of crystallising individual thought' (Barnett 1983: 53). The oppositional and challenging aspect of this poetry was soon realised by the state authorities, and James Matthews's and Gladys Thomas's volume *Cry Rage!* (1972) became the first book of poems to be banned under the Publications and Entertainments Act. Various cultural groups were formed to promote black poetry and drama, amongst which were the Cultural Committee of SASO, the People's Experimental Theatre (or PET, declared subversive in 1975), the Mihloti Black Theatre Group and the Music Drama Arts and Literature Institute (MDALI or Mdali). The lead shown by Mtshali was soon followed by collections by other poets like Serote, Sepamla, Gwala, van Wyk and Madingoane; and, in addition to individual volumes, several important anthologies of resistance poetry have been published, including *To Whom It May Concern: An Anthology of Black South African Verse* (1973), *Black Voices Shout!: An Anthology of Poetry* (1974, banned), *Voices from Within: Black Poetry from Southern Africa* (1982), *The Return of the Amasi Bird: Black South African Poetry: 1891–1981* (1982), *Black Mamba Rising* (1986, banned), *One Day in June: Poetry and Prose from Troubled Times* (1986) and *Ear to the Ground: Contemporary Worker Poets* (1991).

Michael Chapman, who has been one of the champions of the

Soweto poets, has described Soweto poetry as 'the single most important socio-literary phenomenon of the seventies in South Africa'
(Chapman 1982: 11). Prevented from acquiring an extensive knowledge of western literature by the state Bantu Education policies, and
rejecting the cultural forms associated with colonial occupation (as
much out of necessity as out of ideological imperatives), Soweto poets
investigated poetic models in traditional African forms (such as
izibongo, see below), in jazz and blues music, African American
verse, the rhetoric of political manifestos, and even plain speech.
Texts were mostly written in English, reflecting the black consciousness anxiety about using indigenous languages that might deepen
the tribal fissures already exploited by apartheid. Using a racy,
ungrammatical English, the diction drew upon Americanisms, jazz
beats, expletives, slang, 'cat' vocabulary, *tsotsi-taal* (literally 'thug
lingo', or the township patois of the 'tsoti' or street thug) and the
terminology of black power. The poets flouted white norms and practices of linguistic orthodoxy, particularly evident in the poetry of
Sipho Sepamla and Mafika Gwala (and more recently poets like
Lesego Rampolokeng), who are clearly influenced by dub and rap
forms, in volumes like *Horns for Hondo* (1990) and *The Bavino
Sermons* (1999), bleak poems that are obsessed with exploring the
past and the injustices of apartheid as they simultaneously look
forward to a generation standing on the eve of the death throes of a
wounded ideology. As Chapman and other commentators have noted,
Soweto poetry made 'its rejection of Western literary and cultural
continuities almost a stylistic and moral imperative' (Chapman 1982:
13). Certainly, in the struggle against apartheid and colonialism, 'the
return to the vernacular languages has invariably been a political
and cultural gesture' (Alvarez-Pereyre 1984: 6).[4]

A further influential platform for the many voices in the wake of
the 1976 Soweto uprisings was the launch of *Staffrider* magazine by
Ravan Press in 1978. From the outset, *Staffrider* stressed a 'democratic' editorial policy, seeking a 'direct line' to the community: 'We
hope that work appearing in the magazine will be selected and edited
as far as possible by the groups themselves. The magazine is
prepared for publication by Ravan Press, but has no editor or editorial board in the usual sense' (*Staffrider* 1:1, March 1978). As the
emergence of these magazines suggests, Soweto poetry was a
popular, fugitive form speaking in unofficial modes and marginal
spaces. Nadine Gordimer and Piniel Shava both point to the manner
in which poetry emerged as a mode of insinuating political debate
into cultural discourse (Gordimer 1976: 134; and Shava 1989: 71).
Gordimer argued that 'Black writers have had to look for survival
away from explicit if not to the cryptic then to the implicit, and in
their case they have turned instinctively to poetry' (Gordimer 1976:

134). As one critic puts it, Oswald Mtshali's influential volume of poems *Sounds of a Cowhide Drum* (1971) is 'a protest collection, the possibility of censorship and even imprisonment imposing on the poet strategies of obliqueness, allusiveness, symbolism, and irony' (Knipp 1993: 133). Jacques Alvarez-Pereyre's authoritative study *The Poetry of Commitment in South Africa*, also discusses the strategies of adopting poetry as a means for discussion of political events and actions: 'Experience had taught the blacks that prose was a dangerous instrument because too explicit. The government tolerated poetry more readily because it reached a smaller audience. But the poem is also a hiding place, and a marvellous short-cut to saying what is essential with great economy because it expresses the immediacy of emotion in a concentrated form' (Alvarez-Pereyre 1984: 38). Indeed, the title *Staffrider* epitomised this stance of shrewdness and cunning, referring as it did to the black passengers who hitched dangerous and illegal rides on trains by hanging on to the outside of the doors:

> A staffrider is, let's face it, a *skelm* [Afrikaans, pronounced 'skelem', 'a scoundrel', or 'layabout'] of sorts. Like Hermes or Mercury – the messenger of the gods in classical mythology – he is almost as light-fingered as he is fleet-footed. A skilful entertainer, a bringer of messages, a useful person but ... slightly disreputable. Our censors may not like him, but they should consider putting up with him. A whole new literature is knocking at the door, and if our society is to change without falling apart it needs all the messages it can get – the bad as well as the good.
>
> Like him or not, he is part of the present phase of our common history, riding 'staff' on the fast and dangerous trains of our late seventies. He is part of the idiom of this time. (*Staffrider* 1:1, March 1978)

The first issue of *Staffrider* was banned because – it was alleged – some of the poems 'undermined the authority and image of the police'. In his excellent analysis of the central preoccupations of *Staffrider* – blackness, revolt against oppression, the people – Michael Vaughan notes that the undoubted strength of the journal lies in its central role in establishing a new black literature (Vaughan 1984). Nevertheless, he considers the opening issue's self-description of the 'staffrider', the symbolic figure cocking a snook at authority, as indicative of the individualist ideology that pervades the journal, an individualism that Vaughan regards as the journal's weakness.

The poems which appeared in *Staffrider*, and in individual volumes in the aftermath of Soweto 1976, represented departures in form and ideology from those that had been published in *The Purple Renoster*, in *The Classic* and in early collections, such as Mtshali's *Sounds of a Cowhide Drum*. Initially, Soweto poems were aimed at a white, liberal readership, and used poetic techniques not dissimilar to those expected by western-trained readers. Poems such as Mtshali's 'Boy on a Swing' or 'An Abandoned Bundle', for example, might be recognisedly lyric poems. Yet as Chapman observes:

> By the mid-seventies ... the emphasis had shifted with Serote's Black Consciousness voice (predictably less popular with whites) finding its full power in an uncompromising poetry of resistance. This is a mobilizing rhetoric utilizing epic forms (in a highly contemporary, almost Brechtian sense) and traditional African oral techniques of repetition, parallelism and ideophones. By these means the poet seeks to impart to a black communal audience, often in a context of performance, a message of consciousness-raising and race pride. (Chapman 1982: 12)

Mtshali's later collection entitled *Fireflames* (1980) embraces much more combative poems like 'Flames of Fury', 'Hector Peterson – the Young Martyr', '16 June 1979 – a Commemoration in Harlem of the Soweto Uprising', 'I'm a Burning Chimney', and 'The Raging Generation', and throws down the gauntlet of political challenge in a rhetoric of implacable resistance and apocalyptic prophecy. These poems frequently resort to memory as a means to invoke past heroes, past events and censored traditions, as Mtshali seeks to infuse the present with a resistant spirit born of an identifiable cultural past and belonging. Mongone Serote's poetry makes equal invocations of the past and memory as a means of stiffening present political resolve. In later epic works like *Third World Express* (1992) and *Come and Hope With Me* (1994), moments of the past crystallise like epiphanies in memory, in which the past is made tangible again, not black and white but varicoloured, providing mental sustenance against a political system that constantly seeks to erase the past:

> it is simple things which are forgotten
> desecrated
> and defiled
> they are fossilised into a past which is out of reach
> it is in memory that these moments
> crimson
> they dazzle
> they buzz like very long moments of a terribly long day,
> which will not pass.
>
> (Serote 1992: 9)

Alvarez-Pereyre observes that Serote's poems are riddled with expressions of psychological trauma, efforts at memory seeking to recover the past and rewritings of history to include omissions and erasures (Alvarez-Pereyre 1984: 190). Speaking about Serote's earlier epic poem *No Baby Must Weep* (1975), Alex Levumo states that it 'seems to stem from the endless striving of the narrator for an understanding of the burden bequeathed to the current moment by the past. In an intense and concentrated verse that lacks the slyness of Gwala and the humour of Mtsali, Serote tirelessly traces the connection between his subject's current anguish, the suffering of the past and what there may be to hope for in the future' (Levumo 1982: 76). Serote's poem concerns the personal growth and development of the protagonist, who experiences a series of turmoils and oppressions:

> but this wound, this gaping wound, this throbbing wound
> is comfortable at the bottom of my soul
> . . .
> i have pleaded with the voice of this time
> past and coming
> but I shift on this chair
> the wound can't be born
> the soul lies sprawled like a woman defeated by her womanhood.
>
> (Serote 1975)

Quoting this passage, Levumo continues his analysis as a poem about the 'wound': 'Serote embodies the past and all it contains in metaphors drawn from the flesh and the senses. The most important of these is the "wound" that expresses all the particularities that history has impressed onto and into the narrator' (Levumo 1982: 76). Indeed, this theme of the 'wound' surfaces everywhere. Commenting upon the spur to writing injected by the 'trauma' of the 1976 Soweto Uprising, the writers Fhazel Johennesse and Neil Alwin Williams observe that 'From the pain and from the anguish of 16 June comes a new pride. In our work we have not blamed ourselves on history. Instead we have taken our history – personal history and the history of the black struggle – and repossessed it' (Johennesse and Williams 1982: 126). Kelwyn Sole's excellent characterisation of the poetry of the Soweto resistance notes that 'a nostalgia for the black heroes of history is paralleled by a greater interest in traditional forms rather than those of an English literary tradition. Similarly to Negritude, this seems aimed at a rehabilitation of traditional culture and concerns: that is, an attempt at cultural reaffirmation' (Sole 1982: 144). Serote's insistence that 'it is us who will seize history / our freedom' (Chapman 1982: 155) clearly exemplifies the poems' increased 'resistance' rather than 'protest', and marks the shifts that occurred in these later Soweto poems, as Chapman identifies:

> Whereas early Soweto poetry had taken as its highest ideal that Western one of justice, the later poetry, especially that which has appeared since the events of 1976, has rediscovered the highest of African ideals: heroism. Serote, Mtshali and Gwala, as well as many poets writing in *Staffrider* magazine, have begun to focus not so much backwards on a bare Soweto existence as forward to a 'pre-Azanian'

phase of South African history, one wherein the construct of 'the people', including the participatory ideals of black community, has increasingly begun to function as an inspirational myth. (Chapman 1982: 22)

The reception of Soweto poetry has precipitated a discussion about aesthetic propriety and qualitative criteria. The poems have been dismissed by a number of critics as 'poetically inept', 'immature', facile in their treatment of government policies in art form, all of which leads to an attenuation of 'craftsmanship, discipline and art, as well as imagination' (Ullyatt 1977: 58–60).[5] The South African critic and poet Stephen Watson voiced similar aesthetic anxieties in a now infamous retrospective article:

> Today, a coherent 'black aesthetic' remains as remote and unformulated as some mythical 'black value' system. Overwhelmingly, the black poetry of the last two decades consists of a number of half-assimilated European conventions which are frequently patched together in so confused and piecemeal a fashion that one thinks, reading the work, not in terms of a 'renaissance' or 'breakthrough' … or of 'innovations', but rather with anger and dismay at what has happened in this country that such beginnings should have remained largely unfulfilled. (Watson 1987: 23)

Such dismissive comments manifest an ignorance of African forms, a prejudicial commitment to the New Critical model of poetry as opposed to a poetics that departs from its tenets, and a conservative assumption about poetic 'quality', often emanating from a position not dissimilar to that of the colonist's fears of a primitive yet terrifying culture. Aesthetic judgements like these were specifically rejected by the poets themselves, calling as did Mafika Gwala, for 'black standards' that revoke the authority of white culture (Gwala 1982).

Memory and history in Soweto poetry

> only memory can count
> Can score the debt to settle
>   (Sipho Sepamla, 'All That Gold', *The Soweto I Love*)

Many poets explicitly refer to African traditions in their poetry as a refuge from and antidote to the oppressive and debilitatingly censorious white apartheid culture. This fugitive poetry takes many shapes, in terms of both the form and the content of the poetry: the past and memory are resources for the present in a number of different ways. If one opens an anthology like Barry Feinberg's pathbreaking *Poets to the People*, many of the poems are written as *memento moris* to leaders of black political organisations and various 'heroes' and dissidents: dedicated to or about people like Bram Fischer, Denis Goldberg, Arthur Nortje, J. B. Marks, Steve Biko, and

Dennis Brutus's 'For a Dead African', as well as Jack Hodgson (Feinberg 1980: 39), Duma Nokwe (Feinberg 1980: 42), Nelson Mandela (Feinberg 1980: 44), Moses Kotane (Feinberg 1980: 49), Yusuf Dadoo (Feinberg 1980: 49), Walter Sisulu (Feinberg 1980: 49) and Tiro (Feinberg 1980: 45). A poem like 'The Spirit of Bambatha' (Feinberg 1980: 62) apostrophises a whole gallery of ancestors of the struggle and resistance, such as Bambatha, John Dube, Abraham Tiro, Albert Luthuli, Hintsa, Saloojee, Nkosi, Ngudle, Sekukhuni and Makanda. Elsewhere, Lilian Ngoyi is memorialised (Feinberg 1980: 59), Solomon Mahlangu is commemorated (Feinberg 1980: 69), and a poem is written in memory of Joseph Mdluli (Feinberg 1980: 65). Other poems are dedicated to mass events, such as political marches, like the Durban rallies, and commemorate places like Soweto and Sophiatown. Poems invoke past leaders (Feinberg 1980: 46) like Patrice Lumumba, Chief Albert Luthuli and Malcolm X. A. N. C. Kumalo is particularly polemical in his use of past heroes in his poems for inspiring the present, as in, for example, the poem 'A Poem of Vengeance' (Feinberg 1980: 53). Some poems invoke the success of other countries' revolutionary organisations, like Cuba, Vietnam, the MPLA in Mozambique, and the PLO in Palestine, and leaders like Lenin in their struggle against imperialist masters (Feinberg 1980: 48). It becomes clear that here is a whole genre of poems that act as literal – *letteral* – memorials, taking the place of concrete monuments, plaques or busts to mark political and social heroes, in a society that would surely ban or prevent such memorials being erected or built. In this respect, there is a degree of the ritualistic in such poems which include roll-calls of the famous leaders and martyrs of the revolutionary cause. These memorials are partly in compensation for the loss and suffering of the individuals, although they do not aim to vitiate the need for vengeance and retaliation. These narratives of memorial focus upon individuals and write them into a wider narrative of liberation. The poems do not only call upon memories of the past, but are memories themselves. In this way, poems are not meditations or aesthetic beauties but 'weapons', forms of action, like 'Red Our Colour' (Feinberg 1980: 58). Poem after poem in Feinberg's anthology invokes memory, calling upon one to 'Remember ...' (for example, see Barry Feinberg's poem, 'Standing Armed on Our Own Ground', Feinberg 1980: 31). The spear emerges as a central symbol of cultural resistance, partly because of its connection to indigenous cultural history (see the assegai as a weapon at Isandhlwana above), but also because of its symbolic centrality in Zulu and Xhosa cultures and the political insignia of the ANC (Figure III), which is an assegai and a cowhide shield gripped in a fist with a tricolour of gold, green and black.

The colours of the ANC themselves figure prominently in a variety

III ANC symbol

of poems, symbolising as they do the fertility of the land (green), the mineral wealth beneath the soil (gold) and the people (black) of the nation. The colours of the ANC flag were adopted by the ANC in 1925. The spear always acts as an image of past success and power (Feinberg 1980: 63), but it also acts as a symbol of the land, a connection to country, challenging fire, cultural truth and a tool of resistance. Umkhonto we Sizwe, or 'Spear of the Nation', was the name of the military wing of the ANC. A poem like 'Flight of the Spear' (Feinberg 1980: 64) invokes the litany of leaders and connects them to this potent symbol of resistance. Finally, in poems about those in political exile, memory sustains the connection to the land of one's birth in their absence.

Revolutions open up the problem of how to represent change, how to imagine social and political alternatives to the status quo.[6] Some of the poems in Feinberg's anthology are searches for structures upon which to model or figure the anticipated 'revolution', going back to classical patterns to find suitable challenges to authority. For example, David Evans in 'African Prometheus' adapts Prometheus' challenge to Zeus through his theft of fire (Feinberg 1980: 12); while Keorapetse Kgositsile's 'New Age' anticipates a new era structured by memories of the past, with memory as a means of summoning up the lost past, the land as mother and a lost nurturing spirit (Feinberg 1980: 41). The poem invokes the ANC's colours – green, black, gold – as a mantra of liberty, as the turbulence of the past is tamed by liberty, and the future freedom atones for the sins of the past. Kgositsile also invokes memory in his poem 'Open Letter' (Feinberg 1980: 49). As in Barry Feinberg's poem entitled 'A Counterpoint of Marching Feet', memory in this respect is used as a prompt for continuing political action in the face of adversity, and becomes an impetus to unity of action and community. Memory of the past often leads to metaphors of violence or a nurture that is stamped out, such as in 'Mayibuye iAfrika' (Feinberg 1980: 45) and 'Song for Ilva Mackay and Mongone' (Feinberg 1980: 44). 'Mayibuye iAfrika' means 'come back Africa', and is a political slogan that recurs frequently, like 'Amandla! Ngawethu!' ('Amandla': the word for 'power' in Nguni, the Xhosa-Zulu-Swazi-Ndebele sub-class of Bantu languages; *'Amandla ngawethu'*: '[the] power is ours') and others. The phrase suggests the loss of a past nation, identity and people, which is invoked for political unity in the present and future. Retrieving a past tied up in 'mazes of colonial lies' (Feinberg 1980: 46) is also part of memory-work, disentangling a black history from the 'conqueror's' history.

Yet this memory-work does not always result in clearly 'worked-through' outcomes. Essop Patel, a South African Indian poet who emerged in the late 1980s with a volume entitled *The Bullet and the Bronze Lady* (1987), wrote poems which were generally pro-ANC and mixed wry humour with biting derision about the various apartheid laws. Poems depicting the humiliation of the South African Indian population in 'Miriam of Bengal' (Patel 1987: 13) and 'First Insult' (Patel 1987: 14) and describing the social protests in Soweto in 'Necklace' (Patel 1987: 10) and 'State of Emergency' (Patel 1987: 11), jostle with scathingly sarcastic poems about the various apartheid laws in 'Who-zit Elections' (Patel 1987: 28), 'The Right Dishonourable Abuselingumjie Speaks' (Patel 1987: 31) and 'Key-Hole-Peep-In' (Patel 1987: 20), about interracial sex and the Immorality Act. His sequence of poems about Haanetjie, a typical young Afrikaner woman, written in a mixture of Afrikaans and South African slang and colloquialisms, gained some fame for its ironic depictions of her Afrikaner racial prejudices. Yet it is in Patel's concrete-poetry influenced poem 'Afrika!' (Patel 1987: 81) (Figure IV) that he explicitly addresses the problem of reclaiming the past, of grasping the essence of Africa from the past and defining its character in the modern day untainted by the colonial past.

The poem sets out its political commitment from the outset with its dedication to Nat Nakasa, a key figure in the anti-apartheid movement. Reclaiming the indigenous heritage with the African spelling of 'Afrika', the poem's typographical outline of the continent etched against the seas of repetitious 'Afrikas', literally mirrors the 'Africa / emerging from the / colonial haze', as a negative imprint. 'Emerging' is the key word: the continent is literally figured as a white absence emerging from black seas, as African words shape and define the land in a linguistic gesture of tautological affirmation. Yet the attempt to retrieve the continent's obliterated culture in the image of the 'delectable narcissus', a black flower, with an imposing and

AFRIKA!

in memoriam Nathaniel Ndazana Nakasa

```
AFRIKA AFRIKA AFRIKA AFRIKA AFRIKA AFRIKA
AFRIKA AFRIKA AFRIKA AFRIKA AFRIKA AFRIKA
AFRIKA AFRIKA AFRIKA AFRIKA AFRIKA AFRIKA
AFRIKA AFRIKA AFRIKA AFRIKA AFRIKA AFRIKA
AFRIKA A            AFRIKA AFRIKA AFRIKA
AFRIKA              RIKA AFRIKA AFRIKA
AFRIK          Africa      A AFRIKA
AFR'                        A AFRIKA
AF     emerging from the       A AFRIKA
AF   colonial haze;      poised  A AFRIKA
AF     between two oceans        A AFRIKA
AF  detectable as a narcissus  drenched   AFRIKA
AFR    in the morning mist,  her head high AFRIKA
AFRI                          RIKA
AFRIK   her      face impressive      IKA
AFRIKA AFRIKA              but      RIKA
AFRIKA AFRIKA AF          evocative  RIKA
AFRIKA AFRIKA AF   as the         AFRIKA
AFRIKA AFRIKA AF                 AFRIKA
AFRIKA AFRIKA AFR   rapcious      AFRIKA
AFRIKA AFRIKA AFRI      sun—      AFRIKA
AFRIKA AFRIKA AFR'              A AFRIKA
AFRIKA AFRIKA AFR   — Mayibuy'i   A AFRIKA
AFRIKA AFRIKA AFR   Afrika!      KA AFRIKA
AFRIKA AFRIKA AFRI          RIKA AFRIKA
AFRIKA AFRIKA AFRI          RIKA AFRIKA
AFRIKA AFRIKA AFRIK        AFRIKA AFRIKA
AFRIKA AFRIKA AFRIK       A AFRIKA AFRIKA
AFRIKA AFRIKA AFRIKA AFKIKA AFRIKA AFRIKA
AFRIKA AFRIKA AFRIKA AFRIKA AFRIKA AFRIKA
AFRIKA AFRIKA AFRIKA AFRIKA AFRIKA AFRIKA
AFRIKA AFRIKA AFRIKA AFRIKA AFRIKA AFRIKA
```

IV Essop Patel, 'Afrika!'

impressive stature, is somewhat undercut by the ambiguity that
remains in the desperate plea or call in the final line, 'Mayibuy'i
Afrika'. Meaning 'come back Africa', this recall seeks a definition of
the continent but finds instead an outline that vacillates between
whiteness and blackness. In fact, there are several ambiguities in the
poem, questions that seem unanswerable: Why is Africa represented
as a flower on the one hand, and as a 'rapcious sun' (*sic*: presumably
a typographical error) on the other hand, images that seem to be
mutually exclusive? Why is 'evocative' posed as an alternative to
'impressive' by that word 'but'? Why is a 'rapacious sun' 'evocative',
and 'evocative' of what in particular? The poem's figure emerging
from the morning mist is endowed with a certain romantic tinge,
which is reinforced by the stereotypical characterisation of Africa as
a woman – Mother Africa.[7] This common representational motif
juxtaposed with the 'rapacious sun' presents another complexity,
since it situates the female Africa oddly between associations of delicate femininity and rapacious masculinity. Despite these ambiguities
and the ways in which the poem's efforts at identifying the 'pure'
continent are confused by the use of somewhat clichéd images and
tropes, the poem demonstrates the intimate and subtle connection

between affirmation and recollection or memory that permeates the politics of anti-apartheid resistance.

Remembrance then is a key issue for this poetry and there are different roles for memory. Keorapetse Kgositsile's poem 'My People No Longer Sing' enjoins the reader to 'Remember / ... To remind the living / That the dead cannot remember' (Kgositsile 1973: 407). Sipho Sepamla's poetry is suffused with the workings of memory and the past as a resource for ensuring political action in the present. 'History-books Amen!' speaks about the irrelevance of white history to the black population, since their history is not a history of land appropriation or acquisition or colonisation but about the freedom of the land and the animals. White history is distorting and claustrophobic, an 'ominous shadow cast over all my events blurring details of it' (Sepamla 1984: 123). Some poems do evoke famous warriors from the past to invigorate the present, such as 'To Makana and Nongquawuse' (Sepamla 1984: 86), or 'Song of Mother and Child' (Sepamla 1984: 64). 'Now Is the Time' urges that the resources of memory are crucial to spurring the present, remembering 'the remains of bitter memories' (Sepamla 1984: 87) as a source for finding and positioning oneself in a present collective identity, 'To find this us' (Sepamla 1984: 87). Many critics have pointed out how frequently representations of Africans were of a people situated *in* time, rather than possessing a sense *of* time. These representations are effectively part of a conservative and racist ideology that presented Africans as passive rather than dynamic, subject to changeless 'traditions' and 'customs', rather than instrumental in making a history, their own history. The extensive influence of books with a wide circulation such as Dudley Kidd's *The Essential Kaffir*, published in London in 1904, is evidence of the perpetuation and strength of these types of stereotypical representations. So the forging of a specific history, of agency in making that history, and recording a history that is not a 'white history', is a crucial factor in the poetry renaissance in the 1970s and 1980s. Both Alvarez-Pereyre's and Chapman's critical evaluations of the poets of this period repeatedly return to the ways in which, through an ideology of self-assertion, self-determination and choice driven by Black Consciousness, these poets are involved in a Soweto 'renaissance self-fashioning' of black South Africans who are free individuals, responsible for their own destiny as the subjects rather than objects of history. Indeed, many of these poems engage in direct rewritings of history. For instance, Mafika Gwala's 'Afrika at a Piece' is specifically about the writing of history, and the different ways in which history is recorded. Unlike the passive white history entrenched in schoolbooks,

> Our blackman's history
> is not written in classrooms
> on wide smooth boards
> Our history will be written
> at the factory gates
> at the unemployment offices
> in the scorched queues of dying mouths.
>
> (Gwala 1982: 44–6)

Rather then being recorded in the pages of textbooks for children's education, Gwala's history is the various actions of people in the struggle against apartheid and depicted in poems like this one. In 'The Covenant, Whose Covenant?' (Gwala 1982: 47–8), Gwala interrogates the meaning of the Afrikaners' Day of the Covenant, which is the annual day of remembrance on 16 December for the Voortrekkers (the settler ancestors of the Afrikaners) led by Piet Retief, who died at the Battle of Blood River in a fight against the Zulus under King Dingane. Gwala's poem is a reversal of the memory, signifying defiance by remembering other events and days of remembrance, such as the Soweto youth in June 1976, and the anticipation of the institution of a new covenant. The image of the blacks 'twistwrecking "Die Stem" / in "Nkos'ikelele" shebeens', of derailing the Afrikaans national anthem 'Die Stem' into the ANC national anthem 'Nkos'ikelele', is a clear indication of how the poem seeks to work by 'twistwrecking' the Day of the Covenant into a black day of remembrance. This is an example of a transformative memory, where the poem acts like a 'speech act', an act of commemoration in the writing of it, not merely describing the speaker's relation to the past but specifically placing him or her in reference to it, and carrying with it an ethical portent and liability. Elsewhere Gwala writes that 'I am still surviving / the traumas of my raped soil / alive and aware', as the 'wounds' of 'Bullhoek, Sharpeville, Soweto' unwrap 'the dressings of Hope' (Gwala 1982: 7). In its echoes of Serote's thematic of the cultural and racial 'wound', Gwala's poetry repeatedly demonstrates a resistance to the aesthetics of a mannered modernism in its espousal of the morality of race politics in a brash street idiom; and a denunciation of a simple metaphysics of good and evil by its rebellion against the authoritarian Calvinist and Christian orthodoxy. As Jacques Alvarez-Pereyre states, 'By recalling the tragic events that have affected the whole of the South African community – Sharpeville, Langa, Cato Manor, Carletonville, Soweto – and which have inspired still more poems, [poets like Gwala] stand in opposition to the edited official history, which omits any reference to blatant compulsion and the refusal to live as one community. They are writing the history of the South Africa of tomorrow, a *common* history for the nation that must be born' (Alvarez-Pereyre 1984: 259).

Addressing the history of tomorrow also means considering the future generations, and in this respect several poems by Gwala address another key site for this poetics of remembrance: the disproportionate effect of these traumatic race relations on children. For example, 'No More Lullabies', the eponymous title poem of Gwala's *No More Lullabies*, is about the youth who will no longer be coaxed to sleep with lullabies, but given new songs of resistance to sing (Gwala 1982: 91). Whilst there is exhilaration and determination that these future children will grow up free, the poem is nevertheless tinged with regret that children's innocence is tainted by the political system's rude enforcement of an early maturity. In addition to several other commentators, Piniel Shava notes that the corruption of childhood innocence figures large in the poetry, an innocence that is quickly represented as undercut by the corrupting events and effects of apartheid. Rarely is childhood portrayed as a happy memory, a past to which people would wish to return. Oswald Mtshali's *Sounds of a Cowhide Drum* follows themes of poverty, hunger and isolation, especially as they are figured in the lives of children. Daniel P. Kunene's volume *A Seed Must Also Seem to Die and Other Poems* (1981), dedicated to the children of Soweto and all other children in the world from whom tyranny has removed their childhood, contains a hard-hitting introduction about the corruption of childhood: 'In the Year of the Child THEY abolished The Child. Now more than in the fable, the Child confronts and slays the MONSTER which ravishes the earth and napalms the soul … The crimes of the OPPRESSOR are numerous. But to make the child a man, to make the child a woman: This surpasses the ordinary meanings of words' (Kunene, D. 1981: 1). Kunene speaks about the history of birth as the history of death; and in the burial and memorial poem 'The Laying of the Stones' invokes the African warriors who are the forebears and ancestors of the children who died in Soweto in 1976, urging the reader to 'remember the children in the moment of their greatest glory' (Kunene, D. 1981: 7). This collection is permeated by the traumatic experiences of the Soweto children's uprising, such as in the heart-rending 'Prologue', a long dialogue between Death and a 12-year-old girl shot in the 16 June demonstration. Her bewilderment and inability to rationalise the events signify the catastrophic nature of the denial of childhood. Elsewhere, Sipho Sepamla's volume entitled *The Soweto I Love* (1977), dedicated to the 'dead in Johannesburg, Cape Town and elsewhere', contains many examples of the betrayal of childhood innocence. 'I Saw This Morning' depicts the thinly veiled anxiety and distress of daily life in a location as 'rumour' frightens children and an 'unseen monster' stalks the streets (Sepamla 1977: 1). 'A Child Dies' depicts the way in which a child twice described as 'unthinking' is killed in a street as a result of presumed guilt by association and proximity to events, a violence that is meted out on arbitrary and indifferent principles. A 'monster was known to stalk the streets' and there is an ominous pun on the child '*consumed* by curiosity' (Sepamla 1977: 2, my italics). This is a clear example of history or the past creating the traumas of the present. Home is portrayed as a site of internal exile, alienation and unease in 'Home' (Sepamla 1977: 15–16), where names are foreign and the home does not nurture or develop children – it stunts and enwombs them. This loss of innocence is another repetitive sign of the trauma that afflicts black South Africans, as it indicates the ways in which 'normal' psychological development in people is truncated, interrupted and terminated at too early a stage in the emotional and psychological lives of people. This psychological rupture in children continues through into their adult lives, and is also the traumatic rupture that permeates apartheid society as it struggles to 'grow up' or mature into a multicultural consciousness. The writers are set to repeat or stutter similar problems and parallel structures of internal conflict until some form of release occurs, which allows the 'working-through' of the trauma.

Yet if the children have become damaged by this traumatic trunca-tion of their development, they are also regarded as the educators of the present generation. Sepamla has several poems in which he pres-ents the Soweto youths' militant actions as 'teaching' the passive elders about political realities:

> it was on that day children
> excused the past
> deploring the present
> their fists clenched full of the future.
> (Sepamla 1977: 6)

The poem continues to discuss the way in which such action will write off the past, shake off the past, allowing people to begin with a clean slate: 'i shall learn myself anew ...' (Sepamla 1977: 7). Elsewhere, the narrator in 'A Childhood Memory' seeks to distance himself from childhood experiences of racist treatment at a market, and notes how the children of today (i.e. of Soweto) are different – they refuse to be treated in that way (Sepamla 1977: 42–3). The problem is that these children, while providing a salutary example of political action to the older generations, are none the less in that very action also manifesting the damage done to their psyches by apartheid, namely that the truncation in their lives has manifested itself in physical violence and retaliatory justice. In other words, apartheid has been responsible for brutalising the children, forcing them to register the past trauma in gestures of violence and aggres-sion, which partly reinforce the internalisation of the trauma.

Language and memory

Many of the poems in Sepamla's volume are protest poems, but they are not uniformly militant. Several of them are quiet, peaceful and reflective. Many of them are snapshots of daily life in Soweto, depicting its dreariness, its violence, its repetitive actions and deaths. People live moments of unity and triumph only to be reminded of the violence the next morning (Sepamla 1977: 4–5). Some poems seek and invite the peace of humanity. Generally, though, one is left with the impression of 'normal' life being upset, disturbed, or shaken by the violence (physical and psychological) of apartheid. The poems repeatedly return to images of disruption and the inability to make meaningful sense of one's experiences:

> I've tried to piece together
> fragments of the night's act
> but the mind's searing pain refuses.
> (Sepamla 1977: 50)

As with so many of the Soweto poets, Sepamla's poetry returns again and again in a shocked manner to the detail of the overwhelming events, marked as the poems are by an inability to integrate experiences into a completed account of the past. Consequently, there is a close connection between the numbing effect of the experiences and the persistence in endeavouring to represent them. Indicative of this effort to embed memory and to seize an 'impossible history' is the intractability of language. There are many poems that lament the collapse and corruption of language in the state of apartheid, as Essop Patel writes in 'State of Emergency':

> alphabets
> under arrest
> and words in detention:
>   subversive silence
>   in a prison country.
>   (Patel 1987: 11)

These resistance poets are keenly aware of the fact that there is no language to describe the lost (mythicised) past, where a full organic unity existed between people, and between humans and earth. There is a constant inability in the poetry to find suitable words to articulate the experiences of historical loss, cultural alienation and human barbarity under apartheid. As Sepamla states in 'Talk to the Peach Tree', 'words have lost meaning / like all notations they've been misused' (Sepamla 1977: 4); or elsewhere in 'Words, Words, Words', signs are a shifting territory in their denotation, how one definition means another, and how words are 'tossed around' (Sepamla 1977:

40–1). Mongane Serote writes in 'Black Bells' that 'Words, / WORDS, / like thought are elusive, / . . . / I read. / Words, / WORDS. / Trying to get out / Words. Words' (Serote 1972: 52). Similarly, Daniel P. Kunene's poems repeatedly stress the difficulties in articulating atrocities in words – especially the poems 'A Jungle of Words' (Kunene, D. 1981: 51), 'Confuse Conjunctions' (Kunene, D. 1981: 52), 'These Are Not Words' (Kunene, D. 1981: 77), and the general section-title of section V, '. . . metaphors in search of interpretations' (Kunene, D. 1981: 37). The introduction to his volume of poems speaks about the actions that 'surpasses the ordinary meanings of words. We grope in vain. The word has yet to be found' (Kunene, D. 1981: 1).

This literally represents a sort of Kristevan or Lacanian loss of the Real – where the poet no longer has a way back to a fullness of experience and language. Many poems are efforts at wresting back language from the hegemonic processes of semantic definition, and these poems exemplify the sort of struggle over linguistic signs outlined in V. N. Volosinov's *Marxism and the Philosophy of Language*. Volosinov argued that societies were in a state of constant struggle, not merely over the material means of production but over signs. Volosinov suggests that all signs are 'Janus-faced' and are pressurised by the oppressing class for certain associations and meanings (Volosinov 1986: 23). In these poems, this struggle manifests itself most obviously over such signs that denote racial colour and the hierarchies built upon them – white, black, good and evil. This can also quickly transform into a struggle over signs in other discourses which allied to the racial ideology, and that seek to bolster it. For instance, there are numerous poems that challenge white culture through an interrogation of the discourse of Christianity (see, for example, Mafika Gwala, 'Xmas Blues' (Gwala 1982: 20); Sipho Sepamla, 'I Tried to Say' (Sepamla 1984: 84); Daniel Kunene, 'On the Cross' (Kunene, D. 1981: 12); Oswald Mtshali, 'The Shepherd and his Flock', 'An Old Man in Church', 'This Kid is no Goat', 'At Heaven's Door'; and 'Back to the Bush' (Mtshali 1971: 1, 20, 24–5, and 44; and Mtshali 1980: 47–9)). This struggle over signs can be clearly seen in Stanley Motjuwadi's 'White Lies':

> Humming Maggie.
> Hit by a virus,
> the Caucasian craze,
> sees horror in the mirror
> Frantic and dutifully
> she corrodes a sooty face,
> braves a hot iron comb
> on a shrubby scalp;
> I look on.

I know pure white,
a white heart,
white, peace, ultimate virtue.
Angels are white
angels are good.
Me I'm black,
black as sin stuffed in a snuff-tin.
Lord, I've been brainwhitewashed.

But for Heaven's sake God,
just let me be.
Under cover of my darkness
let me crusade.
On a canvas stretching from here
to Dallas, Memphis, Belsen, Golgotha,
I'll daub a white devil.
Let me teach black truth.
That dark clouds aren't a sign of doom,
but hope. Rain. Life.
Let me unleash a volty bolt of black,
so all around may know black right.
                              (Motjuwadi 1974: 12)

This poem clearly involves itself in a struggle over the terms 'white'
and 'black' and their connotations. It seeks to invert the racial association of goodness with whiteness and evil with blackness.
Beginning with the cynical and critical picture of Maggie succumbing
to the 'virus' of aping her white masters by going through the agonies
of bleaching her skin and straightening her hair, the poem moves
into the opposition of white and black in terms of religion, and how
the narrator is condemned by the structures and ideology of
Christianity, with its white angels and black devils, and its symbolic
associations of white peace, black sins, and black evil. The final verse
wrests the religious discourse away from simple oppositions, and
shows that in fact white can be associated with evil, such as the
white assassins of John F. Kennedy (Dallas) and Martin Luther King
(Memphis), and the murderers of the Jews (Belsen) and Jesus Christ
(Golgotha). Using the image of the impending black rain cloud, the
narrator points out how this is a sign of rain, fertility and life, rather
than 'doom', and that the poem constitutes the 'volty bolt of black'
that corrects the oppositional hierarchy and recuperates the signs for
a black world.

Such struggles over the signs and ideologies of Christianity recur
frequently in these poets' work. Yet the Christianity undergoes an
odd yet significant change. Generally, Christian imagery is predicated upon an anticipated movement to salvation – resurrection,
redemption, liberation. Suffering is important to Christianity as a

way forward to this salvation. However, the resistance poets tend to depict suffering for itself: in some of the more cynical and bleak poems, there is no salvation in the future. Mtshali is always critical of Christianity and its lack of application to black South Africans, since the Church teaches resignation and thereby acts as an accomplice of the exploiting state power (Mtshali 1971: 173).

This struggle over signs is also evident in a number of other poems, like Serote's famous poem 'What's in This Black "Shit"?', which seeks to turn the word 'shit' back on whites, and explicitly reasserts the authority of the black writer. As part of this struggle, defamiliarisation is a frequent poetic strategy employed in the poetry, especially as it shocks the reader into a sense of the dissimilar in the familiar. One of Sepamla's poems, 'Like a Hippo', demonstrates this to devastating effect. The poem subtly plays on the animal motif, describing its characteristic lumbering movements 'like a hippo', presenting it as a 'prehistoric monster'. Yet undercutting the animal or nature poem, the poem describes not a hippopotamus but an armoured personnel vehicle that was instrumental in suppressing the civilian uprisings in Soweto and other townships. Its behemoth appearance is 'prehistoric' because 'it is meant to destroy history' (Sepamla 1977: 3) and randomly and arbitrarily 'mows down' everything in its way:

> it tries
> to take us all
> back in time.
> (Sepamla 1977: 3)

The 'animal' is another of those 'monsters' that pervade children's nightmares, 'they scream in the night / as they see it in dreams' (Sepamla 1977: 3). Rather than the somewhat fat yet lovable archetypal animal of the African veld, this 'hippo' is the modern-day reality of African childhood: a tool in apartheid's attempt to suppress social distress, to erase black history and to resist culture.

Oral influences, ancestors and *izibongo*

Not all the poets who wrote poetry during the 1970s and 1980s were explicitly political in their inclination, and nor did they address politics in a sloganeering manner. Nevertheless, their poetry still utilised history and the past as central shaping forces on the present and the ways forward for the black political struggle. One such poet was Masizi Kunene, whose poetry was based on an African consciousness, especially the culture and cosmology of the Zulu. He wrote in Zulu and translated his poetry into English, using Zulu traditions to assert his Africanness. He has written two of the most ambitious epic poems to come from Africa – *Emperor Shaka the Great* (1979) and

Anthem of the Decades (1981). Influenced by Magolwane, the Zulu court-poet to Shaka, and B. W. Vilakazi, the twentieth-century poet, teacher and scholar, Masizi Kunene draws upon Zulu philosophy, imagery and rhetoric, relying heavily on oral traditions of Zulu poetry from the eighteenth century onwards. His volume *The Ancestors and the Sacred Mountains* (1982) concentrates on three main subjects: first, liberation by bloodshed in South Africa; second, looking forward to a time after liberation, and sometimes beyond South Africa to the world at large; and, third, the ecstatic nature of poetry. Prefacing this volume, Kunene writes a long introduction that elaborates upon such issues as individual versus collective effort, of ethics and progressive development, technology, human rights, the philosophy of African literature, and the meeting of European forms and their adaptation. Yet it also contains a major a statement on the African tradition of using the past to illuminate the present: 'Our perspectives are therefore philosophically deeply anchored in the past, which is the *sine qua non* of our present. It is thus unthinkable to view the Ancestors as primitive, uncivilized, backward' (Kunene, M. 1982: xii).[8]

The Ancestors observe and encourage the present, in an omnipresent sense. Rather than seeing them as the inventors of material improvements in the modern world, the Zulus regard the Ancestors as establishing moral and ethical standards and providing guidance and inspiration. The Ancestors are a collective repository of wisdom rather than a group of heroic individuals. The Ancestral Voices emerge in such poems as 'The Rise of the Angry Generation' (Kunene, M. 1982: 3), 'Son of the Beautiful Ones – the Dancer' (Kunene, M. 1982: 6), 'Encounter with the Ancestors' (Kunene, M. 1982: 37), 'After a Dark Season' (Kunene, M. 1982: 39–41), 'The Great Ones' (Kunene, M. 1982: 44) and 'My Forefathers' (Kunene, M. 1982: 49). The poems celebrate the mythical narratives and histories of the Zulu nation, setting out the narrative of creation, the symbols of continuity like the circle, and images of nature and eternity. They endow the people with an epic culture and history, with symbols and images representing the characteristics of greatness, power, heroism and steadfastness. Kunene's poems evoke the contributions of the Ancestors to the cultural heritage and social vision of the present. The Spirits who are symbols or archetypes of ancestral 'beings' emerge to touch the sun, reach to the mountain tops, invoke eagles, slash the earth asunder and generally carry out rituals of celebration, triumph, redemption, rejuvenation and uplifting friendship. Kunene talks about 'the pure gifts of the Ancestral guardians' (Kunene, M. 1982: 12), as the influence of the collective wisdom of past generations on the present and future is established as a cultural fact in 'Return of the Golden Age' (Kunene, M. 1982: 16–17).

Yet despite this latter poem's title, the past does not figure as
nostalgia in his writing, a lost Eden to which black South Africans
ought to be striving to return. On the contrary, as Emmanuel Ngara
has observed, 'In *Zulu Poems*, Kunene uses traditional modes of
thinking and expression without advocating a return to the past, nor
does he necessarily glorify the past like the Senghorian school of
Negritude' (Ngara 1990: 78). Rather, as in 'A Vision of Zosukuma',
the past is like a 'gift' to the present:

> My child takes the poem that is old
> And learns from it our own legends
> To see life with the eyes of the Forefathers.
> (Kunene, M. 1982: 17)

The present generation is regarded as dependent upon the wisdom of
the Ancestors, as the past endows the present with decision, clarity
and identity, as in 'The Great Ones':

> Their memories enter the body of the mountain,
> And they are possessed by the ancient poets
> They sing for us their poem
> They narrate the story of our beginnings.
> (Kunene, M. 1982: 44)

Memory pervades these poems as the pain of past experience spurs
the present generation into ameliorative political action, or resistance to forms of oppression. Tradition is thus a source of political
strength, rather than force for conservative inaction, as Kunene puts
it in a poem entitled 'Breaking Off from Tradition': 'When ultimately
we cut the links of our past, / It is only to trace the path of our deeper
beginning' (Kunene, M. 1982: 55). Acutely conscious of the indebted-
ness to previous political victims and martyrs, Kunene states in 'In
Praise of Ancestors' how 'We sing the anthems that celebrate their
great eras, / For indeed life does not begin with us' (Kunene, M. 1982:
74). Kunene depicts a sense of an organic connection linking the
present with the past in a cyclical movement. Indeed, one of his
poems is entitled 'Cyclic Movement', and it talks of 'the past converging with the present' (Kunene, M. 1982: 56). The past wisdom acts as
a foundation for action in the present:

> He said: 'This shall lead into the memory of endlessness
> To link the past with the present,
> To ensure the continuity of life,
> To bequeath the child with the titles of the sun'.
> (Kunene, M. 1982: 60)

Zulu oral literature functions as a repository of the past, and ancestral wisdom is the inculcator of social ethics. The metaphysical and the mythical consequently exist side-by-side with political poetry.

The poems are structured largely by the techniques of the Xhosa and Zulu praise-poem. This formal aspect is another crucial issue in the recuperation of the past in black poetry. Many colonial western anthropologists regarded African oral cultures as unable to preserve a history or a past without a mechanism of writing. Yet this has been successfully disputed by Africanists since the 1960s, when Jan Vansina's *De la tradition orale* (1961) argued convincingly that even non-literate Africans possessed recoverable histories. Researchers in recent decades such as Ruth Finnegan have regarded oral songs and tales as important as history, a history that must be transmitted to children, because it derives from the ancestors (Finnegan 1970: 19). Such 'maps of experience' embed memories that are important *as* history but also important *in* history (for example, these memories are invoked and manipulated at specific times).

Contemporary praise-poets derive their techniques and practices from Xhosa and Zulu oral traditions, and see their role as eulogisers but also critics and flouters of authority, providing several literate contemporary black South African poets such as Masizi Kunene, Keroapetse Kgositsile, Mafika Gwala and Mongane Serote with a definition of their own social role. Consequently, the significance of orality and oral traditions within Soweto and other resistance poetry written during this period has been the subject of considerable discussion within the past years. The key features are the roles of the *imbongi*, the Zulu court praise-poet and the *izibongo*, the Zulu praise-poem (Cope 1968: 25–31). Developing the roles of these aspects of Zulu oral culture as central to contemporary poets as they turn to more oral and performative modes of poetry, Mbulelo Mzamane counters arguments that some African writers have been westernised to the extent that they have been severed from their cultural roots (Mzamane 1984); quoting Es'kia Mphahlele's words, 'Tradition lives along side the present' (Mphahlele 1972: 144), Mzamane demonstrates in a study of oral forms in the work of B. W. Vilakazi, H. I. E. Dhlomo, A. C. Jordan and Mongane Serote that tradition and western forms coexist. In the case of Serote's poetry, for example, Mzamane demonstrates how his well-known poem 'City Johannesburg' 'despite its urban setting, blends Western influences and traditional elements' (Mzamane 1984: 153). The poem's jazz rhythms, its spirit of celebration (a key element of *izibongo*), the emphasis on the collective over the personal, the salutations and the address to the city ('Jo'burg City'), the showering of praise on the beauty of the city's neon lights, but also the licence to rebuke the exploitation of blacks by white employers, Mzamane maintains that all these are characteristics of the traditional praise-poem, or *izibongo*.

Among others, Duncan Brown has sought to recover the significance of oral performance and the influence of Xhosa and Zulu praise-poetry in the political poetry that has emerged in recent decades in South Africa. He has pointed to the importance of the *imbongi* and the way that the past and history are central to the poetic techniques and shape of *izibongo*, the Zulu epic verse form: 'izibongo ... permits present conduct to be examined in terms of past events, and past events to be re-examined according to the imperatives of the society of the day' (Brown 1998: 109). Brown demonstrates how praise-poetry is an endlessly labile form, adapting to altering social and historical circumstances, shown in the way that *izibongo* were performed in the South African mines, at worker rallies, at the inauguration of Nelson Mandela as President of the Republic and at the first opening of the new South African democratic parliament. Brown cogently argues that the *izibongo* has clearly played an important role in shaping the imperatives, responsibilities and identities of people in the changing state of South Africa, and makes a strong case for the role of these epic poets in forging the nation state and its history with a form that is well suited to vast national changes. Liz Gunner, who has studied the role of orality in South African resistance poetry, regards it as 'part of the "labours of remembrance" used in the turbulent present to recall a perhaps equally turbulent past, but used nevertheless as part of an active remembering of a community's history, and used as part of the way in which it sees itself in the present' (Gunner 1999: 50). Gunner points out how praise-poetry has also functioned as a deeply analytical form and has always been heavily involved in politics, leadership and actions. Part of the adaptation of praise-poetry for resistance purposes has been the harnessing of memory in the service of a 'free nation'. Gunner and Gwala have pointed out how praise epithets used for Shaka in his *izibongo* were used for Chief Albert Luthuli in 1950 during the famous Treason Trial, as the warrior image was impressed for political spheres (see Gunner and Gwala 1994). Gunner is quite clear that the regenerative power of memory is a key feature of *izibongo*, demonstrating an atavistic streak that resists an archaic nostalgia that would effectively marginalise the present. When *imbongi* invoke the names of the past, these names are not directed to the past as history but 'to the present in which elements of the past are embedded and can be reactivated' (Gunner 1999: 55). The form of the *izibongo* is therefore not residual but instrumental in raising political consciousness and recuperating cultural history, in a form that weaves layered intensities of language and image.[9]

   There are a cluster of poets who explicitly develop this oral literary heritage. Duncan Brown has drawn attention to the significant oral performances of the prominent Soweto poet Mzwakhe Mbuli and the Durban- and Natal-based Alfred Qabula (Brown 1996). Despite their differences of emphasis and ideological leanings, both poets draw upon the oral tradition that was excised from South African literary history and that is now being recovered through a revisionist aware- ness of the processes of cultural exclusion, occlusion and effacement that characterised the construction of the white cultural history of South Africa. Another important poet who inherits the mantle of this oral poetry tradition is Ingoapele Madingoane. His principal poem in English entitled *africa my beginnings* (1979) consists of a twenty- one-poem sequence called 'black trial' and a short title poem, 'africa my beginning'. The whole sequence reflects upon the injustices perpetrated on black people as a result of their skin colour. Owing to the banning of the work and as a way of avoiding the editorial stric- tures of largely white control over literary magazines, the poems were performed orally by Madingoane, and township youths could recite whole sections from memory in the late 1970s. As Duncan Brown has convincingly demonstrated, the written text shows how Madingoane uses many of the techniques of the *izibongo*, such as the reiteration of ideas, a loose structure, a cyclical construction, paral- lelism and repetition (Brown 1998: 184–208). 'black trial' puns on ontological existence (life as a trial) and his legal position (he is awaiting trial in South Africa), and traces the spiritual, ideological and historical development of their speaker – a communally defined black man – from a state of self-loathing and passivity to one of self- assertion and social commitment. Madingoane directly denies, Gordimer's assertion that the "'I' is the pronoun that prevails, rather than "we", [where] the "I" is the Whitmanesque unit of multimillions rather than the exclusive first person singular. There is little evidence of group feeling' (Gordimer 1976: 135). 'black trial / *three*' concerns how 'mother africa' is degraded from motherhood and the way apartheid emasculates black men. The poem develops this emas- culation:

> 'cause my african woman
> will always remember
> to call me
> *man.*
>   (Madingoane 1979: 6)

'Man' is a singularly resonant word in this South African context, since part of the white racial ideology worked by constantly infantil- ising and emasculating the black man by calling him 'boy'. To be called a 'man', therefore, is to escape the taint of white racial ideol- ogy, but also to be 'grown up', to have rights, to exercise independ- ence and to have integrity. This issue of determining one's own life and exercising one's rights recurs throughout the sequence: 'black trial / *five*' is about agency, and the need 'to define the value of humanity / to myself' (Madingoane 1979: 5), for freedom to be able to exercise that right. Partly, this occurs through seeking 'salvation' in a return to 'my ancestors'. Indeed, echoing Zulu tradition, the poem shows a conscious return to the ancestral past to find solace and direction for the present:

> i resigned from paradise
> and went back home to africa
> in search of my image
> to dig up the roots
> and burn incense
> to strengthen my stand
> speaking to my ancestors
> in the ancient language of mankind
> i heard the spirits talk back to me
> i felt my soul astir as they led me
> all the way from the black trial
> into the land of sunshine and peace.
> (Madingoane 1979: 9)

Madingoane also summons and evokes the leaders from the heroic past:

> beneath you lie badamo beso   giants
> shaka   africa's warrior
> martyrs
> mashoeshoe from the mountain kingdom
> christians of africa
> khama the great.
> (Madingoane 1979: 31)

This recuperation of the past is a response to deculturation rather than a nostalgic trip to some pre-apartheid Eden. These poems are about cultural 'roots' in Africa (a word used frequently), roots that have been erased, forgotten, censored, buried and suppressed by white culture. The poems seek the solidarity and support not just of South Africans but of the whole continent, as the culminating later sections of the poem envisage an African unity in the future through continental co-operation. Remembrance and memories of past black cultures are keys to the structure of the poem, and the developing movement of the sections mirrors the movement of historical process. As Duncan Brown notes with regard to the poem's disruptive and disrupted textuality, Michael Chapman's comment on Serote may apply equally to Madingoane (Brown 1998: 200):

[He] allows his free-verse lines to stumble, halt and descend to near prose, only to burst into rhetorical climax. He seeks in this way to

convey the idea of historical process itself, its difficulties emphasized in
the broken rhythms and sprawling arrangement of incident, reflection
and prophetic utterance: man is shown subject to all the imperfections
of life, with his struggle sustained over long periods of time despite the
inevitable set-backs. (Chapman 1984: 223, quoted in Brown 1998: 200)

The poetry forces an ethical reassessment of critical vocabulary,
which in a character of authentic analysis, typified by perceptible
dislocations, and visible infelicities of syntax, expression and line,
marks an unevenness of historical certainty and assurance. The past
is therefore embedded in the very form of the writing, structuring the
style and the content. Resistance emerges through reviving and reiterating subjugated histories, substituting a messianic urge for an
analytic deliberation.

Conclusion

These resistance poems are a paradoxical mixture of, on the one
hand, a concrete particularity in their depiction of the details of the
daily lives of black people in the locations, suffering under the
various state laws, and running the gamut of various ill-treatments
at the hands of white people; and, on the other hand, a linguistic slip-
periness, as the poems persistently acknowledge the difficulty of
finding an untainted language to describe daily experiences, the slip-
page in semantic determinacy and the frequent (sometimes wryly
humorous) recognition of the multiple meanings imposed on single
words. 'Left to themselves and under the pressure of circumstances,
these young poets led poetry out of the ghetto in which the purists
and the traditionalist anthologies had imprisoned it, and they gave it
new life' (Alvarez-Pereyre 1984: 40). Critical lexicons have to read-
just as these poets forge new cultural forms to repair the fabric of a
social reality that has been rent asunder by apartheid. As Cindy
Maroleng writes in her poem 'Memories', 'It's only memories / that
are left / of a past / that derided me / even of my own existence / brainwashed' (Maroleng 1991). Always psychologically trapped even when
politically free, memories return to taint a present that has shaken
off the obvious signs of restriction. In terms of registering the traumatic effects of apartheid, this resistance poetry is a complex web of
cathartic experience, a 'working-out' of the trauma, a repetition of
the trauma in its repeated concern with the structures of the past,
and not just a reaction to trauma but also a political battering-ram
attempting to force its way into the political arena and psychological
defences of the hegemonic political structure. Yet rooted in the
censored past and suppressed indigenous traditions, the prophetic
projections of a post-apartheid state embedded in these poems are
not a simplistic projection into a westernised future, as Es'kia

Mphahlele argues: 'The prophetic vision implied in the poetry cannot be interpreted as simply "prediction" or "foreknowledge". It is rather an expression of a sense of the flux of life extending from a past that is reckoned in relation to one's ancestral heritage and actual events experienced by a community, through the present to some infinite time that cannot simply be equated with the western concept of "future". The reason I choose to call it "prophetic" is that it has implications beyond a man's consciousness of the past and the present' (Mphahlele 1979). For Mphahlele, the significance of this poetry appears to lie not in its representations of the daily horrors and unspeakable barbarities of apartheid, important though these are for political motivation. Rather its significance lies in the ways that the poetry strives for a new organic link between the past and the future that has been interrupted, dislocated and arrested by apartheid; and the significance of this 'future' lies in its political visualisation of a remembered past. In their efforts to come to terms with this impossible and unimaginable history and their attempts to assimilate the scraps of overwhelming events, these poets frequently have recourse to deferred memories and images that repeat themselves at a seemingly subliminal level, constantly evoking a missing history that nevertheless seems insistently and pressingly retrievable, and gesturing to a redemptive future that is always just beyond the horizon of consciousness and yet is crucial to the formation of a social and political community that will confront and work through so many of the inequities and exploitations of the past centuries of colonial and racial rule. This poetry is a cultural necessity. It is a political necessity. It is also a psychological necessity. Recollecting that past, gathering those events, remembering that history, is what urges these poets on, all the more so since the process of grappling with finding a means to represent these missing cultural fragments, offers an ethical vision of how the future ought to and should be.

Notes

[1] It is a battle that is conveniently overshadowed in the annals of British military history by the heroic actions that took place several miles away at Rorke's Drift, where a battalion of the 24th Regiment (now The South Wales' Borderers) defended the mission and farmhouse against Zulu impis determined to emulate their fellow warriors' victory at Isandhlwana. The eleven Victoria Crosses awarded for this action earned the Welsh regiment the honour in the imperial history books of the greatest number of Victoria Crosses awarded to a regiment in a single action. It is worth comparing the heroic realism of Fripp's representation of the battle with Jules van der Vijver's densely abstract memorial representation, *Isandhlwana, 1879–1979: No III: The Battlefield* (1980), in Williamson 1990: 16.

[2] See also Horn 1994: 49–62, who argues that there is a distinct shift from a poetry of protest to a poetry of struggle during this period.

[3] Emmanuel Ngara is nevertheless critical of the falsifications of the Négritude idealism of the psycho-physiological qualities of Africa's black people, and is more concerned to point to the poetics that engage with objective realism and economic

socialism, like the work of Kgositsile, Sepamla and Serote (see Shava 1989: 133).

⁴ See also Alvarez-Pereyre's comments on the stylistic features of this poetry. Alvarez-Pereyre 1984: 639–40.

⁵ See also Emmanuel Ngara's assertion that 'The question of what role art can play in the struggle is closely related to the issue of the aesthetics of liberation. In other words, what are the forms of art that are likely to play an effective role in real-ising the goals of the liberation struggle, or what are the forms of representation that make poetry an effective tool of liberation?', in Ngara 1990: 150.

⁶ See, for example, Paulson 1983, and Mehlman 1977, for discussions in relation to the French Revolution, the American Revolution and the Communist Revolution.

⁷ Appropriating Africa anthropomorphically, like the myth of Adamastor, tends to be a white, colonial gesture. The African response is to mythicise Africa as female, and re-appropriate the continent that way. The figure of Adamastor, which looms large in South African literature, makes its grand entrance into literary history in *The Lusiads*, the national epic by the Portuguese poet Camões published in 1512. Adamastor appears in canto V of this great poem, when Vasco da Gama and his fleet approach the Cape of Storms on their historic voyage to India. A cloud in the shape of a monstrous being suddenly towers over them. The giant reproaches the Portuguese sailors for intruding into his domain, and prophesies shipwreck, catastrophe and death for all those bold enough to sail around the Cape. In the famous passage of the 'epic curse', he threatens to unleash his fury on those who come after Da Gama. When Da Gama demands to know who the monster is, he replies bitterly: 'I am that vast, secret promontory / You Portuguese call the Cape of Storms ...' Then follows an account of Adamastor's unhappy fate. He used to be one of the giants of Olympus, he says. He fell in love with a beautiful, seductive sea nymph called Thetis, but she was repulsed by his extreme size and hideous looks. Thetis's mother Doris promised to arrange a tryst for him with her daughter. One night, as Doris had sworn, Thetis appeared. The passionate giant ran towards her and took her in his arms, only to find himself embracing a rock. He was transformed into the Cape – into Table Mountain, to be precise. Stephen Gray has described the Adamastor story as the 'root of all subse-quent white semiology invented to cope with the African experience', in Gray 1979. But, as Gray himself comments more wryly, it is also 'after all, only a highly decorated way of explaining the largeness of Africa and the roughness of rounding the Cape on a bad night'. For further description of the myth and its sources and analogues, see Chapman 1996: 76–7 and notes.

⁸ Masizi Kunene's preface to another volume entitled *Zulu Poems* amplifies on the way the Zulu tradition conceives of the relation of the past to the present: '[The Zulu tradition] interprets, focuses, and analyzes the past as well as the present and then creates a perspective for the future. In African religion, the previous generation, the present generation, and the future generation are seen in terms of an integrated whole, and it is the function of literature to create this connection, this nexus, of the past, present and future' (Kunene, M. 1970: 5). See also Kunene, M. 1976, for the role of the past and history in Zulu traditional culture. See also the excellent chapter on Masizi Kunene in Goodwin 1982: 173–201.

⁹ See Cronin 1990 for an acute analysis of the general poetic features of counter-hegemonic poetic practices under apartheid.

7

On shifting ground: South African fiction in the interregnum

> In short, it is at the heart of the ordinary that the extraordinary is to be found. Post-apartheid writing turns from the fight against apartheid, with its fixation upon suffering and the seizure of power, into just such stories as these: stories which open out to transform the victory over apartheid into a gain for postmodern knowledge, a new symbiosis of the sacred and the profane, the quotidian and the numinous. (Graham Pechey, 'The Post-Apartheid Sublime')

South Africa was often thought of as an appalling test case for the development of a divisive racial politics and writing within the incubator of apartheid. Now South Africa is becoming a test case for the ways in which a nation can overcome a divisive past in order to rebuild for a more socially inclusive future. Under the exigencies of apartheid censorship, many novelists like Lewis Nkosi, Nadine Gordimer, J. M. Coetzee and Christopher Hope saw their project clearly: to use all their writing skills and weapons of representation to combat apartheid in the battle against racism. Yet, since the advent of majority rule within South Africa in 1993, South African fiction has had to reassess its future directions. It would not be exaggerating the matter to say that South Africa has embarked upon a major project to forge a new public sphere since 1993, and a culture and literature that investigate how memory and history are created and inscribed are a key part of this venture. As has been observed, even the new national constitution of South Africa itself embodies the past: it does not purport to be a document that stands above and beyond history, but actively embraces its historical context (Fagan 1998). Yet there is no easy walk to freedom. Strewn as the path is with historical hindrances and ideological impediments, there are many conflicting voices as to the trajectory of writing in the new state. For example, although Bloke Modisane could ironically entitle his autobiography *Blame Me on History* in 1963, now the question has become *whose* history, and how that history is to be represented in the national endeavour to secure a lasting nation of racial equality. On the other hand, the novelist Lauretta Ngcobo argues that the important future lines of division in post-apartheid South Africa are going to be class and gender rather than race (Ngcobo 1992: 167). With the world transfixed upon this experiment in national 'reconciliation', part of whose laboratory has been the national public hearings as well as legal proceedings of the Truth and Reconciliation Commission, the social transformation has been constantly cast in the metaphor of healing a national trauma. As writers who have been part of that trauma seek to extricate the national consciousness from a collective crisis, they have engaged in considerable debate about issues of representation, racial identity and the politics of ethnicity. This chapter will focus on the various trajectories and paths that South African fiction and culture take in this endeavour to examine the country's future, exploring the processes of national 'memory-work' to heal the past through a complicated process of redefinition and reconfiguration.

In this process of forging the public sphere anew, South Africa has engaged in a tricky and complex debate concerning 'nationalism' and constitutionalist politics – over people's rights. Nationalism, so tarred by the apartheid era, is fervently opposed by those seeking a politics of human rights; but in the post-apartheid era nationalist politics has also been espoused by the right-wing Zulu Inkatha organisation, as well as a host of other groups, making it seem that any form of nationalism comes at a considerable ideological cost. The immediate problem appears to be that you can take nationalism out of racial segregation but the question remains as to whether you can ever take racial segregation out of nationalism. Forging anew the public sphere means that this issue needs to be confronted directly, and not sidestepped with some political panacea that convinces everyone in a small way and convinces nobody in a big way. As Ingrid de Kok, a prominent South African poet, says:

> The addressing of public grievance and pain, through legal remedy and transformational social policies, is a proper job for government bureaucracy. But the reparative capacity of government is limited, and no work of mourning, at individual or national level, can take place without recourse to other forms of mediation. Appropriate resources need to be found in civil society itself. Healers, ministers, psychologists, and educators, among others, can mediate between the discourses of the past self and the present self in formalized ways. (De Kok 1998: 60–1)

De Kok concludes that appropriate forms of mediation to accomplish this process of exploring the contradictory voices can be found in the ways cultural institutions and artists produce 'fictions of consolation' and thereby seek to recompose the past, not as a seamless resolution of the problems and ruptures but as a reconfiguration that does not entirely obscure the fractures.

In many quarters, there is the sense that the South African struggle for democracy is 'history' – that is, over and done, finished. Certainly among the media, there are strong pressures for a grand culminating narrative that draws all the elements of South Africa's tumultuous past to a close, thereby allowing South Africa to enter a new global economic and international order with a 'clean sheet'. Indeed, South African history is littered with dates construed as Rubicon crossings: the Treason Trial (1956), the Rivonia Trial (1963), the Sharpeville massacre (21 March 1960), the Soweto Uprising (16 June 1976) and F. W. de Klerk's release of Mandela (2 February 1990).[1] These dates always implied no way back to the 'old days', indicating a past cut off from the present and future. History was cast as a series of irrevocable points of rupture, that prevented the past from returning. South African history has always been written as a series of severances, always impelling itself forward to some 'better' place, some 'morally' superior position. And yet, the practices of race hatred and atrocious material conditions for many black South Africans by and large have not changed: the country is beset by severe internal divisions, material crime is rampant, race-related barbarities persist in certain quarters and a debilitating AIDS epidemic is forecast to have catastrophic effects on the population in the next decade. Sometimes these dates have also been construed as bolts from the blue, actions that have come from nowhere. Yet on the contrary, their occasion was impelled by history, by cause, by preceding events: they are the product of agency and historical processes. As Michael Green points out in his study of history in South African literature entitled *Novel Histories*, the taint of apartheid reaches out beyond the post-apartheid era, and a post-apartheid vision is still defined by strategies and syntactical formulations of the apartheid decades. Indeed, '"History", in line with its problematical conceptual status, is involved in a bewildering array of guises in South Africa fiction' (Green 1997: 8) as various writers and thinkers seek to engage with the legacy of a barbarous episode in the past. Green argues that the only way one can represent the past without appropriating it to one's own position is in 'resistant form', which he describes as an aesthetic form that simultaneously recognises the constructedness of its subject within its own productive processes, yet goes on to create that subject in such a manner that the very terms within which that subject is constructed are challenged – thus resisting the very forms in which it is produced (Green 1997: 6). Green argues that the most successful uses of 'history' in fiction are those 'which allow the past to resist being appropriated by the present. Fiction which recreates the past in its difference powerfully enough to challenge the present shifts us from the rather significant category of "historical fiction" to the more important activity of historicising form' (Green 1997: 174). In his Foucauldian narrative of the necessity of historical discontinuity, Green searches for 'moments when the "historical" becomes more than that, moments when we glimpse a difference that positively erases our sameness ... and alters the position from which we produce our pasts, presents, and future' (Green 1997: 239). In addressing a series of questions about the paradoxes of living in a transition of history, Green proposes that the 'historiographical' novelist rather than the 'historical' novelist is the key writer, that is, the writer who problematises our very concepts of history, like J. M. Coetzee.

Recently, the cat has been set amongst the pigeons by Albie Sachs, an important voice in South African political and literary circles. The ANC had always regarded art as a weapon in the struggle against apartheid. However, writing about the course of South African literature in the post-apartheid era, Sachs whipped up a storm by arguing that writers should stop being political now that apartheid had ceased as a state ideology – writers and artists should surrender their arsenal of artistic weapons and get on with the concerns of writing, freed from the obligations of writing about apartheid (Sachs 1998).[2] Implying that only good art under apartheid *did* have an obligation of writing about apartheid, and that art and politics are separable, this ANC doctrinal position does present a somewhat simplistic and severe polarity of the aesthetic and the politico-ethical: as Benita Parry argues, it poses the 'reification of a stark choice between solipsistic aestheticism and engaged art' (Parry 1992: 129). The question of what constitutes a suitable writing for post-apartheid South Africa was, however, a live one for several decades before Sachs's intervention. In 1970, Es'kia (Ezekiel) Mphahlele in *The African Image* had argued that the function of the black critic in South Africa was essentially restorative, seeking to substitute ordinary life for spectacle (Mphahlele 1974). Njabulo Ndebele has suggested that African writers needed to 'rediscover the ordinary' in their fiction, again eschewing the easy route to the spectacular in their literature (Ndebele 1994). Writers had been discussing this issue since at least the late 1980s, but in 1992 one of South Africa's most eminent literary commentators, Michael Chapman, isolated the issue as an opposition between a literature of 'participatory witness' with 'accountability to progressive forces', and a literature that gives full expression to doubts, ambiguities and complexities of meaning, an aesthetic of verbal iconicity (Chapman 1992: 3). In other words, Chapman asked whether literature should aim for 'relevance' or 'literary excellence'. Taking J. M. Coetzee's fiction as a salient example of a writer confronting race power relations, Chapman critically analyses the novel *Foe*: 'Using his postmodernist allegories to unpick imperial power relations, he has difficulties in knowing what identities need rebuilding. After fragmenting his subject – the white European authority – Coetzee is unable, or unwilling, to turn the African "other" into a new subject. There are no new solidarities' (Chapman 1992: 4–5). Regarding this postmodernist aestheticism as a cul-de-sac for political bridge-building and social reorientation, Chapman urged people to consider how one accounts for restructuration as well as rupture: 'any attempt to reconstruct requires that we accept – pragmatically – the idea of linearities not as inevitable crises, but as necessary master-narratives towards new social and aesthetic relations and ideals' (Chapman 1992: 8). Chapman is extremely concerned that value in post-apartheid South Africa is to do with liberatory politics, with 'justice and compassion in a post-apartheid South Africa' (Chapman 1992: 11). Stephen Gray responded by putting the side of the argument that extols 'literary excellence' and 'autonomous art' (Gray 1992). For Gray, the most significant issue is to produce an art that adheres to an aesthetic integrity, unbetrayed by gestures towards a transient politics or ideology. After Raymond Williams's model of residual, dominant and emergent cultures, Gray proposes that South African culture is always working towards the emergent: 'The emergent in my view is not created seamlessly by transformation; it is created by combating the dominant with selected aspects of the residual. To put this another way, we call on re-visioning the past to forge a future in spite of the present' (Gray 1992: 27). Gray is not naively promoting a dehistoricised aesthetic practice that does not acknowledge the political realities of the day, but rather arguing that an artist's first and foremost loyalty is to the work in hand (whatever that may be), in order to construct the already imagined post-apartheid future(s).

It is this multiplicity of perspective about the future that this chapter seeks to explore. It aims to explore the ways in which different ethnic perspectives treat memory and remembrance in forging the social sphere, and how fiction in particular is intertwined with larger political and social pressures in a post-apartheid era. Benedict Anderson's conception of the 'imagined community' has been the most commonly cited paradigm for the construction of the nation; and indeed the imagined 'nation' has been an important anti-apartheid rallying cry. Yet 'the nation' has also been bedevilled by ideologies of purity, virtuousness and univocal political options, where a lexicon of 'own', 'group areas' and 'group rights' possess a particularly troubled articulation under apartheid. In South Africa's recent examination of the nation as a discursive formation, projections of multiplicity, diversity, plurality and hybridity – Nelson Mandela's invocations and conceptions of the 'rainbow nation' – are broadly a sketch for the future: but it remains broad and provisional, often fragile and vague. In some ways these are uncertain political rhetorics, clinging to old dreams. In the fast-changing political circumstances, it remains important to be labile and sensitive in dealing with future twists and turns on the political helter-skelter of the South African future, and in order to escape the 'discordances' of the past, one needs to find what Ndebele significantly terms a 'point of convergence' that represents a confrontation with history through people 'reinventing themselves through narrative' (Ndebele 1992: 25 and 27). This 'restoration of narrative' as a moral necessity in stimulating people's imaginations towards creating new thoughts and ideas will prove to be an important concept for this chapter.

Monuments and memorials

Close to the little picturesque university town of Stellenbosch where I was born, on the slope of the Paarl mountain range, stands an impressive symbolic monument on a hill overlooking the Paarl and Stellenbosch valleys, and looking south to the wide expanses of the Cape Flats just north of Cape Town. This is the Afrikaans Language Monument, or 'Taalmonument' (Figure V), which was designed and erected in 1975 by the apartheid government as a symbol of the evolution and superiority of the Afrikaans language. Commemorating the centenary of Afrikaans being declared a sepa-

V View of the Afrikaans Language Monument, or Taalmonument, Paarl, South Africa

rate language from Dutch, it is the only major monument dedicated to a language. Among the tapering structures of a convex and concave nature, the phallic splendour of the monument is a testimony to the grandiose self-aggrandisement of the Afrikaner hegemony during the era of apartheid, designed as it is to reflect the ascendancy of Afrikaner culture over all the African cultures, a symbol of European domination of African peoples and the suppression of African languages. As Figure VI shows, the design of three pillars sweeping up to the pillar that represents the purity and preeminence of Afrikaans belittles the indigenous African languages and now stands as a peculiarly tranquil yet moribund relic of a bygone age, when mighty languages such as Xhosa, Zulu and Sotho were mere 'tributaries' to the great South African Afrikaner 'volk'.

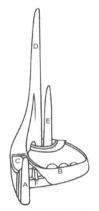

A Clear West

B Magical Afrika

C Bridge

D Afrikaans

E Republic

F Malay language and culture

VI Diagram of the Afrikaans Language Monument, or Taalmonument, Paarl, South Africa, with a key to its symbolic structures

The monument perpetuates the now well-worn stereotypical self-illusion of western rationalism ('Clear West') and the numinous mystical irrationalism of Africa ('Magical Afrika'), both in its nomenclature and in the relative symbolic sizes and features (an upright pillar for the West, and a slouching undulation for Africa). Emblazoned on the pathway leading up to the monument is the phrase 'Dit is ons erns' (roughly 'we are earnest about this'), and a plaque at the entrance of the monument bearing quotations from prominent Afrikaans poets speaks about 'the large, shining West and the magical Africa', 'our imagination' and 'this gleaming vehicle [of Afrikaans]', clearly reinforcing the self-proclaimed dignity, majesty and superior role of Afrikaans in uniting and cementing the cultural pluralities of the southern part of the continent. Ironically, archaeologists have uncovered Arabic scripts in Cape Town's Malay Quarters which proves that, almost in defiance of the Afrikaners' claim to Afrikaans as their 'mother tongue', the Afrikaans language originated amongst the Malay slaves and was not the creation of the Afrikaner tribe. The mix of Dutch and English became further diluted over the years with the addition of African words, and modern linguists contend that it is on the Cape Flats, among the so-called 'coloured' community where Afrikaans is the predominant language, that the 'true' Afrikaans continues to evolve in its pigeon or 'kitchen' form. When apartheid crumbled, part of the post-apartheid debate in the transitional period has had to grapple with the problem of inheriting and accommodating a history that is not one's own: there has been the problem of renaming and rededicating street names saturated with Afrikaans history, such as airports named after apartheid's presidents, or infamous buildings associated with the heinous crimes of apartheid (like John Vorster Square, the notorious police headquarters where Steve Biko among others was interrogated and murdered); and what to do with major national monuments dedicated to the greater glory of the apartheid ideology.[3] Various councils in the new government's Department of Arts and Culture have been established to deal with these renaming and heritage matters, such as the South African Geographical Names Council (SAGNC) and the South African Heritage Resources Agency (SAHRA). The government is renaming some of the metropoles or municipalities: Durban becomes eThekwini, Pretoria becomes Tshwane, and Port Elizabeth becomes the Nelson Mandela Metropole. There is no official new name for Johannesburg yet, but the Zulu name Egoli is one that is being considered. Nevertheless, last bastions of entrenched right-wing Afrikanerdom that resist efforts to promote multiculturalism persist in dark corners of the Republic, even after the historic events of the past decade. Crying the beloved country, these conservatives look set to run full tilt into confrontation with the government. For instance, Radio Pretoria, where apartheid was still revered and the white man reigned supreme, continued to broadcast its steady opposition to racial inter-mingling and the demise of 'separate development', despite its legal confrontation with the Independent Communications Authority in 2003 (Swarns 2002).

South Africa was, and still is to a large degree, a country predicated upon memory and remembrance. As a child at school, I learned that one of the most important national holidays in apartheid South Africa was 16 December, known as Day of the Vow, or the Day of the Covenant. This commemorated the Battle of Blood River, when on 16 December 1838, in Natal, 464 Afrikaner Boers under the command of Andries Pretorius defeated more than ten thousand Zulu warriors. Today the battle site is a monument consisting of 64 replica

Voortrekker wagons cast in bronze and situated just as they were on the day of the famous battle alongside replicas of the three cannons that proved so decisive in halting repeated Zulu charges against the laager. The monument at Blood River is a reminder of the historical battle between the Voortrekkers and the Zulus, which heralded the beginning of the end of the great Zulu kingdom. In preparation for the battle, the Voortrekkers took a vow before God that they would build a church and that they and their descendants would observe the day as one of thanksgiving should they be granted victory: hence, the Day of the Covenant. With the advent of full democracy in South Africa, 16 December retained its status as a public holiday, although now with the purpose of fostering reconciliation and national unity, renamed the Day of Reconciliation. The current schedule of public holidays includes Human Rights Day on 21 March, commemorating the brutal murder of civilians who had gathered together to protest against the Pass Laws under the Native Laws Amendment Act of 1952, at Sharpeville in 1960. In this infamous massacre, police opened fire on peaceful demonstrators, apparently without having been given a prior order to do so, killing 69 people and wounding 180. Other current national holidays commemorate the first democratic elections held in South Africa in 1994 on Freedom Day (27 April), the Soweto Uprising in 1976 on Youth Day (16 June), the day when women participated in a national march petitioning against the Pass Laws in 1956 on National Women's Day (9 August) and a day to celebrate the varied cultures of the nation on Heritage Day (24 September). Appropriately, even daily lived time is etched within history and remembrance.

Significantly, many of the main state monuments inscribe colonial memory: the commanding Voortrekker Monument in Pretoria, the imposing 1820s Settlers Monument in Grahamstown, the grand statue of Jan van Riebeeck outside the Cape Town parliament, the statue of President Paul Kruger in Church Square, Pretoria, the monument commemorating the Battle of Blood River; and, more recently, the establishment of the Robben Island Museum and the District Six Museum in Cape Town as challenges to that memory. As ex-President Nelson Mandela stated in a speech to mark the rededication of the 1820 Settlers Monument in Grahamstown as a national resource for the arts and culture, there are monuments that nurture a particular tradition through the exclusion of others, and 'there are monuments which open the past to scrutiny; recalling it in order to illuminate and transform it into part of our living and changing society; and merging the tradition from which they emerged with the rich diversity of South Africa's culture [which act as] a beacon for the future memory of all our people as much as a memory of the past'.[4]

National myth petrified in stone is always a sculpture of deterioration. Monuments anchor official memory, by acting as material embodiments of versions of the past, which in time become institutionalised as public memory. In this respect, museum policy can aid reconceptualisations of the history of the country that it wants to reflect. South Africa is literally being remade.[5] Refiguring and recoding the past in terms of the imperatives and demands of the present has emerged from a combination of government ideology transformed into social and economic policy. State-funded museums were exhorted by the Ministry of Arts, Culture, Science and Technology to remedy past inequities as part of the national reconstruction and development programme. In other words, state funding has followed projects dedicated to inscribing those disenfranchised and marginalised elements of the community into the national history and transforming the national consciousness about South Africa's past. One example of this approach has been the District Six Museum (1992) which reclaims the social histories of the people who were forcibly removed from the District Six area of Cape Town in the 1960s under the Group Areas legislation, providing a memory bank of human resilience in the face of adversity. The District Six Museum is a typical example of the attempts to recuperate the excised past, declaring that its first exhibition 'was not to recreate District Six as much as re-possess the history of the area as a place where people lived, worked, loved, and struggled'.[6] The District Six Museum is housed in what was once the old Methodist Church, poised on the border between the outskirts of the city centre, Buitenkant Street, and the barren wasteland of District Six. The launch of the *Streets Exhibition: Retracing District Six* in December 1994 provided the idea of establishing a community museum. Central to the museum's purpose is ensuring that the historical memory of dispossessed communities who were forcibly removed by the apartheid government in South Africa endures. According to Vincent Kolbe, an ex-resident and museum trustee, the Museum represents a 'living memorial' and 'is more than just a static display'. The Museum has sought to construct an arena that enables people to reaffirm their identity, celebrate their heritage and confront the complexities of their history. Inspired by this environment of memory and celebration, ex-residents share with museumgoers their stories and experience of District Six. 'We want the Museum to be a place of healing, but we don't want this to happen again. We dare not forget,' says Stan Abrahams, ex-resident and Trustee of the Museum. Among the various reconstructions of District Six, including paintings, prints, photographs, stories and poems, is the 'Memory Cloth', a highlight of the museum, on which are written comments, messages and personal memories by ex-residents of District Six. The cloth is over three hundred metres long and continues to grow, with an additional cloth for visitors on which they can write comments and messages. Nevertheless, the Museum has generated a new complexity in the contested locality, since it has effectively contributed to a reconstrual of District Six as a space collectively owned by all South Africans regardless of race, social status or politics.[7] Other examples of similar institutions and museums setting about the recognition of unwritten pasts are the Mayibuye Centre at the University of the Western Cape which is committed to recovering the history of the liberation movement, and the establishment of the Robben Island Museum, which seeks to preserve in the national consciousness the depths to which apartheid sank in its ideological barbarity. Since 1997, Robben Island has been a National Museum and National Monument, which acts as a focal point of South African heritage running educational programmes for schools, youths and adults, facilitating tourism development, conducting ongoing research related to the Island and fulfilling an archiving function. On 1 December, 1999, Robben Island was listed as a World Heritage Site by UNESCO.

Oppression lingers long in the recesses of the mind, well after the steel shackles have been removed. These reclamations and repossessions of absent memories are clearly part of a process of mourning for the traumatic past that has affected all aspects of the South African population. Rather than promoting a 'monumental memory', which is a memory serving to justify the rememberer's claim to authority and power, these new technologies of memory form part of an 'ethical memory', where memory is put to work in presenting the dead or the past the gift of recollection without waiting for reciprocation. These museums that recover lost histories and communities, and the debates about renaming, provide instructive parallel contexts for much of the fictional strategies of contemporary writers, as they revise the received knowledge of the once-dominant order and unleash the unspoken voices of hitherto silenced subjects. In destabilising the fixity of history and memory, these museums are part of a transformative cultural process of imaginative revision of the past.

The Truth and Reconciliation Commission in literary consciousness

No other African country (apart from possibly Rwanda, Kenya and Zimbabwe) is more intimately concerned with the connection between public memory and a nation's history than South Africa in the post-apartheid era. More than any other ideological change, government initiative or change to the machinery of state, the establishment of the Truth and Reconciliation Commission (TRC) in South Africa in the late 1990s to oversee the transition to democracy through a process of national confession permeated the public imagination and popular consciousness. Arising from the South African Interim Constitution (Act No. 200 of 1993), the TRC was established on the Promotion of National Unity and Reconciliation Act, No. 34 of 1995. As the former Minister of Justice Mr Dullah Omar put it, 'a commission is a necessary exercise to enable South Africans to come to terms with their past on a morally accepted basis and to advance the cause of reconciliation'. The TRC was 'To provide for the investigation and the establishment of as complete a picture as possible of the nature, causes and extent of gross violations of human rights committed during the period from 1 March 1960 to the cut-off date contemplated in the Constitution, within or outside the Republic, emanating from the conflicts of the past, and the fate or whereabouts of the victims of such violation'.[8] In this respect, the TRC was a public rehearsal of memory, where individual traumatic pasts are metonymic of the collective national traumatic past. The TRC's principal action was targeting social memory and making that the site of political transformation. As Kenneth Christie has observed, it was a specific social and political recognition that social memory is a referral to past events and experiences (whether real or imagined), for recalled past experiences and shared images of the historical past are significant for the constitution of social groups in the present and their identity (Christie 2000). In his attention to the importance of embodied habitual practices in sustaining social memory, Paul Connerton has argued that the control of a society's memory largely shapes the hierarchy of social power. The manner in which collective memory is stored is not simply a technical formulation but one that bears directly on the *legitimation* of power relations and what that means: 'Thus we may say that our experiences of the present largely depend upon our knowledge of the past, and that our images of the past commonly serve to legitimate a present social order' (Connerton 1989: 3). Indeed, as Marx's analyses of the eras of Imperial Rome and the French Revolution demonstrated, all political rhetoric utilises the past as a legitimation device. The TRC was an acknowledgement that memory is material. It counts. It serves a purpose. As we have seen, the apartheid state celebrated its own history – through the mechanisms of the mass media, public monuments, museums, educational textbooks. It protected itself with a panoply of statutory powers and spectacular public cultural demonstrations, to prevent any alternative versions of history. The TRC's function was to replace, restore and reinstate a memory rent apart and splintered by apartheid: to prevent the present and future being weighed down by the nightmare of dead generations on the minds of the living. The TRC acknowledged that memory was important, almost as a form of ultimate justice: it captured the gradations of responsibility for the past. In *The Country of My Skull*, Antjie Krog, a well-known South African Afrikaans poet and writer, wrote a minutely detailed record which is a subtle barometer of the daily proceedings of the TRC's work and its results in the media. Krog argued that the TRC would have beneficial social effects only if it construed truth as 'the widest possible compilation of people's perceptions, stories, myths and experiences ... [so that we] can restore to memory and foster a new humanity' (Krog 1999: 23). One has to be careful, however, since the 'politics of memory' can just as easily cause a conflagration of hatred, as testified by the Afrikaners and the Boer War, or the situation in Northern Ireland. Michael Ignatieff saw the processes of the TRC as an effort to decrease the quantity of allowable lies in circulation (Ignatieff 1996). Other commentators remarked on the ways in which the Commission was a public recognition of the inextricable link between public memory and a national past, and the necessity to articulate these hidden memories rather than suppressing them in mortified silence:

> In moving away from the discredited governing consciousness of the past, we will need to build a new, shared and ceaselessly debated memory of that past. Without sustained remembrance and debate, it will be difficult to develop a new South African culture with its various strands intertwined in constructive friction, rather than in mere conflict and mutual strangulation. This talk of shared memory must not be misunderstood or mystified. It is not the creation of a post apartheid *volk* or stifling homogenous nationhood; nor a new fatherland. Nor is it merely the equivalent of every individual's mental ability to retain facts and arguments at the front of her consciousness. Such analogies between individual and collective memory are unhelpful. Rather, shared memory, in the intended sense, is a process of historical account-ability. (Asmal et al. 1996: 9–10)

In the final analysis, the work of the TRC proved to be decidedly controversial, especially in relation to the findings that implicated the African National Congress in unacceptable and questionable breaches of human rights, and the general benefit it brought to the country in its post-traumatic search for identity.[9] Nevertheless, a large consensus of public opinion still appears to regard the processes and proceedings of the TRC as a valuable and necessary national ideological purgation of guilt and shame. The words of the South African Interim Constitution used the words 'ubuntu, not victimisation', thereby promoting the African idea of restorative justice, seeking to include both victim and perpetrator in the resolution of conflicts. Added to this is a discourse of psychological trauma therapy, repeatedly found in the passionate and committed words of Archbishop Tutu, the Chair of the Commission:

> The other reason amnesia simply will not do is that the past refuses to

lie down quietly. It has an uncanny habit of returning to haunt one ...
However painful the experience, the wounds of the past must not be
allowed to fester. They must be opened. They must be cleansed. And
balm must be poured on them so they can heal. This is not to be obsessed
with the past. It is to take care that the past is properly dealt with for
the sake of the future.[10]

Yet for all Tutu's profound emotional appeal and willingness to
efface himself before the other, Jacques Derrida has warned us
about the complexities of 'hauntology' in fixing origins and opening
up new futures very clearly in *Specters of Marx*, specifically with
regard to deferred futures predicated upon cleansed pasts.[11]
Questioning the extent to which South Africa as a 'new nation'
grounds itself in an ethics of responsibility, Ebrahim Moosa has
argued that the TRC structured itself on a lexicon of obligation,
redemption, confession and contrition, unsurprisingly also evident
in Archbishop Tutu's words. Moosa perceives this Christocentric
discourse embedded in the TRC as part of a performative act of
justice, and he regards the TRC as 'an exceptional and extraordinary event because it calls for a "reconciliation with the other"
alongside the normal justice system with its array of sanctions'
(Moosa 2000). Whether or not this Levinasian ethics of alterity
really does underpin the actions of the TRC, it is clear that the
TRC demonstrated that the people of South Africa are serious about
the constitutional commitment to recognise the 'injustices of our
past'.[12] It provided a framework within which victims and perpetrators could begin to deal with the past, exposing a great deal of
suppressed evidence about the private and political state actions in
the apartheid past, and providing catharsis for some victims and
survivors. Yet whilst acknowledging this therapeutic dimension,
Richard Wilson has put forward a strongly sceptical case about the
role of the TRC within the post-apartheid government's exaltation
of the discourse of human rights. Wilson argues that human rights
are a double-edged sword in modern democracies:

> On the one hand, human rights are progressively modernizing and encour-
> age a critical reflection on authority, tradition and patriarchal notions of
> community. Human rights commissions create a space which did not exist
> before where narratives of suffering could emerge and become incorpo-
> rated into the official version of the past ... At the same time, human
> rights are an intrinsic part of the legality of the modern state apparatus
> and as such they constitute an element in the onward march of legal domi-
> nation identified by the sociologist Max Weber in the late nineteenth
> century. They subordinate the lifeworld of social agents to the systemic
> imperatives of nation-building and the centralization of the legal and
> bureaucratic apparatus. (Wilson 2001: 224–5)

With 'Human rights ... entwined with a project of modernist ration-alization', Wilson sees the TRC as 'a process of legal colonization of the realms of personal experience' (Wilson 2001: 225). Within this finely poised context, it is instructive to investigate whether fiction can succeed any more sensitively than the TRC itself, in articulating the tortured intimacies and mournful testimonies of the individual voice without sacrificing them to the greater political exigencies of forging the collective nation.

Gillian Slovo's brisk thriller *Red Dust* (2002) deals with the effects of the TRC in South Africa in the small fictional Eastern Cape town of Smitsrivier that holds an amnesty hearing for the TRC. The novel is about the way the past resurfaces in the present. Prefaced by the poignant quotation from *Henry IV, Part I,* II.4, 'Is not the truth the truth?', the novel is about 'truth': what constitutes 'truth', whether it should be told, indeed whether it can be told, and the effects of what purports to be 'truth'. Slovo initially wanted to entitle the novel 'Complicity', and the incestuous relationship between truth and memory – whether outrightly corrupt, cynically convenient, or trau-matically obliterated – is the overarching idea of this novel. A compelling plot centres upon three different people's anxieties about how their pasts re-emerge to shape their presents in the context of a hearing for the Truth and Reconciliation Commission: Sarah Barcant from New York returns as a top lawyer to her home town; from jail emerges ex-deputy policeman Dirk Hendricks; and situated within the new government comes Alex Mpondo MP, to face his former torturer. Yet the real target of truth is Hendricks's ex-colleague, Pieter Muller, who evaded prosecution and still lives, more or less peacefully, with his strange, invalid wife in Smitsrivier. James Sizela, the obdurate school-headmaster, suspects that Muller – who has not applied for amnesty – murdered his son, Steve. Steve Sizela and his erstwhile comrade, Mpondo, were imprisoned together in the frantic agony of apartheid's dying breath. Only Mpondo was released. Now, fifteen years on, Steve's father is haunted by his inability to account for his missing son with no physical body evident. When James Sizela asks Ben Hoffman, a retired advocate, to help him unravel what happened, the crafty old lawyer calls upon his onetime pupil Sarah to help him to explore the matter.

During the unfolding of the hearing, fragments of the past are pieced together as various accusations and complicities emerge within the fraught political and social divisions wrought by apartheid. In addition, the novel explores the uneasy intimacy that exists between the aggressor and the victim, between the torturer and the tortured. There are numerous types of rhetoric evident in the novel about the discourse of the TRC, which contend and vie with one another for authority. First, there is the Christian rhetoric concern-

ing salvation and psychological catharsis, in which it is suggested
that the ritual enactments of the TRC are symbolically healing to
both perpetrator and victim alike. In this respect, Sarah Barcant
arrives believing in the idealist restorative properties of the TRC
process; although by the end of the novel, she has begun to realise in
her dealings with her mentor Ben that things prove to be far more
complicated:

> 'But the Truth Commission is not about justice,' Ben said. 'It was never
> meant to be.'
>
> 'Well, then, what is it about?' All the frustration that had been build-
> ing up in her seemed suddenly to surface and instead of waiting out
> Ben's reply, she furnished her own: 'Is it about truth?' She laughed out
> loud. 'Hardly. If the new rulers of South Africa think justice is compli-
> cated, well, they should know that he truth is even more elusive. So
> what else is there? Reconciliation? That's what the churchmen preach.
> Good for them, somebody has to. But I defy you to find reconciliation
> between individuals either in this case or in a score of others. Oh, sure
> – there've been the usual heart-warming sentiments from the mouths of
> those wonderful old mamas, the ones who bear the cost of this country.
> They're South Africa's speciality – they make the world feel good about
> its own humanity.'
>
> 'You've got it all wrong,' Ben said. 'The reconciliation the Commission
> talks about is not between individuals.'
>
> 'You're talking about a society-wide reconciliation then. Yes, well,
> perhaps the weight of hearings will help to change perceptions but you
> only have to look at the crime statistics, or even what has happened in
> Smitsrivier since the hearing began, to know how long it's going to take.'
> (*Red Dust*: 318)

Second, there is the urge to just get rid of the past, making a clean
break and closing the book on it. Dirk Hendricks's attitude comes
closest to this line of thinking, largely because he has a good deal to
lose in discoveries being made about the past. Cynical about the 'new
South Africa', Hendricks still clings unrepentantly to his apartheid
beliefs and his unswerving actions in supporting the old regime:

> One thing he knew for sure: the new history of their country could no
> longer fit the old truths ... Dirk knew that no matter how intricate and
> how clever the theories, the so-called experts could never really know
> what it had been like to be caught up in the centre of that whirlwind,
> caught by history in the making and at the same time making history
> and watching it unmade, and all the time having to take decisions like
> where to put the overflow of prisoners, or how to get the information
> before more lives were staked, or how to explain to your kids why you
> turned up from work unable to look them in the eye. (*Red Dust*:
> 198–200)

Hendricks uses perception of being the pawn of history as his escape
clause, ultimately exculpating himself from responsibility as he goes

to prison: 'He had done what he had to do, that was all. It was over now. It had to be. If he dwelt on it, it would drive him mad and that was an option he refused. He would no longer live in memory. It had happened – in the past – and there was nothing to be gained by harping on it. The past was just that – the past: it could not be changed' (*Red Dust*: 336). Against this boorish recalcitrance, there is a demand for reckoning, for a vengeful justice, such as the line that James Sizela takes concerning retaliatory justice for the loss of his son. Finally, reflecting on Sarah Barcant's somewhat naive efforts to prise open the truth, in some ways, Alex Mpondo agrees with Hendricks's attitude about the past: '[Sarah had] forgotten that the story with a beginning, a middle and its own neat ending, which was what she'd tried to give him, was something New York might offer, but not South Africa. There was too much history here, too much bad history, for that kind of completion: all that South Africa could aspire to was a general moving-on' (*Red Dust*: 336–7). Mpondo presents a resigned and acquiescent mood at the completion of the novel, recognising that you cannot take the individual out of history, nor can you take the history out of the individual. Ultimately, *Red Dust* reinforces that there is no way to approach a trauma head-on: testimonies can only offer trauma obliquely and tangentially, in scraps and deferments, in ways that make the initial trauma unrepresentable and inarticulable. Responsibilities for that past are a complex and intricate web of individual and collective, active and passive, deeds and words.

Red Dust's suspension of future resolutions through truth and reconciliation is treated in a more jaundiced way by Achmat Dangor's recently acclaimed novel *Bitter Fruit* (2003). This novel suggests that confessing the truth does not lead to freedom, but rather opens fresh wounds that persist in tainting the present. Combining the intimate secrets of a mixed-race family with the politics of the TRC, the characters in *Bitter Fruit* experience a period where the sins of the fathers are heaped in piles on the present. Silas Ali, a behind-the-scenes broker with the TRC, states: 'We want to forgive, but we don't want to forget. You can't have it both ways' (*Bitter Fruit*: 13). Good as he is at his job, Silas is increasingly weary of 'this country and its contorted history' (*Bitter Fruit*: 223) and progressively suspicious of the ideological validity of the work of the TRC, as he enters an 'ambiguity he sees everywhere ... a growing area of grey, shadowy morality' (*Bitter Fruit*: 164–5). Describing the world of past-apartheid South Africa, *Bitter Fruit* depicts a society underpinned by a fragile foundation of unreachable hurt, where the vestiges of a deeply riven racialised society linger and fester, causing organic matter to ripen, decay and rot. Structured under three sub-sectional headings 'Memory', 'Confession' and 'Retribution', the religious structure of

revelation and reconciliation through public witness permeates the
novel. Yet the family cannot shake off the past through a simple act
of confession, as the son Michael discovers that he is born of a rape
by a white policeman: 'A ghost from the past, a mythical phantom
embedded in the "historical memory" of those who were active in the
struggle. Historical memory. It is a term that seems illogical and
contradictory to Mikey; after all, history *is* memory ... It is as if
history has a remembering process of its own, one that gives life to
its imaginary monsters. Now his mother and father have received a
visitation from that dark past, some terrible memory brought to life'
(*Bitter Fruit*: 32). Mikey is dragged into his past as he becomes
increasingly set on vengeance, as he seeks to keep his future open:
'He is determined not to sink into the melancholy that comes with
reliving the past. He knows that it will not be possible to apply his
golden rule – look to the future, always – with the same single-mind-
edness as before. He can no longer think of the future without
confronting his past' (*Bitter Fruit*: 131). With this traumatic revelation, Mikey also voices a recognition of the compromised situation of
the new ruling party as the flames of its political idealism are gradually guttering, extinguished by egocentric desires for national and
historical acclaim: '"The struggle" sowed the seeds of bright hopes
and burning ideals, but look at what they are harvesting: an ordinar-
iness, but also a vanity fed by sly and self-seductive glimpses in the
mirrors of their personal histories. In each is born a frantic need for
a "legacy", a need to be recognized as a "hero of the struggle". The
world – once more – is full of monument builders and statue erectors'
(*Bitter Fruit*: 168). Not shying away from puncturing certain shibboleths of the new era, *Bitter Fruit* depicts a malaise settling into a new
ruling elite bent on political transformation yet having to compromise its ideals with political realities and personal ambitions (*Bitter
Fruit*: 165).

Since the completion of the TRC's work, it has been repeatedly
noted that the Commission clearly had an institutionalising effect on
the testimonies presented to it: 'In displacing the real bodies of the
nation in order for the imaginary one of the unified nation to take
their places, the official custodians of memory reduce life stories and
testimonies to a pre-inscribed archive' (Grunebaum-Ralph 2001:
208). However, these fictional narratives seek rather to reclaim individual memory from the metanarrative of the nation, from the
abjected realms of negativity, rift and forgetting. The fiction aims to
balance the achievements of publicly recognising hitherto repressed
narratives with holding open the possibilities that these narratives
may well challenge certain clearly defined political and bureaucratic
paradigms of the future inclusive nation. As one critic puts it, 'the
challenge for writers and artists is to tell the story [of trauma] in

such a way that it re-enacts its own paradoxes and displacements, but without displacing the survivors from their own tales altogether, and without locking those survivors into a fixed narrative formula' (Graham 2003: 30). Unlike the TRC, fictions like *Red Dust* and *Bitter Fruit* resist the separation of survivors from their tales, and suspend closure. The fiction maintains a polyvocality about the emergent culture and state; it is a 'working-through' of the traumatic past, without immersing itself in a repetitive melancholy, yet also without committing itself to a singular vision of the future.

Rewriting the Afrikaner past

Red Dust closes with an ambiguous and equivocal glance at the future of South Africa. Steven Clingman suggested that South African fiction of the 1980s showed a marked change, moving from preoccupation with the past and the present to visions of the future (Clingman 1990). Yet even today, contemporary South African fiction seems to be continuing that ambiguous perspective. For example, the novels vying for the prestigious South African Sunday Times Fiction Award 2002 (of which *Red Dust* was one) on the one hand reveal a new willingness to explore South Africa's comic possibilities. Professor Andries Oliphant, one of the judges for the award, observed: 'The South African novel in English is burgeoning. It is now a more differentiated genre compared to a decade or so ago. South African realities are explored from a wider range of perspectives and in a broader spectrum of modalities. There is a new and vivifying comic strain.' Fellow judge and bestselling author Pamela Jooste said: 'Something new seems to be abroad in the land. As writers we seem eventually to be entering the world of the "here" and "now" and there are some very sharp portraits of urban culture.' On the other hand, the third member of the judging panel, Professor Bheki Petersen, notes 'an impressive range of themes' among the contenders, but points out that the present is still informed by the past: 'Most of the entries seemed to explore the continuing salience of past experience on the present.'[13] Despite Clingman's assertion, the long arm of history and the past, as we shall see in this chapter, still claws at contemporary representations of the South African present and the future.

In this context, one of the more urgent cultural efforts in South African fiction has been the attempt to develop a 'non-oppressive' Afrikaans culture. The seeds of this were sewn in the 1960s by the dissident group of Afrikaans writers known as the Sestigers (the 'Sixtiers'), who found their influences in European and American culture and brought a new idiom to Afrikaans literature. The writings were a tremendous shock to people used to old Afrikaans prose, and some people regarded the Sestigers as campaigning to break down the old way of life. In fact, one might argue that they were allowing the twentieth century into Afrikaans prose.[14] Yet latterly there have been other dissenting Afrikaner voices, such as Karel Schoeman (*'n Ander Land*), Wilma Stockenström (*Expedition to the Baobab Tree*, translated by J. M. Coetzee) and Klaas Steytler (*Die Walvisman*). More recently, a new wave of feminist writers like Ingrid Scholtz, Welma Odendaal, Jeanne Goosen and Ingrid de Kok have made an impact; while the new genre somewhat elliptically called 'Grensliteratur' ('border literature') – works associated specifically with the experience of young white conscripts on the borders of Namibia, Angola, Zimbabwe, Mozambique – has emerged, associated principally with Jaap Steyn (*Diary of a Traitor*), Étienne van Heerden (*To A.W.O.L.*) and Alexander Strachen (*A World Without Frontiers*).

Étienne van Heerden, an Afrikaner novelist of increasingly distinguished reputation, has subsequently emerged with short stories and several compelling novels, his most notable being *Ancestral Voices* (1993) and *The Long Silence of Mario Salviati* (2002). *Ancestral Voices* is part ghost story, mysterious and mystical, tracing the present back to an 'origin' that turns out to be an issue less of measurable instigation than of genealogy, the stories being constructed on the basis of a family tree. Linked by narratives rather than biology, family trees attempt to explain events and relationships not in terms of natural causality but in terms of individuals and their actions and the imaginary spurs in their psyches. As Abraham van der Ligt, the investigating magistrate in *Ancestral Voices* observes to himself, 'one form of causality flows into another' (*Ancestral Voices*: 116).

Like *The Long Silence of Mario Salviati*, *Ancestral Voices* is a novel saturated by history and memory, and in particular by the ways in which the past seeps into the present, despite attempts to cauterise and quarantine its effects. The novel focuses upon two families, the Moolmans and the Riets, the former being white and the latter of mixed race, descended from Bushmen and Hottentot crossed with Moolman blood. Interracial anxiety permeates the Moolman family in every aspect of its life. The novel's plot centres upon the ambiguous death of the child Noah ('Trickle') du Pisani, who is the last offspring of the Moolmans, the love-child of CrazyTilly and Dowser du Pisani, and yet another stepchild of the Moolmans. 'Trickle' apparently fell into a water bore-hole and was unable to climb out, and although there is no real mystery about the 'murder' of the child, there was no post mortem and he was not properly buried. Doubt lingers over the death, since after several unsuccessful attempts to extricate 'Trickle', Abel Moolman shot him in the head from above either when he had died or when it was clear that there was no chance of survival. In fact, all that can be ascertained is that there was a gunshot. At the commencement of the novel, this incident had occurred over fourteen months prior to the arrival of the magistrate, Abraham van der Ligt, who has been commissioned to travel to Toorberg and investigate the death of the child, an investigation that embroils him in a complicated exploration of the family's genealogy, the uncovering of a wide range of related family secrets, and serves to subvert his own certainty in his ability to deliver justice. Arguably though the novel is more concerned with the different generations of the Moolmans, whose farm is situated in the shadow of the Toorberg mountain, and was founded by the 'ancestor' FounderAbel. These ancestors appear throughout the novel in the form of 'ghosts' over-looking the current generation's activities, and offering interpreta-tions of their own actions over the decades. They leave their traces all over the homestead, with their 'voices' appearing in the narrative, footprints appearing in the garden, or watching the action at the drill-hole. Yet these and other characters in the novel are dominated by the historic arrival in the area of FounderAbel, and his naming and building of the Toorberg farm. FounderAbel left a clause in his will that each subsequent Moolman in the family was to receive an annual tithe of crops and provisions, and this meant that 'They were the things which would remind the Moolmans of their ancestral home and of their final resting-place' (*Ancestral Voices*: 20). The story is about the ways in which the Moolman family generations have been hedged in by tradition, history and the past, especially the way in which FounderAbel treated his servants and slaves.

Van Heerden prefixes the novel with a family tree of the Moolman and Riet families. The novel charts the genealogy of the Moolmans and their marginalised *skaamfamilie* ('shame-family') that betrays a contaminated parentage. Instead of a straightforward family tree, there are a series of lacunae, as social evils are reproduced down the 'legitimate' and the 'illegitimate' lines of the family. Van Heerden ultimately depicts an Afrikaner family that is unable to come to terms with the fact that its racial heritage is not as pure as it would ideologically like it to be, and that this 'genealogy of shame' is constantly repressed in daily life.[15] 'It would seem', the magistrate writes to his wife, 'that the Moolmans are attempting to escape into a legendary world where normal rules do not apply' (*Ancestral Voices*: 116). The death of a child ultimately forces the family to confront its own psychological blanks and to face up to its past. In South Africa, mixed blood is of course unacceptable blood; and bad blood was regarded as a corruption of the purity of the race. Nevertheless, it transpires that the fulcrum upon which the Moolmans' tragedy pivots is not racial heritage but material avarice: 'the whole district realized that FounderAbel's wealth had affected his head. The consensus was that no man could possess so much and remain sane' (*Ancestral Voices*: 45). The Moolman family is also tainted by sterility. Several male members of the family are said to be sterile, and this is regarded as a further curse of the sins of the father being visited on the sons. This sterility becomes an extended metaphor as Abel Moolman's search for water overshadows life on the farm. The drill-hole into which 'Trickle' falls is part of the family's attempt to find a new source of fertility for the land, since the water from the Toorberg spring initially discovered by FounderAbel has dried up. In fact, the metaphor of water and fertility is secreted into all aspects of the novel: the drilling machine takes on a life of its own in the magistrate's mind; 'Trickle''s eponymous nickname inscribes water, as well as his birth-name Noah, the waterchild, 'the first man who saw a rainbow' (*Ancestral Voices*: 196), and he is said to be fascinated with the bore-drills; while his father Dowser du Pisani makes his living by dowsing for water.

The present is therefore intricately connected to the past; and the past constantly rears its ugly head, even as what appears initially to be a compliment turns into an indication of the ugly hidden past:

> 'Toorberg has a rich history.' . . .
> 'Do you really think,' she asked, 'that ours is a beautiful history?'
> He thought for a moment, letting his eyes run over the portraits. 'The history of the taming of a country,' he said after a while, 'can seldom be completely beautiful.' (*Ancestral Voices*: 147)

Van der Ligt's conversational compliment to Ella Moolman is quickly qualified as the past of FounderAbel's 'taming' of the land and driving out the indigenous Bushmen and Xhosa people emerges, the genocidal history of the Bushmen as the local white farmers killed them off being presented in emphatic manner (*Ancestral Voices*: 202).

The magistrate Abraham van der Ligt persistently senses that his investigative activity is probing histories that are like skeletons hidden in the Moolman family cupboard, tantamount to, as he puts it, raking old chestnuts out of the fire, and that people know more than they are prepared to admit (*Ancestral Voices*: 56). The magistrate considers 'the chain of causality' in the death of 'Trickle' and concludes that 'This may well lead one to the very beginning of the clan itself, to incidents years ago, where history and legend merge in the nightmare of the past' (*Ancestral Voices*: 101). Pursuing this notion of terror and hurt, the magistrate likens delving into the past to picking at an old scab (*Ancestral Voices*: 184). Indeed, the magistrate's letters to his wife (which are never posted) form a sort of clarification of and meditation upon legal process, the issue of whether causality can be demonstrated in this case. Van der Ligt is under tremendous pressure for such a clarification as well; the novel is suffused with references to and incidences of, the mystical, the anti-rational, and the magical: the *'tokoloshe'* who live on the Toorberg, the Malay wizard, the local lores and wisdom, the mysteries of the past associated with CrazyTilly, 'Trickle', and Dowser du Pisani – all these subvert the magistrate's sense of judicial reason. He declares that he discovers 'the unlimited nature, not of the impossible – that which we were never prepared to admit – but the unlimited nature of the possible' (*Ancestral Voices*: 253). Sorting out the rational from the irrational becomes part of van der Ligt's task, as he muses in a further letter to his wife: 'Am I permitting myself to be carried away by this country where the limits of truth and fantasy have long since ceased to be hard-edged?' (*Ancestral Voices*: 116). Elsewhere, the novel admits 'In this territory, when in the intensity of the summer heat when a man's brain simmered in his skull, truth and myth, history and the future, life and death became inextricably entangled' (*Ancestral Voices*: 13).

Van Heerden's novel is clearly an introspective and deeply contemplative account of the Afrikaner past. It places many of the myths about origins, history, family purity, racial superiority, and rational thought, under close scrutiny, and emerges with a series of bits and pieces that do not add up to the narratives that used to be told. On the contrary, the novel exposes all sorts of contradictions, skeletons in cupboards, hidden stories, inconsistencies and irregularities in the cultural framework of the Moolman family, and by extension in Afrikaner culture, that have been buried and ignored through deep shame or guilt.

These themes are repeatedly picked up in van Heerden's other powerful novel, *The Long Silence of Mario Salviati*. This focuses upon the small symbolically named town of Yearsonend in the dry veld of the Karoo, where Ingi Friedländer arrives to buy a sculpture for the new Houses of Parliament. Gradually, she uncovers the intimate secrets and scandals that lie dormant in Yearsonend, maintained by taciturn and tight-lipped inhabitants, especially about a legendary, missing wagon of Boer gold. The least communicative is Mario Salviati, a skilled stonemason and Italian POW, deaf, now blind, and dumb. Throughout the novel, there is an emphasis on the looming influence of history, and the ways in which the past connects, shapes and orders the present, and we are left in no doubt that this is a novel that is dealing, narratively and metaphorically, with 'times when you could sense that things unfolding now would have huge implications for the future' (*Mario Salviati*: 60). Friedländer is quite clear that the repressed silences rearing their head now are part of a traumatic 'working-through':

> Why do I feel as if things that happened so many years ago are unfold-ing in front of me now, and that they have a special meaning for me as

well as everyone around me? Do all these things haunt this place because they've never been talked through to a conclusion? Is it the unfinished past that so stubbornly inhabits the present? The town is glutted with strife and violence and greed, rotten with gossip and inbreeding, yet so much remains unsaid ... There's a feeling that everything has always been this way and will always stay this way, but under the apparent monotony, the energy of repressed memories and frustrations is simmering. (*Mario Salviati*: 271–2)

Everyone is connected to everyone, through stories and narratives. This is figured in a resonant image for Friedländer, that of a tree: 'What I knew of Yearsonend then, and what I know now! It was just a town when I arrived, with dusty streets, water furrows and sluice gates, quiet verandas and curtains drawn against the heat. And now it's like a tree with branches stretching everywhere and tendrils reaching into every house. Every branch grows from another and sends out its own shoots in turn, and when a story is startled from the branches, flying up into the air like a bird, it takes a flock of other stories with it' (*Mario Salviati*: 146–7). This genealogical image echoes van Heerden's working paradigm of the genealogical 'family tree', where once again 'The Yearsonend Blood Tree' prefaces the novel. Friedländer's role is that of reader and listener, as she pieces together the hidden, repressed and censored stories that make up the interrelations of the web of intrigue in Yearsonend. Stories as the repository of memories, which in turn are the cornerstone of the town's history, are frequently alluded to as the repressed element figured in a mirror that carries 'in its memory images of everyone' (*Mario Salviati*: 281), or stones apparently lost by being dropped into dams (*Mario Salviati*: 281). '"Water, gold and feathers", said Meerlust Bergh, ... "These will always be the three main motifs in Yearsonend"' (*Mario Salviati*: 173). The word 'motif' draws attention to the manner in which the story of Yearsonend is 'the artist's story' (*Mario Salviati*: 172). One is persistently made aware that there is a superimposition of cultures in Yearsonend – San, Khoi, Xhosa, Afrikaner – and how the history of the town is intricately connected to the different artists' representations, from the San and Khoi local cave-paintings to the modern fashion-conscious designers of ostrich feather costumes for the European rich and famous. Friedländer observes at one point that the past is a prison (*Mario Salviati*: 138), and she seeks to release this through her investigation of these representations and stories, which 'always came back to water, to gold and to feathers – and to the love affairs that were interwoven with these three things' (*Mario Salviati*: 106). With a sense of inescapable entrapment and fatal circularity, Ingi Friedländer gradually taps into the lifeblood of the town, and pieces together the scraps and fragments that make up the life of Salviati and the inhab-

itants of Yearsonend. That van Heerden recognises the deep structure of trauma in this investigation of the past is made explicit:

> Yes, thought Ingi, we recycle the things that hurt us most, because for
> some reason we need to feel the pain again. Perhaps because we feel
> that a return visit might take the sting out? Or break the spell? Or
> because we bind ourselves to our parents by repeating their mistakes?
> Is it a form of homage or love?
>
> 'That's why the history of a place like Yearsonend keeps on repeating
> itself,' Ingi told Jonty. 'People have to revisit their old wounds over and
> over again, like a murderer compelled to return to the scene of his crime.
> Nothing is ever completed; we're confined like the concentric rings in a
> tree-trunk.' (*Mario Salviati*: 325–6)

Friedländer triggers a 'working-through' of a traumatic, repressed
past, as the inhabitants' complicity and guilt for previous actions are
brought to the surface in one great symbolic dénouement of shame,
pain and remorse.

Shame and guilt are powerful weapons in people's consciousnesses,
especially when any misfortune is treated as a punishment for a sin
committed in the past, and built upon that is the notion that social
position is an expression of value. Exclusion is the tactic and
apartheid became the ideology. Of the plethora of powerful and influential autobiographical journalistic narratives that chronicled the
black South African generations of the 1950s and 1960s in their daily
skirmishes and confrontations with the petty and invasive fingers of
apartheid, one of the most significant is Bloke Modisane's *Blame Me
on History* (1963). An insouciant autobiography and damning critique
of apartheid in the 1950s, the book focuses upon the experiences of
life in Sophiatown, where the lives of the black intelligentsia centred
upon the vibrant and brash magazine *Drum*. Modisane's fictional
gaze oscillates between, on the one hand, the desolation and demoli-
tion of Sophiatown driven by the Nationalist Party's decision to
remove what it perceived to be a metropolitan canker in the 1950s
and to impose a policy of racial sectionalisation and residential separation of the races; and on the other hand, reflecting upon his life
growing up amongst the random violence, the domestic instabilities
and the unexpected acts of courtesy and politeness amongst the
oppressed themselves that characterised life in Sophiatown. Mocking
the logic of apartheid, the book rejoices in his failure to fit the stereotypical role demanded of him by racist white South Africa: 'if I am a
freak, it should not be interpreted as a failure of their education for
a Caliban, but a miscalculation of history' (Modisane 1963: 179). Yet
Modisane's book is principally about the ways in which apartheid
sought to eradicate history, especially the history of black culture,
literally demolishing its physical buildings and spaces, its way of life,
and the places in which it occurred, such as Sophiatown.

History shows that a phoenix does not always arise from the ashes. In the case of Sophiatown, out of the ashes and rubble arose Triomf, a white suburb for housing white working-class Afrikaners built by the social engineers of apartheid authorities. Marlene van Niekerk's *Triomf* (1994) depicts the Benade family, a poor-white family relocated from Vrededorp (where they had been living in cramped, shared squalid conditions after being offered work in Johannesburg when their northern agricultural farm collapsed) to Triomf. One of the first novels to be published in the 'new' South Africa, it incorporates references to the first democratic election in April 1994 as the National Party (the onetime party of apartheid power) attempts to secure the vote of the working-class Afrikaans families in Triomf. The novel depicts the monotonous and mundane lives of this poor-white family, demonstrating how apartheid fell short even to those it was ideologically designed to benefit.

It quickly becomes evident that the Benade family is wholly dysfunctional and completely inept. Their values are warped and misinformed, and their relations with one another and with others are tortuous, vicious and strained. Apartheid ideology has not left them and they retain their racial and social prejudices and wilfully turn their eyes from the transitional political events around them. The old man 'Pop', his 'wife' Mol and their 'relative' Treppie are actually siblings, while the epileptic Lambert is their son (although Pop's or Treppie's fatherhood is left obscure). Unable to function adequately in employment or social situations, the family depends upon social security payments for their living. The plot hinges on the build-up to the possible revelation of Lambert's parentage on his fortieth birthday, although this turns into a farce and eventually a tragic fiasco. In the end, Pop dies and the family are left cowed and unchanged, still trapped in the same economic circumstances and myopically envisaging the unattainable goal of travelling north if 'the shit hits the fan' after the election.

Triomf is replete with symbolic resonance despite its apparently naturalistic style. The incestuous and congenital Benade family metaphorically represents the extremes to which apartheid ideology of racial exclusivity led. Michiel Heyns has called the family 'a vision of the inbred triumph of Afrikaner nationalism' and continues to observe: '*Triomf* is a tentatively transitional novel in that it traces the transition from the "old" South Africa to the "new" in terms of a family that is clearly not going to change radically, although there is some resigned, hardly voluntary, acceptance of the changes around them' (Heyns 2000: 62). Indeed, this is not specifically a novel about history, but it is a novel about memory as it relates to history. As a novel on the cusp of epoch-making political changes in South Africa, it depicts the ingrained attitudes of apartheid in working-class

Afrikaner people, and the ways in which those attitudes are part of the traumatic consequences of apartheid. The depiction of the Benade family as victims of their own social ideology is part of a wider Afrikaner scrutiny of the post-apartheid postcolonial situation in South Africa. Texts by van Heerden, Antjie Krog and Marlene van Niekerk demonstrate an investigation into the complexities of the apartheid postcolonial South Africa and the recesses of the Afrikaner psyche in particular, referred to as 'Afrikaans literature's own truth commission' (Eduan Swanepoel, cited in Viljoen 1996). In posing a paradoxical situation where one's sympathies swivel between loathing and empathy for the incompetent and repugnant Benade family, van Niekerk indicates the weblike connection between the colonial and postcolonial that has to be negotiated in writing about the 'new' South Africa. Extracting the canker of apartheid from the recesses of South Africa is inevitably going to leave the body politic traumatised in a number of different ways and areas, and refusing to acknowledge the past's effects on the present will merely serve to leave the society disabled and resistant to accepting inevitable multi-cultural changes. The colonial cannot merely be eradicated from the postcolonial through easy acts of political forgetting, and the past has to be met head-on rather than sidestepped when forging a post-apartheid discourse in South African literature and culture.

Writing black history

If the Soweto Renaissance and the later resistance poets sometimes displayed the tendency to romanticise and essentialise the past through a simple dichotomy between apartheid and resistance, black South African fiction writers have had to be wary of the same problem over the decades. Unsurprisingly the history of black South African fiction writing is pitted with lacunae, yet recent attempts to rectify omissions have made it plain that there is a strong and vibrant fiction and journalistic tradition, often undertaken despite enormous personal risks and economic hardships. The recent repub-lication of a selection of stories from the hugely influential 1950s and 1960s magazine *Drum* puts in print many of the vivacious, energetic and pulsating writings of people like Henry Nxumalo, Can Themba, Bloke Modisane, Es'kia (Ezekiel) Mphahlele, Nat Nakasa, Richard Rive, Arthur Maimane and Casey Motsisi, some of whom have estab-lished international reputations. Writing about the refreshing vital-ity and professionalism evinced in *Drum*'s articles and stories, John Matshikiza has asserted that 'They are an invaluable part of our missing store of memories – without which we are destined to have no future.'[16] Other writers like Peter Abrahams, Bessie Head, Alex La Guma, Lewis Nkosi and Miriam Tlali have become known internationally partly through the efforts of publishing support outside South Africa. Contemporary black South African novelists such as Lauretta Ngcobo, Mandla Langa, Zakes Mda and Phaswane Mpe have all sought to address the past as a parallel to the present.

Zakes Mda's fiction addresses the culture and history of the Xhosa people in particular. *Ways of Dying* (1995), which won the prestigious South African M-Net Book Prize in 1997, and *The Heart of Redness* (2000), which won the 2001 Commonwealth Writers Prize for the African Region, both address the circumstances of black South Africans in the period of transition to black majority government. *Ways of Dying* was a big hit in South Africa, where it was even adapted into a jazz opera. The novel narrates the quirky and idiosyncratic life of Toloki, who is trying to establish himself as a Professional Mourner and observer of the numerous ways of dying and thereby eking out a meagre living by attending funerals in Cape Town where he lives. In his outworn suit he adds an aura of sorrow and dignity to funerals, often serving as pacifier when arguments ensue: 'One day he would like to have a fixed rate of fees for different levels of mourning, as in other professions ... But for the time being he will accept anything he is given, because the people are not yet used to the concept of a Professional Mourner. It is a fairly new concept, and he is still the only practitioner' (*Ways of Dying*: 17). He encounters Noria, a childhood acquaintance whose son has just died, and the two renew their friendship, finding comfort in reminiscing over the harrowing events of their lives. There are shades of the absurd in Mda's darkly comic descriptions of the crime, poverty, violence and ethnic unrest that plague the characters. Writing from the heart of the new South Africa, Mda tells his country's stories through beautifully realised characters whose search for love and connection takes one up close to the black experience, past and present.

Set in the transitional years before the first democratic elections, the itinerant Cape Town life of Toloki and his romance with Noria, gradually unfold as his village childhood past is juxtaposed in parallel with his present existence on the dockfronts and settlements at Cape Town. As he meets his childhood friend Noria and gradually sets up home with her, the novel charts the lives of the 'squatters', or settlement dwellers in the Cape shanty towns, where lives are constantly threatened by death, and existence is a daily precarious and fragile struggle. As Toloki states: 'Death lives with us everyday. Indeed our ways of dying are our ways of living. Or should I say our ways of living are our ways of dying?' (*Ways of Dying*: 98). The novel is punctuated and studded with random murders, deaths by starvation, sadistic slayings, criminal killings, racial attacks, 'necklacings', tortures, deaths, funerals and fatalities. The different 'ways of dying'

are a testimony to the instability of the society, as well as the consequences of a black South African social network riven by internal
dissension. The irony of the novel and the source of its black satire is
that death becomes a business for many people, such as allowing
Toloki to develop mourning as a profession, and Nefolovhodwe as a
coffin-maker. 'Unlike the village, death was plentiful in the city'
(*Ways of Dying*: 125) and, as Toloki observes, 'Nefolovhodwe had
attained all his wealth through death. Death was therefore prof-
itable' (*Ways of Dying*: 133).

Memory is the eventual sustenance and salvation for both Noria
and Toloki. The novel hinges upon an opposition between traditional
village life and the hurly-burly of modern city existence. The movement from the village to the city for Toloki was an explicit attempt to
forget village life and ostracism by his father Jwara. Yet Toloki's
mind is dogged by the frequent memories of that village life, Noria's
childhood, her mystical powers of song inspiring Jwara's black-
smithing and forging of figurines. These memories both torture
Toloki and keep him rooted in the village ethos and culture, which is
regarded by others as stultifying: 'How was Toloki to know that
homeboys who did well in the city developed amnesia?' (*Ways of
Dying*: 133). Yet meeting Noria and gradually talking through these
memories allows Toloki to reaffirm communal life, and to combat the
alienating existence of the city. Although the narrative acknowledges
that 'The stories of the past are painful' (*Ways of Dying*: 95), and that
the present is structured by death, the novel concludes with hope for
the future born out of the upbeat mood of children's laughter, Toloki's
newfound skill of drawing to Noria's song, and their newborn love.
Yet despite the novel's clear engagement with memory and the resur-
facing past, some are damningly critical of what they perceive to be
Mda's retreat from radical politics in this novel, representing a
'disturbing political neutrality' in the figure of Toloki who is figured
as 'the creative individual who transcends context and political strife
even as he or she is surrounded by the tumultuous workings of
history' (Farred 2000: 186–7). Others find Mda's novel to be the
epitome of contemporary fiction's ability to provide a politically
resistant narrative through its corrosive manipulation of history, 'on
the one hand [offering] an invitation to a conscientious use of the past
that may redeem post-apartheid South Africa ... on the other hand
[offering] a warning that any disregard of the past may result in a
continued form of social, cultural and economic oppression' (Moslund
2003: 117; see also Visser 2002).

Mda's second novel, *The Heart of Redness*, deals with parallel narratives set in the nineteenth and twentieth centuries, and in the face of
the political ambiguity identified with *Ways of Dying*, is far more
explicit in its condemnation of contemporary politics in South Africa.

The nineteenth-century narrative is based upon the manifestations of a divisive prophecy: 'The Strangers said I must tell the nation that all cattle now living must be slaughtered ... The fields must not be cultivated ... When the time is ripe the whole community of the dead will arise, and new cattle will fill the kraals' (*Heart of Redness*: 54). In the mid nineteenth century, in the Eastern Cape village of Qolorha, a young girl called Nongqawuse brought this message from the ancestors to the Xhosa people. As the historical events on which Mda has based the novel demostrate, the prophecy split the nation into Believers and Unbelievers, dividing brother from brother, wife from husband, and the consequences were devastating. One hundred and fifty years later, the feud between the Believers and Unbelievers still simmers in Qolorha, as the villagers take opposing sides on every issue. When plans are mooted to build a vast casino and tourist resort in the village, they once again battle over their future, and face the loss of their heritage. The heart of redness refers to what is at the centre of Xhosa identity, namely the red ochre painted on the bodies in traditional Xhosa dress (*Heart of Redness*: 49). There is a call for the Unbelievers to dispose of traditional dress and adopt a western style:

> 'The Unbelievers stand for progress', asserts Bhonco, to the assenting murmurs of his followers ... 'We want to get rid of this bush which is a sign of our uncivilized state. We want developers to come and build the gambling city that will bring money to this community. That will bring modernity to our lives, and will rid us of our redness'. (*Heart of Redness*: 92)

This belief in modernity proves to be yet another myth, repeating the colonial policies that were designed to undermine the Xhosa nation (see for example, *Heart of Redness*: 134 and 168). Exploring the space between belief and disbelief, Mda is concerned with the power of myth and the dangers in believing it without reflection. The novel explores the ways in which colonial brutality was disguised in trite clichés, such as the advent of a 'civilising mission' that was in actual fact a means of African dispossession. Charting the arrival of the early European settlers through colonisation and local slavery, the depiction of the systematic destruction of indigenous institutions, the dissension sown amongst African people and the policy of divide-and-rule, Mda detonates the historical myths designed to disable and immobilise African communities. Mda interrogates the efficacy of fabricating particular myths in addition to undermining the mythical foundations about race and reason upon which South Africa's history is built. The novel situates many levels of analysis about the significance of history, from those who continually look backward to the past in order to learn lessons from it, to those who want a complete break with the past, regardless of the consequent dangers that such an injunction would imply:

The sufferings of the Middle Generation are only whispered. It is because of the insistence: *Forget the past. Don't only forgive it. Forget it as well. The past did not happen. You only dreamt it. It is a figment of your rich collective imagination. It did not happen. Banish your memory. It is a sin to have a memory. There is no virtue in amnesia. The past. It did not happen. It did not happen. It did not happen.* (*Heart of Redness*: 137)

Yet Mda is not only concerned with the past. He is just as caustic in his exposure of contemporary myths of the post-independence era. He is cynical about the ideas that purport to modernise or develop communities without consulting or involving them in the process. Such *ex cathedra* impositions that do not emerge from the people inevitably lead to problems (for example, the water supply problem). The watchwords of 'black economic empowerment' are scuttled by the corruption and nepotism rife in the cities (*Heart of Redness*: 172) and by banks unprepared to support entrepreneurship in co-op societies (*Heart of Redness*: 179). Ultimately, the book rails against a dependency mentality which has resulted from lack of government foresight (*Heart of Redness*: 180). The book is also critical of the ways in which myths from the past can keep hold of people centuries later, and how these myths perpetuate problematic histories. Indeed, the modern-day clash between the Believers and Unbelievers that has been the source for bitter civil war among Xhosas for decades now manifests itself in an angry conflict between those who support the creation of tourist resorts and gambling casinos in their midst to bring development, and those who regard such processes as an exploitation of local resources, the alienation of local people, and an 'internal enslavement', all camouflaged as 'development'.

Lauretta Ngcobo's novel *And They Didn't Die* (1990) is an interesting alternative to these narratives of the ways in which the past infuses the present, since she concentrates on black South African women's history. The recognition that male history and its past structures most of black South African attempts to rewrite the past makes Ngcobo's novel a refreshing supplement to the archetypal historical narrative about racial marginalisation under apartheid. Jezile, the protagonist whose tragic life is the outcome of negotiating various oppressive systems, has the weight of male history bearing down upon her through her mother-in-law MaBiyela's actions and moral authority:

[MaBiyela] was permanently vigilant, armed with authority and custom. Her vigilance was born of her own embittered life, soured by her own outgrown relationship with her own mother-in-law in her own past. It was the bitterness of generations, from mother-in-law to daughter-in-law. It was the way she perceived her role, the guardian of morality in the absence of the men. (*And They Didn't Die*: 16)

The novel deals with black women's politics and their material conditions. It savagely rails against forms of idealism or metaphysics which stand in for explanations of women's material circumstances. Women are shown to be caught between two forms of oppression. On the one hand, they are prey to the apartheid system of racial oppression: one of Jezile's friends, Nosizwe, explains the economics of rural black women's lives as the reserves for cheap labour for white people's businesses, while other events in the novel lead to explanations about the various ways in which the white medical system interposes itself between women and their indigenous cultural practices, or how the byzantine apartheid bureaucracy of the Bantu Administration and the Pass Laws restrict movement and employment, or how domestic family lives are wrecked by husbands having to work and live separated from their families in the cities, as Siyalo works in Durban while Jezile remains in her village with the children. On the other hand, though, women are also shown to be the victims of their own cultural structures, trapped by customs and hemmed in by patriarchal cultural expectations, such as the way 'many wives were trapped' by babies (*And They Didn't Die*: 18) and 'the web they were caught in' by motherhood (*And They Didn't Die*: 19). Ultimately, Jezile 'felt trapped between the impositions of customary law, state law and migratory practices. And she, the physical creature in between, somehow had to manoeuvre successfully among the threads of the web woven around her by all these' (*And They Didn't Die*: 40).

Jezile's story is about developing both a political consciousness and, for want of a better phrase, a 'women's consciousness'. Attending the village women's meetings to resist the Pass Laws, Jezile gradually comes to a greater politicised understanding of the intricacies of specifically women's oppression under apartheid, which is distinctly different to that of the man. These meetings open up new trajectories in awareness: 'In all their daily chat, for years now, they had concerned themselves only about the past and the present – never asked about the future; it was as though the security of the past ensured the certainty of the future' (*And They Didn't Die*: 50). When different authorities are challenged, and pasts are reconceived, new and different futures open up. Steering between the Scylla of apartheid and the Charybdis of indigenous custom, Jezile establishes her own agency in the face of passivity-inducing structures, albeit at considerable cost to her family life. After Jezile's rape in Bloemfontein by her Afrikaans employer Potgieter, and the birth of their son Lungu, the novel speeds up, showing how Lungu's life is the product of the abominable history of racial separation and division. Cast out and abominated by Potgieter, abhorred by his mother's family, Lungu is a child who fits in nowhere. It is only when Jezile kills a soldier on the point of raping her daughter S'naye, that a reconciliation with her estranged husband Siyalo is effected, as Jezile recounts the truth about Potgieter.

What is noticeable in these narratives is the refusal in fictional form to enforce a similar closure to that of the TRC's final report. These fictional narratives seek in one way or another to hold open possibilities, managing to resist the centrifugal force of political bureaucratic discourse. They are polymorphous and carnivalesque in Graham Pechey's senses, in that their strengths and weaknesses are not reducible to a single narrative in current South African literature (Pechey 1998). In many ways, these black South African novelists are seeking to free themselves from the compulsive fascination with the spectacular that Njabulo Ndebele so presciently identified in 1984, as the reactionary lodestone in the fiction of a changing South Africa (Ndebele 1994). The difficulties with which these writers grapple in envisioning the ethics of what Ndebele terms 'the rediscovery of the ordinary' in place of the persistent captivation with the spectacular, occur within the metamorphoses of a nation that must evade the Manichean trap, avoid the fetishisation of difference, engage in the deconstruction of the term 'post-apartheid' and remain sure-footed on the path towards a cultural integration of widely diverse ethnic groups.

Mandla Langa's fiction of memory

One novelist who appears to be most typically engaged in revivifying memory for the purposes of investigating the present is Mandla Langa, one of South Africa's most respected contemporary novelists. In his short story entitled 'The Naked Song', Langa explicitly deals with the South African past experienced by black people as a trauma that is to be healed in the present (Langa 1996: 67–91). The protagonist Leonard Gama is a psychotherapist who is called upon to heal a onetime musical acquaintance of his, Richard Nkosi, who is suffering from traumatic mute hysteria after years in the ANC resistance and the loss of his lover in what turns out to be a betrayal. Richard's return from political exile as the new democracy takes shape does nothing to alleviate his cataleptic state, and Gama recognises that 'there was no such thing as returning from exile. Exile was not so much a geographic dislocation as a state of mind, something that consumed and branded and left one marked for life. Many, like animals whose limbs were left in a snare, walked through life crippled, their minds locked on that fateful moment of rupture' (Langa 1996: 71).

Retrieving that lost voice from the moment of rupture in the past is an allegory for all of Langa's work, and indeed much of the fiction that is currently being written in South Africa. Langa is the prominent author of a collection of short stories and several novels, including *Tenderness of Blood* (1987) and *A Rainbow on a Paper Sky* (1989), and his most impressive novel to date, entitled *The Memory of Stones* (2000), which analyses the nation as it seeks to define itself as a new democracy. Charting a nation in a state of political transition, the novel is set in the period of the year after Nelson Mandela's release from imprisonment. Ngoza, located in KwaZulu-Natal, South Africa's most chaotic province, is changed beyond recognition when clan leader Baba Joshua dies and his determined and strong-willed daughter confronts the venerable shibboleths held by traditionalists and gangsters alike. This reluctant female protagonist, Zodwa, finds support from improbable quarters. Mpanza, a dejected ex-ANC revolutionary and Venter, a diehard white racist, ally themselves with Zodwa to liberate Ngoza from the reign of terror inflicted by warlord Johnny M. and his thugs. During the course of this action, the novel charts the developing love between Mpanza and Zodwa, and the extraordinary marriage between the Afrikaans policeman Venter and the 'coloured' anti-apartheid activist-in-exile who returns to South Africa, Benedita.

The whole novel is predicated upon the unfettering of the memories of the past. However, this process is never a simple one. From the very outset, Zodwa's memories of the displacement of her people from their land 'to make way for white progress' (*Memory of Stones*: 5), her father's arrival at Ngoza and their subsequent life are described as 'unreliable' (*Memory of Stones*: 5). Nevertheless, memory intimately connects her private self to the larger history of Africa. For example, when she remembers her dead brother Jonah, 'For some reason that escaped her, the memory of Jonah became a memory of the community and her family's exile from Ngoza' (*Memory of Stones*: 9). Zodwa is described as having to make sense of her past in terms of amassing her memories:

> It is in its own way a remarkable dilemma, because human beings always hanker for that memory when things took place and they were too young to reflect on them. Life, being an eternal process of putting pieces of the jigsaw puzzle on the board, is experienced through memory. Zodwa then hugs and takes in the smells of the people, remembering. (*Memory of Stones*: 98)

Memory is later described as a significant means of connecting Zodwa's people to their past: 'We wanted to be able to remember something of ourselves that was left behind' (*Memory of Stones*: 105).

The structure of the novel emerges from the gradual interlocking of several characters and their present lives and their past experiences: Mpanza and UmKhonto we Sizwe (the armed resistance wing of the ANC); Zodwa and her childhood; Venter and Benedita and her anti-apartheid life in London; and Johnny M. and his life of crime. Time and again, the novel returns the reader to the significance of memories of the censored black South African past and its significance for new identity in the present. These memories are mixed up with tradition both as a conservative force pulling people back to restrictive and conformist lives and roles, and also as a counter-force to the repression of black cultures, values and belief systems. For example, in a discussion of the funeral rites upon Baba Joshua's death, Mpanza seems to have an intuitive knowledge of the past:

> Mpanza didn't know how he knew this; it could have sprung from primeval precepts buried deep in his mind, a knowledge imbibed with his mother's milk, like any African child not born into orphanage … While acquainted with the ways of the city, and certainly not a traditionalist, he still held that home was where the umbilical cord was buried. (*Memory of Stones*: 218–19)

The traditional practice of burying a newborn child's umbilical cord in the soil of its home was designed to remind the child and the adult where its closest ties and roots are. The umbilical is a magnet bringing a person home to his or her land, and performs a deep symbolic function. One might argue that, following Kristeva's theories, the umbilical cord is a memory of semiotic existence: the chora pulls the person back!

This deep-seated, almost unconscious connection established with one's land at one's birth is one of the reasons for the traumatic rupture experienced by black South Africans when they were forcibly uprooted and severed from their lands during the system of mass displacements that routinely occurred under apartheid. It can be understood as a severance from one's nurturing, founding point, frequently figured in fiction as a severance from the mother. Indeed, Zodwa's memories of her father are explicitly linked to a traumatic rupture or psychological scar, as she 'wrestled with an unresolved matter. What is extraordinary is that for her time hasn't healed the wounds. The older she gets the more urgently she yearns for an answer' (*Memory of Stones*: 323). Zodwa is a modern woman, educated as a lawyer at the University of Fort Hare, and intending to take up a career as a lawyer in Johannesburg. At university, Zodwa turns her back on her past, thinking that 'Her spirit on campus and the cities of the country, as well as the route to her chosen career, cannot be nurtured in this land of symbols and skins and the stammering memory of stones' (*Memory of Stones*: 106). She is generally portrayed as a woman who cannot understand her past, who cannot make the connection with her land, and finds the past baffling and inexplicable as a result of the rupture of memory, figured as her inability to decipher or decode the language of the 'memory of stones'. Consequently, when the wise old woman Nozizwe takes Zodwa in hand and urges her to take over the leadership of the clan, one of the tasks is to educate Zodwa. Nozizwe tells Zodwa about Zulu history and the threat of the traditionalists, the importance of a single heir, and the crucial significance of clarity of lineage. In order to prevent Zodwa's prevarication over inheriting the leadership of the clan from her father, Nozizwe compares Zodwa's elevation to the chieftaincy with the political leadership of the state, arguing that 'Life can only be lived when people take a chance to weave miracles out of nothing' (*Memory of Stones*: 222). Nozizwe's astute political vision and her sense of the importance of the task in hand urge a politics of risk for future development. The crucial symbolic moment in Nozizwe's guidance of Zodwa and her re-acquaintance with the past occurs when Nozizwe leads Zodwa into the cave to undergo the preparation ritual:

> Nozizwe lights a flare stuck into a wall recess and, as in the song, darkness flies away. The main entrance drops suddenly down to the bottom of the cave, which is some twenty metres below the surface. The chamber is long and seems to entrance the visitor with the play of light on underground lakes and vitreous rock. Everything about the cave speaks of enchantment: the dripstone formation, the large stalactites and their curtains, the limestone, as smooth as glass, formed atop the underlying dolomite rock. The quiet of the underground is eerie and yet, in a strange way, quite arousing, as if it were the last trysting place for ancient lovers fulfilling a suicide pact. Zodwa looks up, hearing the steady dripping of water which, over millions of years, carved these magical shapes.
>
> ... [Nozizwe's] voice sounds ghostly, profane and completely out of place in this cavern whose formations were calcified through innumerable ages by an amalgam of earth, rock fragments and bone material. It is a place that diminishes human beings, humbles them and deepens their understanding that they are but temporary sojourners on this earth. (*Memory of Stones*: 224–5)

With its language of ancient times and primeval knowledge, this passage metaphorically evokes a return to the womb, the return to the 'chora', the semiotic, the regaining of the 'memory of stones', the past life, to equip her for the present and future. Unlike her earlier inability to decode the 'memory of stones', Zodwa now interprets and connects with the stones. Yet the memory of the past becomes conjoined with an ancient, prehistoric mysterious and intangible knowledge, much like Mpanza's knowledge of the umbilical cord ties. This association is made again later in the novel when Zodwa challenges Johnny M. at the Humiliation Tree: at this point the narrative becomes something of a surreal journey into Zulu history, with

Zodwa meeting Dingane and hearing explanations of the ascent and decline of Zulu power, nationalism and history (*Memory of Stones*: 342ff).

The past is repeatedly aligned in parallel with the present as something that cannot be abandoned or neglected, as Zodwa gradually learns:

> 'Why are you so evasive?' Zodwa was genuinely irritated by his attitude. 'We're in the new South Africa now. Secrets are supposed to have died with the past.'
>
> 'That is,' [Mpanza] said gravely, 'if the past is really dead.'
>
> Zodwa seemed to think this over. 'You've got me there, mister,' she said. 'I suppose I am one of the most immediate examples of the past standing in the path of development.'
>
> Her ready admission that the whole system of chiefs was an anachronism surprised him. (*Memory of Stones*: 323)

Ultimately, memory is inescapable, despite being unreliable, erratic and mercurial. Memory needs to be harnessed to future development. Even as the mourning period for her father's death comes to an end, Zodwa realises that memories sustain people in their determination and steadfastness in making changes: 'Looking at the growing things, marvelling at the many disguises nature sometimes wore to introduce herself to the living world, Zodwa found that the memories were the most constant features of her people's lives. They were there, changing all the time, as unreliable as a lover, but they would never escape from you, nor, she realised, could you escape from them. Memory had sustained her kinsmen, who were now more relaxed in their religious beliefs, holding on to some ancient orthodoxy but opening the door to other influences' (*Memory of Stones*: 361). Memory is here likened to an organic entity that needs careful nurturing for growth and change to occur. The clan it turns out is literally sitting on the past, since in the final pages one learns that Zodwa and Mpanza go for 'long walks to the caves where discoveries of prehistoric fossils were being made, it seemed, weekly. They would look at the ancient formations and rejoice that they were part of the living world. Exulting, kissing him, tasting his awful tobacco, Zodwa would know that time would pass and transform them. Perhaps when their graves were dug up in some future millennium, the palaeontologists would comment on their primitive state. But these experts would have had no access to the enduring power of memory' (*Memory of Stones*: 366).

The Memory of Stones is an impressive epic for its time. The novel demonstrates that writing and recording social memory are a crucial aspect of establishing a foundation for the future conduct of a nation. Assuming grand proportions, appropriate at a time of a nation rewriting its history and forging a new national culture, the novel gradually unfolds southern Africa's history: the history of the African National Congress, its period underground with its leaders in exile or in jail and its recent legalisation, rehabilitation and ascent to lead a democratic majority government; the history of apartheid in South Africa; the history of the Afrikaner and the demise of the National Party with its ideology of apartheid; the anti-apartheid movement in Britain; the mighty Zulu nation, its culture, and its recent internecine troubles; the role of the 'coloured' people in South Africa; the political, military and colonial problems in border countries, such as Angola, Guinea-Bissau, Cape Verde and Namibia; and, within the narrative chronological period of two years, the novel's characters are contextualised and explained within the sweep of a history of several places and hundreds of years. Langa shows that Zodwa's emergence as undisputed chief of the clan is a direct consequence of her 'memory of stones'; that without acknowledging one's close-knit ties to one's land, culture and traditions, any hope of forging a viable and credible identity in the future is fraught with the burden of tension and conflict.

Getting beyond apartheid

Commenting upon the history-less and anaemic cultural opening and closing ceremonies of the 1995 Rugby World Cup held in South Africa, J. M. Coetzee says: 'History remains a deeply contentious subject in South Africa. The struggle for the right to make up the story of the country is by no means over' (Coetzee 2001: 352). Indeed, this is a widespread feeling among writers, cultural theorists, and artists more generally. Recently, Njabulo Ndebele has sought to develop the concerns of his *Rediscovery of the Ordinary* (1991), insisting on the necessity of a South African realist fiction, which will piece together the 'real' lives of South Africans through memory. Generally Ndebele finds in favour of the stories told during the course of the Truth and Reconciliation Commission hearings, owing to the fact that they 'represent a ritualistic lifting of the veil and the validation of what was actually seen. They are an additional confirmation of the movement of our society from repression to expression' (Ndebele 1998: 20). Arguing that the testimony of the oppressed is one of the vital conditions for the emergence of a new national consciousness, Ndebele argues that the key for South Africa's future is to reinvent itself through narratives of memory:

> Time has given the recall of memory the power of reflection associated with narrative. Isn't it that there is something inherently reflective about memory, as there is about narrative? If so, narratives of memory, in which real events are recalled, stand to guarantee us occasions for some serious moments of reflection. (Ndebele 1998: 20)

André Brink agrees that new areas of the past are being opened up in contemporary South African fiction and that such explorations are necessary to future national development. However, he disagrees with Ndebele about the mode that is best employed for this retelling of absent or marginalised histories. For Brink, history cannot be separated from language and memory, and, in contrast to Ndebele's realist prescription, Brink proposes a far more postmodernist approach: 'In this activity [of fiction], in other words, history, memory, and language intersect so precisely as to be almost indistinguishable: the "origins" of history, as recovered through memory, are encoded in language, and each of these three moments becomes a condition for the others' (Brink 1998a: 32). Brink points out that various recent books by South African historiographers such as van Onselen's much-discussed *The Seed Is Mine* (1996) have broken down master-narratives of apartheid and have offered 'alternative' accounts of South Africa's past to 'redress unjust emphases and perspectives' and 'a radical new view of the very concept of "history"' (Brink 1998a: 33). In this respect, implicitly echoing Hayden White's conception of history, Brink believes in a 'narrativised past', a 'past that cannot be corrected by bringing to it procedures and mechanics and mind-sets that originally produced our very perception of that past' (Brink 1998a: 33). Rather the past is 'storified', or 'fictified' and the process of its constitution should be constantly foregrounded. Since memory emerges with a whole series of blindspots and gaps, as a mosaic, it cannot produce a whole. Consequently, Brink favours the development of an 'imagined rewriting of history', since 'the best we can do is fabricate metaphors – that is, tell stories – in which, not history, but imaginings of history are reinvented' (Brink 1998a: 42).

It is clear from the foregoing that the role of the fiction-writer is crucial in the development of this new historical narrative. When Nadine Gordimer famously wrote her 1982 paper 'Living in the Interregnum', she defined the South African 'interregnum [as] not only between two social orders, but also between two identities, one known and discarded, the other unknown and undetermined' (Gordimer 1989: 269–70). For Gordimer, it is the novelist's clear and unequivocal role to act as spokesperson for a community's ways of making sense of its social life. These writers need to resist closing down communal understandings and to hold open the possibilities of that as yet unknown and undetermined future. However, in developing its literary and cultural future, South African writers are clearly having to engage in a complex and agonising recasting of the relation between public and private spheres. This problem has a specific intersection with the representation of the past, as the prominent metafictional novelist Ivan Vladislavić acutely observes:

> There seem to be two sets of pressures on writers – institutional pres-
> sures, public pressures. On the one hand, there is the pressure to be
> part of a proposed Renaissance, to present positive images that might
> help to reconstruct our culture. On the other hand, there is an incredi-
> ble stress at the moment on memory – not just in South Africa, although
> it is very strongly developed here – a sense that writers need to remem-
> ber, that one of the things writers can do is keep the past alive. Now it's
> as if writers are being pushed between those two positions, because if
> you lose sight of apartheid, then people say you've forgotten about the
> past, and you're part of the trend towards 'amnesia': on the other hand,
> if you go too deeply into apartheid, they say you're holding onto the past,
> and it's negative, you should be writing about the future. (Vladislavić
> 2000: 279–80)

Skewered on the horns of this dilemma and these problematics, it
may well be that the most searching and most illuminating explorations of the apartheid era are yet to come, and may well be written
decades after the events. Nevertheless, contrary to those who might
favour the amputation of 'traumatic memory' and who adamantly
'refuse to mourn', there are a significant number of contemporary
writers who refuse any precipitate flattening out of real contradictions and favour looking through 'narrative memory' which 'works-
through' the past by recounting comprehensible stories about it.
Absorbing the past into the present is one stage in the process of
healing or making memory; but, as one commentator cautions, 'to
heal, and to remember, is also to find the freedom to ask more questions, to let the unspeakable, both then and now, filter in, to disturb,
to open out consciousness' (Nuttall 1998: 85). Yet in addressing the
crucial issue of what contributions these writers make to an international conscience with regard to apartheid and its aftermath, the
fiction ought not to be valued only in terms of its ability to diagnose
the ills of apartheid and its prognosis for the future. The tensions of
the positions spelled out by Vladislavić are producing numerous
stylistic experiments, searching investigations of language, intrigu-
ing reappraisals of form, and thoroughgoing interrogations of literature's role in contributing to wide-ranging social and public concerns
about culpability, complicity and compromise on a fraught political
stage. Consequently, South African fiction is currently a site of
extraordinary vitality, energy and dynamism, grappling with issues
concerning the ethics of representation, the inheritance, mediation
and dissemination of 'history', all within a confrontation and engagement with multiple languages and cultures. Where South Africa was
once a test case for a divisive racial politics, it is now the site of how
a society can, in the face of a persistence of grave social and economic
inequities and divisions, form and manage the traumatic legacies of
postcolonialism.

In achieving some form of symbolic equilibrium through an articulation of collective memory as a method of successfully 'working-through' that grief, the question is whether one wants to foreclose trauma and conceal scars through commemoration rites, or leave them bare and open to readers. Homi Bhabha regards it as the responsibility of thinkers to contest history's authoritarian tendencies, laying bare the means by which it is produced, exhuming the silenced, problematic and unrepresented pasts which it works to conceal. A novel like *The Memory of Stones* addresses the past not as a set of assimilable facts but as something more problematic. Langa addresses historical questions from the starting point of amnesia, rather than the assumption of knowledge. He starts from the stories of the 'disremembered'. For Michel Foucault, traditional history systematically works to suppress evidence of discontinuities, disjunctions and struggles between rival regimes of knowledge, because its overriding goal is to portray the present as the product of a clear and rational development. Genealogy's counter-historical project is to resist the imperialist and totalising strategies of traditional historical writing. Much of the South African writing I have discussed in this chapter could be construed as 'genealogical', in that it seeks to foreground the counter-historical, the marginal, forgotten, silenced and unacceptable narratives or pasts. South African colonial and apartheid history was a series of ideological and bodily coercions and subjugations, by means of which it sought its own dominance as 'rational', 'true' and 'right'. The novels I have touched upon in this chapter display a 'genealogical consciousness', in that they raise questions about the construction of stable pasts in narrative, about the relationship of pasts and presents to futures, and about the role of such constructions in the formation of national, gender and ethnic identities. In writing counter-memories to the silences imposed by apartheid, these writers have taken up one of the country's most pressing challenges: the task of redefining South Africanness for the twenty-first century.

Notes

[1]   Ironically, President P. W. Botha used the image of the Rubicon in an infamous speech in August 1985, in which he started promisingly with the phrase that South Africa had 'crossed the Rubicon' as a way of staving off international sanctions, but the speech degenerated into a wild condemnation of the western governments and a promise to crack down on dissension in South Africa.

[2]   Originally delivered as 'Perfectibility and Corruptibility – Preparing Ourselves for Power', Inaugural Lecture, University of Cape Town, 20 May 1992.

[3]   See an interesting article about this renaming phenomenon in Donaldson 2001.

[4]   Speech by President Nelson Mandela at the Re-Dedication of the 1820 Settlers Monument, Grahamstown, 16 May 1996.

[5]   See Coombes 2003 for a remarkable study of memorial culture in South Africa since apartheid, foregrounding the political tensions and ambiguities of rehabilitating

traditional monuments as the nation explores old and new histories for a 'new' South Africa. The book covers not merely museums and visual art but national monuments like the Taalmonument, the Voortrekker Monument and Robben Island, in an ethically engaged analysis of the role of public culture in the processes of social and national transformation.

⁶   The source for this information is the District Six Museum website. *District Six Museum*. 25A Buitenkant Street, Cape Town, 8001, South Africa. 18 June 2001 <http://www.districtsix.co.za>.

⁷   See the excellent article on the complex issues of nation, belonging and political contestation that lies at the heart of reconstructing District Six, entitled 'The Politics of Locality: Memories of District Six in Cape Town', Bohlin 1998.

⁸   Act No. 34 of 1995: Promotion of National Unity and Reconciliation Act, 1995. The fact that the full proceedings of the TRC have been loaded on to the World Wide Web suggests that the documentary outcome does fulfil a quasi-governmental role in protecting the past and preserving lost memories. The Truth and Reconciliation Commission, 9th Floor, Old Mutual Building, 106 Adderley Street, Cape Town, 8001, South Africa. 28 January 2002 <http://www.doj.gov.za/trc/>.

⁹   Sanders 2000 provides an exacting enquiry into the TRC's report, dealing with the 'disequilibrium between official record and common memory' and how this 'bear[s] upon literature after apartheid' (p. 15). Sanders concludes that the TRC report sets 'to work an ethics of advocacy, the task of giving the domain of words over to the other' (p. 17).

¹⁰   Archbishop Desmond Tutu, Foreword to the Final Report, Truth and Reconciliation Commission <http://www.struth.org.za/index.pl?&file=report /1chap01.htm>.

¹¹   See Dawes 1997 for a post-structuralist reading of South Africa's inability to free itself from a state of 'immanent melancholy'.

¹²   The Preamble to the Constitution of South Africa, 1996 reads: 'We, the people of South Africa, Recognise the injustices of our past; Honour those who suffered for justice and freedom in our land … We therefore, through our freely elected representatives, adopt this Constitution as the supreme law of the Republic so as to – Heal the divisions of the past and establish a society based on democratic values …' On the subject of responsibility and the TRC, see Libin 2003.

¹³   These judges' views are all quoted from the South African *Sunday Times*, 9 October 2002.

¹⁴   Key writers associated with this group are Breyten Breytenbach, André Brink, Hennie Aucamp, Abraham De Vries, John Miles, Chris Barnard and Etienne LeRoux. For a brief English-language survey of the development of Afrikaans literature see Coetzee 1990.

¹⁵   See the excellent review of the novel in Horn 1995.

¹⁶   Chapman 2001: xii. See also the excellent retrospective article by erstwhile *Drum* editor, Sampson 2001.

8

Intimations of the postmodern

And I feel that it is the symbolic meanings themselves that must change, must be dynamic. (Professor Sackey, in Kojo Laing, *Search Sweet Country*)

In his polemical book *A Mask Dancing: Nigerian Novelists of the Eighties* (1992), Adewale Maja-Pearce admonished his nation's novelists for seeking to flee the complexities and ambiguities that characterised the contemporary fusions evident in African modernity, for the sanctuary of archaic reminiscences and confused cultural primitivisms. Maja-Pearce clearly had not looked beyond his prejudices. For African writers were already rising to this challenge, since during the mid-1980s and early 1990s writers such as Kojo Laing, Ben Okri, M. G. Vassanji, Abdulrazak Gurnah, Nuruddin Farah, Lindsey Collen, Yvonne Vera, Calixthe Beyala, Tsitsi Dangarembga, Damon Galgut, Ivan Vladislavić, Mike Nicol, 'Biyi Bandele-Thomas and Syl Cheney-Coker had published narratives that manifested clear signs of being the products of eclectic, heterogeneous, hybridised consciousnesses. Derek Wright confirms this growth of textual thickening by noting that in

> the second half of the 1980s there appeared in African writing a kind of fiction which challenged the customary ontological boundaries of a hitherto broadly realist mainstream tradition, eroding the lines of demarcation between what, in Western terms, are usually designated as observed and imagined experience, material and magical phenomena, and real and fictional worlds. In this writing different and disparate worlds coexist; the elision of figurative into narrative space leads to a puzzling indeterminacy as regards where literal reality ends and metaphor begins; the relations between history and fiction are problematic; and it is hard to tell in exactly what ways and at what levels human character is constituted. (Wright 1997a: 181)

This chapter will examine the ways in which such African writers have sought to disrupt the politics allied to the conventional realist narrative. By focusing upon the fictions of writers who push at the boundaries of the mythical and real, this chapter will explore the effects and pressures of 'postmodernism' upon the new directions in African writing. Why do some writers resist this term? Why do other writers accept the ideas of a postmodern consciousness? There have been some firm assertions about the fact that postmodernism can prove a disabling distraction to black writing from its vernacular traditions (for example, see Nkosi 1998). Arguments that postmodernism is a perpetuation of colonialism by other means of representation – an imperialism of representation – have in turn been countered by writers who perceive the myriad intertextual relationships of the postmodern text and its ludic inventions as initiating 'strategies of interrogation which prompt the reader to assume a new (moral) responsibility for his/her own narrative, as well as for the narrative we habitually call the world' (Brink 1998b: 23). As André Brink points out, these passages of 'fantasy' are well known in writers like Okri, Tutuola and Coetzee; but they are evident also in such 'realist' writers as Achebe, Soyinka and even Ngugi. The surreal and inexplicable (what many think of as 'magic realism') that lurk uneasily in these texts gesture to a recognition that literature needs to turn to narratives which are not merely located as 'witnesses to history'; that literature need not simply seek to escape the inhibitions and restrictions of apartheid or colonial racism, but needs to construct and deconstruct new possibilities, 'to activate the imagination in its exploration of those silences previously inaccessible; to play with the future on that needlepoint where it meets the past and present; and to be willing to risk everything in the leaping flame of the word as it turns into world' (Brink 1998b: 27).

With their narrative strategies and compositional styles, with their oblique modalities, delays and discontinuities, fragmentation of voices, multiple points of view, recursive time, interweaving of the narrative voice with those of the narrated figures and the commingling of the mundane and extraordinary, these African novelists might give the impression that they are primarily concerned with epistemological problems in much the same manner as American postmodernists. Nevertheless, along with Derek Wright, I think that their primary orientation lies elsewhere. Indeed, Derek Wright makes exactly this point in his very thorough and illuminating discussion of the postmodern aesthetics of various African writers: 'An important difference, however, between these metafictional reinventors of history and their counterparts in American postmodern fiction is that, whereas many of the latter use history to say something about fiction – to display the endlessly fertile, inventive capacities of the literary imagination that compensate for the shortage of verifiable facts – the former use fiction to say something about history, about how and by whom it is written and what social and political imperatives inform the selection processes' (Wright 1997a: 184). This chapter's key focus lies in considering the extent to which African postmodern narratives produce historiographic questioning and metafictional experiments into identity issues and how these address colonial legacies and postcolonial manifestations; indeed, how narrative and representation are perceived to be connected to issues of history and memory in the context of postmodernism. I am less concerned with rehearsing the *applicability* of the term 'post-modern' to certain African texts than I am in considering the ways in which certain African texts often tagged with the label 'postmodern' deal with the role of history and memory. Furthermore, I am inter-ested in exploring the extent to which this handling of history and memory is different from that found in texts of a more recognisably 'realist' genre? Are there particular outcomes of texts that utilise 'postmodern' structures and features, devices and strategies, which are different from the 'realist' texts? Indeed, is it the 'postmodern' that causes history and memory to be such self-conscious issues for contemporary African writers?

Postmodernism in an African literary context

If not literally a four-letter word in relation to African writing, 'post-modernism' has been excoriated by a wide range of writers and critics alike (for example, see Carusi 1990). There are African writers who are very hostile to the notion of the postmodern as it may be applied to their work. In many cases, this is due to the feeling that postmod-ernism is a western aesthetic ideology and set of aesthetic criteria which has little or no place in an African context. Some writers see the association of postmodernism with African literature as a form of neo-colonialism in the cultural sphere, a covert attempt to judge and measure African writing by a commodifying and violent colonial cultural gesture. Such critics as Anjali Roy regard postmodernism as a completely western concept and refuse it because they do not want African work to serve European categories (Roy 2000). Roy nods to Helen Tiffin's caution against the hegemonic application of postmod-ern theory to 'texts outside Europe', since this often occurs without the concomitant self-re-examination of its own epistemological assumptions and is thus tantamount to neo-colonialism (Roy refers to the argument in Tiffin 1988); and Roy particularly fiercely defends Ben Okri from being appropriated by and adopted into western aesthetic categories. Indeed, Helen Tiffin has repeatedly pointed out the paradoxical structure of postmodern criticism arrogating African texts to its own aesthetic and literary criteria:

Given the extent to which European post-modernism and Euro-American poststructuralism have increasingly invested in cultural rela-tivity as a term in some of their most radical insights, it is ironic that the label of 'post-modern' is increasingly being applied hegemonically, to cultures and texts outside Europe, assimilating postcolonial works whose political orientations and experimental formations have been deliberately designed to counteract such European appropriation. (Tiffin 1988: 170)

One clearly needs to be wary about describing African texts as 'post-modernist', since Tiffin convincingly argues that such a gesture conjures up a 'neo-universalism', which 'reinforces the very European hegemony so many of the works ... have been undermining or circumventing' (Tiffin 1988: 171). Tiffin argues that dis/mantling and de/figuring strategies persist in all postcolonial literatures, but with widely differing outcomes despite any superficial similarities. Indeed, similar textual strategies and ideological objectives are prompted by enormously different theoretical assumptions and polit-ical stimuli. Strongly indignant, Tiffin contends that 'otherness' for postmodernism and poststructuralism 'has become that "innocent signifier" enthusiastically embraced by a depleted system' (Tiffin 1988: 172). The same postmodern forms can from a European perspective signal a 'crisis of authority', while from a postcolonial perspective, they 'speak of the erosion of that former authority and a liberation into a world in which one's own identity may be created or recuperated not as an alternative system or fixture, but as a process, a state of continual becoming in which author/ity and domination of any kind is impossible to sustain' (Tiffin 1988: 179).

Others are less forthright in their criticism of postmodernism. Some like Koffi Anyinefa argue for a postcolonial postmodernity (Anyinefa 1998). Elsewhere, Lewis Nkosi, for example, laments the ways in which some African writers have dismissed the usefulness of postmodern theory as an *inevitable* alignment with conservative poli-tics. Nkosi notes that, for even some of its critics, postmodernism is not monolithic, and that it could therefore offer workable or tactical models for African writing in South Africa in particular, and in Africa more generally (Nkosi 1998: 76). On the face of it, Nkosi regards post-modernism as the theory of European academics and theorists eager to provide a focus for various cultural and social issues in contempo-rary western capitalist economies. For countries struggling to shake off colonialism as one would the Shirt of Nessus, postmodern theory might seem to offer little more than poison to the body politic. Nkosi expresses the hope that the post-apartheid situation will set black writing free from a colonial fetter compounded by the coarse mutila-tion and claustrophobia of trivial realism (Nkosi 1998: 77). He clearly sees this perpetuation of realism as a traumatic repetition: '[in] its nightmares and premonitions of a past to be endlessly repeated, black writing shows clearly its relation to this colonial history; the manner, for example, in which it discloses, at the most unexpected moments, its memory of the *sjambok*' (Nkosi 1998: 77). The memory of the piercing slash of the *sjambok*, a leather whip that became an archetypal and symbolic implement of the Afrikaner's brutal and sadistic oppression, recurs in much the same fashion as the irruption into consciousness of a past over which one has no control. In a provocative formulation, Nkosi continues that 'it is important to trace much of the backwardness of black writing to its state of internal isolation and surveillance under the apartheid regime and some of its disabilities to wounds inflicted by cultural deprivation and social neglect' (Nkosi 1998: 79). He is careful to note that pounding postmodernism as unsuitable for black South African writing is to miss the point that what is tired and passé for whites is not so for blacks, since they have not had access to it, or been included in debates about it. Nkosi, therefore, sees postmodernism as a potential opening for black writing, an opening to a set of aesthetic practices and debates from which black writers have hitherto been excluded. Any simple rejection of postmodernism would therefore merely be a perpetuation of internal isolation and cultural deprivation, only now self-inflicted.

Another forthright and outspoken critic on the usefulness of postmodernism in a post-apartheid context is Graham Pechey. More cautious than Nkosi and taking issue with the terms established by Njabulo Ndebele, Pechey argues in his essay 'The Post-Apartheid Sublime' that the usefulness of the everyday is where post-apartheid writing ought to locate its focus:

> In short, it is at the heart of the ordinary that the extraordinary is to be found. Post-apartheid writing turns from the fight against apartheid, with its fixation upon suffering and the seizure of power, into just such stories as these: stories which open out to transform the victory over apartheid into a gain for postmodern knowledge, a new symbiosis of the sacred and the profane, the quotidian and the numinous. (Pechey 1998: 58)

Pechey endorses Njabulo Ndebele's suggestion of looking for a post-apartheid writing in the local, the ordinary, in what Pechey describes as 'the textures of life which have eluded that epic battle and have grown insouciantly in the cracks of the structures that South Africa's fraught modernity has historically thrown up' (Pechey 1998: 57). Pechey argues that South Africa under apartheid was an entry into a late, deferred, phase of neo-colonialism (Pechey 1998: 59), what he calls 'arrested neo-colonialism' (Pechey 1998: 60). Now he is concerned that, in the post-apartheid moment, the critical edge of writing will be nullified by a potentially obsequious strain that merely sanctions the new order, risking 'the danger ... that writing will appear to be aligned with the beneficent moves of the state, seeming to have nothing to do after the end of repression' (Pechey 1998: 63). Nkosi is critical of what he sees as Pechey's failure to explain the material conditions of the 'bifurcation' between black and white writing within a South African context, arguing that Pechey's analysis is ultimately flawed by his misrecognition of the 'limitations imposed upon black writing by its colonial situation' (Nkosi 1998: 78). However, even accepting Nkosi's critique of the contradictions that mar Pechey's argument, nevertheless, Pechey is surely correct in his warning about the ways in which postmodern and post-structuralist approaches would undermine the metanarratives of freedom and liberty that have proved so vital as political rallying narratives to the emancipation of the black majority from the despotism of apartheid (Pechey 1994; see also O'Brien 2001).

African fiction that shows any symptom of linguistic glee or formal innovation must not be treated as a tributary of the mainstream of the English or European novel. Playing with language is a blend of western techniques and African traditions; and denying that African writers can be experimental in their own right enacts a form of 'literary imperialism', where 'Third World' writers are regarded as offshoots of the British or European traditions (Tiffin 1984: 27–8). When one considers certain African authors to be 'postcolonial' or 'postmodern', one needs to use those terms cautiously. Like Stephen Slemon, I would be concerned to maintain the counter-cultural or anti-colonial aspect at work in these texts. This is not to say that other texts displaying more overtly realist or non-modernist characteristics are not anti-colonial; rather, it is to maintain that the intervention made by these postmodern texts as non-realist is of a particular sort – a non-nationalist intervention.

Kwame Anthony Appiah, in 'The Postcolonial and the Postmodern', has analysed the emergence of postmodernism in relation to postcoloniality in African art and fiction. He concludes that all African art has been influenced by a transition through colonialism, but is not necessarily *post*colonial. The 'post' in postcolonial is part of a transcendence of, a going beyond, coloniality, and much of popular culture is unconcerned with such a junction (Appiah 1999: 62). For Appiah, postmodernism is also post-realist, although he argues that African post-realist writers are motivated by impulses different from those of American postmodernist authors like John Barth and Thomas Pynchon. For the African writers, theirs is not the 'literature of exhaustion' and the 'literature of renewal' but part of a distinct challenge to the legitimating procedures of realism's 'return to traditions', a naturalisation of the nationalism that had failed by the late 1960s. This post-realism seeks to delegitimate not only the form but the content of nationalism, and is misleadingly construed as a post-modernism:

> *Mis*leadingly, because what we have here is not postmodern*ism* but postmodernis*ation*; not an aesthetics but a politics, in the most literal sense of the term ... the basis for that project of delegitimation is very much not the postmodernist one: rather, it is grounded in an appeal to an ethical universal ... Postrealist writing; postnativist politics; a *transnational* rather than a *national* solidarity ... Postcoloniality is *after* all this: and its *post*, like postmodernism's is also a post that challenges earlier legitimating narratives ... it challenges them in the name of the suffering victims ... in the name of ethical universal. (Appiah 1999: 69)

These post-realist novelists have eschewed the traditionalism sought and encouraged by the commodifying markets of western aesthetic ideologies, and chosen instead 'the continent and its people' (Appiah 1999: 66). For Appiah, then, postmodernism is not the play of form, the linguistic games, but rather the highly politicised form of questioning the dominance or legitimacy of specific narratives of modernist exclusivity of insight and structure.

Benita Parry has added her voice to the criticism of those who think that a radical writing ought to eschew the metafictional challenges evident in postmodern writing. Parry is critical of the notion that merely a rhetoric of solidarity and militancy, of protest and dissent, is sufficient for constituting a revolutionary literature that might have a transformative impact upon cultural and social politics. Expressive and instantly accessible writing, whose message is transparent and where contest and confrontation is worn on the sleeve of the dustjacket, amounts to nothing more than a politically naive gesture in Parry's opinion. Such writing is 'predicated ... on an instrumental notion of language as the compliant tool of a writer's will or intention' (Parry 2001: 13). Such aesthetic and ideological injunctions merely serve to place writing in a straitjacket. As Parry continues, 'oppositional discourses quickening liberation energies can reside in spaces where there is no obvious correspondence between image and social message, and in articulations which do not register a literal relationship of word to social referent' (Parry 2001: 13). In Parry's opinion, such writing runs the risk, on the one hand, of being prone to offering insipid inventions of the brave and sanguine masses; and, on the other hand, of supplying and consolidating tangible images and symbols upon which a counter-culture can forge its ethic of resistance. Parry is clearly taking direct issue with Lewis Nkosi's position in his early book *Tasks and Masks* (1981), where he approves of social realists for 'their careful *reconstructions* of the precolonial past, in their vivid *chronicling* of the struggle against colonialism', as he commends realism against what he feels to be the titivating and specious stylistic self-indulgence of literary modernism (Nkosi 1981: 55).[1] Parry roundly asserts that there are modes – such as the fantastic and the fabulous, the grotesque and the disorderly, the parodic reiteration or inversion of dominant codes, the deformation of master tropes, the estrangement of received usage, the fracture of authorised syntax – which can act as oppositional and subversive procedures without directly illuminating the struggle or ostensibly articulating dissent and protest.

Any focus upon contemporary innovative developments in African writing must not avoid the historical, regional and contextual circumstances of that writing. Stephen Slemon provides a crucial analysis of the treatment of African texts that are characterised by postmodernist textual forms and paradigms, but which must resist being subsumed into western categories and must retain their geographical and socio-historical contexts (Slemon 1990b). Slemon argues that 'there is the figuration of a reiterative quotation, or intertextual citation, in relation to colonialist "textuality"' (Slemon 1990b: 3) that is very similar to 'the principle of intertexual parody which [Linda] Hutcheon defines for post-modernism' (Slemon 1990b: 5). Despite these similarities, though, there are significant differences. First, 'the location of textual power as an especially effective technology of colonialist discourse means that post-colonial reiterative writing takes on a discursive specificity' (Slemon 1990b: 5); and, second, 'whereas a post-modernist criticism would want to argue that literary practices such as these expose the constructedness of *all* textuality and thus call down "the claim to unequivocal domination of one mode of signifying over another", an *interested* post-colonial critical practice would want to allow for the positive production of oppositional truth-claims in these texts. It would retain for post-colonial writing, that is, a mimetic or referential purchase to textuality, and it would recognize in this referential drive the operations of a critical strategy for survival in marginalized groups' (Slemon 1990b: 5).

This would make post-colonial criticism radically fragmentary and contradictory; 'for such a criticism would draw on post-structuralism's suspension of the referent in order to read the social "text" of colonialist power and at the same time would reinstall the referent in the service of colonized and post-colonial societies' (Slemon 1990b: 5).

History in Kojo Laing and J. M. Coetzee

This dual strategy can be seen inscribed in the so-called postcolonial fiction of Kojo Laing's novels, particularly *Search Sweet Country*, *Woman of the Aeroplanes* and *Major Gentl and the Achimota Wars*. Kojo Laing's writing shows all the hallmarks of postmodernism, with its linguistic pyrotechnics, and its fundamentally fragmented and hybridised representations; its efforts to decentre and decanonise; its enormously self-reflexive and ironic style; and the way it markedly draws upon the devices of 'fiction' to demystify imperialist versions of 'history'. Yet at the same time, it retains the 'recuperative impulse towards the structure of "history" and manifests a Utopian desire grounded in reference' (Slemon 1990b: 6). Laing's *Search Sweet Country* (1986) is concerned with the state of Ghana, what it is and what it will become. The novel is largely about a search for an identity: 'Living on the wondering side of doubt' (*Search Sweet Country*: 6), the protagonist Kofi Loww, for example, who 'cut up his life into little pieces, and did not quite know which piece to pick up first' (*Search Sweet Country*: 114), is searching for his own sense of self-identity, often cast in the form of small epiphanies (*Search Sweet Country*: 24–5) in a larger metaphysical search for self-knowledge: 'Loww begged the universe, and Baidoo begged Accra' (*Search Sweet Country*: 15). Identified repeatedly with the city of Accra (*Search Sweet Country*: 113–14), Kofi Loww sees time as a combination of dead and living, past and present; temporal consciousness is not a series of different 'periods' but superimposed upon one another, interwoven, intermingled (*Search Sweet Country*: 117). Indeed, for the healer turned farmer $1/2$-Allotey, time works very flexibly: 'The future would move back into the past, and deepen and darken as it moved; then it would move sideways into the present, standing in its own deep rind before the raised hands of Allotey' (*Search Sweet Country*: 200). In his anxiety to discern what sort of past he should preserve, or challenge, he argues 'Do not resist, you can neither resist the past nor the future!' (*Search Sweet Country*: 202) as he seeks to 'burst through the propriety of ancient ways' (*Search Sweet Country*: 203).

The central event of the novel that entwines the various characters is Dr Boadi's illegal importation of race horses. In a novel that is unambiguous about the damage done to the nation by political corruption, Dr Boadi appears to be the archetypal traitor; he emerges as a money-oriented man, making money illegally and corruptly, and uses the police force to intimidate and threaten Loww who remains steadfastly incorruptible. Countering Loww's anxiety about a mind/body split when carrying the burdens of the nation, Kofi's father urges him to keep his eyes on process and change with an historical consciousness: 'We are letting our great chance slip in this country. Our war-cry should be, to be histo-, historical and to be smart!' (*Search Sweet Country*: 189). The novel does not really participate in the notion that the nation is a narration of hegemonic conservatism: Ghanaian nationhood is actively sought and defined. In a series of somewhat staged discussions, various protagonists such as Professor Sackey, $1/2$-Allotey, Pinn and Dr Boadi discuss the implications of history for the future of the nation, and in the face of arguments about change, $1/2$-Allotey proclaims: 'We sat down and let the change, the history, be thrown at us! And in spite of over five hundred years of association with foreigners, we have been very stubborn: ... Professor, part of my secret, if it is a secret at all, is that I don't accept that we are still slaves of our own history!' (*Search Sweet Country*: 77). Sackey is given the final voice to criticise a nation undermined by a lack of moral action: 'We really must learn that ideas do not merely exist in relation to the past or to exams, to books, articles, or to other countries. Our soil can grow completely new things here too. The contours of the mind's geography are rather tired here ... the weight of our past seems to be crushing the present ... and the future will not be born' (*Search Sweet Country*: 241). Sackey argues for agency, self-expression, self-determination, initiative actions undefined by the self-interest and structural influences of others.

Ultimately, Laing's fiction is involved in a space-clearing gesture. This is not a sign of manufacturing otherness, and therefore commodifying that otherness as an exotic 'other'. Rather, like Okri, Laing aims to challenge African writers to expand their range of consciousness and exchange of ideas from the 'nativist' paradigm that so dominated the early post-independence nationalist years. Without seeking to impose any structures of closure around purist or traditionalist models of African identity, Laing depicts a hybridised and diverse world. His postcoloniality is an awareness of a destabilised position, a complex state of 'in-betweenness' that experiences the shifting polemics of ethnicity, history, memory, politics, aesthetics, narrative strategy and immigration or exile. Much of the energy in Laing's novel *Search Sweet Country* is directed towards the reinsertion of particular issues into history and those acts and figures of anti-colonialist resistance that imperialist forms of representation have systematically omitted. 'Far from calling down the idea of "history" itself, then, Laing works to map over colonialism's false historicism with a reconstituted, "decolonised" sense of historical event, the result being that the apparently anti-referential display of tropological excess in the narrative is grounded to what I see as an underlying post-colonial realist script' (Slemon 1990b: 6). Hence, the 'project of reiterating the colonialist "pretext" not only involves the figuration of the textual resistance but also the recuperation – the remembering or relearning – of "the role of the native as historical subject and combatant, possessor of another knowledge and producer of alternative traditions"' (Slemon 1990b: 6–7). Slemon cautions western postmodernist readings against overvaluing 'the anti-referential or deconstructive energetics of postcolonial texts that they efface the important recuperative work that is also going on within them' (Slemon 1990b: 7). Ultimately Slemon argues that 'post-modernism joins hands with its modernist precursor in continuing a politics of colonialist control' through a strategic containment of its others when it appropriates their cultural work. Laing's *Search Sweet Country* is motivated not by a desire to interrogate prescribed systems, and characters like Loww and $1/2$-Allotey decide not to slip into binarist thinking but to resist such categorisations: they inhabit the absences of the colonial record, resisting any containing structures, detaching themselves from any neo-universalism that may seek to capture world space for themselves. Invoking the past and memory is one strategy for dealing with the amnesia-inducing colonialist politics, and the traumatic repetition of cultural rupture and historical loss. Any argument that postmodernism signals a forgetting of colonial trauma can be made only because the postmodern is not adequately historicised. For all his postmodern techniques of unhinging foundations, of ontological instability in his characters, of signifiers floating free from signifieds, and assorted disoriented objects, Laing avoids the asocial, apolitical textuality that most people associate with the postmodern. He resists the urge to erase the iniquities of the past (in fact he is constantly haunted by colonialism), and thus does not forget historical trauma but writes from it. As the 'post-memory' fiction of a traumatic survival, Laing's surreal landscapes echo the haunted experiences and weird landscapes identified by Lawrence Langer's analysis of the survivors of the Holocaust survivors: 'the survivor does not travel a road from the normal to the bizarre back to the normal, but from the normal to the bizarre back to a normalcy so permeated by the bizarre encounter with atrocity that it can never be purified again. The two worlds haunt each other' (Langer 1982: 88).

Such a writing might be deemed *allegorical* in its generic approach to the legacy of colonialism. Stephen Slemon has developed ideas about the oppositional impact of postcolonial allegorical writing. He argues that postcolonial treatments of history commonly seek to proceed beyond determinist views of history, 'by revising, reappropriating, or reinterpreting history as a concept, and in doing so to articulate new "codes of recognition", within which those acts of resistance, those unrealised intentions, and those re-orderings of consciousness that "history" has rendered silent or invisible can be recognised as shaping forces in a culture's tradition' (Slemon 1988: 159). Slemon is mostly concerned with the transformative powers of 'imaginative revision' that are evident in allegorical narratives. 'Allegory refocuses our concept of history as fixed monument into a concept of history as the creation of a discursive practice, and in doing so it opens history, fiction's "other", to the possibility of transformation' (Slemon 1988: 161). In particular, Slemon cites the case of

J. M. Coetzee's revision and reappropriation of allegory in *Waiting for the Barbarians*. Many have attacked Coetzee for his use of allegory, arguing that it has a tendency to dehistoricise, to erect a vantage point *outside* history. However, Slemon sees Coetzee as subverting the association of allegory with imperialism and reappropriating it for a politics of resistance. If the allegorical mode is based upon an imperial code of recognition, it can also be seen to be based upon a resistance to totalitarian systems. As far as Slemon is concerned, Coetzee suggests 'that allegory can itself be used to dismantle the system of allegorical thinking that underwrites the act of colonisation' (Slemon 1988: 163). Allegory is thus associated with a belief in the possibility of transformation:

> This characteristic of allegory may have served the ideology of imperialism in legitimising the transformation of the 'other' into colonial subject, and it may continue to underwrite neo-colonial codes. But by foregrounding the fact that history is not a set of immovable past achievements but a discourse, open, as are all discursive practices, to reinterpretation, post-colonial allegorical narratives show that allegorical transformation can also be an effective means of subverting imperial myths. (Slemon 1988: 164)

Ultimately, Slemon argues that 'post-colonial allegories are concerned with neither redeeming nor annihilating history, but with displacing it as a concept and opening up the past to imaginative revision' (Slemon 1988: 165). Postcolonial texts therefore change our ideas not only about history but about the concept of allegory itself. We can add that postcolonial writing not only changes our ideas about history and allegory but also challenges the prevailing assumptions of postmodernism itself.

J. M. Coetzee's writing is indicative of exactly this challenge, raising consciousness about the legitimising roles of history and colonisation. In an interview, Coetzee said that he was inclined 'to see the South African situation [today] as only one manifestation of a wider historical situation to do with colonialism, late colonialism, neo-colonialism' (Watson 1978). The 'postmodern' textual vacillations and indeterminacies that can be identified in Coetzee's fictions have often been regarded critically as an indication of his political quiescence and ideological detachment, rather than as signs of his expression of the ambivalence of the 'coloniser' who repudiates the oppressive system in which he finds himself a component. Others have taken Coetzee's textual reflexivity and his linguistic innovation as indications of his self-indulgence and enchantment with narrative games than with the serious task of combating political inequalities. Yet rather than seeking refuge from history in myth, Coetzee's fiction seeks to draw attention to the matrix of institutionally authorised discursive practices, revealing culture as discourses of ideology and power, as David Attwell seeks to explain (Attwell 1993). His explorations of power and powerlessness in *Dusklands* and *In the Heart of the Country*, and the master–slave relationship in *Foe* and *Disgrace*, illuminate alike the colonising mind and the dissenting colonising mind. In one essay, Coetzee identifies his own procedures as 'fictional rivalry' to historical discourse, in which fiction operates with its own autonomous aesthetic standards and forms in order to challenge the prevailing mythologies embedded in history:

> A novel operates in terms of its own procedures and issues in its own conclusions, not one that operates in terms of the procedures of history and eventuates in conclusions that are checkable by history (as a child's schoolbook is checkable by a schoolmistress). In particular I mean a novel that evolves its own paradigms and myths, in the process (and here is the point at which true rivalry, even enmity, perhaps enters the picture) perhaps going so far as to show up the mythic status of history – in other words, demythologising history ... a novel that is prepared to work itself out outside the terms of class conflict, race conflict, gender conflict or any of the other oppositions out of which history and the historical disciplines erect themselves. (Coetzee 1988: 3)

Anxious to protect the autonomy of the aesthetic and reminiscent of the position adopted by Theodor Adorno in his debates with Georg Lukács over the aesthetic ideologies of realism and modernism, Coetzee seems wary of allowing aesthetic integrity to fall prey to historical and ideological determination. Nor is he enamoured of the aesthetic or political ramifications of realism: 'I don't have much interest in, or can't seriously engage myself with, the kind of realism that takes pride in copying the "real" world' (Morphet 1984: 63). Coetzee is suspicious of the testimonial concept (or the bearing witness to) embedded within realism, and his engagement with history *appears* indirect when put side by side with the staunch realism linked to black prose fiction, or the work of Nadine Gordimer. Nevertheless, as Dominic Head notes, this obliqueness of historical engagement is largely predicated upon a Lukácsian 'critical realism', a realisation of individual characters within an understanding of the historical dynamic which was all too often invoked as the yardstick to assess political value in South African fiction during the height of the apartheid era (Head 1997: 8). As Sue Kossew points out, Coetzee clearly addresses postcolonial concerns in a non-realist, counter-discursive and allegorical style (Kossew 1996: 28). Indeed, Coetzee's first novel, *Dusklands*, provides competing versions of history and colonisation by incorporating 'historical documents' and diaries, while *Waiting for the Barbarians* utilises an allegorical setting to explore the complexities of being a 'liberal' within a tyrannical colonial government that sustains its power by fabricating myths of aggressive 'others' on its borders. Narrative, it would appear, has its own historical logic and can provide a counter-memory to the discourse of history. One of the overriding concerns about writing about African literature ought to be a wariness about homogenising the writings from different parts of Africa, robbing the continent of its textual, cultural, historical and socio-political differences and specificities. Coetzee forces one to be aware of the discontinuities, differences, dispersals and othernesses in African literary pasts in the face of any totalising closure of historiographic forces. To remain alive to the diversity of African literature, one needs to open a space to explore the lineaments of literature and the past, rather than close down or home in on an orthodoxy or a theoretically dogmatic position. The endorsement of an experimentalism that 'shocks' one out of dead familiarities, that affirms indeterminacies and encourages differences in the name of a yet-to-be-realised future, is to be positively encouraged. The postmodern points to such a non-teleological, sporadic narrative of the present. It aims to defy the construction of a 'total history' that would subsume all otherness and difference into the comforting embrace of a legendary mythical postcolonial victory.

Postmodernism brings to the fore a consciousness of history, of historicity. In many respects, postmodernism could be said to focus upon the 'historylessness' of history, the fact that history is not what much of it purports to be – objective, factual, unbiased and without prejudice. In so doing, postmodernism also brings to the fore a consciousness of ethical responsibility. By this, I mean that it forces one to consider the implications of power related to discourse, of covert impulses to aestheticise discourses, of the problems of gaps between events and their representation, and of the disguised motivations of a latter-day imperialism. In other words, this ethical consciousness is *an openness to otherness*. This ethical consciousness is largely to do with strands of postmodernism that insist on opening up a space for the Other in representation, yet without appropriating that Other for the Same. This Levinasian postmodern thought desires to resist the conceptual violence perpetrated by modernity and postmodernity, i.e. a colonisation of the Other. This form of postmodernism emerges as an ethical result of the era of colonisation. Yet this postmodernism has both a negative and a positive impact – it is an effect of western forms and reflects a resistance to those forms. As Jean-François Lyotard's work on the sublime has suggested, postmodernism must be ethical towards the unpresentable. It must demonstrate a respect for the gaps, lacunae, fissures in things – not a filling of the gaps. The risk postmodernism runs though, is a potential for complicity with the structures against which it rails. The complex conjuncture of postmodernism with postcolonialism lies in the distinctions one draws between postmodernism as a politicising aesthetic and postcolonialism as a foregrounding of the contamination of the political, although without losing sight of the social and historical circumstances implicit in that manoeuvre. One needs to be aware of the danger of peddling a syncretisation against a totalising politics and an exoticism of the 'other' that ignores the processes of exploitation themselves and panders to a western cosmopolitanism voracious for escapism. This is the vulnerability of magical realists and African writers attracted to the styles and devices associated with postmodernism. Such writers tack a fine bearing between the Scylla of capturing a political reality disguised by conventional realism and the Charybdis of providing the exotic escape desired by a large proportion of the western market. Laing's and Coetzee's 'post-modernism' would appear not to be that form of celebration of the icon of late capital or consumerised simulacrum evident in so many American postmodernists, but one that brings international globali-sation to the witness box to justify itself to the 'third world'.

M. G. Vassanji's textual pasts

Within the context of Africa, postmodernism is not the 'cultural logic of late capitalism' that it may be in the West. Rather, postmodern textual devices offer an opportunity to challenge the dominant assumptions of western (post)colonial historiography, and these chal-lenges are frequently bound up with portrayals of memory and history. African history figured as a tattered text that is constantly being rewritten or hunted down, sought in every corner of the nation, occurs in M. G. Vassanji's fiction, especially the novels *The Gunny Sack* (1989), *The Book of Secrets* (1994) and his recent *The In-Between World of Vikram Lall* (2003). Narrating 'the crazy dance of history' (*The Gunny Sack*: 10), *The Gunny Sack* focuses upon the foundations, developments and consequences of the historical dispos-session and diaspora of a particular community. The community is that of the Asians in Africa, a community that has a distinctive and particular position within the history and development of East Africa.[2] *The Gunny Sack* relates the unwritten stories that reveal the experiences of an African Asian extended family over four genera-tions in East Africa, during the decades of Tanganyika's emergence as a small colony on the East African coast to its formation as a modern nation of autonomous determination in Tanzania. Recounting the development of cultural and social migrations, border-crossings, hybrid cultures and identities in Dar-es-Salaam and Zanzibar, *The Gunny Sack* worries away at the problems of where one begins, or origins. In this family micro-narrative, the novel also becomes a repository for the collective memory and oral history of many other African Asians. Salim also known as Kala, a Tanzanian Asian and the great-grandson of an African slave, inher-

its the eponymous 'gunny sack' upon the death of his mystical grand-
aunt. Named Shehrbanoo and nicknamed 'Shehru', the gunny sack
unravels a gallery of characters whose stories parallel the emergence
of the modern African nation. The ancient, drab sack is likened to a
Sheherezade of Indian and African settlements in East Africa, a sack
that becomes symbolic of the significance of memory:

> Memory, Ji Bai would say, is this old sack here, this poor dear that
> nobody has any use for any more. Stroking the sagging brown shape
> with affection she would drag it closer, to sit at her feet like a favourite
> child. In would plunge her hand through the gaping hole of a mouth, and
> she would rummage inside. Now you feel this thing here, you fondle that
> one, you bring out this naughty little nut and everything else in it
> rearranges itself. (*The Gunny Sack*: 3)

Memories are treated like a collection of quaint objects that, once
selected, reorganise all other objects in the sack. The gunny sack as
a collection of memories sets in motion a whole set of impulses for the
narrator: 'Images like confetti, like cotton lint in Ji Bai's mattress
shop, drift through my mind haphazardly, each a clue to a story, a
person. A world. Sounds knock in my brain demanding entrance,
rude gatecrashers jostling for right of way, until I in a dizzy spell say,
All right, now what, Shehrbanoo? Leave this magic' (*The Gunny
Sack*: 6). In many respects an African *Midnight's Children*, the
narrative in *The Gunny Sack* is partly an attempt by the narrator to
organise these fleeting memories into a pattern that has meaning,
placing 'wisps of memory. Cotton balls gliding from the gunny sack,
each a window to world ... Asynchronous images projected on multiple cinema screens', arranging a 'frayed remnant of a memory' (*The
Gunny Sack*: 110) in a newly woven text-ile. Yet memories can
produce an infinite variety of patterns:

> Memory, Ji Bai said, is this gunny sack ...
> I can put it all back and shake it and churn it and sift it and start
> again, re-order memory, draw a new set of lines through those blots,
> except that each of them is like a black hole, a doorway to a universe ...
> It can last for ever, this game, the past has no end – but no, Shehrbanoo,
> you will not snare me like that, let it end today this your last night. (*The
> Gunny Sack*: 266)

Tied up with the legitimation of beginnings, origins, identity and
story, memory propels the narrative forward yet always hovers
around the events as a trace of the past. Indeed, as the novel opens,
Kala is presented with a question by his schoolteacher: '"Where do
you come from?" and later would say, "Begin at the beginning"' (*The
Gunny Sack*: 6). Like Saleem in *Midnight's Children*, beginning at
the beginning is Kala's great difficulty: attempting to fix what is
transient, what is always slipping away, the novel offers a backward

perspective in tracing the generations of his ancestors (Kala's family genealogical tree prefaces the narrative), yet eventually it gets to the point of resisting the pull of history for a more forward, optimistic outlook: 'The running must stop now, Amina. The cycle of escape and rebirth, uprooting and regeneration, must cease in me. Let this be the last runaway, returned, with one last, quixotic dream. Yes, perhaps here lies redemption, a faith in the future, even if it means for now to embrace the banal present, to pick up the pieces of our wounded selves, our wounded dreams, and pretend they're still intact, without splints, because from our wounded selves flowers still grow' (*The Gunny Sack*: 268–9). Part of the problem for Kala is not merely remembering the past, but how to forget it, how to shake off the effects of the traumatic memory (*The Gunny Sack*: 183). When Kala first visits Matamu, it is described in precisely these terms:

> Matamu. Sweet; but what? Opinions vary; it is now part of the character of this town, this question asked only half seriously. Sweet, but what? It's the water, some will say, from the nearby Mnene, the fat stream; others will point to one of the numerous fruits you can find here. Ma-tamu. The name always had a tart sound to it, an aftertaste to the sweetness, a far off echo that spoke of a distant, primeval time, the year zero. An epoch that cast a dim but sombre shadow on the present. It is the town where my forebear unloaded his donkey one day and made his home. Where Africa opened its womb to India and produced a being who forever stalks the forest in search of himself. It is where Bibi Taratibu, given as a gift for cold nights, was so used and discarded, and then disappeared. Only traces of that past, are visible here. It is almost a ghost town, barely hanging together, where one stops for a drink of cold water on a hot day, but not for too long, and buys some fruit it it's not too softened from lying all day in the sun. (*The Gunny Sack*: 39–40)

History is always missing, both the recent past and the distant past. Ruptured from any easy connection with the present, Matamu bears vestigial presences that haunt the consciousness of the narrator. As the narrator observes at another moment, 'The past is just this much beyond reach, you can reconstruct it only through the paraphernalia it leaves behind in your gunny sack ... and then who would deny that what you manufacture is only a model ...' (*The Gunny Sack*: 127). History is intimately tied up with reconstruction, yet as a replica of history, narrative is never wholly adequate or representative as a replacement or substitution for the past. The text always threatens to implode or collapse. Indeed, Vassanji's presentation of the past is never crystal clear: 'the past in [*The Gunny Sack*] is deliberately murky to some degree. I did not see, nor wanted to give the impression of, a simple, linear, historical truth emerging. Not all of the mysteries of the past are resolved in the book. That is deliberate. It's the only way' (Kanaganayakam 1991: 22). As Kala notes, memory is always a manifold complex: 'I stopped to examine the collective memory – this spongy, disconnected, often incoherent accretion of stories over generations' (*The Gunny Sack*: 66). Vassanji's concern is repeatedly how history affects the present and how personal and public histories can overlap (Malak 1993: 279). Personal histories, reclaimed through memory, are juxtaposed with the contemporary, reminding us that, after all, remembering is something done *now*, not *then*. Memories and histories become part of the field of the novel, not as things to which the novel refers.

The Gunny Sack is thus dominated by the issue of subjectivity and how it is constructed or associated with the past, or history. Alternative readings are given throughout the novel of past events, raising interesting questions about the *meaning-then/meaning-now* dichotomy. Undecidability is the only means of understanding realities – deferred allusions and misreadings create multiple perspectives suggesting the unreliability of the text as a means of presenting the past as real. The past is always rewritten therefore as a misreading – always as a present. Kala does not think that the world operates in terms of a surface and deep structure whose fragments connect at a quintessential level, whose surface absurdities disappear into a unified order and vision. Kala realises that he needs to make the past tangible, to acknowledge that the past has something important to say, in order for him to construct the present: 'Thus the disposition of the past. To be remembered and acknowledged' (*The Gunny Sack*: 268). Simply becoming an amnesiac and *forgetting* the past do not adequately account for his equal responsibility to the present. Yet retrospective processes of interpretation result not in reconstructing the truths of the past, but in misreadings. This is not just ambiguity; the apparent irreconcilability of the readings and misreadings are a major deconstructive process resting on a recognition that language – discourse – compels all readings to be misreadings. The story that emerges is thus a continual ambivalence deferring its own resolution. As the novel outlines, there are so many stories to tell …. The past is consumed into the present so that the narrator – the fiction – becomes responsible for the past because it exists only in fictions; and with Kala as narrator, as an insecure narrator, all illusion is insecurity. Reality, Kala argues, is metaphorical. His past family members can be made to represent many things, according to one's point of view: they can be seen as the last throw of everything antiquated and retrogressive in his myth-ridden nation, whose defeat was entirely desirable in the context of modernising, twentieth-century economy; or as the true hope of freedom, which is now for ever extinguished. Memory has a special kind of truth all its own. It selects, eliminates, alters, exaggerates, minimises, glorifies; and vilifies also; but in the end it creates its own reality, its heterogeneous but usually coherent version of events; and no sane human being ever trusts someone else's version more than his or her own. The different parts of Kala's somewhat complicated life refuse, with wholly unreasonable obstinacy, to stay neatly in their separate compartments. Reality is a question of perspective; the further you get from the past, the more concrete and plausible it seems – but as you approach the present, it inevitably seems more and more incredible. All of this causes a collapse of linear models of narrative: indeed, as Kala at one point indicates, the entire model of time needs to be reconceptualised. This narrative structural challenge to linear temporality, Linda Hutcheon argues, is also a challenge to totalisation. Kala does not hide the narrativisation of past events: the events no longer seem to speak for themselves, but are shown to be consciously composed into a narrative, whose constructed – not found – order is imposed upon them, often overtly by the narrating figure. Consequently, Kala's discourse is plagued by the worry of the necessity for meaning, and whether this inevitably leads to a distortion of things, to the degree that he rewrites the whole of history in order to place himself in the central position and role. Kala constantly perceives analogues, parallels and patterns between apparently diverse material. The function of chance or randomness, Kala argues, is critical in a narrative or life. Without a *why*, life appears terrible: all actions become futile and accidental. So the text constantly battles between the imposition of an order, and the emergence of a 'natural' pattern, a narrative which signals its own rather than another's pattern. As with so much of postmodern fiction, this does not in any way rule out the actuality of the past reality, 'but it focuses attention on the act of imposing order on that past, of encoding strategies of meaning-making through representation' (Hutcheon 2002: 67). What Kala discovers is that the 'forces of history are not controlled by destiny or regulative mechanisms, but respond to haphazard conflicts. They do not manifest the successive forms of a primordial intention and their attraction is not that of a conclusion, for they always appear through the singular randomness of events' (Foucault 1980: 154). Instead, he produces a history which is perceived to be the result of his personal actions within African-Asian society, a history which is closely tied to the personal, a history or knowledge derived from perspective. Similarly, associated with the birth of a nation, Kala's subjectivity is inherently multiple, bearer as he is of the multiple voices of the emerging people and the multiple hopes of Tanzanian independence. This opens up the text as a specific representation of how a nation is made, of the narration of a nation to pinch Homi Bhabha's phrase. Edward Said, a theorist of the processes and implications of colonialism, discussed the formation of the modern nation as a 'secular horizontal space', in which

'The fundamental thing is that history and human society are made up of numerous efforts crisscrossing each other, frequently at odds with each other, always untidy in the way they involve each other' (Said 1985: 145). Yet in this context, argues Said, 'no single explanation sending one back immediately to a single origin is adequate. And just as there are no simple dynastic answers, there are no simple discrete formations or social processes' (Said 1985: 145). The space of a modern nation is never horizontal. In order to construct the temporality of representation that moves between cultural formations and social processes without a centred causal logic (and all the power implications that goes along with that) requires a kind of "doubleness" in the writing of the nation. It is this 'doubleness' that Vassanji seems to try to achieve in *The Gunny Sack*, as Kala tries to hold two or more narratives, subjectivities, histories, together at once. And this it seems to me can be assimilated to a theory and strategy of counter-imperialism. Such a strategy implicates both history and space: 'The politics of imperialism and colonialism is thus a politics which is founded not just upon geography but also upon a series of temporal factors ... It does what the periphery has always silently and powerlessly done: it decentres the centre' (Docherty 1993: 445). Reading *The Gunny Sack* demonstrates that global truths are of little use in describing non-European strategies for self-determination. Universalist essentialism is pointless. Yet what is of value is understanding local, temporary 'truths'. Therefore, we are forced into making critical decisions about whose or what perspective we are going to adopt.

The colonial history of Kenya and Tanzania also serves as the backdrop for his later novels, *The Book of Secrets* and *The In-Between World of Vikram Lall*. Both novels are structured by forms of inter- and intra-textuality, leading to specific conclusions about the nature of the pasts that they invoke. *The Book of Secrets* is the personal history contained in the diary of Alfred Corbin, a British East African colonial administrator, that fuels the story. While the narrator, a retired schoolteacher, reads the diary and attempts to trace the events that occur after the diary stops, he eventually finds himself revisiting his own personal history: 'And so I would construct a history, a living tapestry to join the past to the present, to defy the blistering shimmering dusty bustle of the city life outside which makes transients of us all' (*The Book of Secrets*: 8). Developing as a book-within-a-book, the narrator/author becomes 'captive to the book', 'exposed to my own inquiry', and subject to 'the hidden longings of my past' (*The Book of Secrets*: 8). Interleaving Corbin's observations with extracts from official government statements about policies towards the African population (for example, *The Book of Secrets*: 31, 32, 40), the novel situates itself ironically at odds with

Corbin's experiences, opening up fissures between what passes for official science or knowledge of Africans and the experiences of Corbin's daily life as Deputy Assistant District Commissioner. Corbin eventually glimpses the illusion of 'this little England in Africa', sensed by him to be 'fraudulence in the sense of a conjuring trick' (*The Book of Secrets*: 63). He understands that Nairobi 'was not an homogenous society' (*The Book of Secrets*: 63), as one is constantly aware of the stratified white society, the mixture of Muslims and Africans, and the different hierarchies between these peoples. Corbin's realisation of his awkward position in relation to the African cultures over which he presides eventually comes to a head: 'admin-istration's all right, but how the devil do you deal with another culture's ghosts?' (*The Book of Secrets*: 72). At the end of the diary entry, the novel turns into a detective story, as the narrator senses his textual/text-ile task: 'Like a snoop, I must follow the threads, expose them in all their connections and possibilities, weave them together. What else is a historian but a snoop?' (*The Book of Secrets*: 91). When the narrator goes in search of the characters in Corbin's diary, he finds the ways in which the present is still intricately connected to the colonial past as it resurfaces in the contemporary world – how the events surrounding the life of Corbin's servant Mariamu, which resurface in relation to Corbin's friends or people who know about Corbin (or the diary). Yet the interesting perspective is that the past is constantly figured as 'writing', as a text, a testa-ment and record. Ultimately, the narrator recognises that history is a flimsy reconstruction, entirely dependent upon fleeting textual evidence and ephemeral signs: 'But there is no sign of the war here, no sign of the past. History drifts about in the sands, and only the fanatically dedicated see it and recreate it, however incomplete their visions and fragile their constructs' (*The Book of Secrets*: 175). This preoccupation is continued in *The In-Between World of Vikram Lall*, in which the eponymous protagonist, vacillating between the worlds of Kenya-then and Canada-now, the present and the past, reflects upon his upbringing and life in Kenya during the pre- and post-inde-pendence years from the perspective of his self-imposed exile in Canada in the 1990s. Concerned with how to represent that past – with all the experiences of colonial racism, the complex Mau-Mau politics, the differing allegiances to friends and family, the corrup-tion of the Kenyatta neo-colonial period – the novel is studded with reflections on the nature of 'pastness', often with more than a hint of Proustian poignancy: 'There are wonderful moments sometimes – a splash of colour, the sweet taste of icy kulfi on a Sunday afternoon, the feel of hot steam on the face and arms from a gasping locomotive – that stand out purely in themselves, sparkles of childhood memory scattered loosely in the consciousness. They need not tell a story, yet moments lead from one to another in this tapestry that is one's life; and so we feel bound, unhappy adults, to look past and around those glimmer points in our desperate search for nuance and completeness, for coherence and meaning' (*Vikram Lall*: 56). The metaphor of history as an interlaced textile persists, as Vikram Lall seeks through the power of memory to extricate random shards from the debris of the past and to weave them into a 'tapestry' that portrays the trajectory of his life to the present.

Vassanji's fiction presents one with the 'ambivalent affiliations' of the 'double exile', and is, ultimately, concerned with celebrating 'multiple identities': 'The appeal of Vassanji's work thus mainly resides in its ironic ridicule of the claim of ethnic or religious purists: half-castes, mixed ancestries, syncretic ideologies and beliefs (Shamsi rituals being an interbreed between Hinduism and Islam [*The Gunny Sack*: 7–8]), and cross-cultural relationships or marriages preoccupy his narrative with varying degrees of prominence' (Malak 1993: 281). Otherness is not bracketed off, demarcated and cauterised as a separate space from the real, but situated within the familiar and the known. Vassanji's metafictional characteristics bleed dry the ideology of realm embedded within western cultural imperialism, and focus a fiction that 'works-through' a series of racial and national ruptures or traumas, that forces the bringing together of the many facets of overwhelmingly complicated events. In so doing, Vassanji distils complex experiences into more understandable packages, allowing people to gradually move beyond the trauma. As with much postcolonial writing, it characterises a movement away from anthropological interests in 'structure' to more political and psychological interests in 'agency', the crucial issue of being in control and managing one's self-direction.

Conclusion: what future postmodernism?

Brenda Cooper's *Magical Realism in West African Fiction* examines the cultural politics of magical realism, arguing that it arises out of postcolonial, unevenly developed societies, that are the product of ancient and modern, and scientific and magical, views of the world that coexist. In her very engaging analysis of the role of magical realism in relation to African writing, Cooper argues that 'magical realists strive towards incorporating indigenous knowledge in new terms, in order to interrogate tradition and to herald change. Thus upholding the indigenous as a justification in itself for returning to ancient values and customs, without ironic distancing, is inimical to magical realism. Rather, such a position will tend to promote the fiction of cultural nationalism, which employs myth and legend, deities and spirits, rituals, proverbs, and injunctions. This is in distinction to one of magical realism's defining features – its hybridity that contests boundaries and violates them' (Cooper 1998: 49). The porousness of literary boundaries, of temporal limits, and margins of literary styles, is widely recognised in contemporary literary debates. Within this hybridised state of representation, the role of memory in negotiating the past and present is of particular interest, and one that has been the subject of considerable debate in recent years. One of the key contributors to this debate is Andreas Huyssen, whose book *Twilight Memories* contributes a powerful and sustained analysis of the ways in which our very notions of temporality have changed, the vicissitudes of nationalism, and the ways in which 'the mode of memory is *recherche* rather than recuperation' (Huyssen 1995: 3):

> At a time when the notion of memory has migrated into the realm of silicon chips, computers, and cyborg fictions, critics routinely deplore the entropy of historical memory defining amnesia as a dangerous cultural virus generated by the new media technologies. The more memory stored on the data banks and image tracks, the less of our culture's willingness and ability to engage in active remembrance, or so it seems.
>
> Remembrance shapes our links to the past, and the ways we remember define us in the present. As individuals and societies, we need the past to construct and anchor our identities and to nurture a vision of the future. In the wake of Freud and Nietzsche, however, we know how slippery and unreliable personal memory can be; always affected by forgetting and denial, repression and trauma, it, more often than not, serves a need to rationalize and maintain power. But a society's collective memory is no less contingent, no less unstable, its shape by no means permanent. It is always subject to subtle and not so subtle reconstruction. A society's memory is negotiated in the social body's beliefs and values, rituals and institutions. In the case of modern societies in particular, it is shaped by such public sites of memory as the museum, the memorial, and the monument. Yet the permanence promised by a monument in stone is always built on quicksand. Some monuments are joyously toppled at times of social upheaval, and others preserve memory in ossified form, either as myth or as cliché. Yet others stand simply as figures of forgetting, their meaning and original purpose eroded by the passage of time. As Musil once wrote: 'There is nothing in the world as invisible as monuments.'
>
> But does it even make sense to oppose memory with forgetting, as we so often do, with forgetting at best acknowledged as the inevitable flaw and deficiency of memory itself? Paradoxically, is it not the case that each and every memory inevitably depends both on distance and forgetting, the very things that undermine its desired stability and reliability and at the same time are essential to the vitality of memory itself? Isn't it a constitutive strength of memory that it can be contested from new perspectives, novel evidence and from the very spaces it had blocked

out? Given a selective and permanently shifting dialogue between the present and the past, we have come to recognize that our present will inevitably have an impact on what and how we remember. It is important to understand that process, not to regret it in the mistaken belief that some ultimately pure, complete, and transcendent memory is possible. It follows that the strongly remembered past will always be inscribed in our present, from feeding our unconscious desires to guiding our most conscious actions. At the same time, the strongly remembered past may turn into mythic memory. It is not immune to ossification, and may become a stumbling block to the needs of the present rather than an opening in the continuum of history. (Huyssen 1995: 249–50)

Albeit a lengthy quotation, this succinctly sums up many of this book's preoccupations; and although Huyssen is speaking about the cultural and political situation in westernised societies, especially in the light of the fall of the Berlin Wall, nevertheless his meditation upon the relationship between memory and amnesia is instructive for a post-independence, new millennial, African context. Although Africa's cultures are very far from being dominated by silicon chips, computers, cyborg fictions, databanks and image tracks, the important lesson is the delicate balance needed between memories acting as the motivations for guiding nations' visions of their futures, and the warnings about memories being ossified into mythic deceptions.

Again and again, critics like Fredric Jameson point to the way in which postmodern fictions dehistoricise. Resisting a simple endorsement of multiplicity, which can also be an ethically vacuous plurality (often overlooked in the approbation for postmodern fragmentation), those African texts repeatedly marked out as 'postmodernist' do not abandon history: if anything, they intensify the issue of history and memory, inserting politics into the very heart of their aesthetic styles and ideological concerns. Biodun Jeyifo notes the 'the imperialism of representation', a struggle that 'has continued as a central problematic of post-colonial discourse'. Many of the important theorists and critics of postcolonial writings are involved in this 'vast project of demythologisation' (Jeyifo 1991: 56). In this project, these postmodern postcolonial fictions bring about an encounter between the dominant symbolic order and that which threatens its stability. Indeed, one might turn this perspective around. Instead of arguing that one has western history forming, influencing or affecting African literature and forms, rather one could see it as African literature and forms shaping western forms of history. In other words, one might regard the case not as another example of the active West working on a passive Africa, but as an active Africa using its initiatives, its agency, its activity to work on the shapes, structures, and orders of western history. Yet more than this, it is finally a rejection of that history: since to see it as a working on western history suggests that that model of history is what is kept and important. Rather, African literatures are engaged in establishing their own history, their own models, their own structures. Ultimately, the agency puts in place its own structures rather than simply *responding* to a pre-given. Christopher Miller argues that the concept of projection is crucial to this ethical responsibility in African literatures, of projecting one's voices and ideas into new situations, thereby opening and bringing into being a wider consciousness of liberation (Miller 1990: 63). However, since human experience is itself subject to change and rein-terpretation, what seems usual for us may well have registered as traumatic for earlier generations. Robert Young's analysis of the interrelationship between postmodernism and postcolonialism in *White Mythologies: Writing History and the West* considers the case of cosmopolitan postcolonialism within a postmodern context. He concludes that 'deconstruction involves the decentralization and decolonization of European thought', especially the category of 'the West'. Postmodernism 'becomes a certain self-consciousness about a culture's own historical relativity' resulting in 'the loss of the sense of an absoluteness of any Western account of History' (Young 1990: 18 and 19). The historical transformation of the notions of the 'ordi-nary' are what are at the root of this. The principal criticism of post-modernism in relation to postcolonial politics is that it refuses to acknowledge all efforts at political change and voices that speak of origins, collectivities or determinate historical projects. There is a mesmeric pull towards a powerful revival of ethnicity by way of exca-vating the past, which is itself part of a politics of decolonisation and national reconstruction. In the face of this magnetic force, what have been at stake in this book are the epistemological possibilities and the moral necessities of considering the poetic and fictional represen-tations of *unresolved past experience(s)*, whether it be the fragmenta-tion of the self or the horrors of the legacy of the colonial regimes, within an African literary context.

Notes

[1] See Lewis Nkosi's rebuttal of Parry's critique, in Nkosi 1998: 82–3.
[2] For a fuller discussion of this subject, see Sarvan 1976; and Sarvan 1985.

Works cited

Achebe, Chinua (1958), *Things Fall Apart*, London, Heinemann.
——, (1964a), 'The Role of the Writer in a New Nation', *Nigeria Magazine*, 81, 157–60.
——, (1964b), *Arrow of God*, London, Heinemann.
——, (1966), *A Man of the People*, London, Heinemann.
——, (1975a), 'The Novelist as Teacher', in *Morning Yet on Creation Day*, London, Heinemann, pp. 42–5.
——, (1975b), *Morning Yet on Creation Day*, London, Heinemann.
——, (1984), *Anthills of the Savannah*, London, Heinemann.
——, (1988), *Hopes and Impediments: Selected Essays, 1965–1987*, London, Heinemann.
——, (2000), *Home and Exile*, New York and Oxford, Oxford University Press.
Adam, Ian and Helen Tiffin (eds) (1990), *Past the Last Post: Theorizing Colonialism and Post-Modernism*, Calgary, University of Calgary Press.
Adedji, Joel A. (1976), 'The Genesis of African Folkloric Literature', *Yale French Studies*, 53, 5–18.
Adichie, Chimamanda Ngozi (2004), *Purple Hibiscus*, London, Fourth Estate.
Adorno, Theodor W. (1986), 'What Does Coming to Terms with the Past Mean?' (1959), in Geoffrey Hartmann (ed.), *Bitburg in Moral and Political Perspective*, Bloomington, Indiana University Press, pp. 114–29.
——, (1991), 'The Position of the Narrator in the Contemporary Novel', in *Notes to Literature*, Vol. I, ed. Rolf Tiedemann, and trans. Shierry Weber Nicholsen, New York, Columbia University Press, pp. 30–6.
——, (1992), 'Commitment', in *Notes to Literature*, Vol. II, ed. Rolf Tiedemann, and trans. Shierry Weber Nicholsen, New York, Columbia University Press, pp. 76–94.
Afejuku, Tony (1990), 'Autobiography as History and Political Testament: Ngugi wa Thiong'o's *Detained*', *World Literature Written in English*, 30:1, 78–87.
Ahmad, Aijaz (1995), 'The Politics of Literary Postcoloniality', *Race and Class*, 36:3, 1–20.
Aidoo, Ama Ata (1977), *Our Sister Killjoy*, Harlow, Longman.

Alvarez-Pereyre, Jacques (1984), *The Poetry of Commitment in South Africa*, trans. Clive Wake, first published in French 1979, London, Heinemann.

Amadi, Elechi (1970), *The Great Ponds*, first published in 1969, London, Heinemann.

——, (1978), *The Slave*, London, Heinemann.

Amuta, Chidi (1981), 'Ayi Kwei Armah and the Mythopoesis of Mental Decolonization', *Ufahamu*, 10:3, 44–56.

Anderson, Linda (2001), *Autobiography*, London, Routledge.

Aniebo, I. N. C. (1978), *The Journey Within*, London, Heinemann.

Anyidoho, Kofi (1981), 'Historical Realism and the Visionary Ideal: Ayi Kwei Armah's *Two Thousand Seasons*', *Ufahamu,* 11:2, 108–30.

——, (1992), 'Literature and African Identity: The Example of Ayi Kwei Armah' in Wright 1992: 34–47.

Anyinefa, Koffi (1998), 'Postcolonial Postmodernity in Henri Lopes's *Le pleurer-rire*', *Research in African Literatures*, 29:3, 8–20.

Appiah, Kwame Anthony (1992), *In My Father's House: Africa in the Philosophy of Culture*, New York and Oxford, Oxford University Press.

——, (1999), 'The Postcolonial and the Postmodern', in Olu Oguibe and Okwui Enwezor (eds), *Reading the Contemporary African Art from Theory to the Marketplace*, London, Institute of International Visual Arts, pp. 48–73.

Armah, Ayi Kwei (1968), *The Beautyful Ones Are Not Yet Born*, London, Heinemann.

——, (1969), *Fragments*, Boston, Houghton Mifflin.

——, (1973), *Two Thousand Seasons*, London, Heinemann.

——, (1979), *The Healers*, London, Heinemann.

——, (1985), 'Teaching Creative Writing', *West Africa*, 20 May, 994–5.

——, (1995), *Osiris Rising*, Popenguine, Per Ankh.

——, (2000), *KMT: In the House of Life: An Epistemic Novel*, Popenguine, Per Ankh.

Ashcroft, Bill, Gareth Griffiths and Helen Tiffin (1989), *The Empire Writes Back: Theory and Practice in Post-colonial Literatures*, London, Routledge.

Asmal, Kader, Louise Asmal and Ronald Suresh Roberts (1996), *Reconciliation Through Truth*, Cape Town, David Philip.

Atta, Seffi (2004), *Everything Good Will Come*, Northampton, MA, Interlink Books.

Attridge, Derek and Rosemary Jolly (eds) (1998), *Writing South Africa: Literature, Apartheid, and Democracy, 1970–1995*, Cambridge, Cambridge University Press.

Attwell, David (1993), *J. M. Coetzee: South Africa and the Politics of Writing*, Berkeley, University of California Press.

Awoonor, Kofi (1971), *This Earth, My Brother . . .*, London, Heinemann.

Ayivor, Kwame (2003), '"The Beautyful Ones Were Born and Murdered": Armah's Visionary Reconstruction of African History and the Pan-Africanist Dream in *Osiris Rising*', *Journal of Commonwealth Literature*, 38:3, 37–69.

Bâ, Mariama (1981), *So Long a Letter*, trans. Modupé Bodé-Thomas, first published in French 1980, London, Heinemann.

Bakhtin, M. M. (1981), *The Dialogic Imagination: Four Essays*, trans. Caryl

Emerson and Michael Holquist, Austin, TX, University of Texas Press.

Barnett, Ursula (1983), *A Vision of Order: A Study of Black South African Literature in English (1914–1980)*, London, Sinclaire Browne.

Benjamin, Walter (1992), *Illuminations*, ed. Hannah Arendt, first published in 1973, London, Fontana.

Beyala, Calixthe (1996a), *The Sun Hath Looked Upon Me*, trans. Marjolijn de Jaeger, first published in French 1987, London and Portsmouth, NH, Heinemann.

——, (1996b), *Your Name Shall Be Tanga*, trans. Marjolijn de Jaeger, first published in French 1988, London and Portsmouth, NH, Heinemann.

Biko, Steve (1979), *I Write What I Like*, ed. Aelred Stubbs, London, Heinemann.

Blanchot, Maurice (1986), *The Writing of Disaster*, trans. Ann Smock, Lincoln, University of Nebraska Press.

Boesak, Allan (1978), 'Introduction: A Farewell to Innocence', in *Black Theology Black Power*, first published in 1976, London and Oxford, Mowbrays, pp. 1–7.

Bohlin, Anna (1998), 'The Politics of Locality: Memories of District Six in Cape Town', in Nadia Lovell (ed.), *Locality and Belonging*, London and New York, Routledge, pp. 168–88.

Booker, Keith M. (1998), *The African Novel in English: An Introduction*, Oxford, James Currey.

Booth, James (1981), *Writers and Politics in Nigeria*, London, Hodder and Stoughton.

Boyce Davies, Carole (1994), *Black Women, Writing and Identity: Migrations of the Subject*, London, Routledge.

——, and Anne Adams Graves (eds) (1986), *Ngambika: Studies of Women in African Literature*, Trenton, NJ, Africa World Press.

Bremen, Paul (ed.) (1973), *You Better Believe It: Black Verse in English*, Harmondsworth, Penguin.

Brennan, Timothy (1990), 'The National Longing for Form', in Homi Bhabha (ed.), *Nation and Narration*, London, Routledge, pp. 44–71.

Breytenbach, Breyten (1984a), *The True Confessions of an Albino Terrorist*, London, Faber.

——, (1984b), *Mouroir: Mirrornotes of a Novel*, London, Faber.

Brink, André (1998a), 'Stories of History: Reimagining the Past in Post-Apartheid Narrative', in Nuttall and Coetzee 1998: 29–42.

——, (1998b), 'Interrogating Silence: New Possibilities Faced by South African Literature', in Attridge and Jolly 1998: 14–28.

Brodsky, Joseph (1996), Foreword to Siobhan Dowd (ed.), *This Prison Where I Live: The PEN Anthology of Imprisoned Writers*, London, Cassell.

Brown, Duncan (1996), 'South African Oral Performance Poetry of the 1980s: Mzwakhe Mbuli and Alfred Qabula', in Ngara 1996: 120–48.

——, (1998), *Voicing the Text: South African Oral Poetry and Performance*, Oxford, Oxford University Press.

—— (ed.) (1999), *Oral Literatures and Performance in Southern Africa*, Oxford, James Currey.

Brown, Lloyd W. (1981), *Women Writers in Black Africa*, Westport, CT, and London, Greenwood Press.

Brydon, Diana and Helen Tiffin (1993), *Decolonising Fictions*, Sydney and Hebden Bridge, Dangaroo.

Bush, Barbara (1996), 'History, Memory, Myth? Reconstructing the History (or Histories) of Black Women in the African Diaspora', in Stephanie Newell (ed.), *Images of African and Caribbean Women: Migration, Displacement, Diaspora*, Occasional Paper No. 4, University of Stirling, Centre of Commonwealth Studies, pp. 3–28.

Carnochan, W. B. (1995), 'The Literature of Confinement', in N. Morris and D. J. Rothman (eds), *The Oxford History of the Prison: The Practice of Punishment in Western Society*, New York, Oxford University Press, pp. 427–56.

Carusi, Annamaria (1990), 'Post, Post and Post; Or, Where Is South African Literature in All This?', in Adam and Tiffin 1990: 95–108.

Caruth, Cathy (ed.) (1995), *Trauma: Explorations in Memory*, Baltimore, MD, Johns Hopkins University Press.

——, (1996), *Unclaimed Experience: Trauma, Narrative and History*, Baltimore, MD, Johns Hopkins University Press.

de Certeau, Michel (1984), *The Practice of Everyday Life*, Berkeley, University of California Press.

Chapman, Michael (1982), *Soweto Poetry*, Johannesburg, McGraw-Hill Book Company.

——, (1984), *South African English Poetry: A Modern Perspective*, Johannesburg, Ad Donker.

——, (1992), 'The Critic in a State of Emergency: Towards a Theory of Reconstruction', in Holst Petersen and Rutherford 1992: 1–13.

——, (1996), *Southern African Literatures*, London, Longman.

—— (ed.) (2001), *The Drum Decade: Stories from the 1950s*, introduced by John Matshikiza, first published in 1989, Durban, University of Natal Press.

Chennells, Anthony (1996), 'Authorizing Women, Women's Authoring: Tsitsi Dangarembga's *Nervous Conditions*', in Ngara 1996: 59–75.

Chinweizu, Onwuchekwa Jemie and Ihechukwu Madubuike (1983), *Toward the Decolonization of African Literature: African Fiction and Poetry and Their Critics*, Washington, DC, Howard University Press.

Christie, Kenneth (2000), *The South African Truth Commission*, Basingstoke, Palgrave.

Clayton, Cherry (1991), 'Post-colonial, Post-apartheid, Post-feminist: Family and State in Prison Narratives by South African Women', *Kunapipi*, 13:1–2, 136–44.

Clingman, Stephen (1990), 'Revolution and Reality: South African Fiction in the 1980s', in Trump 1990: 41–60.

Coetzee, Ampie (1990), 'Literature and Crisis: One Hundred Years of Afrikaans Literature and Afrikaner Nationalism', in Trump 1990: 322–66.

Coetzee, J. M. (1980), *Waiting for the Barbarians*, London, Secker and Warburg.

——, (1986), *Foe*, London, Secker and Warburg.

——, (1988), 'The Novel Today', *Upstream*, 6:1, 2–5.

——, (1996), 'Breyten Breytenbach and the Reader in the Mirror', in *Giving*

Offense: Essays on Censorship, London and Chicago, University of Chicago Press, pp. 215–32.

——, (1999), *Disgrace*, London, Secker and Warburg.

——, (2001), *Stranger Shores: Essays, 1986–1999*, London, Secker and Warburg.

Collen, Lindsey (1994), 'The Rape of Fiction', *Index on Censorship*, 23:4/5 (Sept./Oct.), 210–12.

——, (1995), *The Rape of Sita*, London, Minerva.

Coly, Ayo Abiétou (2002), 'Neither Here nor There: Calixthe Beyala's Collapsing Homes', *Research in African Literatures*, 33:2, 34–45.

Connerton, Paul (1989), *How Societies Remember*, Cambridge, Cambridge University Press.

Cook, Allen (1974), *South Africa: The Imprisoned Society*, London, International Defence and Aid Fund.

——, (1982), *Akin to Slavery: Prison Labour in South Africa*, London, International Defence and Aid Fund.

Coombes, Annie E. (2003), *History After Apartheid: Culture and Public Memory in a Democratic South Africa*, Durham, NC, and London, Duke University Press.

Cooper, Brenda (1998), *Magical Realism in West African Fiction: Seeing With a Third Eye*, London, Routledge.

Cope, Trevor (ed.) (1968), *Izibongo: Zulu Praise-Poems*, Oxford, Clarendon Press.

Coundouriotis, Eleni (1999), *Claiming History*, New York, Columbia University Press.

Cronin, Jeremy (1987), *Inside*, first published in 1983, London, Jonathan Cape.

——, (1990), '"Even under the Rine of Terror ...": Insurgent South African Poetry', in Trump 1990: 295–306.

Dangarembga, Tsitsi (1988), *Nervous Conditions*, London, Virago.

——, (1992), Interview in Wilkinson 1992, pp. 188–98.

Dangor, Achmat (2003), *Bitter Fruit*, first published in 2001, London, Atlantic Books.

Darlington, Sonja (2003), 'Calixthe Beyala's Manifesto and Fictional Theory', *Research in African Literatures*, 34:2, 41–52.

Dathorne, O. (1971), 'Amos Tutuola: The Nightmare of the Tribe', in King 1971: 64–76.

Davies, Ioan (1990), *Writers in Prison*, Oxford, Blackwell.

Dawes, Nicholas (1997), 'Constituting Nationality: South Africa in the Fold of the "Interim"', *Jouvert*, 1:2 <http://social.ncsu.edu/jouvert/v1i2/Dawes>.

Dingake, Michael (1987), *My Fight Against Apartheid*, London, Kliptown Books.

Diop, David (1975), *Hammer Blows*, first published in French as *Coups de Pilon*, 1956, trans. Simon Mpando and Frank Jones, London, Heinemann.

District Six Museum, 25A Buitenkant Street, Cape Town, 8001, South Africa. 18 June, 2001 <http://www.districtsix.co.za>.

Dlamini, Moses (1984), *Robben Island Hell-Hole: Reminiscences of a Political Prisoner*, London, Spokesman.

Docherty, Thomas (1993), Introduction to 'Periphery and Postcolonialism', in

Postmodernism: A Reader, Hemel Hempstead, Harvester Wheatsheaf, pp. 445–7.

Donaldson, Andrew (2001), 'Oom Bey Is Streets Ahead in the Renaming Stakes', South Africa *Sunday Times*, 7 October <http://www.suntimes.co.za/2001/10/07/insight/in06.asp>.

Dove-Danquah, Mabel (1947), 'Anticipation', in Charlotte H. Bruner (ed.) (1983), *Unwinding Threads: Writing by Women in Africa*, London, Heinemann, pp. 6–10.

Driver, C. J. (1975), 'The View from Makana Island: Some Recent Prison Books from South Africa', *Journal of South African Studies*, 2, 109–19.

Dunton, Chris (1997), 'To Rediscover Woman: The Novels of Calixthe Beyala', in Wright 1997b: 209–19.

Eaglestone, Robert (2004), *Holocaust and the Postmodern*, Oxford, Oxford University Press.

Eakin, John Paul (1985), *Fictions of Autobiography*, Princeton, Princeton University Press.

Echewa, T. Obinkaram (1986), *The Crippled Dancer*, London, Heinemann.

Edkins, Jenny (2003), *Trauma and the Memory of Politics*, Cambridge, Cambridge University Press.

Ekpa, Anthonia Akpabio (2000), 'Beyond Gender Warfare and Western Ideologies: African Feminism for the 21st Century', in Emenyonu 2000: 27–38.

Ekwensi, Cyprian (1975), *Jagua Nana*, first published in 1961, London, Heinemann.

Elder, Arlene A. (2000), 'Narrative Journeys: From Orature to Postmodernism in Soyinka's *The Road* and Okri's *The Famished Road*', in Wylie and Lindfors 2000: 409–16.

Ellmann, Maud (1993), *The Hunger Artists: Starving, Writing and Imprisonment*, London, Virago.

Emecheta, Buchi (1980), *The Joys of Motherhood*, first published in 1979, London, Heinemann.

——, (1983), *Double Yoke*, New York, Braziller.

Emenyonu, Ernest N. (ed.) (2000), *Goatskin Bags and Wisdom: New Critical Perspectives on African Literature*, Trenton, NJ, Africa World Press.

Erikson, Kai (1995), 'Notes on Trauma and Community', in Caruth 1995: 183–99.

Eyerman, Ron (2001), *Cultural Trauma: Slavery and the Formation of African American Identity*, Cambridge, Cambridge University Press.

Fagan, Edward (1998), 'The Constitutional Entrenchment of Memory', in Nuttall and Coetzee 1998: 249–62.

Fanon, Frantz (1970), *Toward the African Revolution*, first published in 1964, Harmondsworth, Pelican.

Farah, Nuruddin (2000a), *Maps*, first published in 1986, New York, Penguin.

——, (2000b), *Gifts*, first published in 1992, New York, Penguin.

——, (2000c), *Secrets*, first published in 1998, New York, Penguin.

Farred, Grant (2000), 'Mourning the Postapartheid State Already? The Poetics of Loss in Zakes Mda's *Ways of Dying*', *Modern Fiction Studies*, 46:1 (Spring), 183–206.

Farrell, Kirby (1998), *Post-Traumatic Culture: Injury and Interpretation in the Nineties*, Baltimore, MD, Johns Hopkins University Press.

Feinberg, Barry (ed.) (1980), *Poets to the People*, first published in 1974, enlarged ed., London, Heinemann.

Felman, Shoshona and Dori Laub (1992), *Testimony: Crises of Witnessing in Literature, Psychoanalysis and History*, New York and London, Routledge.

Finnegan, Ruth (1970), *Oral Literature in Africa*, Oxford, Clarendon Press.

First, Ruth (1982), *117 Days: An Account of Confinement and Interrogation under the South African 90–Day Detention Law*, first published in 1965, Harmondsworth, Penguin.

Foster, Don H., with Dennis Davis and Diane Sandler (1987), *Detention and Torture in South Africa: Psychological, Legal and Historical Studies*, London, James Currey.

Foucault, Michel (1979), *Discipline and Punish*, Harmondsworth, Penguin.

——, (1980), *Language, Counter-memory, Practice: Selected Essays and Interviews*, ed. with an introduction by Donald F. Bouchard, Ithaca, NY, Cornell University Press.

Fraser, Robert (1980), *The Novels of Ayi Kwei Armah: A Study in Polemical Fiction*, London, Heinemann.

Freud, Sigmund (2001a), 'Remembering, Repeating and Working-Through', in *The Standard Edition of the Complete Psychological Works of Sigmund Freud, Volume XII (1911–1913): Case History of Schreber, Papers on Technique and Other Works*, trans. under general editorship of James Strachey, first published in 1958, London, Vintage, Hogarth Press, pp. 145–56.

——, (2001b), 'Mourning and Melancholia', in *The Standard Edition of the Complete Psychological Works of Sigmund Freud, Volume XII (1914–1916): On the History of the Psycho-Analytic Movement, Papers on Metapsychology and Other Works*, trans. under general editorship of James Strachey, first published in 1958, London, Vintage, Hogarth Press, pp. 237–60.

Gakwandi, S. A. (1977), *The Novel and Contemporary Experience in Africa*, London, Heinemann.

——, (1992), 'Freedom as Nightmare: Armah's *The Beautyful Ones Are Not Yet Born*', in Wright 1992: 102–15.

Gikandi, Simon (2000), *Ngugi wa Thiong'o*, Cambridge, Cambridge University Press.

Gilmore, Leigh (1994), *Autobiographics: A Feminist Theory of Women's Self-Representation*, Ithaca, NY, Cornell University Press.

Goodwin, Kenneth (1982), *Understanding African Poetry: A Study of Ten Poets*, London, Heinemann.

Gordimer, Nadine (1974), *The Conservationist*, London, Cape.

——, (1976), 'Writers in South Africa: The New Black Poets', in Rowland Smith (ed.), *Exile and Tradition: Studies in African and Caribbean Literature*, London, Longman and Dalhousie University Press, pp. 132–51.

——, (1980), *Burger's Daughter*, first published in 1979, London, Penguin.

——, (1989), 'Living in the Interregnum', in Stephen Clingman (ed.), *The Essential Gesture: Writing, Politics and Places*, London, Penguin, pp. 261–84.

——, (1998), *House Gun*, New York, Farrar, Straus and Giroux.

Graham, Shane (2003), 'The Truth Commission and Post-Apartheid

Literature in South Africa', *Research in African Literatures*, 34:1, 11–30.

Gray, Stephen (1979), 'The White Man's Creation Myth of Africa', in *Southern African Literature: An Introduction*, Cape Town, David Philip, pp. 15–37.

——, (1992), 'An Author's Agenda: Re-Visioning Past and Present for a Future South Africa', in Holst Petersen and Rutherford 1992: 23–31.

Green, Michael (1997), *Novel Histories: Past, Present, and Future in South African Fiction*, Johannesburg, Witwatersrand University Press.

Griffiths, Gareth (2000), *African Literatures in English: East and West*, Harlow, Pearson Education.

Griswold, Wendy (2000), *Bearing Witness: Readers, Writers and the Novel in Nigeria*, Princeton, NJ, Princeton University Press.

Grunebaum-Ralph, Heidi (2001), 'Re-Placing Pasts, Forgetting Presents: Narrative, Place, and Memory in the Time of the Truth and Reconciliation Commission', *Research in African Literatures*, 32:3 (Fall), 198–212.

Gunner, Liz (1999), 'Remaking the Warrior? The Role of Orality in the Liberation Struggle and in Post-Apartheid South Africa', in Brown 1999: 50–60.

——, and Mafika Gwala (eds) (1994), *Musho!: Zulu Popular Praises*, Johannesburg, Witwatersrand University Press.

Gwala, Mafika (1982), 'Black Writing Today' (1979), in Chapman 1982: 169–75.

——, (1982), *No More Lullabies*, Johannesburg, Ravan Press.

Hall, Stuart, Chas Critcher, Tony Jefferson, John Clarke and Brian Roberts (1978), *Policing the Crisis: Mugging, the State, and Law and Order*, Basingstoke, Macmillan.

Harlow, Barbara (1987), *Resistance Literature*, London and New York, Methuen.

Hartman, Geoffrey (1994), 'Public Memory and Its Discontents', *Raritan*, 13, 24–40.

Head, Bessie (1972), *Maru*, first published in 1971, London, Heinemann.

——, (1974), *A Question of Power*, London, Heinemann.

Head, Dominic (1997), *J. M. Coetzee*, Cambridge, Cambridge University Press.

van Heerden, Étienne (1993), *Ancestral Voices*, trans. Malcolm Hacksley, first published in 1986, London, Allison and Busby.

——, (2002), *The Long Silence of Mario Salviati*, trans. Catherine Knox, London, Sceptre.

Henke, Suzette (1999), *Shattered Subjects: Women's Life-writing and Narrative Recovery*, Basingstoke, Macmillan.

Herman, Judith (2001), *Trauma and Recovery*, first published in 1992, London, Pandora.

Herreman, Frank (ed.) (1999), *Liberated Voices: Contemporary Art from South Africa*, New York, Museum for African Art.

Heyns, Michiel (2000), 'The Whole Country's Truth: Confession and Narrative in Recent White South African Writing', *Modern Fiction Studies*, 46:1 (Spring), 42–66.

Himunyanga-Phiri, Tsitsi V. (1992), *The Legacy*, Harare, Zimbabwe Publishing House.

Hirsch, Marianne (1997), *Family Frames: Photography, Narrative and Postmemory*, Cambridge, MA, Harvard University Press.

Holst Petersen, Kirsten and Anna Rutherford (eds) (1992), *On Shifting Sands: New Art and Literature From South Africa*, Portsmouth, NH, Heinemann, and Sydney, Dangaroo Press.

hooks, bell (1990), 'Choosing the Margin as a Space of Radical Openness', in *Yearning: Race, Gender and Politics*, Boston, South End Press, pp. 145–53.

Horn, Peter (1994), *Writing My Reading: Essays on Literary Politics in South Africa*, Amsterdam and Atlanta, GA, Rodopi.

——, (1995), 'The Genealogy of Shame', *Southern African Review of Books*, 36 (March/April).

Horowitz, Sara (1997), *Voicing the Void: Muteness and Memory in Holocaust Fiction*, Albany, SUNY Press.

Hove, Chenjerai (1990), *Bones*, first published in 1988, London, Heinemann.

——, (1991), *Shadows*, Harare, Baobab Books.

——, (1996), *Ancestors*, London, Picador.

Hutcheon, Linda (2002), *The Politics of Postmodernism*, London, Routledge.

Huyssen, Andreas (1995), *Twilight Memories: Marking Time in a Culture of Amnesia*, London, Routledge.

Ignatieff, Michael (1996), 'Articles of Faith', *Index on Censorship*, 25:5 (Sept./Oct.), 110–22.

Innes, Lyn and Caroline Rooney (1997), 'African Writing and Gender', in Msiska and Hyland 1997: 193–215.

Irele, Abiola (ed.) (1977), *The Selected Poems of Léopold Sédor Senghor*, Cambridge, Cambridge University Press.

——, (1981), *The African Experience in Literature and Ideology*, London, Heinemann.

Irlam, Shaun (1998), 'Mariama Bâ's *Une si longue lettre*: The Vocation of Memory and the Space of Writing', *Research in African Literatures*, 29:2, 76–93.

Iroh, Eddie (1979), *Toads of War*, London, Heinemann.

Iyayi, Festus (1986), *Heroes*, Harlow, Longman.

——, (1987), *Violence*, first published in 1979, Harlow, Longman.

Izevbaye, D. S. (1992), 'Ayi Kwei Armah and the "I" of the Beholder', in Wright 1992: 22–33.

Jacobs, J. U. (1986), 'Breyten Breytenbach and the South African Prison Book', *Theoria*, 68 (December), 95–105.

——, (1991), 'Confession, Interrogation and Self-Interrogation in the New South African Prison Writing', *Kunapipi*, 13:1–2, 115–27.

——, (1992), 'Narrating the Island: Robben Island in South African Literature', *Current Writing*, 4:1 (October), 73–84.

JanMohamed, Abdul (1983), *Manichean Aesthetics*, Amherst, MA, University of Massachusetts Press.

Jenkin, Tim (1987), *Escape from Pretoria*, London, Kliptown Books.

Jeyifo, Biodun (1991), 'For Chinua Achebe: The Resilience and the Predicament of Obierika', in Kirsten Holst Petersen and Rutherford (eds), *Chinua Achebe: A Celebration*, London, Heinemann, pp.51–70.

Johennesse, Fhazel and Neil Alwin Williams (1982), 'Statement', in Chapman 1982: 126.

Johnson, Richard, et al. (eds) (1982), *Making Histories: Studies in History-Writing and Politics*, London, Hutchinson and Centre for Contemporary Cultural Studies.

Jolly, Rosemary (1996), 'Breyten Breytenbach's Prison Writings', in *Colonization, Violence, and Narration in White South African Writing: André Brink, Breyten Breytenbach, and J. M. Coetzee*, Athens, Ohio University Press, pp. 60–109.

Kanaganayakam, Chelva (1991), '"Broadening the Substrata": An Interview With M. G. Vassanji', *World Literature Written in English*, 31:2, 19–35.

Kanneh, Kadiatu (1998), *African Identities: Race, Nation and Culture in Ethnography, Pan-Africanism and Black Literatures*, London, Routledge.

Kgositsile, Keorapetse (1973), 'My People No Longer Sing', in Bremen 1973: 407.

Killam, G. D. (ed.) (1984), *The Writing of East and Central Africa*, London, Heinemann.

King, Bruce (ed.) (1971), *Introduction to Nigerian Literature*, Lagos, University of Lagos and Evans Bros Ltd.

Knipp, Thomas (1993), 'English-Language Poetry', in Oyekan Owomoyela (ed.), *A History of Twentieth Century African Literatures*, Lincoln, University of Nebraska Press, pp. 103–37.

de Kok, Ingrid (1998), 'Cracked Heirlooms: Memory on Exhibition', in Nuttall and Coetzee 1998: 57–71.

Kortenaar, Neil ten (1997), 'Doubles and Others in Two Zimbabwean Novelists', in Wright 1997b: 19–41.

Kossew, Sue (1996), *Pen and Power: A Post-Colonial Reading of J. M. Coetzee and André Brink*, Amsterdam and Atlanta, GA, Rodopi.

Krog, Antjie (1999), *The Country of My Skull*, first published in 1998, London, Vintage.

Kunene, Daniel P. (1981), *A Seed Must Also Seem to Die and Other Poems*, Johannesburg, Ravan Press.

Kunene, Masizi (1970), *Zulu Poems*, New York, Africana Publishing Corporation.

——, (1976), 'South African Oral Traditions', in Christopher Heywood (ed.), *Aspects of South African Literature*, London, Heinemann, pp. 24–41.

——, (1982), *The Ancestors and the Sacred Mountain*, London, Heinemann.

LaCapra, Dominick (1994), *Representing the Holocaust: History, Theory, Trauma*, Ithaca, NY, Cornell University Press.

——, (1998), *History and Memory After Auschwitz*, Ithaca, NY, Cornell University Press.

——, (2001), *Writing History, Writing Trauma*, Baltimore, MD, Johns Hopkins University Press.

Laing, B. Kojo (1986), *Search Sweet Country*, London, Heinemann.

——, (1988), *Woman of the Aeroplanes*, London, Heinemann.

——, (1992), *Major Gentl and the Achimota Wars*, London, Heinemann.

Langa, Mandla (1996), *The Naked Song and Other Stories*, Johannesburg, David Philip, and Boulder, CO, Lynne Rienner.

——, (2000), *The Memory of Stones*, Johannesburg, David Philip, and Boulder, CO, Lynne Rienner.

Langer, Lawrence (1975), *The Holocaust and Literary Imagination*, New

Haven, Yale University Press.

——, (1982), *Versions of Survival: The Holocaust and the Human Spirit*, Albany, SUNY Press.

——, (1991), *Holocaust Testimonies: The Ruins of Memory*, New Haven, Yale University Press.

Laplanche, J. and J.-B. Pontalis (1973), *The Language of Psycho-Analysis*, first published in 1967, New York, W. W. Norton & Co.

Lazarus, Neil (1990), *Resistance in Postcolonial African Fiction*, New Haven and London, Yale University Press.

——, (1992), 'Pessimism of the Intellect, Optimism of the Will: A Reading of Ayi Kwei Armah's *The Beautyful Ones Are Not Yet Born*', in Wright 1992: 157–87.

Le Goff, Jacques (1992), *History and Memory*, trans. Steven Rendall and Elizabeth Claman, New York, Columbia University Press.

Levumo, Alex (1982), 'Mongane Serote's *No Baby Must Weep*', in Chapman 1982: 76.

Lewin, Hugh (1989), *Bandiet*, Claremont, South Africa, David Philip.

Leys, Ruth (2000), *Trauma: A Genealogy*, Chicago, University of Chicago Press.

Libin, Mark (2003), 'Can the Subaltern Be Heard? Response and Responsibility in *South Africa's Human Spirit*', *Textual Practice*, 17:1, 119–40.

Lindfors, Bernth (1980), 'Armah's Histories', *African Literature Today*, 11, 85–96.

Lovesey, Oliver (1995), 'Chained Letters: African Prison Diaries and "National Allegory"', *Research in African Literatures*, 26:4, 31–45.

——, (1996), 'The African Prison Diary as "National Allegory"', *Studies in English and Comparative Literature*, 10, 209–18.

Low, Gail (2002), 'In Pursuit of Publishing: Heinemann's African Writers Series', *Wasafiri*, 37 (Winter), 31–5.

Madingoane, Ingoapele (1979), *africa my beginnings*, Johannesburg, Ravan Press.

Maja-Pearce, Adewale (1992), *A Mask Dancing: Nigerian Novelists of the Eighties*, London and New York, Hans Zell Publishers.

Malak, Amin (1993), 'Ambivalent Afflictions and the Postcolonial Condition: The Fiction of M. G. Vassanji', *World Literature Today*, 67:2 (Spring), 279–82.

de Man, Paul (1979), 'Autobiography as De-Facement', *Modern Language Notes*, 94, 919–30.

Marcus, Laura (1994), *Auto/biographical Discourses: Theory, Criticism, Practice*, Manchester, Manchester University Press.

Maroleng, Cindy (1991), 'Memories', in Anon (ed.), *Ear to the Ground: Contemporary Worker Poets*, Johannesburg, COSAW/COSATU, pp. 52–5.

Mashinini, Emma (1989), *Strikes Have Followed Me All My Life*, London, Women's Press.

Matlho, Duncan (1980), 'Isandlhwana', in Feinberg 1980: 136–7.

Mazrui, Ali A. (1986), *The Africans: A Triple History*, Boston, Little, Brown.

McWilliams, Sally (1991), 'Tsitsi Dangarembga's *Nervous Conditions*: At the Crossroads of Feminism and Post-Colonialism', *World Literature Written in English*, 31:1 (Spring), 103–12.

Mda, Zakes (1995), *Ways of Dying*, Cape Town, Oxford University Press.

——, (2002), *The Heart of Redness*, first published in 2000, New York, Farrar, Straus and Giroux.

Mehlman, Jeffrey (1977), *Revolution and Repetition*, Berkeley, University of California Press.

Meyer, Lisa (1999), 'Fragmented Homeland, a Vocal Critic; A Somali Writer Dissects His Country's Civil War, Dictatorial Past, and Neocolonial Present', *Los Angeles Times*, 15 March.

Michael, Cheryl-Ann (1995), 'Constructing the Self, Inventing Africa', in Julia Swindells (ed.), *The Uses of Autobiography*, London, Taylor and Francis, pp.73–80.

Middleton, Peter and Tim Woods (1999), *Literatures of Memory*, Manchester, Manchester University Press.

Miller, Christopher L. (1990), *Theories of Africans: Francophone Literature and Anthropology in Africa*, Chicago, University of Chicago Press.

Millett, Kate (1994), *The Politics of Cruelty: An Essay on the Literature of Political Imprisonment*, London, Penguin.

Modisane, Bloke (1963), *Blame Me on History*, London, Thames and Hudson.

Mogale, Dikobe wa (1984), *baptism of fire*, Johannesburg, Ad Donker.

Moosa, Ebrahim (2000), 'Truth and Reconciliation as Performance: Spectres of Eucharistic Redemption', in Charles Villa-Vicencio and Wilhelm Verwoerd (eds), *Looking Back Reaching Forward: Reflections on the Truth and Reconciliation Commission of South Africa*, Cape Town, University of Cape Town Press, and London, Zed Books, pp. 113–20.

Morphet, Tony (1984), 'An Interview with J. M. Coetzee', *Social Dynamics*, 10:1, 62–5.

Moslund, Sten Pultz (2003), *Making Use of History in New South African Fiction: Historical Perspectives in Three Post-Apartheid Novels*, Copenhagen, Museum Tusculanum Press.

Moss, Laura (2000), '"The Plague of Normality": Reconfiguring Realism in Postcolonial Theory', *Jouvert*, 5:1 <http://social.chass.ncsu.edu/jouvert/v5i1/moss.htm>.

Motjuwadi, Stanley (1974), 'White Lies', in Robert Royston (ed), *Black Poets in South Africa*, first published in 1973, London, Heinemann, p. 12.

Mpe, Phaswane (2001), *Welcome to Our Hillbrow*, Pietermaritzburg, University of Natal Press.

Mphahlele, Es'kia [Ezekiel] (1972), *Voices of the Whirlwind and Other Essays*, London and Basingstoke, Macmillan.

——, (1974), *The African Image*, rev. ed., London, Faber.

——, (1979), 'The Voice of Prophecy in African Poetry', *English in Africa*, 6:1, 34–5.

Msiska, Mpalive-Hangson (2000), 'Issues in African Literary Criticism', *The European English Messenger*, 9:1 (Spring), 9–19.

——, and Paul Hyland (eds) (1997), *Writing and Africa*, London, Addison Wesley Longman.

Mtshali, Oswald Joseph (1971), *Sounds of a Cowhide Drum*, Johannesburg, Renoster Books.

——, (1980), *Fireflames*, Pietermaritzburg, Shuter and Shooter.

Mudimbe, V. Y. (1988), *The Invention of Africa: Gnosis, Philosophy, and the Order of Knowledge*, Bloomington, Indiana University Press.

Mungoshi, Charles (1975), *Waiting for the Rain*, London, Heinemann.

Munonye, John (1971), *Oil Man of Obange*, London, Heinemann.

Murray, Michael (1987), *South Africa: Time of Agony, Time of Destiny*, London, Verso.

Mzamane, Mbulelo (1984), 'The Uses of Traditional Oral Forms in Black South African Literature', in Landeg White and Tim Couzens (eds), *Literature and Society in South Africa*, London, Longman, pp. 147–60.

——, (ed.) (1986), *Hungry Flames, and Other Black South African Short Stories*, London, Longman.

Naidoo, Indres (1982), *Island in Chains: Ten Years on Robben Island*, London, Penguin.

Nasta, Susheila (1991), 'Introduction', in Susheila Nasta (ed.), *Motherlands: Black Women's Writing from Africa, the Caribbean and South Asia*, London, Women's Press.

Ndebele, Njabulo (1994), 'The Rediscovery of the Ordinary: Some New Writings in South Africa', in *South African Literature and Culture: Rediscovery of the Ordinary*, Manchester, Manchester University Press, pp. 41–59.

——, (1998), 'Memory, Metaphor, and the Triumph of Narrative', in Nuttall and Coetzee 1998: 19–28.

Neale, Caroline (1986), 'The Idea of Progress in the Revision of African History, 1960–1970', in B. Jewsiewicki and D. Newbury (eds), *African Historiographies: What History for Which Africa?*, London, Sage, pp. 112–22.

Newell, Stephanie (1997), 'Introduction', in Stephanie Newell (ed.), *Writing African Women: Gender, Popular Culture and Literature in West Africa*, London, Zed Books.

Newmark, Kevin (1995), 'Traumatic Poetry: Charles Baudelaire and the Shock of Laughter', in Caruth 1995: 236–55.

Nfah-Abbenyi, Juliana Makuchi (1997), 'Calixthe Beyala's "femme-fillette": Womanhood and the Politics of (M)Othering', in Nnaemeka 1997b: 101–13.

Ngara, Emmanuel (1982), *Stylistic Criticism and the African Novel*, London, Heinemann.

——, (1990), *Ideology and Form in African Poetry*, London, James Currey.

——, (ed.) (1996), *New Writing from Southern Africa*, London, James Currey.

Ngcobo, Lauretta (1990), *And They Didn't Die*, London, Virago.

——, (1992), 'Impressions and Thoughts on the Options of South African Women', in Holst Petersen and Rutherford 1992: 165–9.

van Niekerk, Marlene (2000), *Triomf*, first published in 1994, London, Abacus.

Nietzsche, Friedrich (1909), 'The Use and Abuse of History', in *Thoughts Out of Season*, Vol. 2, Part II, 1873, trans. Adrian Collins, 3rd ed., London, George Allen and Unwin, Ltd, pp. 1–100.

Nkosi, Lewis (1981), *Tasks and Masks: Themes and Styles of African Literature*, Harlow, Longman.

——, (1998), 'Postmodernism and Black Writing in South Africa', in Attridge and Jolly 1998: 75–90.

Nnaemeka, Obioma (1997a), 'Urban Spaces, Women's Places: Polygamy as

Sign in Mariama Bâ's Novels', in Nnaemeka 1997b: 162–91.

——, (ed.) (1997b), *The Politics of (M)Othering: Womanhood, Identity and Resistance in African Literature*, London and New York, Routledge.

Nuttall, Sarah (1998), 'Telling "Free" Stories: Memory and Democracy in South African Autobiography Since 1994', in Nuttall and Coetzee 1998: 75–88.

——, and Carli Coetzee (eds) (1998), *Negotiating the Past: The Making of Memory in South Africa*, Oxford, Oxford University Press.

Nwachukwu-Agbada, J. O. J. (2000), 'Nigerian Literature and Oral Tradition', in Emenyonu 2000: 67–89.

Nwahuunanya, Chinyere (1995), 'The Writer as Physician: The Therapeutic Vision in Ayi Kwei Armah's *The Healers*', *Neohelicon*, 22:2, 141–54.

Nwapa, Flora (1966), *Efuru*, London, Heinemann.

——, (1986), *Women Are Different*, Enugu, Nigeria, Tana Press.

——, (1992), *This Is Lagos and Other Stories*, Trenton, NJ, Africa World Press.

Obiechina, Emmanuel (1975a), *Culture, Tradition and Society in the West African Novel*, Cambridge, Cambridge University Press.

——, (1975b), 'Amos Tutuola and the Oral Tradition', in Bernth Lindfors (ed.) *Critical Perspectives on Amos Tutuola*, Washington, DC, Three Continents Press, pp. 123–44.

O'Brien, Anthony (2001), *Against Normalization: Writing Radical Democracy in South Africa*, Durham, NC, Duke University Press.

Ogot, Grace (1966), *The Promised Land*, Nairobi, East African Publishing House.

——, (1968), *Land Without Thunder*, Nairobi, East African Publishing House.

——, (1976), *The Other Woman*, Nairobi, Transafrica.

Ogude, James (1999), *Ngugi's Novels and African History*, London, Pluto Press.

Ogundele, Wole (2002), 'Devices of Evasion: The Mythic versus the Historical Imagination in the Postcolonial African Novel', *Research in African Literatures*, 33:3, 125–39.

Ogundipe-Leslie, Omolara (1987), 'The Female Writer and Her Commitment', in Eldred Jones, Eustace Palmer and Marjorie Jones (eds), *Women in African Literature Today*, London, James Currey, and Trenton, NJ, Africa World Press, pp. 5–13.

Okara, Gabriel (undated), *Cultural Events in Africa*, No. 102, 4.

——, (1970), *The Voice*, first published in 1964, London, Heinemann.

——, (1973), 'African Speech ... English Words', in G. D. Killam (ed.), *African Writers on African Writing*, London, Heinemann, pp.137–9.

Okonkwo, Christopher (2003), 'Space Matters: Form and Narrative in Tsitsi Dangaremgba's *Nervous Conditions*', *Research in African Literatures*, 34:2 (Summer), 53–74.

Okpewho, Isidore (1980), 'Rethinking Myth', *African Literature Today*, 11, 5–23.

——, (1983), 'Myth and Modern Fiction: Armah's *Two Thousand Seasons*', *African Literature Today*, 13, 1–23.

Okri, Ben (1991), *The Famished Road*, London, Jonathan Cape.

Okurut, Mary Karooro (1998), *The Invisible Weevil*, Kampala, Uganda, Femrite.

Olney, James (1972), *Metaphors of Self: The Meaning of Autobiography*,

Princeton, NJ, Princeton University Press.

Opoku-Agyemang, Naana Jane (1997), 'Recovering Lost Voices: The Short Stories of Mabel Dove-Danquah', in Newell 1997: 67–80.

Ousmane, Sembene (1962), *God's Bits of Wood*, London, Heinemann.

Palmer, Eustace (ed.) (1972), *An Introduction to the African Novel*, London, Heinemann.

Palumbo-Liu, David (1996), 'The Politics of Memory: Remembering History in Alice Walker and Joy Kogawa', in Amritjit Singh, Joseph T. Skerrett Jr and Robert E. Hogan (eds), *Memory and Cultural Politics*, Boston, Northeastern University Press, pp. 211–26.

Parry, Benita (1992), 'Culture Clash', *Transition*, 55, 125–34.

——, (2001), 'Some Provisional Speculations on the Critique of "Resistance" Literature', in Elleke Boehmer, Laura Chrisman and Kenneth Parker (eds), *Altered State? Writing and South Africa*, Sydney, Dangaroo Press, pp. 11–24.

Patel, Essop (1987), *The Bullet and the Bronze Lady*, Braamfontein, Skotaville.

Paulson, Ronald (1983), *Representations of Revolution*, New Haven, Yale University Press.

p'Bitek, Okot (1984), *Song of Lawino and Song of Ocol*, first published in 1966, London, Heinemann.

Pechey, Graham (1994), 'Post-Apartheid Narratives', in Francis Barker, Peter Hulme and Margaret Iversen (eds), *Colonial Discourse/Postcolonial Theory*, Manchester, Manchester University Press, pp.151–71.

——, (1998), 'The Post-Apartheid Sublime: Rediscovering the Extraordinary', in Attridge and Jolly 1998: 57–74.

Pheto, Molefe (1983), *And Night Fell: Memoirs of a Political Prisoner in South Africa*, London, Heinemann.

Priebe, Richard (1976), 'Demonic Imagery and the Apocalyptic Vision in the Novels of Ayi Kwei Armah', *Yale French Studies*, 53, 102–36.

——, (1988), *Myth, Realism, and the West African Writer*, Trenton, NJ, Africa World Press.

Reiter, Andrea (2000), *Narrating the Holocaust*, New York, Continuum.

Richards, Colin (1999), 'About Face: Aspects of Art History and Identity in South African Visual Culture', in Olu Oguibe and Okwui Enwezor (eds), *Reading the Contemporary African Art from Theory to the Marketplace*, London, Institute of International Visual Arts, pp. 348–73.

Ricoeur, Paul (1985), *Time and Narrative*, Vol. 3, trans. Kathleen Blamey and David Pellauer, Chicago, University of Chicago Press.

Rive, Richard (1987), *Buckingham Palace: District Six*, first published in 1986, London, Heinemann.

Roberts, Sheila (1985), 'South African Prison Literature', *Ariel*, 16:2, 61–73.

——, (1986), 'Breyten Breytenbach's Prison Literature', *Centennial Review*, 30:2, 304–13.

Roth, Michael S. (1995), *The Ironist's Cage: Memory, Trauma, and the Construction of History*, New York, Columbia University Press.

Rothberg, Michael (2000), *Traumatic Realism*, Minneapolis, University of Minnesota Press.

Roy, Anjali (2000), 'Post-Modern or Post-Colonial? Magic Realism in Okri's

The Famished Road', in Daniel Gover, John Conteh-Morgan and Jane Bryce (eds), *The Post-Colonial Condition of African Literature*, Trenton, NJ, African World Press, pp. 23–39.

Russell, Diane E. H. (ed.) (1990), *Lives of Courage: Women for a New South Africa*, London, Virago.

Sachs, Albie (1990), *The Jail Diary of Albie Sachs*, first published in 1966, London, Paladin.

——, (1998), 'Preparing Ourselves for Power', in Attridge and Jolly 1998: 239–48.

Said, Edward W. (1985), 'Opponents, Audiences, Constituencies and Community', in Hal Foster (ed.), *Postmodern Culture*, London, Pluto Press, pp.135–59.

Sampson, Anthony (2001), 'And the Beat Goes On', *The Guardian Weekend* (24 March), 9–16.

Sanders, Mark (2000), 'Truth, Telling, Questioning: The Truth and Reconciliation Commission, Antjie Krog's *Country of My Skull*, and Literature After Apartheid', *Modern Fiction Studies*, 46:1, 13–41.

Saro-Wiwa, Ken (1995), *A Month and a Day: A Detention Diary*, London, Penguin.

Sarvan, C. P. (1976), 'The Asians in African Literature', *Journal of Commonwealth Literature*, 11, 160–70.

——, (1985), 'Ethnicity and Alienation', *Journal of Commonwealth Literature*, 20, 100–20.

Scarry, Elaine (1985), *The Body in Pain*, Oxford, Oxford University Press.

Schalkwyk, David (1994), 'Confession and Solidarity in the Prison Writing of Breyten Breytenbach and Jeremy Cronin', *Research in African Literatures*, 25:1, 23–45.

——, (2001), 'Chronotopes of the Self in the Writings of Women Political Prisoners in South Africa', in Nahem Yousaf (ed.), *Apartheid Narratives*, Amsterdam and New York, Rodopi, pp. 1–36.

Schipper, Mineke (1987), 'Mother Africa on a Pedestal: The Male Heritage in African Literature and Criticism', in Eldred Jones, Eustace Palmer and Marjorie Jones (eds), *Women in African Literature Today*, London, James Currey, and Trenton, NJ, Africa World Press, pp. 35–54.

——, (1989), *Beyond the Boundaries: African Literature and Literary Theory*, London, Allison and Busby.

Schreiner, Barbara (ed.) (1992), *A Snake With Ice Water: Prison Writings by South African Women*, Johannesburg, COSAW.

Schwartz, Daniel R. (1999), *Imagining the Holocaust*, London, Palgrave.

Schwartzman, Adam (ed.) (1999), *Ten South African Poets*, Manchester, Carcanet Press.

Sedlak, Werner (1996), 'Prison Memoirs by African Writers (Ngugi, Pheto, Soyinka)', in P. O. Stummer and C. Balme (eds), *Fusion of Cultures?*, Amsterdam, Rodopi, pp. 183–92.

Sepamla, Sipho (1977), *The Soweto I Love*, London and Cape Town, Rex Collings and David Philip.

——, (1984), *Selected Poems*, Johannesburg, Ad Donker.

Serequeberhan, Tsenay (ed.) (1998), *African Philosophy: An Anthology*, Oxford, Blackwell.

Serote, Mongane Wally (1972), *Yakhal'inkomo: Poems*, Johannesburg, Renoster Books.

——, (1975), *No Baby Must Weep*, Johannesburg, Ad Donker.

——, (1992), *Third World Express*, Johannesburg and Cape Town, David Philip.

Serumaga, Robert (1970), *Return to the Shadows*, first published in 1969, London, Heinemann.

Shava, Piniel Viriri (1989), *A People's Voice: Black South African Writing in the Twentieth Century*, London, Zed Books.

Simatei, Tirop Peter (2001), *The Novel and the Politics of Nation Building in East Africa*, Bayreuth African Studies, 55, Bayreuth University, Bayreuth.

Slemon, Stephen (1988), 'Post-Colonial Allegory and the Transformation of History', *Journal of Commonwealth Literature*, 23:1, 157–68.

——, (1990a), 'Unsettling the Empire: Resistance Theory for the Second World', *World Literature Written in English*, 30:2, 30–41.

——, (1990b), 'Modernism's Last Post', in Adam and Tiffin 1990: 1–11.

Slovo, Gillian (2000), *Red Dust*, London, Virago.

Smith, Angela (1989), *East African Writing in English*, London, Macmillan.

Smith, Sidonie and Julia Watson (2001), *Reading Autobiography: A Guide for Interpreting Life Narratives*, Minneapolis, University of Minnesota Press.

Sole, Kelwyn (1982), 'Changing Literary Activity in Black South Africa, Pre- and Post-Sharpeville', in Chapman 1982: 144.

Solzhenitsyn, Alexander (1963), *One Day in the Life of Ivan Denisovich*, first published in 1962, Harmondsworth, Penguin.

Soyinka, Wole (1970), *The Interpreters*, first published in 1965, London, Heinemann.

——, (1972), *The Man Died: Prison Notes of Wole Soyinka*, New York, Noonday Press, Farrar, Straus and Giroux.

——, (1976), *Literature, Myth and African World*, Cambridge, Cambridge University Press.

——, (1999), *The Burden of Memory, the Muse of Forgiveness*, Cambridge, MA, Harvard University Press.

Sprinker, Michael (1980), 'Fictions of the Self: The End of Autobiography', in James Olney (ed.), *Autobiography: Essays Theoretical and Critical*, Princeton, Princeton University Press, pp. 321–42.

Stratton, Florence (1994), *Contemporary African Literature and the Politics of Gender*, London, Routledge.

Sugnet, Charles (1997), '*Nervous Conditions*: Dangarembga's Feminist Reinvention of Fanon', in Nnaemeka 1997b: 33–49.

Swanepoel, Eduan (1996), 'Helende terapie', *De Kat* (April 1995), 102.

Swarns, Rachel L. (2002), 'In a New South Africa, an Old Tune Lingers', *The New York Times*, 7 October.

Tadjo, Véronique (1986), *A Vol d'Oiseau*, Paris, Nathan.

Tal, Kalí (1996), *Worlds of Hurt: Reading the Literatures of Trauma*, Cambridge, Cambridge University Press.

The Truth and Reconciliation Commission, 9th Floor, Old Mutual Building, 106 Adderley Street, Cape Town, 8001, South Africa. 28 January 2002 <http://www.doj.gov.za/trc/>.

Thiong'o, Ngugi wa (1965), *The River Between*, London, Heinemann.

——, (1967), *A Grain of Wheat*, London, Heinemann.

——, (1972), *Homecoming*, London, Heinemann.

——, (1977), *Petals of Blood*, London, Heinemann.

——, (1981a), *Detained: A Writer's Prison Diary*, London, Heinemann.

——, (1981b), *Writers in Politics*, London, Heinemann.

——, (1986), *Decolonising the Mind: The Politics of Language and Literature*, London, James Currey.

——, (1987), *Matigari*, London, Heinemann.

Thomas, Dylan (1952), Review of Amos Tutuola's *The Palm-wine Drinkard*, *The Observer*, 8405, 6 June.

Thomas, Sue (1992), 'Killing the Hysteric in the Colonized's House: Tsitsi Dangarembga's *Nervous Conditions*', *Journal of Commonwealth Literature*, 27:1, 26–36.

——, (1997), 'Memory Politics in the Narratives of Lindsey Collen's *The Rape of Sita*', in Wright 1997: 123–37.

Tiffin, Helen (1984), 'Commonwealth Literature and Comparative Methodology', *World Literature Written in English*, 23:1, 26–30.

——, (1988), 'Post-Colonialism, Post-Modernism and the Rehabilitation of the Post-Colonial History', *Journal of Commonwealth Literature*, 23:1, 169–81.

Tlali, Miriam (1975), *Muriel at Metropolitan*, Johannesburg, Ravan Press.

——, (1989), *Footprints in the Quag: Stories and Dialogues from Soweto*, Cape Town, David Philip.

Tonkin, Elizabeth (1992), *Narrating Our Pasts: The Social Construction of Oral History*, Cambridge, Cambridge University Press.

Trump, Martin (ed.) (1990), *Rendering Things Visible: Essays on South African Literary Culture*, Athens, Ohio University Press.

Tutu, Archbishop Desmond, Foreword to the Final Report, Truth and Reconciliation Commission <http://www.struth.org.za/index.pl?&file=report/1chap01.htm>.

Tutuola, Amos (1961), *The Palm-wine Drinkard and His Dead Palm-wine Tapster in the Deads' Town*, first published in 1952, London, Faber.

Ullyatt, A. G. (1977), 'Dilemmas in Black Poetry', *Contrast*, 44, 51–62.

United Nations, *Declaration on the Protection of All Persons from Being Subjected to Torture and Other Cruel, Inhuman or Degrading Treatment or Punishment*, adopted by General Assembly resolution 3452 (XXX) of 9 December 1975.

Vansina, Jan (1965), *Oral Tradition: A Study in Historical Methodology*, London, Routledge and Kegan Paul.

Vassanji, M. G. (1989), *The Gunny Sack*, Portsmouth, NH, Heinemann.

——, (1996), *The Book of Secrets*, first published in 1994, London, Picador.

——, (2004), *The In-Between World of Vikram Lall*, New York, Alfred A. Knopf.

Vaughan, Michael (1984), '*Staffrider* and Directions Within Contemporary South African Literature', in Landeg White and Tim Couzens (eds), *Literature and Society in South Africa*, London, Longman, pp. 196–212.

Vera, Yvonne (1994), *Nehanda*, first published in 1993, Toronto, Tsar Books.

Vice, Sue (1999), *Holocaust Fiction*, London, Routledge.

Viljoen, Louise (1996), 'Postcolonialism and Recent Women's Writing in Afrikaans', *World Literature Today*, 70:1 (Winter), 63–72.

Visser, Irene (2002), 'How to Live in Post-Apartheid South Africa: Reading Zakes Mda's *Ways of Dying*', *Wasafiri*, 37, 39–43.

Vladislavić, Ivan (2000), Interview, by Christopher Warnes, *Modern Fiction Studies*, 46:1 (Spring), 273–81.

Volosinov, V. N. (1986), *Marxism and the Philosophy of Language*, first published in 1929, Cambridge, MA, Harvard University Press.

Wangusa, Ayeta Anne (1998), *Memoirs of a Mother*, Kampala, Uganda, Femrite.

Watson, Stephen (1978), 'Speaking: J. M. Coetzee', *Speak*, 1:3, 23–4.

——, (1987), 'Shock of the Old: What's Become of "Black" Poetry?', *Upstream*, 5:2 (Autumn), 22–6.

Webb, Hugh (1980), 'The African Historical Novel and the Way Forward', *African Literature Today*, 11, 24–38.

Werbner, Richard (ed.) (1998), *Memory and the Postcolony: African Anthropology and the Critique of Power*, London, Zed Books.

Wilkinson, Jane (ed.) (1992), *Talking with African Writers*, London, James Currey, and Portsmouth, NH, Heinemann.

Williams, Patrick (1999), *Ngugi wa Thiong'o*, Manchester, Manchester University Press.

Williams, Raymond (1984), *The English Novel from Dickens to Lawrence*, London, Hogarth Press.

Williamson, Sue (ed.) (1990), *Resistance Art in South Africa*, London, CIIR.

Wilson, Richard A. (2001), *The Politics of Truth and Reconciliation in South Africa: Legitimizing the Post-Apartheid State*, Cambridge, Cambridge University Press.

Wright, Derek (1987), 'The Well-Worn Way: Armah's Histories', *Wasafiri*, 6–7, 11–13.

——, (1989), *Ayi Kwei Armah's Africa: The Sources of His Fiction*, London, Hans Zell.

——, (1990), 'Ayi Kwei Armah and the Significance of His Novels and Histories', *International Fiction Review*, 17:1, 29–40.

——, (ed.) (1992), *Critical Perspectives on Ayi Kwei Armah*, Washington, DC, Three Continents Press.

——, (1994), *The Novels of Nuruddin Farah*, Bayreuth African Studies 3, Bayreuth University, Bayreuth.

——, (1997a), 'Postmodernism as Realism: Magic History in Recent West African Fiction', in Wright 1997b: 181–207.

——, (1997b), *Contemporary African Fiction*, Bayreuth African Studies 42, Bayreuth University, Bayreuth.

Wylie, Hal and Bernth Lindfors (eds) (2000), *Multiculturalism and Hybridity in African Literatures*, Trenton, NJ, African World Press.

Young, Robert (1990), *White Mythologies: Writing History and the West*, London, Routledge.

Žižek, Slavoj (1989), *The Sublime Object of Ideology*, London, Verso.

Zwelonke, D. M. (1973), *Robben Island*, London, Heinemann.

Index

Note: 'n.' after a page reference indicates the number of a note on that page